The Central and Eastern European Countries and the European Union

T0328850

The accession of ten new members to the European Union on 1 May 2004 is among the most significant developments in the history of European integration. Based upon studies conducted by the European Forecasting Network, this book analyses key aspects of the impact of this recent enlargement with reference to eight of the ten new Member States, namely the Central and Eastern European countries (CEECs). It demonstrates that the enlargement could have profound consequences on both the new Member States and on the pre-accession members of the Union, given the unparalleled magnitude of the enlargement, the fact that the CEECs have levels of prosperity and economic development well below the Union average, and their history of participation in centrally planned regimes. The contributions examine regional policy, the debate about accession to the EMU, the macroeconomic trajectories of the Central and Eastern European economies to date and their likely future development.

MICHAEL ARTIS is Professor at the University of Manchester and Professorial Fellow at the European University Institute in Florence.

ANINDYA BANERJEE is Professor at the European University Institute and a Fellow of Wadham College, Oxford.

MASSIMILIANO MARCELLINO is Professor of Econometrics at Bocconi University in Milan.

The Central and Eastern European Countries and the European Union

Edited by

Michael Artis

Anindya Banerjee

Massimiliano Marcellino

CAMBRIDGE
UNIVERSITY PRESS

CAMBRIDGE UNIVERSITY PRESS
Cambridge, New York, Melbourne, Madrid, Cape Town, Singapore,
São Paulo, Delhi, Dubai, Tokyo

Cambridge University Press
The Edinburgh Building, Cambridge CB2 8RU, UK

Published in the United States of America by Cambridge University Press, New York

www.cambridge.org
Information on this title: www.cambridge.org/9780521142052

First published 2006
This digitally printed version 2010

A catalogue record for this publication is available from the British Library

Library of Congress Cataloguing in Publication data

The Central and Eastern European countries and the European Union /edited
by Michael Artis, Anindya Banerjee, Massimiliano Marcellino.
       p. cm.
    Includes bibliographical references.
    ISBN-13 978-0-521-84954-8 (hardback)
    ISBN-10 0-521-84954-3 (hardback)
   1. European Union – Europe, Eastern. 2. European Union – Europe, Central.
3. Europe, Eastern – Economic policy – 1989– 4. Europe, Central –
Economic policy. I. Artis, Michael J. II. Banerjee, Anindya. III.
Marcellino, Massimiliano. IV. Title.

HC240.25. E852C46 2006
337.1'42'0943–dc22 2005022421

ISBN 978-0-521-84954-8 Hardback
ISBN 978-0-521-14205-2 Paperback

Contents

Contents   ix

Figures

Tables

Notes on the contributors

MANUEL ARTÍS is Professor at the Department of Econometrics, Statistics and Spanish Economy at the University of Barcelona, and Director of the AQR Group (Grup d'Anàlisi Quantitativa Regional), a research unit integrated into the Department.

MICHAEL ARTIS is Professor of Economics at the University of Manchester, and Professorial Fellow of the European University Institute. Michael Artis has previously held posts at Swansea University College, the National Institute of Economic and Social Research in London, Adelaide and Flinders Universities in Australia, and the Oxford University Institute of Economics and Statistics. He has also held fellowships from the Nuffield Foundation and from the Economic and Social Research Council as well as at the Bank of England, the University of Otago and the University of Indiana. He is a Fellow of the British Academy and is a Research Fellow of the CEPR.

ANINDYA BANERJEE is Professor of Econometrics at the European University Institute, on leave from the University of Oxford where he is Barnett Fellow in Economics in Wadham College. He has previously held positions at the University of Florida, the John F. Kennedy School in Harvard, Queen's University, Canada, and the University of Canterbury in New Zealand.

MOHAMED HEDI BCHIR is an economist with the CEPII, and is currently completing his PhD on pension problems in France, directed by Toufik Rajhi at the University of Paris I.

MICHELE BOLDRIN is Professor and Director of Graduate Studies at the Department of Economics of the University of Minnesota, and holds a post at the Research Department of the Federal Reserve Bank of Minneapolis. Michele Boldrin is a Research Fellow of the CEPR.

LIONEL FONTAGNÉ is Director of the CEPII. He is a member of the Conseil d'Analyse Economique (Council of Economic Analysis) and

Professor in Economics at the University of Paris I Panthéon-Sorbonne. He was formerly at the University of Nantes. He is also an adviser to the International Trade Center UNCTAD–WTO (CCI) in Geneva.

ELIANA LA FERRARA is Associate Professor at the Department of Economics of Bocconi University, Milan.

ENRIQUE LÓPEZ-BAZO is Professor in Applied Economics at the Department of Econometrics, Statistics and Spanish Economy at the University of Barcelona, and Coordinator of the AQR Group.

MASSIMILIANO MARCELLINO is Professor of Econometrics at the Department of Economics of Bocconi University, Milan, where he also holds the post of Deputy Director of the IGIER. Massimiliano Marcellino is a Research Fellow of the CEPR.

IGOR MASTEN is Assistant Professor at the Department of Money and Finance in the University of Ljubljana.

TONI MORA is Professor in Statistics, Econometrics and Applied Mathematics at the Department of Social and Economic Sciences at the Universitat Internacional de Catalunya.

ROSINA MORENO is Professor at the Department of Econometrics, Statistics and Spanish Economy at the University of Barcelona, and Research Fellow at the AQR Group.

CHARLES MOVIT is Research Director at the "Emerging Europe, Country Intelligence Group" of Global Insight, Inc.

TOMMASO PROIETTI is Professor of Economic Statistics at the Department of Statistical Sciences at the University of Udine.

RAÚL RAMOS is Associate Professor in Applied Economics at the Department of Econometrics, Statistics and Spanish Economy at the University of Barcelona, and Research Fellow at the AQR Group. Raúl Ramos is also a member of the Grup d'Innovació Docent per a l'Anàlisi de Dades en Economia i Empresa.

EMILIO ROSSI is Managing Director at the "European Consulting Group" of Global Insight, Inc.

JORDI SURIÑACH is Professor at the Department of Econometrics, Statistics and Spanish Economy at the University of Barcelona, and Director of the AQR Group.

ZBYSZKO TABERNACKI is Chief Economist at Global Insight, Inc.

ESTHER VAYÁ is a Research Fellow of the AQR Group.

PAOLO ZANGHIERI is an economist at ANIA (Associazione Nazionale tra le Imprese di Assicurazione), and has previously worked at the CEPII.

Acknowledgments

With one exception, the chapters contained in this book derive from papers originally prepared by the authors under the auspices of the European Forecasting Network (EFN). This network, set up in response to a competition sponsored by the European Commission, had as one of its objectives to provide regular forecasts for the European economy (such forecasts are still produced in regular sequence and may be consulted on the EFN's website at http://www.efn.uni-bocconi.it) and, as another, to provide reports on policy areas of concern to the Commission. Thus the Commission was responsible for suggesting to the EFN that it should generate reports on the Central and Eastern European countries. The EFN, in turn, saw this reference as a means to use best-practice forms of analysis on a unique data set; in particular, some of the techniques incorporated in the book found their first expression in earlier reports for the Commission on other issues - prominent examples being the use of factor analysis in forecasting (Chapter 4) and the methods used for business cycle identification and dating (Chapter 5). Whilst the reports provided the basis for the chapters published here, the latter represent an evolution of the former – an evolution that benefited greatly both from discussion of the original reports with Commission economists in EFN meetings and subsequently from the careful refereeing that the Commission supplied. We are very grateful to Peter Weiss for having organized this process for us; and to Jurgen Kroeger who represented the Commission to the EFN. Perhaps needless to say, but important to reiterate, the Commission bears no responsibility either for the views expressed here or for any remaining errors; these are the individual responsibility of the authors named.

We also owe a great debt of gratitude to the secretaries at Bocconi, Ornella Bissoli and Nicola Scalzo, who serviced the EFN.

Most of all, in relation to the preparation of this book, we wish to thank Helen Wallace, Director of the Robert Schuman Center for Advanced Studies, and her staff for their support and for providing a wonderfully congenial home for the EUI-component of the EFN network. We also thank the Research Council of the European University Institute for their generous financial assistance. Finally, it is a pleasure to acknowledge the dedicated work of Peter Claeys who worked with us, meticulously and tirelessly, to keep the widely dispersed authors together and to organise the revised papers for publication here, and of Tomasz Kozluk who helped with correcting the proofs.

Introduction

Michael Artis, Anindya Banerjee and Massimiliano Marcellino

This book is about the subset of eight of the European Union's ten new Member States admitted in the most recent (1 May 2004) enlargement. These are the countries collectively known as the Central Eastern European countries (or CEECs, for short). They comprise: Hungary and Slovenia, the Czech Republic and Slovakia, Poland and the three Baltic countries Estonia, Latvia and Lithuania. Shortage of data is one of the reasons for excluding consideration of Cyprus and Malta, the other two countries admitted in the 2004 enlargement.

Earlier enlargements brought with them distinct challenges and opportunities both for the new participants and for the existing members of the Union. The one we are concerned with here is no exception.

In particular, the latest enlargement is unparalleled in terms of the *number* of countries involved, provoking the need for a change in the governance structure of the European Union (EU). Otherwise the enlargement could be seen as leading to paralysis in decision-making. Secondly, the average level of prosperity and economic development of the new Member States is clearly well below that of the Union average and by a larger margin than had been seen in any previous enlargement. The extent to which the epithet 'poorer and more rural' applies to this set of countries can be judged from Table 0.1.

It is easy to see from the table that, with the exception of Slovenia, GDP per head was lower in the CEECs in 2003 than it was in Portugal, the least developed EU-15 member, on this measure. Compared to the average for the new enlarged Union of twenty-five, it can be seen that four of the CEECs were only half as prosperous, whilst even the more advanced among them – Slovenia, the Czech Republic and Hungary – fell below the level recorded for Greece, the next poorest country of the EU-15. The proportion of the employed workforce working in agriculture (which includes fishing and forestry) – with the single exception of the Czech Republic – was everywhere above the average for the original EU-15, in some cases (Poland, Lithuania, Latvia) markedly so.

1

2   *Artis, Banerjee and Marcellino*

Table 0.1. *Poorer and more rural*

Country	GDP per head, 2003 PPS[a]	Employment, % agriculture 2003
Germany	108	2.4
Italy	107	4.4
France	111	4.1
UK	119	0.9
EU-15	109	4.0
EU-25	100	5.2
Portugal	75	12.6
Greece	81	14.6
Slovenia	77	11.0
Czech Republic	69	3.9
Hungary	61	5.5
Slovakia	52	4.4
Poland	46	19.3
Estonia	49	6.0
Lithuania	46	17.8
Latvia	41	13.3

[a] Purchasing Power Standard (PPS) comparisons are used to allow for price variations between countries. Thus one PPS buys the same given volume of goods and services in all countries, whereas different amounts of national currency units are needed to buy this same volume of goods and services in individual countries, depending on the price level.

Another characteristic shared by these countries is that all had been to a greater or lesser extent subject to the central planning regimes of the Soviet bloc and have only recently recovered from the transition recession. Taken together, these characteristics might suggest that the impact of membership for the countries in question – and perhaps for some countries of the pre-existing Union – could be profound.

The EU response to the governance issue is represented in the proposed Constitution for the European Union, whose fate is still unsettled as this book goes to press; meanwhile, the partial responses agreed upon at the Treaty of Nice hold sway. However, governance is not one of the issues addressed by this book. Rather, the papers presented here represent a response to the second aspect of the enlargement. They attempt to describe the economic situation in these countries and its likely development and outline the nature of the impact that membership of the EU may involve. They provide answers to a number of pertinent questions and respond to some of the apprehensions that enlargement has brought with it; and they provide essential background material that might be used to help answer yet other questions not directly posed in the book. As clarified further below, the authorship of this book is multinational, drawing upon the resources of the European Forecasting Network (EFN). The EFN is briefly described in the acknowledgments which precede this introduction, and the authors, with their institutional affiliations, are listed on pp. xvii–xix above.

The rest of this introductory chapter proceeds by identifying some of the principal issues that arise in this enlargement, and explains how the subsequent chapters cast light on them. Four such broad themes are identified. First, there is the overarching issue of the impact of the enlargement and its distribution; secondly, there is the issue of regional policy and the handling of structural funds from which the new Member States can hope to benefit considerably; thirdly, we look at the macroeconomic trajectories of these economies to date and their likely future development; fourthly and finally, we bring together the analyses to be found in the subsequent chapters in so far as they relate to the debate about accession to the European Monetary Union (EMU).

The overall impact

Despite the stark contrast between the CEECs and most of the existing Member States in terms of their levels of prosperity and development, there are a number of reasons for thinking that the apprehensions of a large impact on *existing* member states are mistaken. There are three simple and straightforward reasons for thinking this. The first is that a great deal of what it means to be a member of the EU had already been achieved by the CEECs in the years before formal membership – trade flows for example had all been substantially freed of tariffs and controls. Secondly, the largest immediate effect about which there was (and remains) serious apprehension is the prospect of a substantially freer flow of labour from the CEECs to the existing Member States, but for most Member States special transitional arrangements have suspended this likelihood. We have not investigated, here, what will happen when these transitional arrangements expire. (Much economic analysis has used the evidence from previous enlargements to argue that the effects on labour migration might not be large and the prospects for further rapid growth in the CEECs should blunt the desire to migrate; and it may be that the transitional arrangements could be extended in some form for as long as deemed necessary.) Thirdly, there is the fact that the CEECs, with the exception of Poland, are small in size relative to the EU-15; big impacts for them may translate to only small impacts for the existing Member States. The issue is dealt with formally in detail and in a sophisticated way by the authors – Bchir, Fontagné and

Zanghieri – of Chapter 2 here. These authors apply a computable general equilibrium (CGE) model to generate estimates of the effects on trade, output and welfare over a period of time; the model gives multi-sectoral detail and incorporates an assumption of imperfect competition outside the agricultural sector, yielding predictions for the number and size of firms in specific sectors. By rehearsing different scenarios the authors are able to point out that the further impacts to come from more liberalized trade alone are relatively small – relative, that is, to a baseline which already incorporates the continuation of established trends in expanding trade. However, more is to be expected from the subsequent adjustment in market structure and specialization, and (largely speaking) more again from the effects of admitting the countries to a modified form of the Common Agricultural Policy (CAP), the form agreed upon at the Copenhagen Summit. By 2015 and relative to the base line, the authors predict large expansionary impacts on the output and welfare of most of the CEECs – in the order, for GDP, of 7–8%. The Baltic countries form the exception, their pattern of industrial specialization inhibiting them, according to the model, from making rapid gains (and possibly producing losses). By contrast, the impacts on the pre-existing members of the EU are, overall, reckoned to be slight – in terms of GDP a possible fall of less than 1 per cent.

Regional policies and the structural funds

The large gap in output levels between the new Member States and the existing EU members (see Table 0.1 above) is an immediate indication that the CEECs might expect to be the recipients of substantial structural fund disbursements. Several issues then arise: are the aims and objectives of EU regional policy proper concerns, and is the policy well conducted with respect to its declared aims? What does past experience in similar situations tell us about the optimality (or otherwise) of these policies? Is it true that public sector infrastructure investment, a strong candidate for stimulus, can provide the kind of boost to growth that some economic theory (e.g. endogenous growth theory) suggests? Finally, will the diversion of funds from existing recipient regions to the new ones in the new Member States represent a strongly negative factor for those States?

The authors of Chapter 3 – Mora, Vayá and Suriñach – concentrate initially on estimating specialization and concentration indices using gross-value-added data for a large number of regions, examining first what can be said about the change in these measures over the period from 1985 to 1995. This period is selected to start before the EU's

Iberian enlargement as a way of mimicking the period to follow the latest enlargement. In key respects the earlier experience should provide a model for the later – the development disparities are similar and the policies to be followed perhaps not much different. The first result obtained is that at the level of broadly defined sectors ('agriculture, forestry and fishery products', 'building and construction' etc.) there is not a great deal of difference to be found between the indices for 1985 and for 1995: there is no sweeping tendency to a 'core and periphery' dichotomy to be found, nor indeed the contrary tendency to greater equalization. The authors are concerned that the results obtained for broadly defined sectors and summarized in the indices employed may conceal some movements of interest that would be evident in a more detailed look at the relevant distributions. Kernel density functions are estimated to probe for the presence or new formation of 'regional clubs' in particular industrial sectors. Indeed, some bimodality is evident in some of their plots, consistent with this idea and tests for spatial dependence are quite positive. In an extension to this exercise the authors augment their data base with data for a (super-) enlarged EU of twenty-seven members (including also Romania and Bulgaria). The comparison of the EU-15 and this EU-27 suggests an increase in the sectoral specialization coefficient for agriculture, forestry and fisheries, which is hardly surprising, but relatively little change elsewhere. Chapters 11 (Moreno, López-Bazo and Artís) and 12 (La Ferrara and Marcellino) use evidence from the experience of other countries, with some claim to be 'representative', to analyse issues of relevance for the form of regional policy. In Chapter 12 the authors use regionally disaggregated data for the Italian regions to discover whether public sector infrastructure investment is favourable for total factor productivity, output growth and cost efficiency. The results show that public sector infrastructure investment scores favourably on all counts, but more so in the regions of the Centre and South than in those of the North; this might be regarded as a good augury for the relative value of making public sector infrastructure in the CEECs rather than in the older Member States of the Union. The authors of Chapter 11 look to the experience of Spain for comparable instruction. They take a sample period which predates Spain's accession to the EU to examine the effect of public sector infrastructure investment on regional output, using a data base which contains data for fifty regions (provinces). Public sector infrastructure investment is divided into two categories – transport and other: one of the features of the results is that the returns seem larger for the latter type of investment rather than for the more glamorous transportation sector (which is also the one favoured by EU-related and funded projects). Relative to some earlier studies, the positive effects estimated for public sector infrastructure investment are not large, but they are positive and they are obtained in a context where suitable controls can be, and are, used in the estimation. The author of Chapter 13 – Boldrin – takes a different tack. Whilst arguing that the CEECs are indeed in much the same position, relative to the rest of the EU, as were Spain, Greece and Portugal at the earlier enlargements, he is inclined to attribute little if any of the catch-up in growth that these countries have shown to the effects of the structural funds disbursements. These are liable to result in a lack of 'additionality', as recipient States effectively spread the funds received over their own project-portfolio, undermining any EU-inspired sense of priorities. In the limit they become pure income transfers. At the same time, he argues, these policies can have negative political side-effects in encouraging rent-seeking and policies aimed at attracting income transfers at the expense of activities which could lead to sustained economic development. The Mezzogiorno is cited as a standing example of the 'dark side' of regional economic transfers.

The macroeconomic trajectory

Several chapters in this volume, starting with Chapter 1 (Rossi and Tabernacki), review the trajectory of macroeconomic development of the CEECs. All these countries experienced a recession of greater or lesser degree in association with their transition from the preceding centrally planned regime but have since embarked on a relatively un-interrupted expansionary path. For the analysis of cycles, as the authors of Chapter 5 (Artis, Marcellino and Proietti) point out, the combination of a short sample period free of structural break and the sequence of transition recession and growth mean that the concept of the classical cycle is hardly useful. The classical cycle requires for an upper turning point to be identified a succeeding period of absolute decline in eco-nomic activity. On this basis, some of the CEECs exhibit no, or only one, cycle. The concept of the deviation cycle is more productive as variations in the growth of output are pervasive: the authors examine especially carefully the co-movements of output growth within the group of the CEECs. They discover that there is little such concordance between the CEECs in their business cycle developments – nor, with a few excep-tions, is there much concordance between their cycles and those of the Euro area or leading Euro area economies. Good forecasting is an essential input to good macro-policy making. Chapter 4 (Banerjee, Marcellino and Masten) aims to uncover what the CEECs can hope for, in this respect. The short sample period of relevant, post-transition data and experience inhibits reliance on standard time series methods. The authors therefore explore carefully how well dynamic factor models can perform, given that these have the potential to exploit a wider range of data points, with encouraging (though variable) results. Zanghieri's Chapter 9 aims to analyse the current account dynamics likely to apply to these countries. The emergence of chronic balance of payments deficits – already visible – is liable to continue. It is to be expected that economies in course of development and catch-up will have justifiable investment needs well beyond their savings capabilities, implying the need to import capital and correspondingly to run a deficit on the current account. This process should be a virtuous one, with the investments 'paying off' the cumulated deficits in the course of time. There are possible problems to be faced though – an excessive build-up of debt might trigger doubts about sustainability and precipitate a crisis; on the other hand, excessive confidence might appreciate the exchange rate to such an extent that competitiveness is prejudiced. In the case of the CEECs also the prospect of future accession to the Euro area throws its shadow into the present though the effects are equivocal in principle and depend greatly on the form of interim exchange rate regime chosen. The author suggests that the quality (or type) of capital inflow may be critical – a high proportion of FDI is stabilizing to the extent that FDI does not add to the financial debt burden. Meanwhile, and into the medium term (up to 2007), the authors of Chapter 1 suggest that output growth will continue to remain strong, if not outright spectacular, with the Baltic countries leading the way on growth rates in the 6% range, whilst other countries in the bloc may grow at more modest rates of 3.5 to 5%.

EMU accession

Several papers in this volume relate to the issue of the EMU participation of the CEECs. An interesting first observation is that those chapters which provide evidence that might be used, on traditional optimal currency area (OCA) grounds, to support or oppose EMU accession (these are Chapters 5, 6 and 7), would provide a lot of evidence *against* accession. This is because these chapters show that the business cycles of the CEECs are not (with a few exceptions) strongly correlated with those of the Euro area (Chapter 5: Artis, Marcellino and Proietti), whilst the stochastic experience of the CEECs examined by Ramos and Suriñach in Chapter 6 likewise displays little or no relationship to that of the Euro area. These findings are partly modified by those of Chapter 7 (again by Ramos and Suriñach) where the monetary transmission mechanism in the new potential members is found not to differ greatly from that in the Euro area – suggesting that at least asymmetric shocks arising from the exercise of a common monetary policy need not be anticipated. Still, according to traditional OCA theory, findings like these suggest that Euro-area monetary policy would be ill-adapted to the needs of most of the CEECs, and EMU participation is counter-indicated. This, however, is to assume that the CEECs have in substantial degree the option of a well-adapted stabilization policy by staying out of EMU. But this is something which is widely doubted for countries with small domestic capital markets and little reputation, where highly mobile financial capital has the potential to disrupt the best attempts at autonomous stabilization policy. (Chapter 5 considers this literature and gives some references on it.) Whether for this reason or for some others, it is clear enough that the CEECs themselves are to the contrary quite intent on joining EMU. Already three of them (Slovenia, Latvia and Lithuania – the latter two have particularly low business cycle synchronization with Euro area countries) have entered the ERM II, which is the antechamber for entrance into EMU, whilst others among the group have evinced a strong desire to participate. Whilst these countries are not yet members of the Euro area, however, the opportunity remains for the European Commission and the European Central Bank to 'call the shots' – notably the section of the reform of the Stability and Growth Pact which observers saw as the most effective is the part that refers to the EMU qualification of non-members. This must still involve satisfying the Treaty of Maastricht, including its fiscal criteria. The CEECs' particular history raises special concerns about their ability to meet these criteria: Chapter 8 (Rossi and Tabernacki) reviews the problems facing Hungary, Poland and the Czech Republic in some detail, in recognition of the special salience of this issue. Chapter 10 (Movit) contributes a timely analysis also of the problem of banking stability in the CEECs. From the transition the banking systems of these countries have had to move rapidly across unfamiliar territory to a situation where they can cope with possible shocks and continued pressures from the integration of their economies into the global scene. Accession to EMU requires particular attention be paid to the stability of these systems.

The eastern expansion of the EU continues a story of progressive enlargement of the Union. The incorporation of the CEECs undoubtedly presents some novel and important challenges both for the existing members of the Union and for the acceding countries themselves. The chapters presented in this book, we hope, will help fulfil the need for more information and more perspective on some of the issues arising.

1 New Member States: macroeconomic outlook and forecasts*

Emilio Rossi and Zbyszko Tabernacki

1.1 The recent economic recovery in the new Member States

The entry of the new Member States into the European Union (EU) on 1 May 2004 marked the culmination of a historic process of economic transition that commenced with the fall of Communism in 1989. Fifteen years after the initiation of far-reaching reform in Eastern Europe, eight of the formerly centrally planned economies together with Cyprus and Malta joined the existing fifteen EU members in the largest EU enlargement to date. And, while the combined economic weight of the new members might seem relatively small compared to the EU-15, the dynamics of growth, commitment to internal reforms, and the desire to close the income gap with the rest of the EU, may well provide a key impulse to future economic development in Europe.

From the cyclical perspective, the new Member States are entering the EU with indisputably strong growth dynamics. Following the economic slowdown of 2001 and 2002, caused both by the unaccommodating external environment and serious domestic policy mistakes, and the moderate recovery of 2003, the first half of 2004 marks the first period of very strong growth across most of the region, in particular in the largest economies. More importantly, with only a few exceptions, the current growth recovery is overwhelmingly broad based, combining the benefits of stronger demand in the traditional Western European export markets with steady growth in private consumption, and, even more importantly, with a gradual recovery in domestic capital spending. This structure of growth makes the current recovery less sensitive to the potential reversal in European economic fortunes as global economic growth starts to decelerate in 2005.

* The projections and forecasts reported in this chapter are based on the analysis of Global Insight, with information available until the first quarter of 2004. These were contained in the Autumn 2004 Report of the European Forecasting Network.

9

The unexpectedly strong acceleration in growth rates in the largest economies of the new Member States is clearly the most positive development of the last few quarters. Poland, Hungary, Slovakia and, to a lesser extent, the Czech Republic have reported very strong growth entering 2004. Economic growth in the Baltic States and Slovenia also exceeded our preliminary expectations, boosting the annual average growth forecast for the new Member States to 5.2% year on year in 2004, well in excess of the 1.8% year-on-year growth for the Euro area.

In Poland, the largest of the new Member States, economic growth has accelerated from 4.7% in the last quarter of 2003 to 6.9% year on year in the first three months of 2004, and is expected to average 6.4% in the first half and around 6.0% for the full year 2004. These rates of growth will propel Poland again to the position of indisputable pacesetter within the region, the position the country enjoyed for most of the mid-1990s. Growth in Poland has been supported by a very strong net export component of national accounts, as local exporters enjoying the benefits of a weaker currency for most of 2003, as well as through accelerated internal restructuring, found ways to increase their market share in the key EU markets. Import growth, although accelerating gradually into 2004, remained relatively subdued on the back of a still only modest pick-up in investment spending. On the other hand, personal consumption continued to expand at an average annual rate in excess of 4.0%, complementing exports as a key driver of growth.

Slovakia, another growth leader in the region, features an economy that in 2003 was driven almost entirely by exports. Personal consumption and gross fixed investment actually declined moderately. GDP still managed to expand by 4.2%, an impressive performance, although considered a disappointment by the Slovak government. The growth in consumption was severely restricted by Slovak tax reform, which raised VAT, resulting in an inflationary surge, as well as by the cabinet's fiscal reform plans. While a broadening of the growth base in the coming years is expected, net exports are likely to determine Slovakia's growth pattern in the nearest future. As elsewhere among the new Member States, the success in expanding exports to the EU-15, despite rather lacklustre developments in aggregate demand in that region, was aided by the increasing integration of their economies with those of Western Europe. In Slovakia, this has had a particular focus in the automobile industry. In addition to the expansion of the crucial investment in the automotive sector by Volkswagen AG, two other large greenfield auto manufacturing plants will be coming on line in the next two years that will convert the Slovak economy into one of the largest car producers in the world.

Faced with a rather unaccommodating external environment with regard to its key export markets in Western Europe, the Hungarian economy turned in a rather disappointing performance in 2003, expanding by an estimated 2.9%, down from a revised 3.5% year on year in 2002. However, the first signs of more robust growth were already visible in the last three months of 2003, leading to a 4.2% growth spurt in the first quarter of 2004, on the back of an 18.9% year-on-year surge in investment spending. And, while such rates of growth are unlikely to be recorded again any time soon, they should provide the basis for solid growth in industrial production and exports that will take over as key drivers of growth into the future, with growth already accelerating to around 3.6% year on year in 2004.

A spurt in investment spending and a rebound in external sales are also likely to be responsible for a modest acceleration in growth in the Czech Republic from 3.1% year on year reported for 2003 to around 3.6% in 2004. Meanwhile, the 3.9% growth in household consumption reported in the first quarter is likely to moderate somewhat in the remaining months of 2004, partly due to higher VAT rates and rising inflation.

Among the smaller new Member States, the three Baltic economies of Estonia, Latvia and Lithuania have been by far the fastest growing for some time now. This remained the case in the first quarter of 2004, as annual growth rates ranged from 6.8% year on year in Estonia to 8.8% year on year in Latvia. The broad expansion in almost all sectors of these economies has characterised the Baltic miracle. This pattern of growth is not likely to change substantially in the coming years, although the pressures on their external accounts due to rapidly growing domestic economic activity remain severe and require the governments to address the boom in bank lending. The remaining three new Member States, Slovenia, Cyprus and Malta, continue to underperform in terms of growth rates due to a combination of reduced inflows from tourism and moribund personal consumption.

The Global Insight forecast for growth in 2004 and beyond is more optimistic. Growth has surprised many observers on the upside in the first half of 2004, mostly in the case of the economies that have relied on net exports as the key driver of growth in the last several quarters. The delayed rebound in investment spending has not precluded Poland and Slovakia from recording solid expansion, based predominantly on identifying and exploiting existing niches in Western European markets despite still lacklustre growth in demand for imports there. When supported by an anticipated boom in investment spending that should be at least partially supported by funding from the EU's regional and cohesion

12   *Rossi and Tabernacki*

funds, the outlook for growth for all of the new Member States is very optimistic with annual rates in the 4–4.5% range in the coming years.

1.2   Inflation's temporary resurgence not yet a concern

In the EFN Spring Report for 2004, Global Insight reported the emerging short-term inflationary risks prevalent in most economies in the region. Following impressive declines during 2002 and early 2003, mainly due to rapid drops in the prices of food products, delays in more aggressive increases in administratively controlled prices and strengthening currencies, performance on inflation has been considerably more mixed since the summer months of 2003 and into 2004 (see Table 1.1).

The delayed effects on the prices of food products of drought conditions across the continent in the summer of 2003 and the ensuing disappointing grain harvests continued to influence inflationary pressures in early 2004. In addition, and by far more importantly, world market crude oil prices edged up to levels considered very high even by historical standards, as the tensions in Iraq and short-term supply shortages from other markets persisted. Many of the new Member States also embarked on a major process of adjustments in VAT and excise tax rates in order to harmonise their tax regimes with EU requirements. Finally, the EU accession itself resulted in a short-lived surge in prices for selected products, mostly food. All these factors together led to a modest acceleration of inflation in all of the new Member States. In the two countries that entered 2004 with the highest rates of inflation, Slovakia

Table 1.1. *Summary of indicators for the new Member States*

	Real GDP growth in %		Avg. CPI inflation in %		Unemployment rate in % of labour force		Public sector deficit in % of GDP	
	2003	2004	2003	2004	2003	2004	2003	2004
Cyprus	2.0	3.5	4.1	2.0	3.3	3.2	−5.9	−3.6
Czech Republic	3.1	3.6	4.1	2.0	9.9	10.3	−13.0	−5.4
Estonia	4.9	6.4	1.3	2.3	10.0	9.5	2.6	1.2
Latvia	7.5	7.4	2.9	4.7	8.6	9.2	−1.8	−1.7
Lithuania	9.0	6.6	−1.2	0.9	12.4	11.8	−1.7	−1.3
Hungary	2.9	3.6	4.7	6.9	5.9	5.9	−5.9	−5.1
Malta	3.4	3.3	1.3	2.6	5.3	5.1	−9.7	−5.5
Poland	3.7	6.0	0.7	3.6	20.0	19.2	−5.3	−5.7
Slovakia	4.2	4.6	8.5	7.6	15.2	14.6	−3.5	−3.8
Slovenia	2.3	3.5	5.6	3.9	6.7	6.7	−1.8	−1.4

and Hungary, declines in inflation were inhibited by the new circumstances discussed above. Even in Lithuania, which experienced consumer price deflation for most of 2003, prices have been clearly on an upward trend in the last several months.

Despite these recent developments, the risk of a major resurgence in inflation in the new Member States is not significant in the short- to medium-term future. Despite the persistently high cost of oil in international markets, the inflationary pressures in the global economy remain subdued. Monetary authorities in many leading economies around the world have started to tighten monetary conditions, and, while the European Central Bank has not yet followed suit, the period of extraordinarily low interest rates is clearly coming to an end. The same applies to most of the economies of the new Member States. With the exceptions of Hungary and Slovakia, where excessively high interest rates are still providing the authorities with room to manoeuvre, other central banks are reviewing their relatively lax policies. The Czech and Polish central banks have already acted to bring interest rates up between 50 and 125 basis points since the beginning of 2004.

Although much remains to be done to remove the risks of undesirable inflationary pressures stemming from deferred increases in administratively controlled prices, predominantly in the service sector, overall inflation rates are likely to peak sometime later in 2004 and start declining again in 2005 and beyond. In most cases, inflationary performance is not likely to constitute an obstacle in the new Member States' quest for future membership in the EMU. In the longer run, however, we cannot rule out the possibility that headline inflation will rise in some countries. Wage pressures could be much greater in the Central and Eastern European region than in the Euro area, as citizens in the new Member States demand purchasing power closer to that of their new compatriots. The volatility in exchange rates for some of the most open Central European economies could result in temporary drops in the value of local currencies, although this volatility would most likely be short-term in nature.

1.3   The rush to the euro: a dose of realism

For the new Member States, entry into the European Union is considered only a stepping stone towards further economic integration that would culminate in the adoption of the euro and full membership in the EMU. The obvious advantages of entering the EMU are viewed as outweighing the challenges along the way. Among these challenges, achieving the nominal convergence of key economic indicators with those of the other countries in the Euro area is still a distant prospect for many countries. While the smaller new Member States, such as the Baltic States, Slovenia, Cyprus and Malta, can conceivably adopt the euro as early as 2007–8, the four largest, Poland, the Czech Republic, Hungary and Slovakia, have their work cut out for them for the next several years, with the prospect of adopting the euro now being pushed back as far as 2010. While it should be noted that, for the current participants in the EMU, the Maastricht criteria with respect to government deficits and public debt have been interpreted quite flexibly, continued problems in containing fiscal deficits are nevertheless at the core of the challenge for the new Member States (see Table 1.1 above). For these economies, the chances of bringing public sector deficits below 3% of GDP in the near future are becoming increasingly remote. Although the sources of the underlying problems (structural fiscal rigidities relating to bloated and inefficient social security systems and bureaucratic waste) are well known to them, these governments have found it quite difficult to tackle the problems faced by them. In our Spring 2004 report, we indicated that the fiscal situation across the region was not very rosy. This continues to be the case.

In Poland, the 2004 budget shows a general government deficit of 45.3 billion zlotys, considerably higher than the 36.9 billion zloty deficit reported for 2003. According to Polish officials, the increase in the deficit stems from, among other things, the need to pay EU membership fees and to co-finance EU-funded projects. In reality, for yet another year, the budget fails to reflect any sizeable reduction in fixed expenditures and serious budgetary reform has been deferred until later in this decade. While the improved economic environment in the first half of 2004 permits the government to be roughly on or even slightly below target in 2004, this mainly reflects improved tax collection. The ratio of public debt to GDP is rapidly nearing the 55% of GDP mark, and is on track to reach the constitutionally set maximum level of 60% by 2006. The complete package of reform presented by the Miller government, which has since left office, is aimed at cutting the deficit by 3.1% of GDP by 2007, but has not been fully approved by the parliament. In fact, some of its provisions have been watered-down in order to secure the appointment of the new cabinet of Marek Belka in May 2004. Under the most optimistic scenario, Poland could possibly bring the deficit under 3% of GDP by 2007–8. That would be soon enough to adopt the euro by 2010.

The situation is even less promising in the Czech Republic. A release by Eurostat in mid-March 2004 showed that the Czech public finance deficit had soared to 328.5 billion koruna in 2003, or 13.0% of revised

GDP, significantly higher than in the other new Member States. The Czech finance ministry disputed these figures, claiming instead that the deficit amounted to only 5.3% of GDP, but still a much less favourable development than in the other countries. The Czech National Bank and the government acknowledged in a document approved in October 2003 that Prague will be unable to accede to the Euro area before 2009 or 2010. The country may decide to adopt the euro even later if the eurosceptic opposition Civic Democrats (ODS) emerge as the dominant governing party after the next parliamentary election in 2006. Even the current goal of adopting the euro by 2010 would require profound fiscal reforms during the coming years. The parliament approved the first phase of the reforms in September 2003, including a rise in the retirement age, cuts in sickness pay, and increases in excise duties, in addition to a gradual decline in the corporate income tax rate. The final phase of reforms to be launched by the cabinet before the end of its current term in 2006 would involve much-delayed changes to the pension, social security and health systems. The government's proposals introduced to date have been characterised as haphazard and insufficient, as the public finance deficit is still expected to remain at 3.8% of GDP in 2006.

Following a disastrous budget performance in 2002 (the deficit reached 9.3% of GDP), and an equally disappointing deficit of 5.9% of GDP in 2003 which led to the resignation of Finance Minister Csaba László, the Hungarian government published a new detailed projection for the 2004 budget in late March 2004. At first glance, the projection is very optimistic, particularly with regard to revenue estimates. While it was expected that value added tax collection would be moderately lower in May and June immediately after the EU entry, the plan assumes that 62% of all VAT receipts will be received by the budget in the second half of 2004. It is therefore likely that the government will have to undertake major spending cuts, in addition to those already announced. The implementation of the budget in the first seven months of 2004 (the deficit reached 90.5% of the annual figure) does not provide us with much optimism. Furthermore, the expected shift to the left within the ruling Socialist party may signal a more lenient approach to fiscal consolidation. According to our forecast, the Hungarian budget deficit will reach 3.0% of GDP only by 2007, or even 2008, delaying the adoption of the euro until 2010.

The Slovak centre-right government that took office in September 2002 soon put forward wide-ranging reforms in the area of taxes, pensions, health care and social policy, aimed at bringing down the public finance deficit, while at the same time simplifying the taxation system, preventing tax evasion and promoting investment. As a result, in 2003,

Slovakia's public finance deficit fell to a surprisingly low 3.5% of GDP. After climbing slightly to an expected 3.8% of GDP in 2004, the Finance Ministry is projecting the public finance deficit to rise to 4.0% of GDP in 2005, before falling to 3.0% of GDP by 2007. As a result of the reform, Slovakia is likely to be the first of the big four new Member State economies to adopt the euro in 2008–9.

The current fiscal ills in the region are not going to disappear in the short- to medium-term unless growth reaches 4–5% annually across the region and budget spending is seriously curtailed. Furthermore, transfers from the EU will require the governments to allocate amounts of matching funds within the budget, putting an additional strain on public finances.

1.4   Fiscal challenges and interest rate convergence

Having switched to a more cautious approach to interest rate reductions during 2003, the monetary authorities in most of the new Member States set a steady course in late 2003 and early 2004 by keeping rate adjustments to an absolute minimum. While there is arguably still room for further interest rate cuts in many of the countries, most notably Slovakia and Hungary, the authorities could not ignore the first signs of gathering inflationary pressures and the fact that the region's economies are either recording robust growth or signalling that a recovery from the lacklustre performance of 2003 and 2004 is well underway. Countries that have successfully applied inflation targeting have watched price developments with moderate concern and are trying to estimate the destabilising monetary impact of increased credit activity or weakness in the local currencies.

Among the largest economies, Poland has maintained the policy interest rate at 5.25%, for a long time after June 2003. With the real rates dropping rapidly due to an increase in inflation, Polish monetary authorities first warned of the possibility of switching from a neutral to a tightening bias in their interest rate outlook. That was followed by a cumulative rise in interest rates by 125 basis points in June–August 2004, with warnings that more hikes were probably on the way. In the Czech Republic, the central bank brought down the rates to the European Central Bank-equivalent level of 2.00% by August 2003. The policy rate has remained stable until two hikes moved the rate up to 2.5%. Due to the rapid rise in headline consumer price inflation caused by the introduction of tax and price hikes, the National Bank of Slovakia opted to run a very cautious interest rate policy in 2003. However, in 2004, the policy rate was slashed significantly to counteract the appreciation pressures on the koruna. In Hungary, the policy rate remained above 10% for several quarters and is not likely to drop rapidly until inflation normalises and the public finance situation is brought under control.

In all new Member States, the authorities are attempting to maintain a balance between the expectation of nominal convergence in inflation, exchange rates, and long-term interest rates to EU levels, with the need to counteract excessive market volatility due to external shocks, the unstable situation in public finances, and the influence of the opening of local capital markets on currency stability. In all of these cases, a moderate tightening of monetary conditions would have a marginally negative effect on economic growth rates.

1.5   Country overviews

1.5.1   Poland's expansion to continue beyond 2005

The Polish economy grew very rapidly in the first half of 2004 (see Table 1.2). GDP expanded by a stunning 6.9% in the first quarter and the second-quarter growth likely exceeded 6.0% year on year as well. Strong growth in industrial output, retail sales and exports continues unabated. This fast-paced recovery is poised to continue throughout 2005 and beyond. A more sizeable rebound in investment spending will accompany private consumption and net exports as key drivers of expansion, broadening the base for growth. Public spending is also expected to expand for yet another year in 2004, a result of a rather lax budget presented by the ruling SLD–UP coalition. Poland will also benefit from a healthy outlook for the global economy. An improvement in consumer and business confidence domestically should create conditions for rapid expansion in both the industrial and services sectors.

Similar to 2003, growth in the first quarter of 2004 was driven by the continued strengthening of the net exports component of national accounts. However, domestic demand also rose in the period, by an impressive 5.7% year on year. Following a seasonal pattern, gross accumulation jumped 21.8% year on year, caused by restocking of inventories, but also due to a more substantial 3.5% year-on-year growth in investment spending. Although still below the high single-digit growth rates in late 2004, this development in investment spending was a marked improvement over the paltry 0.1% year-on-year growth in the fourth quarter of 2003. Investment growth confirms the long-awaited turnaround in corporate investment activity that is likely to strengthen further into 2004. Even more importantly, household consumption

Table 1.2. *Economic developments in Poland to 2007*

		1996	2001	2002	2003	2004	2005	2006	2007
GDP, total	billion current euro	110.6	207.3	202.4	185.4	193.7	216.8	234.5	255.9
Per capita GDP	current euro	2863	5367	5243	4813	5032	5632	6095	6654
GDP, growth rate	per cent	6.0	1.0	1.4	3.7	6.0	5.4	4.9	4.9
Average annual inflation	per cent	19.9	5.5	1.9	0.7	3.6	3.2	2.6	2.2
Population, end-year	thousands	38639	38632	38610	38514	38500	38492	38478	38463
Unemployment rate	per cent	13.2	19.4	20.0	20.0	19.2	18.5	17.4	16.0
Exchange rate, end-year	zloty/EUR	3.62	4.03	4.71	4.50	4.52	4.45	4.40	4.40
Public finance deficit (ESA-95)	% of GDP	NA	−4.8	−5.5	−5.3	−5.7	−4.9	−4.4	−3.4
Net foreign debt	% of GDP	20.4	24.4	28.0	23.9	19.3	16.8	15.1	13.7
Exports	million euro	18810	46535	49372	53841	59326	63681	69396	72364
Imports	million euro	25101	55090	57028	58894	63541	68205	73988	77152
Current account balance	% of GDP	−1.0	−2.9	−2.6	−1.9	−1.8	−1.7	−1.6	−1.6

growth maintained its pace, rising modestly from 3.9% year on year in the fourth quarter of 2003 to 4.0% year on year in the first quarter of 2004, widely attributed to a strong pre-EU spending splurge by Polish households. In terms of GDP by sector of origin, growth was clearly driven by 14.5% year-on-year growth in gross value added in industry and a 5.7% year-on-year increase in value added by market services. However, the construction sector continued to falter, with another decline in output in the first quarter of 2004, this time by 3.9% year on year.

In the longer term, annual growth rates should average 3.8–4.5%. The return to the extremely high growth rates reported for 1994–7 is likely to be only temporary and not stretch beyond the first half of 2004. Assuming steady growth in private consumption and a diminishing role for public spending in generating growth, the recovery in the Polish economy will have to come from renewed investment spending and expanding exports. On both fronts, the news is quite encouraging. Exports continue to grow very strongly. The improved environment in the Euro area resulted in an improved outlook for exports as well. The weak zloty during most of 2003 and early 2004, slow wage growth, and the internal restructuring undertaken by Polish exporters in the last several years, have created an excellent basis for further export expansion. Poland's share in Western European markets has been expanding, and the new distribution channels are starting to bear fruit. In fact, Polish exports to the European Union grew by 18.7% year on year in January–May 2004, exceeding, in terms of the dynamics of export growth to the European Union, even China.

While capital spending fell sharply during the downturn and continued to contract throughout the first three quarters of 2003, it turned positive right at the start of 2004 and should accelerate throughout 2005. Annual growth rates in investment should reach as high as 7.0–10.0%, with companies rebuilding inventories, upgrading machinery and equipment, and broadening production capacity. The increased flow of FDI following Poland's accession to the EU should further contribute to a rapid growth in investment spending. While the corporate credit market remains moribund, the first signs of improvement are visible. The medium-term outlook for economic growth in Poland will increasingly be determined by the country's membership in the European Union. In 2004–8, Poland's main financial indicators will gradually converge with levels currently observed in Western Europe.

After reaching all-time lows at 0.7% on an annual average basis in 2003, consumer price inflation accelerated strongly in the first half of 2004. The authorities closely monitored any attempts by producers and retailers to inflate prices artificially around the time of the EU accession in May, but were only partially successful in preventing increases, especially with respect to food prices. Finally, persistently high prices of fuels in international markets constitute yet another factor keeping headline inflation a bit higher in 2004 than in 2003. By May, headline consumer price inflation broke through the ceiling of the central bank's 1.5–3.5% medium-term inflation target range and reached 4.4% year on year. Core inflation indicators also jumped markedly, forcing the central bank to react with a cumulative increase in interest rates of 75 basis points in June and July.

However, even taking all of this into account, as long as inflationary expectations by households are not being bumped up markedly, the inflationary environment should be described as moderately benign. This assumes that the central bank should have no problem in keeping consumer prices under control in 2005 in preparation for the accession to the EMU and adoption of the euro. Most of the factors contributing to higher inflation in 2004 have been supply-driven. As a result, the authorities are more likely to bring inflation under control, but not earlier than in the second half of 2005. According to our forecast, average annual inflation will reach 3.6% year on year in 2004 and inch back gradually to around 2.5% year on year by 2006–7.

1.5.2   The Czech Republic to rely on external demand and investment

After a moderate increase in economic growth in 2003, a further acceleration is projected in 2004 (see Table 1.3). Key determinants of the country's macroeconomic development in 2004 and beyond include the success of the government's plan for public finance reform, the value of the koruna, and wage growth. External factors will also be important. While GDP was boosted in the past several years by a loosening of monetary and fiscal policy, room for manoeuvre in 2004 is more limited in those areas. As a result, economic growth will depend more on external demand and business investment, both of which should be positively affected by the Czech Republic's accession to the European Union on 1 May. Investment in the Czech Republic should strengthen over the coming years due in part to continued inflows of FDI. The Czech Republic remains a very attractive location for foreign firms, given its favourable geographic location, relatively good infrastructure, and skilled labour force. Gross fixed investment should rise rapidly in the coming years, based in part on lower tax rates for firms operating in the Czech Republic. In line with the government's first phase of fiscal reforms, the corporate tax rate was cut from 31% to 28% in January

Table 1.3. *Economic developments in the Czech Republic to 2007*

		1996	2001	2002	2003	2004	2005	2006	2007
GDP, total	billion current euro	44.4	68.0	77.9	79.2	84.8	93.4	101.0	103.9
Per capita GDP	current euro	4306	6661	7636	7754	8310	9170	9920	10214
GDP, growth rate	per cent	4.3	2.6	1.5	3.1	3.6	4.0	4.3	4.0
Average annual inflation	per cent	8.8	4.7	1.8	0.1	2.8	2.8	3.2	3.0
Population, end-year	thousands	10312	10206	10203	10211	10201	10191	10180	10170
Unemployment rate	per cent	3.5	8.5	9.2	9.9	10.3	10.1	9.6	9.3
Exchange rate, end-year	koruna/EUR	34.6	32.0	31.6	32.4	31.5	30.7	30.2	29.1
Public finance deficit (ESA-95)	% of GDP	NA	−6.5	−6.4	−13.0	−5.4	−4.7	−3.8	−3.3
Net foreign debt	% of GDP	8.3	13.0	4.4	8.8	9.7	10.2	11.0	12.0
Exports	million euro	17294	37301	40653	43000	50999	55045	62076	63504
Imports	million euro	21514	40736	43028	45221	53282	57921	65153	66638
Current account balance	% of GDP	−7.4	−5.4	−5.6	−6.3	−5.8	−5.3	−5.1	−4.6

2004, and is scheduled to decline gradually to 24% by 2006. Personal consumption growth is projected to moderate in 2004, as higher VAT and excise duties send inflation upward. In the medium term, however, household demand should contribute to driving steady economic growth. Meanwhile, government spending will be limited during the next several years, as the cabinet tries to get the country's fiscal situation under control. By sector, industry will play an important role in growth in the medium term, as production is driven by rapid inflows of FDI that have materialised over the past several years.

GDP growth accelerated in 2003 and should continue to rise during the next several years. Czech GDP figures are often subjected to substantial revision, making forecasting difficult. Although preliminary data put 2003 GDP growth at 2.9%, that figure was later pushed up to 3.1%, when the Czech Statistical Office revised its figures according to ESA-95 methodology. Currently, we are projecting that GDP growth will accelerate to 3.6% in 2004, driven by a recovery of investment and external demand (particularly in terms of services), coinciding with the Czech Republic's accession to the European Union on 1 May and the improved economic situation in Western Europe. Investment should also be boosted by the decline in corporate tax rates. According to preliminary estimates, GDP rose 3.1% year on year in the first quarter of 2004, by far the lowest rate in Central Europe. As we had expected, gross fixed investment was the key driver of growth, rising by 9.5%, up from a revised 7.4% rate for all of 2003. That corresponded with the strong growth in the construction sector during the first quarter, as building was spurred by anticipated changes in VAT as of 1 May. Net exports continued to have a negative impact on growth, despite the improvement in the nominal first quarter trade deficit, with real exports and imports rising 8.3% and 11.3% year on year, respectively. Meanwhile, the growth rate in household consumption slowed somewhat, but remained relatively strong, at 3.9% year on year. Household consumption should moderate during the remainder of 2004, partly due to higher VAT and excise duties, which are contributing to rising inflation. Higher levels of unemployment and the expected increase in interest rates in the second half of 2004 made Czech consumers more cautious.

After a deceleration in consumer price inflation during 2003 and 2004, partly in connection with the completion of major energy price deregulations, price growth is speeding up in 2004. Consumer price inflation reached an annual average of 0.1% in 2003, the lowest rate in the history of the independent Czech Republic. Prices were pulled downward primarily by falling food and recreation prices, although food prices did start to recover in the latter part of 2004 partly due to the poor state of the agricultural sector.

In 2004, administrative measures were pushing up consumer prices considerably. In the first half of that year, headline inflation jumped to 2.5% on average, driven by a shift of some goods and services from the lower category of value added tax to the upper one, as well as by a rise in regulated utility prices and a hike in excise taxes on tobacco, alcohol and fuel, all of which took effect at the start of the year. In May, administrative prices rose again, as the VAT was hiked on certain services in connection with the country's EU entry, although the effects were not as strong as expected. Overall, the Czech Republic's entrance into the European Union has had only a marginal impact on consumer prices thus far. In terms of market prices, inflation has been particularly strong in automotive fuel. Czech inflation is projected to rise gradually in the second half of 2004 affected in part by growing producer price inflation. Consumer price inflation is widely expected to surpass 3% in the second half of 2004. Nonetheless, the slower than expected inflation to date has already led the Finance Ministry to reduce its average inflation forecast for 2004, from 3.1% to 2.9%. Given the relatively positive results for the first half, we have lowered our forecast for average annual inflation in 2004 to just 2.7%. In subsequent years, average inflation is projected to remain at close to 3.0% annually. In fact, in March 2004, the central bank set its inflation target at 3.0% for the period beyond January 2006. According to the central bank, that should allow the Czech Republic to fulfil the monetary side of the Maastricht convergence criteria, while bringing the economy toward real convergence with the rest of the European Union in the long term.

1.5.3 Hungary's manufacturing sector and investment are driving accelerated growth

Following a disappointing performance in the last two years, mainly due to unaccommodating external conditions, Hungary's economic growth is likely to accelerate markedly in 2004 and beyond (see Table 1.4). After 2.9% in 2003 we forecast GDP growth accelerating to 3.6% in 2004 and 3.7% in 2005. This represents a slight upward revision to our growth forecast and reflects much stronger growth in investment in the first quarter of 2004. This expansion pushed GDP up by an unexpectedly strong 4.2% year on year in the first quarter. The investment boom that has begun to support the rapid expansion in the manufacturing sector took shape as companies needed to add capacity in response to growing

Table 1.4. *Economic developments in Hungary to 2007*

		1996	2001	2002	2003	2004	2005	2006	2007
GDP, total	billion current euro	34.5	57.9	68.6	73.0	80.2	89.2	96.8	102.2
Per capita GDP	current euro	3391	5690	7130	6159	5805	6681	7508	10033
GDP, growth rate	per cent	1.3	3.8	3.5	2.9	3.6	3.7	3.8	3.5
Average annual inflation	per cent	23.6	9.2	5.3	4.7	6.9	4.6	3.5	2.8
Population, end-year	thousands	10174	10175	10154	10090	10026	9962	9899	9835
Unemployment rate	per cent	9.9	5.7	5.8	5.9	5.9	5.8	5.8	5.8
Exchange rate, end-year	forint/EUR	208.1	247.7	235.9	262.2	248.0	245.0	242.0	245.0
Public finance deficit (ESA-95)	% of GDP	NA	−4.4	−9.3	−5.9	−5.1	−4.2	−3.7	−3.2
Net foreign debt	% of GDP	38.8	44.1	45.1	36.2	29.3	24.9	28.7	31.7
Exports	million euro	10111	34062	36268	37491	39933	42864	46178	47929
Imports	million euro	12468	37617	39727	41944	43906	46914	50658	52335
Current account balance	% of GDP	−2.7	−6.2	−7.2	−8.9	−8.0	−6.8	−6.9	−6.5

demand from the Euro area. Capital spending is estimated to have surged 18.1% year on year, even taking into account that the seasonal adjustment was up 4.6%. Moreover, the construction sector also rebounded strongly with a 21.9% year-on-year increase. Following this impressive first quarter performance, the Hungarian economy continued to expand at a steady pace in April–June as well. The growth outlook for the next several quarters is quite positive. On the one hand, private consumption should continue to support growth, but annual rates are likely to decline in response to weaker growth in wages and fiscal tightening. On the other hand, a rebound in exports will gain traction.

The outlook for 2004 will be increasingly determined by a combination of developments in private consumption and fixed capital investment and an ongoing recovery in industrial activity. While wages are still growing strongly and retail sales continue to surprise on the upside, we expect growth in those sectors to moderate gradually. Growth in private consumption is likely to slow from 6.5% in 2003 to 4.6% in 2004. The government's plans to reduce the budget gap, while originally estimated to result in a modest 1.0% contraction in public sector spending, will most likely cut growth in this category of the national accounts to around 1.0%. As evidenced by the rising spending on new machinery and equipment in the first quarter of 2004, annual growth in fixed capital investment will likely accelerate from 3.0% reported for 2003 to around 5.8% in 2004. The National Bank of Hungary (NBH) will keep a close watch over the fiscal performance by the government in order to make sure that the ambitious inflation targets are met. Most of the work, however, will have to be undertaken by the government.

The 2004 rebound in exports, combined with steady increases in industrial output and investment, should secure growth in 2004 at 3.6% and in 2005 to 3.7%. Public consumption will grow only very moderately in 2004 as the government is forced to curtail spending to reduce budget deficits. We expect fiscal policy to be tightened considerably in 2004–6. In the second half of 2004 and beyond, much stronger growth in Western Europe will keep Hungary on course to record annual GDP growth rates of around 3–4% during 2004–7. Thanks to extensive FDI that has modernised the manufacturing, energy and financial sectors, Hungary's export competitiveness and performance should continue to improve, although excessive wage growth needs to be curtailed. Pressures from financial markets and the EU to keep fiscal balances in order and foreign debt under control will ensure that Hungary's external imbalances do not reach threatening proportions. Going forward, Hungarian economic policies will increasingly be determined by membership in the EU in 2004 and the need to meet Maastricht criteria for Euro area accession just several years later.

Headline consumer price inflation in Hungary reached its low at 3.6% year on year in May 2003, and has gradually risen ever since. In addition to the weakening of the forint, since last summer, the adjustment in VAT rates to align them with EU levels effective on 1 January 2004 added 1.2–1.5% to headline inflation early in 2004. The surge that started in 2003 brought inflation to 7.6% year on year in May 2004. However, July 2004 inflation had already dropped to 7.2% year on year, and the outlook for inflation for the remainder of 2004 and 2005 is actually much more benign than it was just a few months ago. This is not to say that inflationary risks are not skewed upwards. It is currently still difficult to assess to what extent the period of higher headline inflation will translate into increased inflationary expectations among the population.

The central bank hopes to cut inflation down to 4.0% by the end of 2005, and Global Insight originally concurred that this target seemed realistic. However, the price developments in the first half of 2004 mean that reaching this target would require substantial discipline on the part of the government and the NBH to keep a very close eye on price developments, making necessary adjustment along the way. We forecast 4.2% consumer price inflation at the end of 2005, and an average annual rate of 4.6%. In the medium term, inflation will decline gradually, to 2.5–3.0% by 2007, in preparation for the Euro area entry in 2010–11.

1.5.4 Fiscal reforms place Slovakia as the most progressive country in Central Europe

The benefits of Slovakia's tax reforms that were implemented in January 2004, as well as the country's accession to the European Union in May, will help to foster an acceleration of growth in 2004 and beyond (see Table 1.5). Although the implementation of a flat-rate income tax is giving many consumers more room for spending, personal consumption will rise only moderately in 2004, as the final set of major regulated energy price hikes took effect on 1 January and the lower rate of VAT was raised. Meanwhile, corporate tax cuts should help trigger a jump in investment spending, spurring new hiring. Growth in government spending, in contrast, will be weak during the next several years, based on the current cabinet's fiscal reforms.

Inflows of FDI will be particularly important in driving growth, especially in manufacturing, financial services, and communications, all of which are areas where privatization and restructuring have moved

Table 1.5. *Economic developments in Slovakia to 2007*

		1996	2001	2002	2003	2004	2005	2006	2007
GDP, total	billion current euro	15.7	23.3	25.5	28.7	33.2	36.9	40.8	44.2
Per capita GDP	current euro	2933	4336	4750	5334	6161	6838	7557	8200
GDP, growth rate	per cent	5.8	3.8	4.4	4.2	4.6	5.0	5.8	4.7
Average annual inflation	per cent	5.8	7.3	3.3	8.5	7.6	3.8	2.9	2.5
Population, end-year	thousands	5379	5379	5379	5380	5385	5391	5393	5394
Unemployment rate	per cent	11.3	18.3	17.8	15.2	14.6	14.0	13.3	12.6
Exchange rate, end-year	koruna/EUR	40.3	42.8	41.7	41.2	39.6	38.9	38.0	38.0
Public finance deficit (ESA-95)	% of GDP	NA	−6.0	−5.7	−3.5	−3.8	−4.1	−4.0	−3.0
Net foreign debt	% of GDP	7.5	21.4	11.6	14.9	9.2	2.1	−1.3	−4.1
Exports	million euro	6837	14189	15292	19381	22969	24881	29917	33550
Imports	million euro	8528	16406	17564	19949	23918	26308	30745	33995
Current account balance	% of GDP	−10.2	−8.4	−8.0	−0.9	−2.1	−2.5	−1.6	−0.7

rapidly. The cabinet's fiscal reforms, which have helped to present Slovakia as the most progressive country in Central Europe, are already helping to attract higher inflows of FDI. Early in 2003, Slovakia was chosen as the location of a new PSA Peugeot Citroën plant, which at the time was the largest greenfield project in Slovak history. The plant, which is scheduled for completion in 2006, should have an annual capacity of 300,000 cars and will employ an estimated 3,500 workers, in addition to indirect employment of 6,000–7,000. The PSA Peugeot Citroën investment alone is expected to add as much as 1 percentage point to GDP by 2006. In March 2004, Slovakia again won out over its neighbours in attracting another automobile producer, Hyundai/Kia. That firm will open a plant worth €1.2 billion, also scheduled to begin operation in 2006.

First quarter 2004 GDP growth reached 5.5%, the highest rate since the same period of 1998. In its February forecast, the Finance Ministry was projecting GDP growth of just 4.1% in 2004, rising to 4.3% in 2005, and 5.0% in 2006. However, in its most recent forecast, released on 28 July, those projections were raised to 4.7%, 4.5% and 5.1%, respectively, with growth reaching a high of 5.4% by 2007. The Finance Ministry's projection is now roughly in line with the Global Insight 2004 projection. Despite the first quarter surge, the 2004 GDP growth forecast remains steady at 4.6%. The healthier economic base should help to trigger new hiring and higher wages, thereby raising household consumption. As a result of those factors, GDP growth should gradually accelerate to a high of nearly 6.0% by 2006. In subsequent years, GDP growth should slow to more sustainable rates. Slovakia's current over-reliance on a few major firms makes the economy sensitive to fluctuation; however, in the medium term, the country will gradually become more diversified, as the government lays the groundwork for a more business-friendly environment for small- and medium-sized enterprises and the country becomes increasingly integrated with the European Union.

Fiscal reform remains the most pressing economic problem facing the country, but the centre-right government that took office following the September 2002 election seems ready for the challenge and has already made considerable headway in pushing its proposals for tax, pension and healthcare reform through the parliament. We assume that Slovakia will meet the Maastricht criteria for entry into the Euro area by 2007, at the latest, with accession in 2009. Unemployment is another of Slovakia's most difficult medium- and long-term problems, despite a significant decline in 2003. On 1 July 2003, new changes in the labour code took effect that should make firms more flexible in hiring new employees. It is also hoped that upcoming large-scale injections of foreign investment will eventually help to bring down the jobless rate.

After surging from 3.3% in 2002 to 8.5% in 2003, consumer price inflation is forecast to slow gradually over the next several years to reach 2.5% by 2007, as Slovakia attempts to meet the Maastricht criteria for entry to the EMU. In 2003, the consumer price index rose, mainly due to administrative measures that were put in place on 1 January. In 2004, average annual inflation is projected to slow to about 7.5–7.8%, as the last of the major regulated price hikes are implemented and the lower rate of VAT is raised. Slovakia's accession to the European Union in May 2004 had little effect on market prices in May and June. Consumer price inflation is projected to slow in the latter part of the year. This is particularly true given the strong base related to excise tax hikes that were implemented in August 2003. Nonetheless, prices will be pushed up by the recovery of domestic demand in connection with rising real wages and the recent cuts in interest rates. The Finance Ministry is projecting average annual inflation of 7.8% in 2004 while we are forecasting a somewhat slower rate of 7.6%.

Inflation should drop again in subsequent years, as the country prepares for entry into the EMU. According to its medium-term outlook, the central bank expects headline inflation to fall below 4.0% by early 2005, before approaching Euro area levels later that same year. We project that year-on-year inflation will fall to 2.5% in 2007, allowing Slovakia to meet the Maastricht criteria for entry into the Euro area. This is precisely in line with the Finance Ministry's forecast from July 2004.

1.5.5   Slovenia looks to net exports to boost growth

In the medium term, Slovenian GDP growth is expected to strengthen to between 4.0% and 4.5%, allowing Slovenian GDP per capita to close the gap with the EU average (see Table 1.6). An improvement in net exports will be the primary engine behind the more vigorous economic growth through the next several years. The combination of exports and imports of goods and services is larger than the country's total domestic demand. In 2003, net exports subtracted 1.8 percentage points from overall economic growth, its first negative contribution since 1999. In the first quarter of 2004, the negative effect of net exports lessened significantly, reducing overall economic growth by 1.1 percentage points. The modest improvement contributed to an acceleration of GDP expansion to 3.7% year on year in the first quarter of 2004. Within domestic demand, a sharp acceleration of fixed capital formation growth, from 5.5% in 2003 as a whole to 8.0% year on year in January–March 2004 was a

Table 1.6. *Economic developments in Slovenia to 2007*

		1996	2001	2002	2003	2004	2005	2006	2007
GDP, total	billion current euro	14.5	21.8	23.2	24.2	25.7	27.3	29.1	31.0
Per capita GDP	current euro	7293	10939	11646	12101	12908	13751	14713	15706
GDP, growth rate	per cent	3.5	2.9	3.2	2.3	3.5	3.7	3.9	4.1
Average annual inflation	per cent	9.9	8.4	7.5	5.6	3.9	3.5	2.8	2.3
Population, end-year	thousands	1991	1994	1995	1997	1990	1984	1979	1974
Unemployment rate	per cent	7.3	6.4	6.3	6.7	6.7	6.6	6.7	6.6
Exchange rate, end-year	tolars/EUR	178.6	221.4	230.3	236.7	239.5	239.7	239.6	239.5
Public finance deficit (ESA-95)	% of GDP	NA	−2.7	−1.9	−1.8	−1.4	−1.5	−1.6	−1.9
Net foreign debt	% of GDP	−0.8	17.6	17.3	23.9	29.8	33.9	33.3	29.8
Exports	million euro	6425	10435	11060	11410	12895	12805	13850	14296
Imports	million euro	7060	11127	11322	11960	13597	13514	14575	14958
Current account balance	% of GDP	0.2	0.2	1.4	0.1	−0.4	−0.2	−0.1	0.0

significant boost to overall economic growth. Private consumption growth, meanwhile, also accelerated, from 3.0% in 2003 to 3.7% year on year in the first quarter of 2004. Net exports will likely continue to hurt overall GDP growth in the short term, as demand for capital goods keeps import growth higher than export growth. Mitigating that negative trend, however, is a potential dip of imports from the Balkan Peninsula in the second half of 2004 through 2005. Slovenia had previously maintained several unilateral free trade agreements with other Balkan countries, a condition not allowed in the EU. Upon accession, Slovenia was forced to abandon these agreements, making imports from this area more expensive. After a few years in the EU, import demand for capital goods should level off, allowing net exports to begin to exert a positive influence on the economy once again through the medium and long term.

A recovery of demand from Slovenia's primary export market, the EU, will provide impetus to export growth through the medium term. At the same time, import growth should slow from its recent highs, as investment demand eases and world energy prices cool. These factors should lead to a slow improvement of the current account balance through the medium term, as well. In 2004, the balance is expected to fall into deficit, but begin to improve in 2005. In the short term, any modest current account deficit should be easily financed by growing investment inflows. Domestically, fixed capital formation will drive economic growth, as new opportunities for foreign investors have been opened now that the country has entered the EU, eliminating previous restrictions on foreign capital inflow. Private consumption will be a drag on overall economic growth, as labour market improvements will be modest and monetary policy will be tight.

The importance of trade movements to Slovenia's economic health has driven Slovenian officials to set an aggressive timetable for the adoption of the euro. In June 2004, Slovenia entered an ERM-II exchange rate regime, with an eye towards adopting the euro at the beginning of 2007. While in the ERM-II, the tolar is vulnerable to speculative attacks. However, the Bank of Slovenia is well positioned to defend such attacks, and will focus monetary policy through the medium term on the stabilisation and protection of the tolar/euro tie. Adopting the currency of its single largest trade partner will reduce Slovenia's risk exposure to foreign exchange movements. Prior to adopting the euro, however, the country must meet all of the Maastricht criteria. Although Slovenia is arguably among the best prepared of the new Member States to meet the criteria, the primary problem going forward is an inflation rate that is 1–2 percentage points too high.

Although inflation has cooled substantially from the beginning of 2003 to mid-2004, more progress must be made. In order to meet the targets, monetary policy will likely be reined in from its slightly more accommodative phase of recent months and fiscal policy will remain tight. In recent years, the government has shown admirable fiscal restraint, keeping budget deficits to less than 2% of GDP. In 2004, it has kept down all administratively controlled prices in hopes of reaching its inflationary target. Despite these positive steps, upward pressure on prices from stronger consumer demand and high world energy prices will prevent the country from meeting its 2004 inflationary target. In addition, lingering structural problems, such as an inflexible labour force and continued wage indexation, will make the reduction of inflation difficult both in 2004 and over the next couple of years, until these problems can be addressed. Accordingly, the country will not enjoy true success at significantly reducing inflation to the targeted level until 2006 at the earliest.

1.5.6   *The Baltic again to set the pace for economic growth among the new Member States*

Estonia   Estonia's economy is currently in good shape as it becomes aligned with the business cycle of the EU to an increasing extent. Remaining a healthy margin above the EU's average GDP growth in the medium to long term, we believe Estonia will continue to catch up with Western Europe in terms of per capita income. On the production side, the share of transport and communications in total value added will increase further. EU membership, as well as Estonia's sophisticated Internet penetration, which is already quite high, will propel growth of transport as well as communication services (see Table 1.7).

According to the forecasts of Global Insight, on the expenditure side, the development of private consumption is crucial for the medium-term sustainability of Estonia's external balances. Demand pressure on the current account will be alleviated gradually over the next three years, and private consumption is forecast to grow around 5% at the same time, significantly lower than in 2000–2. Gross fixed capital formation almost stagnated in the first quarter of 2004, but will nevertheless resume strong expansion in the remainder of 2004 and beyond, while growth of government consumption will decelerate again in the medium term. However, due to fiscal obligations to NATO, as well as those related to EU membership, public expenditures will be kept growing despite the government's efforts to curb the spending spree.

Table 1.7. *Economic developments in Estonia to 2007*

		1996	2001	2002	2003	2004	2005	2006	2007
GDP, total	billion current euro	3.4	6.7	7.4	8.0	8.8	9.5	10.4	11.4
Per capita GDP	current euro	2288	4892	5482	5935	6483	7095	7798	8549
GDP, growth rate	per cent	3.9	6.4	7.2	4.9	6.4	5.9	5.7	5.6
Average annual inflation	per cent	23.1	5.8	3.6	1.3	2.3	3.4	3.8	3.6
Population, end-year	thousands	1476	1367	1361	1356	1351	1344	1338	1331
Unemployment rate	per cent	10.0	12.6	10.3	10.0	9.5	9.3	9.1	8.9
Exchange rate, end-year	kroon/EUR	15.6	15.6	15.6	15.6	15.6	15.6	15.6	15.6
Public finance deficit (ESA-95)	% of GDP	NA	0.3	1.8	2.6	1.2	0.3	-0.2	-0.2
Net foreign debt	% of GDP	7.3	41.8	45.9	53.8	48.9	46.6	45.4	43.3
Exports	million euro	1576	3691	3633	3997	4661	5069	5448	5857
Imports	million euro	2446	4791	5080	5738	6460	6896	7309	7749
Current account balance	% of GDP	-9.2	-5.7	-11.4	-12.6	-10.4	-8.5	-7.9	-7.3

A major revision of national accounts data lifted GDP growth for 2003 upwards, to 5.1%. Exports grew quite robustly in 2003, yet were somewhat slower than imports, so that net trade continued to be a drag on economic growth. According to the current projections of Global Insight, GDP growth will equal 6.4% in 2004, as Estonia's key export markets will further recover in the second half of the year. The overall growth outlook for Estonia is favourable in the medium term as well, and GDP will record 5.7% average annual growth in 2005–7. The benefits of privatization and restructuring will result in higher productivity and rapid growth in industrial output for several years. Estonia's manufacturing sector already appears to be well positioned for the strong competition of the EU's internal market as well as for the world market. Manufacturing will remain strong, but will nevertheless record declining growth rates, roughly at parity with overall GDP expansion. During the next three years, Global Insight forecasts annual growth rates in industry at 5.2% on average. Services, including transport and communications, generate around half of Estonia's GDP, and it may be assumed that these sectors will enjoy higher rates of growth through the medium term, supplanting manufacturing as a key driving force for economic growth to some extent. Domestic trade is projected to grow at least 7% each year until 2007. The construction sector will continue to grow rapidly in line with strong investment. Transport and communications, as well as construction, will rise faster than GDP, at 7.5% and 6.9%, respectively, on average during that period. The Estonian government is more pessimistic about this year's economic growth, forecasting 5.3% real GDP expansion, but its projections for 2005–7 almost match our own, according to the 2004 Convergence Program released in May.

Estonia has recorded comparably low inflation during the transition period, in large part due to the successful currency board arrangement for the kroon. Average annual inflation reached a record-low 1.3% in 2003. However, while upward adjustments for administratively regulated prices, energy prices and certain kinds of excise taxes had already taken place before Estonia's EU accession, common EU rules require further adjustments.

Moreover, the government has noted that the continued harmonization of Estonia's tax regime with that of the EU will make further increases in VAT rates necessary. In addition, Estonian energy will need to achieve significant price increases over the next few years in order to finance the level of investment needed. For 2004, the company has already sought to increase its electricity tariff by 15%. While adjustments of regulated prices as well as excise taxes will lead to an increase of the headline inflation rate, core inflation measures will indicate that consumer price changes remain quite moderate and only slightly above the average of the European Union and the Euro area, in particular.

Global Insight forecasts consumer price inflation to accelerate slightly to 2.3% in 2004, and to reach 3.6% on average in the three years beyond, peaking in 2006 with 3.8%. While this inflation rate is supposed to come close to the ceiling of the applicable Maastricht criterion, we nevertheless believe that Estonia's EMU membership will not be impaired by too high an inflation rate at any time during 2006–8. Moreover, changes in the monetary environment related to the accession to the EMU are quite unlikely to have any negative effects on price stability in Estonia, since the country is already *de facto* a member of the Euro area as the kroon was tied to the euro under the currency board arrangement.

Latvia Among the three Baltic States, Latvia still has the lowest per capita income. In order to approach per capita income levels recorded in other new EU Member States, not to mention Western Europe, Latvia has to grow significantly faster for an extended period. In 2003, GDP growth picked up to 7.5%, after a slowdown in 2002. We have raised our forecast for 2004, to 7.4%, but currently maintain our projection of 6.1% average GDP growth during 2005–7 (see Table 1.8).

Manufacturing, a key driver for growth in 2003, will decelerate slightly in 2004, while domestic services, in particular retail trade, will continue to record robust growth in the medium term. Value added from the transport sector, which still depends heavily on the transit of goods to Russia, is expected to accelerate expansion in the medium term, outperforming the services average. Modernisation of infrastructure, adjustment in charges, and higher quality services will make Latvia a more competitive trade route for goods to and from Russia. Competition from ports in Russia will result in better services and lower prices in Latvia rather than reduced trade. Moreover, the country could benefit significantly from enhanced cooperation and integration with Russia, mainly because of its geographic location, as a bridge between Russia and Western Europe in terms of oil transport.

Global Insight forecasts gross fixed capital investment to increase at an average of 7.0% in 2005–7. Net exports, on the other hand, will continue to serve as a drag on GDP growth into the medium term, as the import of capital goods and, with increased significance, consumption goods will remain strong. The current account deficit will remain a threat to the country's external stability in the medium term. Yet, the government has ignored calls for a tightening of the fiscal budget in order to rein in domestic demand. However, with even closer economic integration after

Table 1.8. *Economic developments in Latvia to 2007*

		1996	2001	2002	2003	2004	2005	2006	2007
GDP, total	billion current euro	3.9	9.2	9.7	9.8	10.7	11.3	12.3	13.3
Per capita GDP	current euro	1588	3885	4147	4198	4604	4928	5376	5862
GDP, growth rate	per cent	3.7	8.0	6.4	7.5	7.4	6.3	6.1	5.9
Average annual inflation	per cent	17.6	2.5	1.9	2.9	4.7	3.5	2.3	2.1
Population, end-year	thousands	2468	2366	2346	2332	2319	2303	2287	2271
Unemployment rate	per cent	7.2	7.7	8.5	8.6	9.2	9.0	8.8	8.7
Exchange rate, end-year	lats/EUR	0.702	0.561	0.610	0.674	0.687	0.687	0.687	0.687
Public finance deficit (ESA-95)	% of GDP	NA	-1.6	-2.7	-1.8	-1.7	-1.8	-1.5	-1.5
Net foreign debt	% of GDP	18.9	52.9	61.2	69.5	63.4	63.5	63.7	61.9
Exports	million euro	1110	2235	2408	2556	3002	3272	3616	3855
Imports	million euro	1784	3915	4268	4632	5324	5747	6188	6455
Current account balance	% of GDP	-5.5	-8.9	-7.0	-8.6	-9.0	-8.9	-8.5	-7.7

EU accession buoying Latvian exports, the deficit will probably be kept at bay. Moreover, Latvia expects to receive sizeable funds from the EU's structural programmes. After a current account deficit of 9.0% of GDP in 2004, Global Insight projects a gradual decline in 2005–7. On average, the current account deficit will total 8.4% of GDP, and an accelerating inflow of FDI will finance roughly 60.00% of the deficit in that period.

Despite strong growth in revenues, the general government's budget recorded a deficit of 1.8% in 2003. Claiming social responsibility as a top policy priority, the government is unlikely to significantly reduce the deficit in the medium term. NATO and EU membership will add further spending pressure. Bearing in mind that GDP growth remains robust in the medium term, Global Insight forecasts the budget deficit to record an average of 1.6% in 2005–7.

Inflation has returned recently as a cause for concern. A mix of supply-side factors as well as strong domestic demand has driven consumer prices upwards. Upward price and tax adjustments will continue to influence inflation significantly, and Global Insight raised its inflation forecast for 2004 to 4.7%. The government still regulates prices on one quarter of all goods and services in the consumption basket, including energy, water and telecommunications. Going forward, it will be difficult to further reduce inflation in the near term, as remaining administered prices need to be adjusted to cost-recovery levels, an important step for Latvia in the medium term to ensure that its economy is competitive. In April 2003, for example, the public services regulatory panel noted that a 16.5% increase of natural gas tariffs over the following three years could push up overall inflation by 0.5%. Additional inflationary pressures will come from wages. However, while consumer price inflation will remain a considerable margin above the EU average, we believe that it will not rule out membership in the EMU within the medium term. According to our projection, inflation will average 2.7% per year in 2005–7.

Lithuania Lithuania achieved a stunning 9.0% growth rate in 2003 (see Table 1.9). Surprisingly, the strong growth was achieved along with a modest decline in the level of consumer prices. In fact, consumer prices decreased at 1.2% on an annual average basis in 2003. The overall economic expansion will moderate hereafter and inflation will turn positive again in 2004, but there are no signs pointing towards a major change in the underlying trends. For 2004, we have maintained our projection for GDP growth of 6.6%. In the medium term, economic growth will slow slightly, but remain strong. We are forecasting 5.6% annual GDP growth during 2005–7, as further economic rebounds in

Table 1.9. *Economic developments in Lithuania to 2007*

		1996	2001	2002	2003	2004	2005	2006	2007
GDP, total	billion current euro	6.1	13.3	14.8	16.1	17.6	18.7	19.9	21.4
Per capita GDP	current euro	1635	3809	4288	4665	5131	5457	5803	6249
GDP, growth rate	per cent	4.7	6.4	6.8	9.0	6.6	5.3	5.1	6.3
Average annual inflation	per cent	24.6	1.5	0.3	-1.2	0.9	1.1	1.2	1.2
Population, end-year	thousands	3712	14444	16152	18413	20250	21390	22411	23935
Unemployment rate	per cent	7.1	12.5	13.8	12.4	11.8	11.2	10.9	10.5
Exchange rate, end-year	litas/EUR	5.0	3.5	3.5	3.5	3.5	3.5	3.5	3.5
Public finance deficit (ESA-95)	% of GDP	NA	-2.1	-1.4	-1.7	-1.3	-0.8	-0.3	0.0
Net foreign debt	% of GDP	19.7	30.3	26.9	28.4	26.0	27.3	28.9	29.3
Exports	million euro	2581	5119	5864	6397	6467	6689	7389	7848
Imports	million euro	3507	7096	8126	8692	8686	9238	9884	10306
Current account balance	% of GDP	-9.2	-4.8	-5.2	-6.7	-6.1	-5.9	-5.6	-5.4

key export markets, as well as the high price of oil, will give the economy an additional boost. The Finance Ministry was even more upbeat than our projection, forecasting 7.0% growth for 2003, and 6.7% during 2005–7, based on the favourable external environment and strong consumer demand at home.

Industrial output growth should fluctuate around 6% annual through 2007, due to continued privatization and restructuring, further boosted by growing integration with the EU market. Growth will remain strong in the medium term due to the restructuring that has already taken place in Lithuania's industry and the impact of foreign investment on the economy. In addition, continuing privatization will benefit the overall economy by attracting better management and more investment. However, economic expansion in 2005–6 will be negatively impacted by the planned closure of the Ignalina nuclear power plant. Construction activity will continue to experience robust growth rates. Indeed, we forecast construction value added to rise 7.3% on average in 2005–7, thanks to inflows of structural funds from the EU. Growth of aggregate demand will decline, from 10.7% in 2003 to an average 5.7% during 2005–7. At the same time, however, structural changes within domestic demand are underway: while personal consumption growth is projected to decelerate considerably, gross fixed investment will pick up, with growth rates ranging from 7.0% to 9.5%. Over the long term, though, investment growth will fall back again below 5%.

Our medium-term forecast assumes that the fortunes of Mazeikiai Nafta, Lithuania's sole petroleum refinery and a very significant contributor to aggregate output, improve further, recovering from the low operating margins and the disruption at the company's Butinge terminal in 2002. Nonetheless, in case of falling oil prices, the performance of Lithuania's oil refining sector, and hence industry, would have to be downwardly revised again. But, at present, a major drop in oil prices is not on the cards. Global Insight does not expect a decline in the currently extraordinarily high world market price of crude oil before the second half of 2005 and even then the decline will be at only a moderate pace.

Lithuania's current account deficit relative to GDP was just half the size of Estonia's, but was nevertheless a concern at 6.7% in 2003. FDI inflows contracted sharply, so that financing the deficit has become more difficult. Nevertheless, we expect the gap to decline gradually during the medium term, as export growth accelerates and, as a result of relatively low import growth, the trade deficit shrinks. Transfers from the EU's structural funds will also help to reduce the deficit. According to our forecast, the current account balance should equal 5.4% of GDP in 2007.

Without doubt, a more restrictive fiscal policy stance would help to rein in domestic demand and, as a result, the large trade deficit too. Despite sustained strong overall growth, though, it is unlikely that the fiscal deficit will be reduced to somewhere near balance in the medium term. Indeed, the upgrading of administrative and military capacities in line with EU and NATO accession, as well as the requirements for the co-financing of EU-related structural projects, will put additional pressure on fiscal expenditures.

In 2003, Lithuanian consumer price deflation was achieved thanks to increased competition and greater productivity which offset the impact of robust domestic demand.

However, consumer prices will rebound in 2004 due to administrative and EU-related price changes. Increases in excise tax rates on cigarettes and fuel will exert upward pressure on prices. In addition to rising taxes, administered prices need to be raised towards cost-recovery levels. Rising wages and convergence with EU prices will also put modest upward pressure on prices. Consumer price inflation will end up at 1.6% year on year in December, but prices are projected to rise only 0.9% for the year on average. A peak will be reached in 2006 and 2007, at an annual average of 1.2%. Lithuanian officials project somewhat more significant upward pressure on consumer prices in the medium term: the Finance Ministry forecasts a 1.4% rise in consumer prices in 2004, and in 2005–7 consumer prices are projected to rise 2.3% on average.

1.5.7   Cyprus and Malta

Cyprus   The medium-term development of Cyprus' economy will be largely shaped by the country's recent accession to the EU. While further integration of the Cypriot economy with Western Europe will help to boost exports and tourism, growth will be tempered by several factors, including the government's need to take fiscal austerity measures aimed at meeting EMU membership targets, as Cyprus will be committed to adopting the euro within the medium-term horizon. The country will remain highly dependent on tourism revenues, which currently generate around one-fifth of Cyprus' GDP. The performance of the agricultural sector, which is highly dependent on weather conditions, will also remain an important factor in the country's growth outlook.

In line with the slow recovery in the global economy, GDP growth slowed to 2.0% in both 2002 and 2003, compared with a revised 4.0% for 2001 (see Table 1.10). Declines in tourism and export revenues

Table 1.10. *Economic developments in Cyprus to 2007*

		1996	2001	2002	2003	2004	2005	2006	2007
GDP, total	billion current euro	6.8	10.2	10.7	11.3	11.9	12.0	12.7	13.3
Per capita GDP	current euro	9241	13394	13887	14626	15266	15286	16059	16770
GDP, growth rate	per cent	1.9	4.0	2.0	2.0	3.5	3.3	3.2	3.2
Average annual inflation	per cent	3.0	2.0	2.8	4.1	2.0	2.2	1.9	1.9
Population, end-year	thousands	738	762	768	773	778	783	788	793
Unemployment rate	per cent	3.4	3.1	3.5	3.3	3.2	3.2	3.1	3.1
Exchange rate, end-year	pounds/EUR	0.592	0.579	0.516	0.526	0.596	0.625	0.604	0.613
Public finance deficit (ESA-95)	% of GDP	-3.4	-2.8	-3.6	-5.9	-3.6	-3.1	-3.0	-1.8
Net foreign debt	% of GDP	NA	NA	NA	NA	NA	NA	NA	NA
Exports	million euro	1070	1090	891	812	838	862	903	913
Imports	million euro	3064	4398	4313	3961	4466	4589	4796	4852
Current account balance	% of GDP	-9.2	-4.8	-5.2	-6.7	-6.1	-5.9	-5.6	-5.4

contributed to the weaker performance. Tourism revenues fell 10.96% in 2002, and remained weak in 2003, decreasing by a further 4.8%.

Growth in 2004 is benefiting from the pickup in the global economy, but the growth of the Cypriot economy will be tempered by several factors: the government's fiscal austerity measures aimed at meeting the Maastricht requirements for EMU membership and reining in a surging fiscal deficit and the uncertain geopolitical environment that has continued to affect tourism. Growth is projected to rebound to 3.5% in 2004 but will moderate slightly to a more sustainable growth rate of 3.0–3.2% in the medium term and beyond.

Cyprus' annual inflation rate has generally been relatively low, averaging less than 4.0% during the 1990s and only 2.7% during 1995–2001. In 2002, inflation increased to 2.8%, up from 2.0% a year earlier, but still below the 4.0% inflation rate registered in 2000. Inflation was subsequently boosted by crude oil prices and increases in certain taxes, including VAT rates, resulting in a rebound in the average rate of increase of consumer prices in 2003 to 4.1%. Consumer prices were not under substantial upward pressure in the first half of 2004, but with industrial producer price inflation boosted by record high world market prices for oil and metals, some acceleration in consumer price inflation growth is anticipated in the succeeding months. We project average annual consumer price inflation at only 2.0% in 2004, accelerating modestly, however, to 2.2% in 2005, but decelerating slowly thereafter through the medium term in line with trends in Western Europe.

Malta Malta's economic performance faltered in 2003 (see Table 1.11), with GDP declining in real terms after moderate growth in 2002. While 2002 growth was driven by net exports and consumer spending, both of those categories recorded disappointing results in 2003, particularly in the latter case, as exports declined. On a positive note, gross fixed investment surged in 2003, following two years of declines, signalling that overall GDP growth should pick up in 2004. That is particularly true in light of the projected revival of external demand and tourism. Malta's accession to the European Union on 1 May 2004 has provided the basis for sustained growth in the medium to long term. Nonetheless, the country must deal with its fiscal challenges, as its public debt was the highest among all ten accession countries in 2003, while its public finance deficit was second highest as a percentage of GDP.

Malta's National Statistical Office has revised its GDP data in line with ESA-95 standards, and figures for the first quarter of 2004 have yet to be released. However, after the decline in GDP registered in 2003, we

Table 1.11. *Economic developments in Malta to 2007*

		1996	2001	2002	2003	2004	2005	2006	2007
GDP, total	billion current euro	2.5	4.1	4.1	4.0	4.3	4.5	4.8	5.0
Per capita GDP	current euro	6754	10313	10371	10050	10611	11222	11822	12353
GDP, growth rate	per cent	4.0	-1.1	2.3	-1.7	3.4	3.3	3.2	3.1
Average annual inflation	per cent	2.5	2.9	2.2	1.3	2.6	2.3	2.5	2.0
Population, end-year	thousands	380	393	396	399	401	403	406	408
Unemployment rate	per cent	5.0	5.2	5.6	5.3	5.1	5.1	5.0	5.0
Exchange rate, end-year	lira/EUR	0.454	0.400	0.418	0.432	0.425	0.418	0.414	0.417
Public finance deficit (ESA-95)	% of GDP	-7.7	-6.4	-5.7	-9.7	-5.5	-4.5	-3.5	-3.0
Net foreign debt	% of GDP	NA	NA	NA	NA	NA	NA	NA	NA
Exports	million euro	1331	2239	2383	2213	2322	2570	2779	2839
Imports	million euro	2150	2873	2821	2818	2892	3134	3397	3480
Current account balance	% of GDP	-12.2	-4.5	-1.2	-6.0	-5.1	-4.6	-4.1	-3.5

are projecting a recovery in 2004, with growth reaching a rate of 3.4%. That revival should be based on a recovery in external demand and tourism. A recovery of exports will be crucial in 2004 and beyond. Customs data for the first four months of 2004 revealed a 3.6% year-on-year rise in lira exports and a 1.5% decline in imports.

Retail price inflation reached an annual average of 1.3% in 2003. Nonetheless, price growth sped up significantly in the last months of the year, to a year-end rate of 2.4%. In 2004, prices have continued to rise relatively rapidly, with year-on-year inflation reaching 2.7% in the first half. For the full year 2004, Global Insight now projects inflation on an annual average basis at double the 2003 rate, reaching 2.6%.

Malta's public finance deficit jumped to 9.7% of GDP in 2003, far above the 3.0% limit required for entry to the EMU. That was the second highest deficit among the ten EU accession countries. Prior to the release of the latest figures, the budget deficit was projected to fall to 5.4% of GDP in 2004, and to 2.8% by 2006. However, there remains considerable doubt as to whether the budget targets can be reached, particularly in light of 2003's worse than expected results. Another problem facing Malta in that regard is that end-2003 public debt rose to 1.3 billion lira, or 72% of GDP, the highest of the ten accession countries and far above the 60% requirement for entry to the Euro area.

2 The asymmetric impact of enlargement on old and new Member States: a general equilibrium approach

Mohamed Hedi Bchir, Lionel Fontagné and Paolo Zanghieri*

2.1 Introduction

Notwithstanding the historical opportunity to achieve the unification of Europe on the basis of values such as democracy, competition and social welfare, is the recent enlargement of the European Union (EU) good news for the economies of the old Member States?

This enlargement has raised several concerns among EU-15 members. First, this enlargement episode has involved a large number of countries and thus raised institutional issues. Secondly, the new Member States have per capita income levels much lower than the old Member States' average, which has raised among the latter the issue of social competition and the fears of a massive relocation of industries or massive migrations. In addition, political sustainability of the enlargement will imply sizeable transfer payments associated with structural policies, whereas the effectiveness of such transfers in promoting the catching-up process has been challenged by empirical analysis (e.g. Boldrin and Canova, 2003 and Chapter 13 below). Since catching-up is not proved to be an automatic process for new members, internal reforms should be promoted (Kaitila, 2004). Last but not least, the agricultural sector represents a disproportionate share of GDP and employment in certain new Member States, which has raised the issue of the Common Agricultural Policy (CAP) and how it will be adjusted in order to take into account the enlargement.

Some issues such as the EU budget and the impact of enlargement on immigration have been extensively dealt with in the last few years. The reader should, however, keep in mind that these studies did not incorporate certain important decisions on the EU budget, the CAP and

* The authors acknowledge helpful comments by three anonymous referees. The traditional disclaimers apply.

EU structural funds, which were taken at the Copenhagen Summit in December 2002. This issue, in particular concerning the CAP, will be dealt with in section 2.4 below.

To start with institutional issues related to the draft of the Constitution, increasing the number of Member States to twenty-five (possibly twenty-seven in 2007) is likely to raise problems with the way the European Council takes decisions. Baldwin *et al.* (2000) show that, with the current voting rules, an increase in the number of EU members will lead to a jump in the probability of having coalitions blocking important decisions and to a much bigger risk of the decision-making process being slowed down by the polarization between the block of richer Northern European countries and that of less-well-off Southern and Eastern European States.

Concerning the expected impact on the European budget, a comprehensive survey can be found in Weise (2002), which also presents some simulations. A great deal of discussion is centred on the effect on the CAP. The size of the farming sector (both as a percentage of GDP and as the number of people employed) in the new EU members would call for a sizeable transfers of funds, under the current CAP rules. In 2000, 21.6% of the labour force in the candidate countries was employed in agriculture, compared to only 4.3% in the EU-15. Provided that increasing the funds needed to finance the CAP without resorting to co-financing by single Member States appears politically unfeasible, enlargement is likely to provoke a redistribution of resources at the expense of old Member States. The EU-15 had agreed a temporary rural development package, involving direct aid for the new members for a total amount of €5.1 billions for 2004–6. Afterwards, direct aid will be phased in over ten years. These funds can be topped up to some extent by Member States' rural development funds. The farmers from the new states will be entitled to full and immediate access to CAP market measures. If no changes had been made to current CAP rules, some problems would have arisen, even if we leave aside any consideration about the European budget. Farm support via direct payments to farmers would have caused problems with WTO rules. A set of new rules was, however, adopted in January 2005. Ten Member States will apply the new Single Payment Scheme (SPS) for EU farmers, which is decoupled, i.e. independent of production, and which allows for a reduction in direct payments for bigger producers.[1] To date, none of the new Member States, with the exception of Malta and Slovenia, has decided

---

[1] However, limited coupled elements could be maintained to prevent abandonment of production. The Tobacco, olive oil and cotton sectors will join the system in 2006.

to join this system.[2] The other new Member States will stick to a different system until 2009 at the latest, namely the Single Area Payment Scheme (SAPS). The latter system is based on uniform per-hectare entitlements granted within any one region from regional financial envelopes.

At the same time, the huge disparities between new and old Member States in terms of per capita income and infrastructures will entail a major reallocation of structural funds. As Weise (2002) points out, as a consequence of enlargement, average GDP per capita in the EU will drop by roughly 10-15%. Consequently, all old EU regions have mechanically improved their relative position, which is a key issue for regions previously benefiting from Objective 1, and risk losing EU structural funds. Back-of-the-envelope calculations show that nearly 50% of the Objective 1 regions (concentrated mainly in Germany, Greece and Italy) run this risk. Moreover, enlargement will change the way the EU budget is financed: assuming no dramatic changes in agricultural policy, the burden of enlargement will be split in quite an inequitable way (see Weise (2002) Table A2), with Germany being particularly badly affected.

Regarding immigration and the impact on the labour markets, Boeri and Brücker (2000) stress that the very slow convergence in per capita income will surely trigger migration to old EU members, once the barriers to labour movements from Central and Eastern European countries are lifted. However, assuming that the pattern of migration follows that observed in post-war Europe, huge flows of immigrants should be ruled out. Boeri and Brücker (2000) estimate that a peak in migration will be reached within thirty years from the lifting of the barriers and that immigrants will represent no more than 1.1% of the EU-15 population. Such a relatively small flow can be explained by the high adjustment cost immigrants have to bear. Moreover, it is likely that they will compete not only with unskilled labour, as it is commonly imagined, but also with other skill groups, given the generally high level of formal education immigrants from accession countries show.

Sinn (1999) developed a theoretical model of capital and labour migration, based on the German reunification experience. The result he obtained was that labour migration to current EU Member States would only be temporary. While capital has only set-up costs, slowing down installation without affecting the long-run allocation, immigrant workers must bear permanent costs lasting for the whole period they live and work abroad, consisting of higher rents, the discomfort of not

---

[2] These two countries will adopt the system in 2007.

living at home and the costs of regular visits home. While not influencing the short-term reallocation of labour across countries, these last factors, according to Sinn (1999), are likely to affect the long-term equilibrium, tending to stabilize the initial allocation of labour. In the end, the adjustment process would lead to a first-best factor allocation, and therefore governments should not intervene to slow down migration. However, these results are somewhat weaker once minimum wage and welfare payments in current EU members are taken into account.

Lastly comes the issue of specialization and the relocation of industrial activity eastward. Given the very large gap in per capita income and factor endowments, one concern is that EU enlargement will dramatically alter the specialization pattern in the continent, with old Member States suffering the largest reallocation costs. In particular, a clear risk commonly envisaged is that labour-intensive industry will relocate massively to new Member States, where wages are on average 15% at current exchange rates (or one-quarter at purchasing power parity levels) of the EU average. Such a dramatic shift would possibly harm blue-collar workers within old Member States who would face a drastic reduction in wages or (more probably, given the characteristics of the labour market) mounting unemployment.

The potential impact should be different for new Member States since they will join a hugely integrated area, which is much more than simply entering into a free trade arrangement. It is very difficult to draw a precise picture, since previous episodes of enlargements hardly provide comparisons. For instance, combining transition and enlargement can have interesting outcomes associated with imperfect competition mechanisms: Boeri and Oliveira-Martins (2002) point out that taking into account the 'love for variety' of consumers profoundly affects conclusions. In the same way, it is difficult to assess *a priori* what would be the behaviour of firms in response to a dramatic change in the scale of their playing field, in terms of investment, mark-ups, etc. On top of that, it is important to stress the role joining the euro could have. Frankel and Rose (2002) show that the size of the gains in terms of increase in trade volumes can be huge. In total, economic analysis indicates that the expected impacts of enlargement should be smoothed by two elements. First, the competitive pressure is already faced by the industries of the old Member States. The latter have been increasingly confronted with competition from Eastern European producers over the last decade; adjustments have taken place, mostly via FDI flows and plant relocation. One could argue that this has been a great opportunity for European producers to enhance their competitiveness by relying on new suppliers and cheaper locations. In the same way, the expected convergence of new Member States will reduce the competitive pressure and enlarge the markets opened to incumbent countries' producers. In addition to this catching up process, the adoption of the 'acquis communautaire' is a key mechanism here.

How will old and new Member States be affected in the end? Are the fears raised by enlargement in old Member States motivated by sound economic analysis? If it is rather elementary to compute how the EU budget will be affected by this enlargement, it is much more difficult to assess how economies will be affected at the macroeconomic as well as sectoral levels. It is even more difficult to address the issue of competition among firms or the change in the specialization of countries and its induced impact on the labour markets.

In order to address properly the fears raised in old Member States, it is worth tackling all these issues by focusing on general equilibrium mechanisms. It allows us to take full account of the relationships between goods and factor markets, while accounting for the sizes of the countries considered, which is a very important determinant of the magnitude of the impacts to be expected. Hence, this is the approach that will be adopted in the current chapter, relying on a dynamic Computable General Equilibrium (CGE) model allowing for imperfect competition in all sectors but agriculture (MIRAGE).

We identify the following regions: the Euro area, the rest of the old Member States, Hungary, Poland, the Baltic, the rest of the new members, and the rest of the world. The sectoral breakdown identifies Agriculture, plus eight industrial sectors (Machine and tools, Automobile, Textile and clothing, Wood and wood products, Electronics, Chemicals, Metal products, Other industries) and lastly two service sectors (Transport, and Other services). We rely on GTAP[3] data, with the exception of tariffs for which MAcMap[4] is utilized. Three scenarios are considered. In a first scenario, where formal trade obstacles are removed while the market remains loosely integrated, all remaining trade barriers identified at the detailed level of some 5,000 product categories are removed.[5] In a second scenario, inspired by Smith and Venables (1988), the market is fully integrated and firms do take their decisions on this basis, in old as well as in new Member States. In a last scenario, new Member States accede to the CAP mechanisms, along the lines of the Copenhagen agreement. We are interested in the percentage deviations

---

[3] Global Trade Analysis Project: http://www.gtap.agecon.purdue.edu.

[4] Market Access Map has been developed by ITC (UNCTAD and WTO, Geneva) and CEPII. See Bouët *et al.* (2004).

[5] Product categories are defined at the 6-digit level of the Harmonised System.

from the baseline in 2015, as well as in the full dynamics of key macro-economic variables, of market structures, and the associated impacts on the labour market.

This chapter is organized as follows. In section 2.2 we provide a brief description of the trade relations between new and old Member States. Section 2.3 illustrates the general equilibrium dimensions of the integration process and describes MIRAGE, the CGE model we employ in order to assess the quantitative implications of EU enlargement. The results of the simulations are presented and commented on in section 2.4 and are compared with similar studies in section 2.5. Section 2.6 concludes.

2.2   The pre-enlargement situation

With the exception of agriculture and anti-dumping, new Member States had been granted free access to the EU-15 market long before their accession. The reverse is not true, however, as some accession countries kept some transitional import restrictions. Accordingly, East–West trade patterns have already dramatically changed over the last decade. The EU was already the main trading partner of the new Member States before their accession, absorbing roughly 68% of their total exports. Of course, given the difference in economic sizes, the reverse is not true: only 4% of EU-15 total imports were shipped by these countries. However, as a consequence of the transition to market economies and of the ongoing integration into the rest of Europe, the economies of the new Member States have recorded deep changes in production structures prior to accession. Redirecting resources towards sectors in which accession countries are granted a comparative advantage has been only part of the story. As highlighted in various studies on European integration, intra-industry trade, defined as two-way trade in (horizontally or vertically) differentiated products, has been a byproduct of integration (Fontagné *et al.*, 1998; Freudenberg and Lemoine, 1999). For instance, at the six-digit level of the nomenclature of traded products, the share of intra-industry trade in total trade for the Czech Republic is equal to the EU average, and is increasing at a high pace in each of the new Member States.

The increasing bilateral trade integration has thus led to an increasing share of intra-industry trade reflecting the move from a trade based upon low wage costs in new Member States towards a specialization based on more diversified and catching-up economies. Benefits from the latter class of trade relationships are theoretically higher, because of the presence of increasing returns to scale. Also, adjustment costs associated with such trade are expected to be much more limited

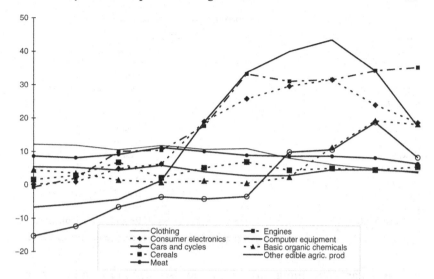

Figure 2.1. Hungary: revealed comparative advantage (unit: per thousand of GDP; source: CEPII CHELEM: 1993–2002).

(Fontagné and Freudenberg, 2002). This is why the impact on wages in new Member States is not necessarily detrimental to their low-skilled labour force: in sectors characterised by increasing returns to scale, imperfect competition and cross-hauling, the impact on blue-collar wages is more complex than is suggested by the traditional Stolper-Samuelson view. The same reasoning applies to blue-collar workers competing in old Member States with imports of labour-intensive goods produced in new ones.

These developments are reflected in the rapid evolution of the specialization of new Members' economies in the recent period, as measured by their revealed comparative advantage (defined as the contribution of each sector to the trade balance).[6] Hungary (Figure 2.1) has been specializing in Computers, Consumer electronics and Engines and to a lesser extent Cars and cycles. A recent reversal of these trends,

---

[6] These evolutions have been largely documented in the literature. Accordingly, rather than documenting each new Member State separately, we will stick to the countries for which detailed simulations are provided below: Hungary, Poland and the Baltic States. This breakdown has been suggested by a combination of CGE modelling constraints, the breakdown in the GTAP database, and lastly the enlargement itself. Accordingly, Bulgaria and Romania are dropped in 'the Rest of the world', the Czech Republic, Slovakia, Slovenia and Malta are aggregated with the 'Rest of new Member States' (see Table 2.1).

Table 2.1. *Geographical breakdown of Eastern European countries (and Malta)*

GTAP 5-2 Database	Current exercise
Bulgaria	Rest of the world
Czech Republic	Rest of new Member States
Hungary	Hungary
Malta	Rest of new Member States
Poland	Poland
Romania	Rest of the world
Slovakia	Rest of new Member States
Slovenia	Rest of new Member States
Estonia	Baltic
Latvia	Baltic
Lithuania	Baltic
Rest of CEECs	Rest of new Member States

in particular concerning the electronics sector, must, however, be stressed. In contrast, Poland (Figure 2.2) has traditionally been largely specialized in (unskilled) labour-intensive activities such as Clothing, Furniture, or Primary products (Coal). An emerging specialization in Consumer electronics is observed, while the specialization in the Clothing sector is decreasing. Coke, Shipbuilding, Iron and steel, Metallic structures also characterise a specialization in production inherited from the previous regional division of labour. However, this specialization is declining over time. Contemplating this specialization, much higher transition costs are expected for Poland than for Hungary in the future.

Lastly, the specialization of Baltic countries (Figure 2.3) is very specific: Refined oil and Non-edible agricultural products, and to a lesser extent Clothing, are the sectors in which these countries have increasingly allocated their resources in the recent period. Other fields of specialization comprise Furniture, Knitwear, Wood articles, Coal, Fertilisers, and Non-ferrous and ferrous ores. Telecommunication equipment is the only dynamic sector in which the Baltic countries are positioned.

2.3   General equilibrium dimensions of enlargement

As far as the old Members' economies are concerned, the big differences in size with respect to the new Member States and the pronounced asymmetry in the trade structure hints at a very limited impact of trade integration.

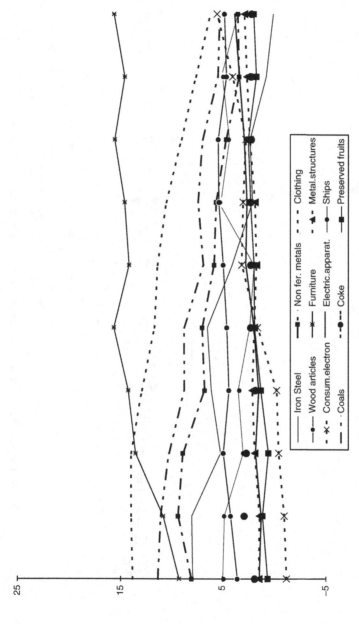

Figure 2.2. Poland: revealed comparative advantage (unit: per thousand of GDP; source: CEPII CHELEM: 1993–2002).

Legend:
- Iron Steel
- Wood articles
- Consum.electron
- Coals
- Non fer. metals
- Furniture
- Electric.apparat.
- Coke
- Clothing
- Metal.structures
- Ships
- Preserved fruits

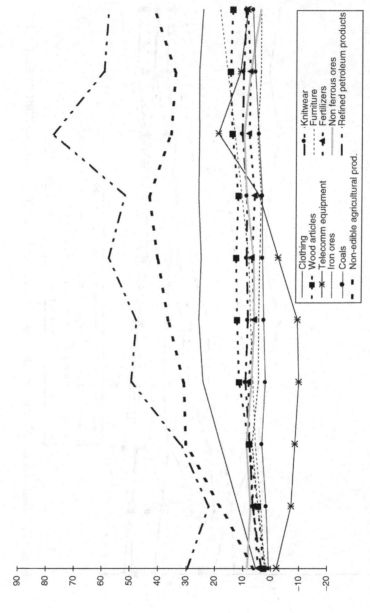

Figure 2.3. Baltic States: revealed comparative advantage (unit: per thousand of GDP; source: CEPII CHELEM: 1993–2002).

Legend:
- Clothing
- Wood articles
- Telecomm equipment
- Iron ores
- Coals
- Non-edible agricultural prod.
- Knitwear
- Furniture
- Fertilizers
- Non ferrous ores
- Refined petroleum products

On the contrary, the effects on new Member States will be large. At this stage, these countries have already reaped the short-term benefits from trade agreements with the EU-15 signed before their accession, as they have been trading increasingly freely with the old members for a decade or so.[7] However, the medium-run adjustment is likely to have at least two adverse consequences for new Member States. First, the removal of the remaining trade barriers will entail a deterioration in their terms of trade. The second, and probably more important, consequence is that a higher exposure to international competition will harm those sectors still showing large inefficiencies. Substantial and painful adjustment is expected, notably in sectors characterized by sizeable increasing returns to scale. Following such adjustments, however, the efficiency gains are expected to increase overall welfare.

A full account of the integration dynamics and the quantification of its effects needs to take into account a wide range of transmission channels. Moreover, one has to control for the general equilibrium effects of the changes in production trade patterns, the role played by market structures (i.e. the type of competition), the degree of factor specificity (which is very important for agriculture) and the degree of substitutability across goods from different sectors and/or country of origin.

In order to meet these needs, we undertake the analysis using MIRAGE (see Bchir et al., 2002, for a detailed description of the model), a multi-region, multi-sector CGE model, developed by CEPII and devoted to trade policy analysis. Data on trade barriers are provided by MAcMap (Bouët et al., 2004).[8]

MIRAGE has a sophisticated treatment of market structure, where products are differentiated by variety and by quality. Imperfect competition is modelled in an oligopolistic framework, in which firms exploit their market power and adopt a pricing-to-market strategy.[9] Horizontal product differentiation is associated with varieties as well as with geographical origin. There is also vertical differentiation; the elasticity of substitution is higher for goods having the same quality level. Thus, for example, a firm located in a Member State will face much harder competition from other EU-25 firms than from firms in developing

---

[7] Adopting the Common External Tariff should also have an impact on their trade, however.

[8] MAcMap includes ad valorem tariffs, ad valorem equivalent of specific tariffs, tariff quotas, and anti-dumping duties, on bilateral and tariff line level. We rely on 2001 data. The methodology used here is slightly different from the one used for the GTAP version of the database finalised in July 2004.

[9] Competition is à la Cournot: firms do not take into account the impact their decision might have on competitors or on the global level of demand.

countries. The number and the size of firms by sector adjusts progressively to market conditions.[10] This change in the number of firms is associated with pro-competitive effects: mark-ups are affected, as well as returns to scale. Consumers are affected too, given the *love for variety* assumption made. Capital accumulation is gradual and subject to adjustment costs. Agriculture is modelled as a perfectly competitive sector, and farm support is explicitly taken into account.

2.4   From trade liberalization to deep economic integration

Enlargement has had at least two different meanings. First, trade liberalization has involved the break-up of the residual tariffs and non-tariffs (essentially anti-dumping) protection, and the application by new members of the same common external tariff as the existing EU countries as well as the trade agreements with other areas (for example, some Mediterranean countries). Secondly and more importantly, it has meant deep economic integration, in line with the completion of the Single Market: accordingly, firms will now take their production decision considering an enlarged market of twenty-five members. Products from the new Member States will be regarded by consumers as belonging to the same quality range as old Members' products. The end of market fragmentation will make competition harder, pushing mark-ups down. On average, firm size will increase. The magnitude of these effects is bound to vary greatly across industries, with the difference between fragmented and segmented sectors playing a crucial role.

The assumptions about product differentiation play a key role in determining the results of economic integration. Where vertical differentiation is concerned, a process of integration in which goods from entrant countries will share the same quality as those from incumbent countries will increase greatly the level of competition faced by entrant countries' firms, thereby lowering mark-ups. The assumption is central as well for the behaviour of firms in the new Member States. Full entry in the EU increases their share in this area, thus enabling them to increase their mark-up in this market. On the other hand, fiercer competition with EU firms on their domestic market will oblige them to reduce the mark-up there, with beneficial welfare effects. Here we use a specific development inspired from Smith and Venables

---

[10] Each sector has a specific market structure: in some sectors, called 'fragmented', growth increases the number of firms; in others, called 'segmented', it is the size of existing unit that expands (see, for example, Sutton (1991) and Oliveira-Martins *et al.* (1996)). Profits are thus driven to zero much faster in fragmented than in segmented sectors.

(1988) in which economic integration eventually translates into the elimination of firms' ability to price-discriminate between different national markets.

Increased capital mobility is modelled as a reduction in the required rate of return for investment in the new Member States. Migration between the old and new EU Members is assumed to reflect income disparities. The sensitivity of migration to income disparities is assumed to follow the results of Boeri and Brücker (2000).

Three scenarios will be considered in order to disentangle the various effects of accession. The first attempt will be to identify the basic mechanisms associated with the removal of formal trade barriers alone. We cancel all remaining barriers at the date of enlargement but leave the markets fragmented from a competition point of view. In addition, new Member States adopt the Common External Tariff. This first scenario will be referred to as 'trade liberalization'. This is a kind of pre-Single Market situation in which formal barriers are abolished but where markets are still hardly integrated.

The second scenario aims at shedding light on the key influence on the economies of Member States in a framework of imperfect competition, namely market structures. In this 'market integration' scenario, firms take their decisions in a fully integrated European market, which affects the degree of competition they face on domestic as well as foreign markets, their pricing behaviour and lastly their size and the benefits to be reaped from increasing returns in industry and services. Moreover, since the perceived quality of goods produced in new Member States is the same as that of goods produced in old Member States, the former countries will face much higher competition from firms belonging to the latter. In both scenarios, the CAP remains unchanged and acceding countries do not benefit from it.

In the third scenario, we combine economic integration with farm support in new Member States. This scenario will be referred to as 'accession'.[11] The comparison with the outcome of the previous scenario sheds light on the specific impact of the policies pursued regarding farm support. In this scenario, all countries contribute to the CAP according to their GDP, a sum which is augmented by EU-25 tariff revenues on agricultural products. This amount is then shared among old and new Member States in proportion to their agricultural output, as follows: old Member States receive the full amount immediately,

[11] Notably, structural funds are not modelled here: our guess was that the *regional* impact of these transfers should be the issue to address; in addition, working with structural funds would imply a specifically modelled public sector in the CGE model.

whereas new Member States receive only 30% in 2005, increasing progressively up to 100% in 2012 on a linear basis.

For each scenario, the percentage deviations from the baseline (no-integration) solution, in 2005, 2010 and 2015, are provided. Our aim is to answer three basic questions:

- What is the impact on production and microeconomic equilibrium, i.e. the size and efficiency of firms, and the number of varieties produced and offered to consumers?
- What are the macroeconomic effects in terms of trade welfare and factor prices (especially skilled and unskilled workers' wages)?
- What are the most affected sectors and to which countries will production relocate?

2.4.1   'Trade liberalization'

Trade liberalization alone has a negligible impact on firms within the Euro area: markets were already wide open to exports from the new Member States before enlargement, with the exception of agriculture and a limited range of sensitive products. Hence, the change in the volume of trade does not affect market structure and mark–up behaviour. And, if new Member States open their markets, which were even more protected, their size is too limited to have an impact on old Member States. Hence, even if trade liberalization may foster trade, microeconomic efficiency gains will be limited. This is confirmed by a glance at the size of the firms in the various industries after all adjustments have taken place: output per firm changes by no more than 2%, positive or negative. With the exception of Metal products in Hungary (output per firm increases by +6.5%) and of Metal products and Automobiles in Poland (respectively +9.2% and +7.6%), as well as Machines and tools in the rest of the new Member States (+6.7%), economies of scale cannot be achieved as a result of trade liberalization.[12]

As far as the macroeconomic impact is concerned, the effects are highly asymmetric, as expected. This first scenario has a negligible impact on welfare in the Euro area, as the decrease (−0.05%) in the short run, which is reversed afterwards when adjustments have taken place, is very limited. The real exchange rate adjusts in order to balance the current account in value terms. The impact on wages is less intuitive: there is no sizeable impact on unskilled wages, even in the long run,

---

[12] We refer to percentage change as compared to the baseline in 2015, if not otherwise specified.

whereas a negligible decrease of the skilled wages is to be expected (−0.2%). This is the result of the slight change of the pattern of old Member States' exports, and of the real exchange rate appreciation with respect to the Euro area's main trading partners, the trade with which consists mainly in skilled labour-intensive goods. The only sizeable impact is on land's rate of return, as a result of our set of assumptions: both Euro area and new Member States are cancel their tariffs in agriculture (in fact its ad valorem equivalent of tariffs and tariff quotas). But the difference is that initially new Member States protected their agriculture by means of tariffs only, whereas Euro area members relied largely on domestic support. Since the latter is neither dismantled nor extended to new Member States in this first scenario, old Member States benefit from a competitive advantage which is beneficial to the specific factor used in agriculture.

The effect is similar for the rest of the old Member States, although somewhat more unfavourable in terms of GDP (−0.06%) and welfare (−0.1%) as a result of a slight trade diversion.

The macroeconomic impact is much more pronounced for new Member States as a result of limited initial efficiency, greater liberalization, and limited economic size. It is important to notice that most of these countries (especially Poland and Hungary) will experience a trade boom: this is due not only to increased trade with old Member States, but also to the non-negligible effects of new Member States adopting the EU external tariff system. The static effect[13] is detrimental to GDP (−0.5% in Hungary, up to −1.8% in Poland, −1.2% for the rest of the new Member States) and the real exchange rate has to adjust in order to balance the current account. Unskilled and skilled wages decline during the adjustment process and recover only in the long run. The impact on agriculture is highly detrimental: this is due to the set of assumptions used here: in this first scenario, taken as a benchmark, new Member States do not benefit from any payment associated with the CAP. Hence, one should not pay too much attention to this result at this stage: these figures simply confirm that these countries could not have joined without receiving support in the agricultural sector. Land return increases by 3.0% in the Euro area, which is to be compared with a 50% decrease in Hungary for instance, provided that no compensatory policy is implemented. We will come back to this issue below. In the long run, GDP is 2.6% above the baseline in Hungary but only 1.4% in Poland and 4.0% in the rest of the new Member States. It must be stressed that, if the evolution of factor incomes is detrimental

---

[13] Percentage change in 2005 as compared to the baseline.

to unskilled labour in Hungary and Poland, skilled wages are 3.1% above the base line in Hungary and 5.6% in Poland in the long run. In contrast, unskilled wages remain below their baseline in these countries (respectively −2.7% and −3.5%).

A glance at the results for Baltic countries reveals a different evolution. The static effect is positive (0.4%), but the dynamic and long-term effect is detrimental: GDP (−0.7%) and skilled wages (−2.6%) below their baseline, contrasted with increased unskilled wages (+3.0%). This is due to the very peculiar pattern of specialization they have (see Figure 2.3).

The results shown here are obtained despite a sizeable increase in trade flows (up to +20% in Poland), which are magnified in the long run. In total, we can expect a potentially adverse macroeconomic effect that should be taken into account by policy makers: there is a case for a transitory support to these countries. However, before addressing such issue, it must be kept in mind that integration is more than simply trade liberalization. Additional mechanisms associated with full market integration will now be taken into account in a second scenario.

2.4.2   'Market integration'

From a microeconomic point of view, this scenario highlights the changes in market structures and the induced responses of firms. Mark-ups are similar over the whole (enlarged) Single Market: there is no country-specific price discrimination. At the same time, the number of competitors is changing. These changes affect more new Member States than old ones: given their small domestic market before market integration, the competitive shock is much larger in the new Member States. For the older Member States, on the contrary, the only significant economic impact is observed in the Automobile industry, and is slightly negative (output per firm is decreasing by 2.5%). In Poland, large gains in efficiency are obtained for Metal products (+15.3%), Wood (+8.2%) and Other services (+24.9%). In Hungary, the size of the representative firm increases by 25% for Wood, Metal products and in Other services; sizeable efficiency gains are also recorded in the Automobile industry (+12.9%). For the Baltic countries, a similar evolution is recorded (Wood: +22.4%; Other services: +23.0%).

In terms of macroeconomic effects, for the Euro area, as well as for the rest of the old Member States, this new set of assumptions does not change the results significantly and we can rely on previous comments: accession is a negligible shock to old Member States. In the steady state, GDP recovers after a marginal decline during the adjustment process.

Sizeable differences with the previous scenario are in contrast observed for new Member States. First, GDP no longer declines as a result of the shock in the short run. Even the static impact is slightly positive (+0.5%) in Hungary, whereas the adverse evolution is smoothed in Poland (−0.7% instead of −1.8%). Similarly, the adverse effect on unskilled wages is much more limited than in the previous scenario (−1.4% in Hungary, −2.1% in Poland). This means that skilled and unskilled wages are above the level reached in the previous scenario in the long run. This scenario is also beneficial to the Baltic countries: GDP increases more in the short run (+2.0%) and stays above the baseline in the long run (+0.4%), in contrast to the previous scenario. For the rest of the new Member States, the positive impact on GDP and wages (skilled and unskilled) already observed in the previous scenario is confirmed.

The reasons explaining these favourable outcomes have already been stressed above: under imperfect competition full market integration leads to a reduction in mark-ups, a reduction in the number of firms, and an increase in the size of firms. All this turns into efficiency gains thanks to increasing returns. In total, the positive impact of efficiency overcompensates the negative impact on welfare of the reduction in the number of varieties offered to consumers.

2.4.3 'Accession'

In this scenario, new Member States are eligible to participate in the CAP, in accordance with the agreement reached in Copenhagen. They contribute to the European budget in proportion to their GDP and income from tariff duties on agricultural products, and CAP payments (modelled as a negative tax on production) are increasing progressively to the levels suggested by their agricultural output according to the rules for the old EU members, on a linear basis between 2004 and 2006.

At the microeconomic level, the results in terms of firm size, displayed in Table 2.2 are roughly the same as in the previous scenario, with a slight increase in the magnitude of the deviation from the baseline.

In this scenario, the negative impact for the Euro area is slightly more pronounced, but still modest: −0.7% of GDP in 2015 (Table 2.3). The outcome for the other old Member States (Table 2.4) is even less pronounced (−0.1%).

In contrast, the macroeconomic gains are much larger for the new Member States except the Baltic States (Tables 2.5 to 2.8). Important gains in terms of GDP are likely to materialise in the medium to long run, as the boom in domestic demand will offset the huge increase in imports. Hungary's GDP increases by 3.0% in the short run and 7.6% in

Table 2.2. *Accession: effects on firm size*[a]

Sectors	Euro area	Rest EU-15	Hungary	Poland	Baltic	Other new Member States
Machine and Tools	-0.45	-0.13	-0.58	3.69	-0.42	0.90
Automobile	-1.73	-0.76	4.97	14.14	NA	7.18
Textile Clothing	-0.04	-0.03	-0.81	0.92	-0.40	2.07
Wood	-0.48	-0.05	8.41	22.42	22.00	34.60
Electronics	-0.24	-0.24	0.82	0.95	-0.93	0.39
Chemicals	-0.26	-0.13	2.28	6.28	-1.86	2.55
Metal Products	-0.92	-0.21	13.68	23.17	2.07	28.35
Transport	-0.18	-0.24	2.24	1.67	-7.25	-2.62
Other industry	-0.07	-0.05	1.75	5.94	1.50	4.51
Other services	-0.16	-0.11	25.00	24.84	21.67	23.03

Notes: (a) % deviation from baseline in 2015.

Table 2.3. *Accession: effects on the Euro area*[a]

	2005	2010	2015
Welfare	-0.72	-0.82	-0.93
GDP (volume)	-0.50	-0.64	-0.73
Terms of trade	-0.19	-0.34	-0.41
Real exchange rate	-0.09	-0.24	-0.28
Unskilled wage	1.10	0.72	0.53
Skilled wage	-0.51	-0.91	-1.13
Return to capital	-0.20	-0.06	0.12
Land return	2.94	1.97	1.98
Exports (volume)	-0.01	0.05	0.16
Imports (volume)	-0.84	-1.10	-1.29

Notes: (a) % deviation from baseline.

the long run. The corresponding figures are 0.9% and 6.9% in Poland, and 3.1% and 7.2% in the rest of the new Member States. The most surprising result is accordingly the substantial welfare loss incurred by the Baltic States (-11.9% in the short run and even more in the long run). The explanation has to do to a large extent with the perverse effect CAP funds will have on their pattern of specialization. The full adoption of the EU tariff system will entail a sizeable loss in tariff duties. At the same time, CAP flow will lead to a shift of resources to the agricultural

Table 2.4. *Accession: effects on the rest of the old EU members*[a]

	2005	2010	2015
Welfare	−0.57	−0.66	−0.74
GDP (volume)	0.11	−0.04	−0.12
Terms of trade	−0.04	−0.11	−0.15
Real exchange rate	0.14	0.06	0.02
Unskilled wage	0.28	0.08	0.00
Skilled wage	−0.15	−0.44	−0.62
Return to capital	0.41	0.55	0.74
Land return	8.94	8.10	8.86
Exports (volume)	−0.14	0.29	−0.43
Imports (volume)	−0.05	−0.16	−0.32

Notes: (a) % deviation from baseline.

Table 2.5. *Accession: effects on Hungary*[a]

	2005	2010	2015
Welfare	3.44	4.90	6.67
GDP (volume)	3.02	5.79	7.59
Terms of trade	1.20	1.35	1.81
Real exchange rate	−1.32	−0.24	0.93
Unskilled wage	−4.14	−2.32	−0.23
Skilled wage	1.80	3.23	6.26
Return to capital	0.27	−0.95	−0.86
Land return	−40.50	−30.80	−28.40
Exports (volume)	−0.64	1.60	2.64
Imports (volume)	12.22	16.86	20.25

Notes: (a) % deviation from baseline.

sector (in which the Baltic States are less efficient than the rest of the EU) at the expense of the rest of the economy.

How differently the sectors will be affected by enlargement can be illustrated by simulated changes in trade flows. Table 2.9 illustrates for instance the sizeable changes in trade flows to be expected in certain sectors as a result of Hungarian accession. First, Agriculture will be significantly affected, since a 143% increase in Euro area exports appears in the accession scenario, starting from limited levels however. This should not be surprising: the CAP is still stimulating trade in agricultural products among Member States, even for old Members. The reverse

Table 2.6. *Accession: effects on Poland*[a]

	2005	2010	2015
Welfare	−1.10	1.81	4.33
GDP (volume)	0.91	4.57	6.98
Terms of trade	−3.15	−1.22	−0.11
Real exchange rate	−5.14	−2.42	−1.13
Unskilled wage	−9.52	−5.75	−3.13
Skilled wage	−1.09	3.50	8.09
Return to capital	−3.32	−3.42	−3.65
Land return	−4.86	−6.92	−6.89
Exports (volume)	12.12	10.30	8.76
Imports (volume)	21.13	26.39	29.38

Notes: (a) % deviation from baseline.

Table 2.7. *Accession: effects on the Baltic States*[a]

	2005	2010	2015
Welfare	−11.90	−17.60	−20.60
GDP (volume)	0.89	−1.11	−3.36
Terms of trade	0.88	−1.33	−1.79
Real exchange rate	−1.40	−3.00	−2.99
Unskilled wage	9.24	5.84	3.44
Skilled wage	−1.79	−12.60	−18.20
Return to capital	6.18	7.25	10.54
Land return	48.70	61.58	64.15
Exports (volume)	11.99	−1.23	−5.93
Imports (volume)	−8.32	−12.70	14.90

Notes: (a) % deviation from baseline.

flow increases only by 45–50%. Other sectors affected to an important degree are Automobile and Electronics; Automobile exports shipped to Hungary by plants located in the Euro area will be severely reduced (up to −32% in 2015), while exports from Hungary to the Euro area in the same sector will progressively increase (+4% in 2005; +25% in 2015). In Electronics, Euro area exports will be only slightly reduced (−3% in 2015), while Hungarian exports will increase by 9% in 2005 and up to 41% in 2015. Accordingly, Hungary will benefit from a sizeable trade surplus in the latter sector. In contrast, Hungarian exports of

Table 2.8. *Accession: effects on the rest of the new Member States*[a]

	2005	2010	2015
Welfare	4.51	5.62	6.70
GDP (volume)	3.15	6.17	7.22
Terms of trade	1.28	1.28	1.51
Real exchange rate	−0.94	−0.49	−0.02
Unskilled wage	2.97	4.34	5.31
Skilled wage	5.37	6.61	8.55
Return to capital	3.01	1.71	1.07
Land return	−11.20	−0.19	1.48
Exports (volume)	−2.35	−0.94	−1.13
Imports (volume)	16.88	19.87	21.69

Notes: (a) % deviation from baseline.

Textile and clothing will progressively decline (−3% in 2005; −26% in 2015). These changes in bilateral trade flows are one among the numerous impacts affecting production on both sides. In Agriculture, the output is in total only slightly affected within the Euro area (+1.8%). The Automobile sector is more severely impacted (−4.8% in 2015). Metal products, Electronics or Machine tools record a 2% decrease in their output, and Textile and clothing a 1% decrease only.

Given the difference in economic sizes, the changes are much more sizeable in Hungary. Agricultural output is reduced by 24%, while Automobile production increases by 25% in 2015, Electronics by 39% and Metal products by 30%. The only exception to this general mechanism is observed in the Textile and Clothing sector where production will be declining in Hungary (−1.0% in 2005; −11.9% in 2010; −22.1% in 2015).

2.4.4 Comparison of dynamics across scenarios

In order to evaluate the relative contribution of the different elements of economic integration, Figures 2.4 to 2.6 show the impact on GDP of the three different scenarios.

The most striking effect is the impact CAP rules would have on most new members. Agricultural subsidies will amplify the beneficial effect of full market integration. By contrast, the CAP will only be responsible for the small GDP loss the old Member States will face. The same applies for the Baltic States, for which the most beneficial situation is the one

Table 2.9. *Accession: effects on bilateral trade between the Euro area and Hungary*

Sectors	Euro area to Hungary				Hungary to Euro area			
	Initial level[a]	2005[b]	2010[b]	2015[b]	Initial level[a]	2005[b]	2010[b]	2015[b]
Agriculture	520	143.06	140.78	137.52	1125	44.94	48.63	50.44
Machine and Tools	3408	0.77	4.23	6.98	2279	6.08	8.91	1.67
Automobile	2050	20.65	-24.79	-32.37	1788	4.41	20.19	25.98
Textile Clothing	1385	1.18	5.71	9.41	1519	-3.35	-15.57	-26.67
Wood	195	-16.13	-6.04	3.94	369	-4.65	-15.39	-25.99
Electronics	1612	-1.26	-0.19	-3.25	2115	9.37	31.79	41.22
Chemicals	2249	-5.19	-1.17	5.16	1082	-0.78	-2.30	-8.77
Metal Products	1047	-23.59	-20.14	-16.84	951	0.92	7.67	8.77
Transport	148	3.02	9.87	16.11	284	-0.26	-5.65	-10.00
Other industry	923	-4.18	-0.57	5.69	514	3.35	0.21	-7.20
Other services	1116	-22.39	-13.43	-5.87	1177	-19.68	-24.82	-28.72

Notes: (a) initial level in 1997, USD million; (b) % deviation from baseline.

Table 2.10. *Accession: effects on production by sector, Euro area*

Sectors	Initial level[a]	2005[b]	2010[b]	2015[b]
Agriculture	87.50	1.78	1.89	1.82
Machine and Tools	54.84	−1.57	−2.32	−2.29
Automobile	42.72	−1.90	−3.15	−4.83
Textile Clothing	25.18	−1.75	−1.76	−1.17
Wood	11.88	−0.72	0.29	0.65
Electronics	30.19	−1.30	−1.59	−1.84
Chemicals	76.65	−0.86	−0.74	−0.55
Metal Products	48.49	−1.73	−1.97	−1.88
Transport	48.35	−0.39	−0.22	−0.18
Other industry	56.96	−0.81	−0.55	−0.37
Other services	634.20	−0.59	−0.62	−0.71

Notes: (a) initial level in 1997, USD million; (b) % deviation from baseline.

Table 2.11. *Accession: effects on production by sector, Hungary*

Sectors	Initial level[a]	2005[b]	2010[b]	2015[b]
Agriculture	1.23	−24.60	−23.60	−24.10
Machine and Tools	0.37	6.10	9.41	3.18
Automobile	0.33	8.12	22.86	25.11
Textile Clothing	0.26	−1.05	−11.90	−22.10
Wood	0.08	5.00	−1.32	−7.88
Electronics	0.36	8.84	30.43	39.41
Chemicals	0.55	5.12	6.24	3.33
Metal Products	0.32	13.81	25.57	30.81
Transport	0.47	2.61	2.26	2.24
Other industry	0.36	4.81	4.22	1.13
Other services	4.07	7.53	9.03	9.79

Notes: (a) initial level in 1997, USD million; (b) % deviation from baseline.

not including the CAP. Then come the dynamics *per se*: in Poland, positive impacts would be postponed to 2010 if trade integration alone were at stake (Figures 2.4 to 2.7). In the rest of the new Member States, the benefits of the accession are fully reaped within a seven-year period only, while these are much more longstanding for countries like Poland and Hungary.

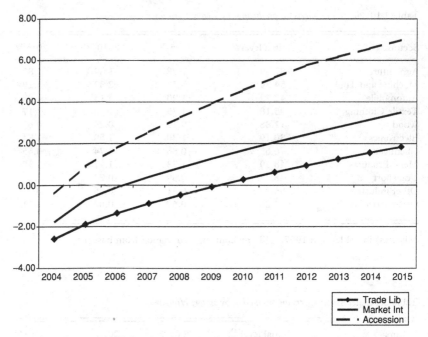

Figure 2.4. Poland: impact on GDP of different enlargement scenarios.

2.5   Comparison with other studies using a similar methodology

There have been numerous recent studies of enlargement relying on a CGE methodology. Bchir and Maurel (2002), Lejour *et al.* (2001) and Maliszewska (2002) all raise the issue of integration aspects going beyond the reduction of formal tariffs: full entry means accession to the internal market (and thus a reduction in border formalities or decisions taken by firms on a different geographical scope, for instance) and eventually of migration flows. Bchir and Maurel (2002), using the MIRAGE model, develop three scenarios, namely trade integration, economic integration, and economic convergence in line with Total Factor Productivity (TFP) catch-up. Their geographical breakdown identifies Hungary and Poland among CEECs, and France or the rest of EU-15 on the other side. Lejour *et al.* (2001) start by assessing the impact of the accession to the internal market by estimating gravity equations at the industry level. This first step is used as an input in a second step in which this trade potential is used in a CGE model of the

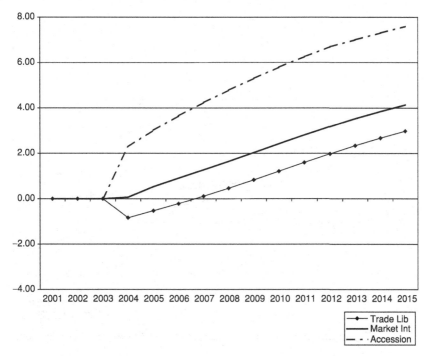

Figure 2.5. Hungary: impact on GDP of different enlargement scenarios.

world economy. Maliszewska (2002) focuses on Single Market-related mechanisms.

As far as agriculture is concerned, the final impact is highly sensitive to the type of assumption made on transfer payments and farm support granted to new members. Assumptions can range from zero to full benefit; in the latter case, one can either redistribute the shares of the pie, or increase the size of the pie with constant shares (Bach *et al.*, 2000; Bchir and Maurel, 2002). A key assumption is the magnitude of the output changes in accessing countries when farm support is introduced, namely the elasticity of production. Reciprocally, any general increase in the output in agriculture should be constrained by the availability of arable land and other resources used. Depending on the set of assumptions made, the change in output can be either limited or very large.

According to Vaittinen (2002), EU enlargement will have a significant economic impact on the new Member States, with GDP 10% above its

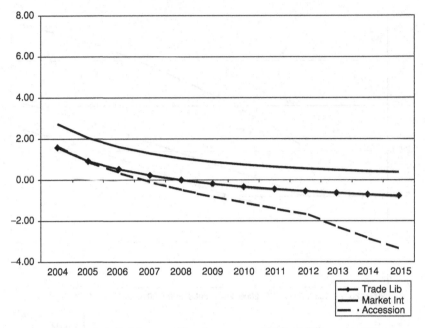

Figure 2.6. Baltic countries: impact on GDP of different enlargement scenarios.

baseline within ten years. This is qualitatively the same result as ours, but quantitatively much larger (+2–7% at most in our simulations). In both cases, the models are dynamic. These differences are due to different basic assumptions: we do consider that rigidities and factor specificity impede the reallocation of factors. We do not allow for migrations, since huge migrations (up to 5.6 million migrants over ten years in Vaittinen (2002)) would certainly not be easily accepted by the incumbent countries concerned and, moreover, have not been recorded in the past, as discussed above. In addition, there has been so far evidence of limited mobility of labour in the new Member States. Lastly, we do not take into account foreign investments, due to a lack of reliable data and the fact that firms have already anticipated this accession and largely invested in new Member States (in Hungary, for instance). In contrast, Vaittinen (2002) finds that a large share of the increased output is generated by FDI and that increase in per capita consumption is partially driven by migration flows towards old Member States that decrease the labour force faster than the GDP. Furthermore, Vaittinen (2002) introduces a 10% cut in transportation costs associated with integration,

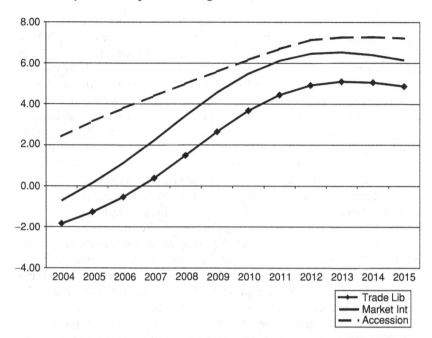

Figure 2.7. Rest of the new Member States: impact on GDP of different enlargement scenarios.

in addition to immediate benefits of CAP payments for new members and structural funds.

Maliszewska (2002) finds gains for the new Member States more in line with our own estimates. She evaluates the implications of enlargement by focusing on Single Market-related mechanisms such as the removal of border costs and reduced costs for achieving national standards. The volume of GDP increases by 1.4–2.4% in new Member States as a result of these mechanisms. After adjustment of the capital stock, these static gains are more than doubled.

Both Vaitinnen (2002) and Maliszewska (2002) confirm our results of quite a small impact of enlargement on old members as a whole, given the large difference in economic size.

2.6   Conclusions

The simulation shows that the impact of enlargement on the economy of EU-15 members taken as a whole is negligible, because of the relatively small economic size of the new Member States and the new opportunities Western European firms will find in the Eastern European markets. Therefore, the fears of eastward integration producing massive relocation of firms and hurting low skilled workers appear excessively pessimistic. However, as pointed out for example by Boeri and Brücker (2000), some effects on specific sectors or on some neighbouring regions cannot be ruled out. This could call for some specific policy interventions. In contrast, while the impact on the new Member States will be sizeable and highly positive in the medium-to-long run (with the exception of the Baltic States), the transition is unlikely to be smooth. Sizeable reallocation of factors (especially labour force) across sectors is to be expected. This is likely to create temporary unemployment and public policy will be needed in order to smooth the effects of the integration.

Another issue concerns exchange rates. Market integration will provoke swings of relative prices and large changes in the real exchange rate. Such phenomena should be taken into account by the new Member States for their decision about exchange rate arrangements, and especially on the timing of the adoption of the euro. If, on the one hand, the adoption of a common currency has been proven to boost trade and economic integration, on the other losing monetary freedom too quickly could be harmful for countries undergoing big macroeconomic and structural adjustments.[14]

We cannot conclude without stressing the drawbacks of our approach. As already recalled, MIRAGE does not take into account the externalities openness and integration create in recipient economies, such as technological spillovers, which might affect dramatically the economic structure. Moreover, a key domain for future improvement of such approaches is to model properly the labour market and to assess the differences in labour market flexibility which could favour the adjustment process and bring about more favourable outcomes than those obtained by our simulations. The latter remark is only one aspect of a multi-faceted issue: the same structural model is applied in MIRAGE to each economy. This is of course a very strong hypothesis: regulated prices are more relevant in new Member States than in old ones, the capacity to finance new investments and thus to allocate resources towards new sectors might be temporarily constrained, etc. However, relying on a general equilibrium framework imposes some simplifications: the purpose here was not to forecast, but to shed light on certain

---

[14] Larèche-Révil and Ëgert (2003) estimate real equilibrium exchange rates for five accession countries (Czech Republic, Slovakia, Slovenia, Poland and Hungary), finding that some currencies are strongly overvalued with respect to the euro and the dollar.

mechanisms and magnitude of effects too often misunderstood. Regional impacts should finally be addressed in order to have a full assessment of the expected impacts of enlargement on new Member States. This will be done in the next chapter.

References

Bach, C., Frandsen, S. and Jensen, H. 2000. 'Agricultural and Economic-Wide Effects of European Enlargement: Modelling the Common Agricultural Policy'. *Journal of Agricultural Economics*, vol. 51, pp. 162–80.

Baldwin, R., Berglöf, E., Giavazzi, F. and Widgrén, M. 2000. 'EU Reforms for Tomorrow's Europe'. CEPR Discussion Paper, No. 2623.

Bchir, M., Decreux, Y., Guérin J. and Jean, S. 2002. 'MIRAGE, A General Equilibrium Model for Trade Policy Analysis'. CEPII Working Paper, No. 17.

Bchir, M. and Maurel, M. 2002. 'Impacts économiques et sociaux de l'élargissement sur l'Union Européenne et la France'. CEPII Working Paper, No. 3.

Boeri, T. and Brücker, H. 2000. *The Impact of Eastern Enlargement on Employment and Labour Markets in the EU Member States*. Berlin: European Integration Consortium.

Boeri, T. and Oliveira-Martins, J. 2002. 'Transition, variété et intégration économique'. *Economie et Prévision*, vols. 152–3, pp. 55–69.

Boldrin, M. and Canova, F. 2003. 'Regional Policies in the Light of the EU Enlargement'. European Forecasting Network report, Chapter 8, www.efn. uni-bocconi.it/Annex_to_chapter_8.pdf.

Bouët, A., Decreux, Y., Fontagné L., Jean, S. and Laborde, D. 2004. 'A Consistent, Ad Valorem Equivalent Measure of Applied Protection Across the World: The MAcMap-HS6 Database'. CEPII Working Paper, No. 22.

Fontagné, L. and Freudenberg, M. 2002. 'Long-Term Trends in IIT', in Lloyd, P. and Lee, H. (eds.), *Frontiers of Research on Intra-industry Trade*, Basingstoke: Palgrave Macmillan, pp. 131–58.

Fontagné, L., Freudenberg, M. and Péridy, N. 1998. 'Intra-Industry Trade and the Single Market: Quality Matters'. CEPR Discussion Paper, No. 1959.

Frankel, J. and Rose, A. 2002. 'An Estimate of the Effect of Common Currencies on Trade and Income'. *Quarterly Journal of Economics*, vol. 117, pp. 437–66.

Freudenberg, M. and Lemoine, F. 1999. 'Central and Eastern European Countries in the International Division of Labour in Europe'. CEPII Working Paper, No. 5.

Kaitila, V. 2004. 'Convergence of Real GDP Per Capita in the EU-15: How Do the Accession Countries Fit in?' ENEPRI Working Paper, No. 25.

Lahrèche-Révil, A. and Égert, B. 2003. 'Estimating the Fundamental Equilibrium Exchange Rates of Central and Eastern European Countries: The EMU Enlargement Prospect'. CEPII Working Paper, No. 5.

Lejour, A., de Mooij, R. and Nahuis, R. 2001. 'EU Enlargement: Economic Implications for Countries and Industries'. CESifo Working Paper, No. 585.

Maliszewska, M. 2002. 'Eastern EU Expansion: Implications of the Enlarged Single Market for Current and New Member States'. mimeo.

Oliveira-Martins, J., Scarpetta, S. and Pilat, D. 1996. 'Mark-up Ratios in Manufacturing Industries – Estimates for 14 OECD Countries'. OECD Economics Department Working Paper, No. 162.

Sinn, H. 1999. 'EU Enlargement, Migration and Lessons from German Unification'. CEPR Discussion Paper, No. 2174.

Smith, A. and Venables, A. 1988. 'Completing the Internal Market in the European Community: Some Industry Simulations'. *European Economic Review*, vol. 32, pp. 1501–25.

Sutton, J. 1991. *Sunk Costs and Market Structure*. Cambridge: MIT Press.

Vaittinen, R. 2002. 'Eastern Enlargement of the EU: Factor Mobility and Transfers – Which Matters Most?' mimeo.

Weise, C. 2002. 'How to Finance Eastern Enlargement of the EU: The Need to Reform EU Policies and the Consequences for the Net Contributor Balance'. ENEPRI Working Paper, No. 14.

3 Changes in the spatial distribution patterns of European regional activity: the enlargements of the mid-1980s and 2004

Toni Mora, Esther Vayá and Jordi Suriñach *

3.1 Introduction

The deepening of the integration process and the continued expansion of the European Union (EU) over the last two decades have unavoidable consequences for both the spatial configuration of activity and the regional convergence process. As far as the convergence process is concerned, there is no consensus on whether integration is a positive phenomenon. Following a neo-classical view, the elimination of internal boundaries for the mobility of capital and labour will enhance the relative advantages of peripheral regions (that is, their lower salaries) inducing industry to spread to these regions. At the same time, integration may allow a better allocation of resources, leading to an increase in overall efficiency. Additionally, the enlargement of commercial links could promote convergence, at least between the regions most closely related in trade (Ben-David, 1994). Moreover, the small size of the companies in the South of Europe (unlike the North) means that they probably stand most to gain from the integration process (Neven, 1990). However, other authors do not share these optimistic views.

Thus, despite the lower salaries in the South, the core regions retain additional advantages: more accessibility to large markets, better infrastructure and human capital endowments, strong internal and external economies of scale, and so on. Furthermore, according to Krugman and Venables (1990) and Krugman (1991a, 1991b), insufficient integration (not enough reduction of the barriers) increases the concentration of the activity in the core and regional inequalities thus persist. So it could be inferred that further reductions in trade costs in Europe would lead to

* The authors acknowledge financial support from the Ministerio de Ciencia y Tecnología, Plan Nacional de Investigación Científica, Desarrollo e Innovación Tecnológica, SEJ 2005–04348/ECON.

75

considerable centripetal shifts in the European industry. In this scenario, we would expect an increased concentration of scale-intensive production in the EU core, while the periphery would specialise in manufacturing activities not characterised by scale economies, and non-manufacturing activities. In any case, it seems that the final result (persistence of the core-periphery scheme or a more equal distribution) will depend on both the strength of the centripetal and centrifugal forces and the ability of each European region to capitalise on their own advantages (see Illeris, 1993;[1] and Suarez-Villa and Cuadrado-Roura, 1995). Indeed, it seems clear that a simple division into core and periphery is no longer an accurate description of a complex society.

During the period considered, the services sector has grown quickly, in terms of both output and employment (Molle, 1996). This development has had major consequences for the division of labour (Hansen, 1990). However, underlying the increase in services is a significant degree of heterogeneity between the types of services involved. While high-quality, dynamic services (financial and enterprise services) are concentrated in certain areas in the core of Europe, the most backward and peripheral regions have increased their involvement in precarious services with low productivity, salaries and qualifications (Rodríguez-Pose, 1995).

Reports in the literature have traditionally applied concentration measures with the aim of evidencing changes of sectoral concentration. The spatial distribution of the activity has not been tested in depth. In addition, overall concentration measures do not identify partial changes in the distribution of specialisation. Here, in order to overcome these limitations in previous analyses, we will study the evolution of sectoral specialisation/concentration by estimating kernel density functions and by performing an exploratory spatial analysis. In this way, we hope to identify the lessons to be learnt from the EU enlargement of the mid-1980s, in order to try to calibrate future scenarios after the latest enlargement in 2004. This chapter will therefore focus on the changes in the distribution of product. The spatial distribution of economic activity and the estimation of kernel density functions will explain the evolution of the concentration of economic activity that complements the previous empirical evidence. This is one reason why we look at the shares of the top and bottom percentiles of distribution, which may not be moving in

---

[1] Illeris (1993) defined two factors to consider: the structural composition of the economy of each region plays a role in its development; whether a region gains or loses depends largely on the local conditions, such as political institutions, regional policy assistance, infrastructures, supply of skilled labour, social qualifications, factor prices and population density.

the direction that the inequality coefficient expresses. Additionally, the main contribution of the chapter is the analysis of the spatial distribution of product at regional level (the literature usually applies these techniques at national level). A study at regional level will provide the chance to consider new policy decisions, and the inclusion of Eastern regions provides us with a wide-ranging sample giving an overview of the European Union after the most recent enlargement.

The chapter is structured as follows. The next section will discuss both theoretical aspects and empirical contributions from the New Economic Geography perspective. Section 3.3 defines the sample used and the specialisation and concentration indices computed. In section 3.4, the changes in the distribution of these indices during the enlargements of the 1980s are analysed for EU-12 regions. Section 3.5 presents a picture of the distribution of regional and sectoral concentration when Eastern regions are considered jointly with EU-15 regions. Finally, section 3.6 concludes.

3.2   Spatial agglomeration models: theoretical aspects and empirical evidence

3.2.1   What have we learned from spatial models?

The earliest New Economic Geography models offered an endogenous explanation for the agglomeration of activity in a territory. Following on from the seminal papers of Krugman (1991a, 1991b), these models explained the regional distribution of industry as the result of the tug-of-war between forces that tend to promote geographical concentration (centripetal forces) and those that tend to oppose it (centrifugal forces).

Among the forces that contribute to agglomeration, we include the three traditional Marshallian sources of external economies: backward and forward linkages between firms[2] (the consequence of input–output linkages), the existence of a thick and immobile local labour market (under the assumption of inter-regional mobility)[3] and the presence of external economies via information spillovers.[4] By contrast, the presence

---

[2] See Krugman and Venables (1995) and Venables (1996).
[3] Puga (1999) introduces the hypothesis of intersectoral mobility as well as inter-regional mobility to Krugman's model (1991a, 1991b). The benefit obtained by the R&D labs from input differentiation plays a role in Martin and Ottaviano (1999), which is equivalent to that of inter-regional labour mobility in Krugman (1991b) and that of input–output linkages in Venables (1996) and Krugman and Venables (1996).
[4] In the words of Ottaviano and Puga (1997), technological externalities arising from personal interactions matter more for small-scale agglomerations, while to explain

of immobile factors (certain land and natural resources and indeed people, in an international context), the high rents on land characterised by a notable concentration of economic activity, and external diseconomies (such as congestion) are the main centrifugal forces working against industrial concentration. Economic agglomerations may occur at various levels of aggregation: from small-scale agglomerations of clearly defined sectors (for instance, highly specialised industrial districts) to large-scale agglomerations that cut across state boundaries.[5]

Looking at this last case, economic integration may have an impact on the eventual spatial location of economic activities given that it affects the equilibrium between the forces of dispersion and agglomeration. In the first stages of integration (characterised by high trade costs), the need to supply markets locally encourages firms to locate in different regions, leading to a stable, symmetric equilibrium. However, as integration processes advance (leading to intermediate trade cost values) and under the hypothesis of increasing returns, the incentives for self-sufficiency weaken, leading industry to concentrate in regions with the largest market size. Then, pecuniary externalities take over, firms and workers cluster together and the cumulative causation process begins, leading regions to differentiate endogenously into an industrialised core and a de-industrialised periphery.

However, the relationship between the integration process and agglomeration is far from monotonic or linear. In fact, it is an inverted U-shape: the prices of local factors (land rents and wages) and goods tend to rise wherever agglomeration takes place. This is particularly relevant if they involve certain immobile factors that are important for production (for instance, labour) or non-tradable goods that are important for consumption (for instance, housing). In this case, as further integration reduces the importance of pecuniary externalities, differences in the prices of immobile goods and factors take over. As a consequence, industry spreads to less developed regions, reducing the previous spatial divergence in the distribution of activity throughout the territory. Puga and Venables (1996) described a gradual process of industrialisation where, after a critical mass is reached, firms move from the core to other regions some distance away to avoid the high wages present in the centre, but close enough to it in order to benefit from its advantages in terms of agglomeration economies (positive pecuniary externalities created by inter-firm linkages). The process may then

---

large-scale agglomerations, we must either look to other technological externalities whose effectiveness does not decrease sharply with distance, or turn to pecuniary externalities.
[5] See Krugman (1991a, 1991b, 1998).

repeat itself, so industrialisation takes the form of a sequence of waves, with industry spreading from country to country.[6]

3.2.2 What does the previous evidence of empirical spatial specialisation suggest?

We will now look at previous empirical papers on patterns of specialisation, an early stage in terms of the theoretical aspects discussed above. A European analysis can be found in Molle *et al.* (1980), Brülhart and Torstensson (1996), Brülhart (1998), Amiti (1999), Haaland *et al.* (1999) and Midelfart-Knarvik *et al.* (2000). Davis and Weinstein (1998, 1999) deals with prefectures in Japan and twenty-two OECD countries, Aiginger *et al.* (1999) considers US regions, while Longhi *et al.* (2003), Hallet (2000) and Altomonte and Bonassi (2002) considers Eastern candidate regions, EU-15 regions and a sample of European regions (French, Italian and Spanish), respectively. These analyses vary in focus, examining employment, production or trade to consider industrial specialisation patterns, and they also apply different specialisation indices. European Commission (2003) provides a recent empirical report.

The literature therefore explores different samples of countries or regions, different periods and different databases, most of them referring to the national level. Considering only European analyses, it has been detected that the overall specialisation of EU countries rose during the 1970s, and for most countries in the 1990s (Amiti, 1999; Brülhart, 1998; Walz, 1999). Haaland *et al.* (1999) detected a rise in concentration of about 11.4% (for a 1985–93 sample period) in the average industry, and Midelfart-Knarvik *et al.* (2000) found a significant effect of geographical aspects on the evolution of industrial concentration. At the same time, these authors concluded that dissimilarities in industrial patterns have continued since the 1980s. However, empirical evidence indicates that not all industries were analogously concentrated (slow-growing and unskilled-labour-intensive industries became more concentrated whereas industries with large economies of scale became more dispersed), without any limit in the evolution of dissimilarities. Additionally, production specialisation has increased while trade specialisation has decreased (Amiti, 1999 or Midelfart-Knarvik, 2000).

As regards the regional analysis, there seems to have been an increase in localisation of the manufacturing sector as a whole during the 1970s

[6] See Krieger-Boden (2002) for a brief summary of the New Economic Geography hypothesis.

and 1980s (Molle *et al.*, 1980; Brülhart, 1998; Walz, 1999). Altomonte and Bonassi (2002) confirmed the existence of a perverse specialisation of regions that were lagging behind (only regions from France, Italy and Spain were considered). On the other hand, in a study of seventeen branches of activity from EU-15 regions, Hallet (2000) found an increasingly similar pattern for most regions, reflecting a structural change from manufacturing to services; agricultural and day-to-day services are spatially dispersed, while industries with high economies of scale are concentrated in a few locations, and there is a tendency towards stability for the concentration of branches (period 1980–95). A further analysis is found in Brülhart and Traeger (2003), where a decomposition of entropy measures of concentration is applied. The study detects both between-country and within-country indices. In addition, the authors compute centre–periphery gradients, finding that manufacturing has become gradually more concentrated, though the location bias towards central regions has become weaker. Krieger-Boden (2002) analysed the evolution of specialisation compiling regional employment data for France (from 1973 to 1996) and Spain (from 1981 to 1992). Using a high degree of sectoral desegregation (thirty-five and eighty manufacturing branches for France and Spain respectively), the author concluded that during the European integration process changes in the specialisation patterns were slow and that there was no obvious trend towards either increase or decrease (though there is a slightly elevated probability for an increase). In addition, Krieger-Boden (2002) found that the typical intensive returns to scale industries as a whole tended to disperse during the period, and that a certain catching-up process exists.

With respect to the Eastern economies, the empirical evidence also differs according to whether the focus is national or regional. In a study based on trade data, Landesmann (1995) reports that these countries tend to specialise in labour-intensive sectors following an inter-industry trade pattern. At a regional level, Longhi *et al.* (2003) finds evidence of increasing specialisation in Bulgaria and Romania during the early 1990s. In contrast, Hungarian regions show no changes during the first half and a decrease in the second half of the decade, leading to a homogenisation of the spatial concentration of activity. According to Petrakos (1999), transition increases dissimilarities, favouring countries near the East–West border. Resmini's (2002) findings support this notion. Regions bordering the EU, with higher wages, a more skilled labour force and a well-developed service sector show the highest growth rates. Several factors may explain these results. Altomonte and Resmini (1999) stress the significance of foreign direct investment (FDI) for shaping regional specialisation. Landesmann (2003) notes the importance of FDI and education levels. Therefore the experience of certain regions seems to confirm the presence of the Gerschenkron hypothesis (i.e. the advantage of backwardness). In 1999, FDI was strongly concentrated in a few regions in specific countries (Poland, Czech Republic and Hungary accounted for 62% of overall FDI in 1999).

3.3   Defining data and indices

Our analysis is based on a study of a set of 180 regions from the EU-27, incorporating the entire EU-15 territory as well as regions from the ten new Member States plus Bulgaria and Romania (henceforth, Eastern regions). The regions studied in Portugal (five regions), Spain (seventeen), France (twenty-one), Italy (twenty-nine), Greece (thirteen), Sweden (eight), Finland (six), Austria (three), Czech Republic (eight), Hungary (seven), Poland (sixteen), Romania (eight), Slovakia (four), Denmark, Ireland, Estonia, Latvia, Lithuania, Bulgaria, Slovenia, Cyprus and Malta, were all NUTS II in the regional classification level, and those for the UK (eleven), Belgium (three), Holland (four), Germany (sixteen) and Luxembourg were NUTS I.

The EUROSTAT REGIO database provides us with Gross Value Added (GVA) data. The data available from this database on this variable is not complete, so our evidence does not aim to examine the evolution over the entire period. We aim to focus on two time points: 1985, in order to obtain an initial spatial picture of the regional specialisation pattern before the integration of the poorest EU-15 countries, and 1995, in order to assess the final achievements of integration. The period can be considered a time of particularly strong policy-led integration. As we compute specialisation indices by means of GVA data, the results may differ with regard to employment data.[7] For the EU-12 regions, a NACE-R17 sectoral classification has been used, while the lack of data obliges us to use only nine sectors for EU-27 regions. In the latter case, the analysis is done for 1995, since no GVA data are available for more recent years.

In order to characterise the distribution of the product in the sectors analysed, we calculated three different indices. The first is a sectoral concentration coefficient (L_j), which informs us whether one sector j is highly concentrated in a few regions $(L_j \rightarrow 1)$ or if, on the contrary, it has a more equilibrated distribution $(L_j \rightarrow 0)$.

[7] The lack of completed employment data for NACE-R17 sectoral classification at regional level leads us to study the specialisation pattern only with GVA data.

$$L_j = \frac{1}{2} \sum_{i=1}^{N} \left(\frac{x_{ij}}{x_{\cdot j}} - \frac{x_{i\cdot}}{x} \right), \quad i = 1, ..., N; \; j = 1, ..., R \qquad (1)$$

where x_{ij} is the GVA in the region i in the sector j; $x_{i\cdot}$ ($x_{\cdot j}$) the total GVA in the region i (sector j); and x is the total GVA. We also computed a regional specialisation coefficient (L_i), in order to determine whether a region i is extremely specialised in certain sectors ($L_j \rightarrow 1$) or if the distribution of its GVA is diversified ($L_j \rightarrow 0$). The regional specialisation coefficient is:

$$L_i = \frac{1}{2} \sum_{j=1}^{R} \left(\frac{x_{ij}}{x_{i\cdot}} - \frac{x_{\cdot j}}{x} \right), \quad i = 1, ..., N; \; j = 1, ..., R \qquad (2)$$

The final index is a regional-sectoral concentration coefficient, L_{ij}. From this index, we know whether one sector j is highly concentrated in region i in comparison with overall EU value ($L_{ij} > 1$) or if, on the contrary, a small proportion of the GVA of j is located in this region, $L_{ij} < 1$ in relation to the EU average. The specialisation patterns are normalised in accordance with this EU average. The regional-sectoral concentration coefficient is defined as follows (its elements have the same meaning as before):

$$L_{ij} = \frac{x_{ji}/x_i}{x_j/x}, \quad i = 1, ..., N; \; j = 1, ..., R \qquad (3)$$

In addition, from the last coefficient, we computed three average concentration indices: one for services with the highest levels of technological intensity (Transport and communication; and Credit and insurance institutions), another for low-technology industries (Food, beverages, tobacco; Textiles and clothing, leather and footwear; and Paper and printing products) and, finally, another for high-technology industries (Chemical products; Transport equipment; and Metal products, machinery, equipment and electrical goods).

3.4   Analysis of the distribution of the evolution of spatial activity, 1985–95

Table 3.1 summarises the results for overall sectoral concentration (L_j evolution). Our results show that concentration indices for the final period are similar to the initial figures (as was the case in Hallet, 2000). In addition, the results do not differ from the evidence in the

Table 3.1. *Sectoral concentration coefficients* (L_j)*: EU-12 regions (1985–95)*

Sector	1985	1995
Agricultural, forestry and fishery products	0.328	0.343
Fuel and power products	0.225	0.181
Ferrous and non-ferrous ores and metals, other than radioactive	0.344	0.362
Non-metallic minerals and mineral products	0.199	0.201
Chemical products	0.215	0.203
Metal products, machinery, equipment and electrical goods	0.213	0.202
Transport equipment	0.241	0.233
Food, beverages, tobacco	0.164	0.171
Textiles and clothing, leather and footwear	0.346	0.384
Paper and printing products	0.184	0.194
Products of various industries	0.196	0.202
Building and construction	0.074	0.078
Recovery, repair, trade, lodging and catering services	0.076	0.076
Transport and communication services	0.108	0.093
Services of credit and insurance institutions	0.140	0.139
Other market services	0.084	0.081
Non-market services	0.102	0.115

literature on the sectors with the highest concentration: the sectors depending on the location of natural resources (Agriculture, Ferrous and non-ferrous ores and metals and Fuel and power products) together with the Textile sector and the Transport equipment sector. In contrast, the sectors with the lowest concentrations are related mostly to the Services sectors. As regards the changes in concentration indices during the period analysed, slight enhancements are recorded in the agricultural and low-technology industries sectors, while the sectors with lower indices are those grouped in our high-technology industrial and services classification.

However, some of these results may hide partial sectoral evolutions. We will now estimate kernel density functions in order to analyse the distribution of regional sectoral concentration indices (L_{ij}). Quah (1997) proposed this technique to consider intra-distributional mobility as a factor that could affect inequality or concentration measures. This is a relevant factor given that inequality or concentration measures only include differences with a single value and do not capture the overall intramobility distribution (Quah, 1997; Atkinson, 2002). In the literature there are many evaluations of this option for the analysis of GDP per capita (López-Bazo *et al.*, 1999 or Magrini, 1999, among others). The analysis of the density functions of the regional and sectoral concentration indices allows us to consider any specific changes in certain percentiles of the distribution. In this regard, a widening of the density function would be taken to indicate a greater heterogeneity among sectoral specialisation indices. Thus, each region would be highly specialised after integration, and the concentration of the GVA distribution increases. However, heterogeneity may appear just for a particular club of regions. This would be detected by expanding the probability masses for a few percentiles. In this way, we can detect those regions that are changing their overall distribution (below, around or above the average specialisation level). This would show, for example, that, although there may be an overall process of lower concentration, some regions might show a higher partial concentration. In this regard, Brülhart and Traeger (2003) estimated centre–periphery gradients in sectoral location patterns in order to detect the presence of a geographical concentration of sectors in order to consider the feature called 'anonymity' in the distribution literature. But their analysis is applied taking into account the region's market potential and the fact that it belongs to an EU Member State. Our belief is that perfect anonymity can be only evidenced by kernel density functions.

We therefore analyse the evolution of sectoral patterns of concentration and specialisation in a regional classification derived from the enlargement of the mid-eighties (Figures 3.1 and 3.2). This will help to predict the consequences of the new enlargement. For the EU-12 case we will compare the 1995 distribution of economic activity with the initial distribution in 1985, prior to the second enlargement of the European Community. These figures present comparable distributions[8] and show probability measures related to an average value of the indices (unity). An estimation of this kind illustrates the distribution of specialisation indices, which helps to identify the regions that have altered their global concentration magnitudes (enhancing the lower or upper quartiles).

Results from Figures 3.1b, 3.1c, 3.1d correspond to distributions at initial and final period for the cases of average specialisation indices (L_{ij} for high-tech industries, low-tech industries and high-tech services) and Figure 3.1a reflects the regional specialisation index evolution (L_i). This last figure shows a clear tendency to narrow the range of the distribution due to the lower specialisation level of those regions above the average. So, though we note a catching-up approach, bimodality seems to persist as a consequence of the existence of a club of regions[9]

---

[8] Kernels are estimated applying the Silverman option, and results have been obtained with Gary King's procedure in Gauss.

[9] This club is mainly composed by Greek regions jointly with most of the Portuguese regions and some Spanish and Italian regions.

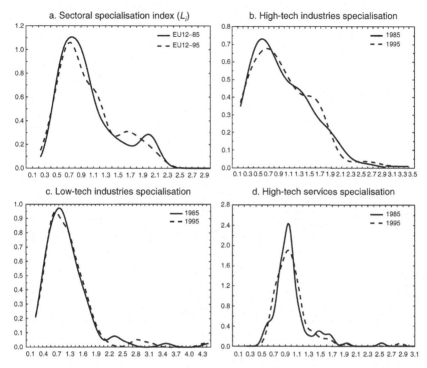

Figure 3.1. Distribution of specialisation indices: EU-12 (1985–95).

that are highly specialised in some sectors (in relation to the EU average). Thus, Figure 3.1a seems to confirm the empirical evidence in the literature of the presence of an overall concentration specialisation pattern for European regions.

The estimation of partial sectoral density functions for our averaged indices or specific sectoral ones will contribute to explaining the relevance of some sectors in concentration after integration. Figures 3.1b, 3.1c, 3.1d seem to show the concentration pattern detected, but a bimodality tendency is more evident for the case of high-technology industrial specialisation indices (Figure 3.1b). However, Figure 3.1c shows a mass of probability rising slightly above the average. Therefore, regions with a higher level of low-technology industries specialisation seem to be moving towards higher levels of specialisation (upper cue).

However, regions differ in their sectoral specialisation within our average specialisation indices. So these indices may not reflect overall regional sectoral patterns. We are therefore interested in knowing the evolution of specialisation distribution for those sectors with high or

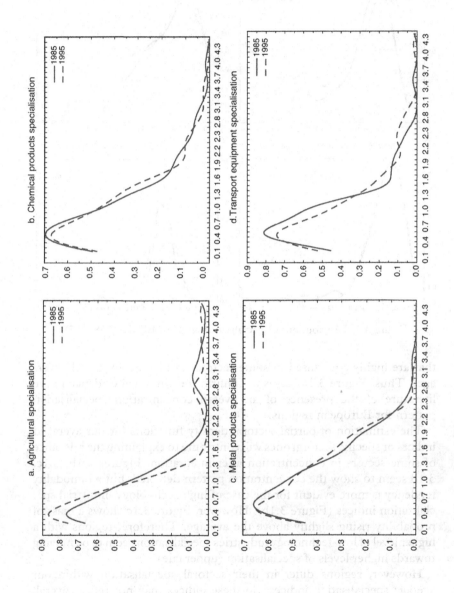

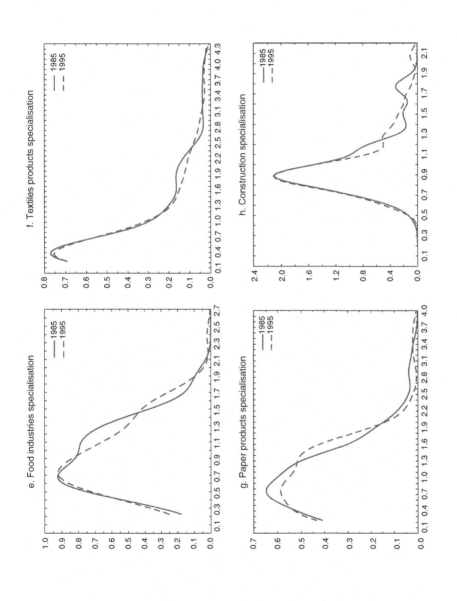

e. Food industries specialisation

f. Textiles products specialisation

g. Paper products specialisation

h. Construction specialisation

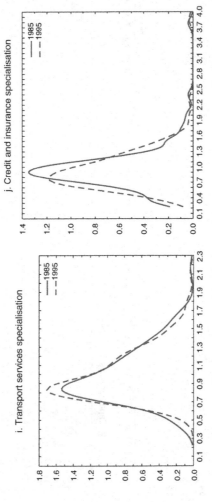

i. Transport services specialisation

j. Credit and insurance specialisation

Figure 3.2. Distribution of regional sectoral concentration indices (L_{ij}): EU-12 (1985–95).

low technological classification. Partial kernel density functions are estimated comparing the time period 1985–95.

In this regard, Figure 3.2 shows the evolution in distribution of the L_{ij} coefficient for some specific sectors.[10] On the one hand, Agricultural sector specialisation (Figure 3.2a) tends towards greater homogeneity due to the presence of a clear tendency towards a concentration of distribution (narrowing towards the average). However, some regions are trapped in higher degrees of specialisation in this sector.[11] Secondly, regarding high-tech industries, the Chemical and Metal products sectors show slight movements in distribution percentiles (Figures 3.2b and 3.2c).[12] In contrast, Figure 3.2d shows that Transport equipment is the sector with the greatest changes in specialisation distribution, leading to a more heterogeneous situation. The upper cue shows enhanced probability masses for the group of regions[13] which are above the average level of specialisation in 1995. Thus, these regions seem to have experienced a higher relative degree of specialisation after the integration process in this sector, though a decrease in the overall concentration degree is detected by means of the L_j coefficient. This may mean that the overall specialisation pattern for high-tech industries has increased.

Regarding the changes experienced in low-tech industries, Figures 3.2e, 3.2f and 3.2g show that most of the changes were due to the performance of the Food, beverages and tobacco and Paper and printing products sectors, whereas the Textile sector underwent only a slight movement. Figure 3.2e shows that the Food sector reduces its bimodality due to the performance of the regions slightly above the average level. However, the upper relative levels of specialisation enhance its mass of probability,[14] and a higher concentration level appears in this sector. With regard to the Paper and printing products sector, the greater heterogeneity is clear. Finally, Figure 3.2h shows that the Building and construction sector becomes more concentrated due to the regions in the upper cue.[15]

Figures 3.2i and 3.2j show the changes in the high-tech services sectoral concentration (Transport and communication services sector

[10] Results for all sectors could be provided by the authors upon request.
[11] Specifically Greek and Portuguese regions that increase their relative specialisation in this sector during the period.
[12] Figure 3.2b detects that the chemical sector shows a slight enhancement in upper cue probability mass (higher regional concentration for a few regions in this sector). Figure 3.2c shows that the metal products sector would have become less concentrated for those regions below the average level.
[13] Basilicata, Navarre, Niedersachsen, Aragon, Saarland, West Midlands, Baden-Württemberg, Castile and Leon and Piemonte.
[14] Lisbon e Vale do Tejo, Navarre, Bretagne, Castile and Leon, Norte, Cantabria and Dytiki Makedonia.
[15] Results for all sectors could be provided by the authors upon request.

and Services of credit and insurance institutions). Whereas Transport services becomes slightly more homogenous (lower concentration), the Credit and insurance sector shows a higher heterogeneity in its distribution at both cues. In the latter case, the upper percentiles seem to reflect the evolution of certain capital regions (Luxembourg, Brussels, Madrid and Ile de France).

At this point another question arises: do the changes in the above indices during the period (measured by variation rates for the period 1985–95) follow a spatial pattern? Are these changes spatially concentrated? To answer this question, a global spatial association analysis of the distribution of the changes in the indices was carried out (see Anselin 1988; Vayá and Suriñach, 2003). This kind of analysis overcomes one of the major shortcomings of the traditional concentration indices, that is, it takes into account the space in which each region is located, considering it as an isolated unit and ignoring any possible links with neighbouring regions.[16] By computing the global spatial association test, it is possible to know if the changes in the specialisation patterns have been randomly distributed in space (no spatial dependence) or whether, on the contrary, there is a significant trend towards spatial clustering (positive spatial dependence) or dissimilar (negative spatial dependence).

A Moran I test (Moran, 1948; Anselin, 1988), the best-known spatial dependence test, has been computed using a spatial weight matrix based on the inverse of the distance between each pair of regions (Table 3.2). As can be seen, there is a significant trend towards clustering of similar changes in the regional specialisation coefficient (L_i) between 1985 and 1995 in nearby regions. A highly significant positive spatial association is also detected between nearby regions when analysing the spatial distribution of changes in regional specialisation indices in the following sectors: Agriculture; Chemical products; Metal products, machinery, equipment and electrical goods; Textiles and clothing, leather and footwear; Products of various industries; and Building and construction, and in all the services sectors analysed (with the exception of the Transport and communication services). In contrast, the spatial distribution of changes in the rest of the sectors is random. So, the changes in terms of more and less relative specialisation in these sectors have followed a clearly spatial pattern, evidencing the existence of certain clusters of neighbouring regions with similar evolutions in their sectoral structure. This shows that space still matters.

---

[16] Neighbouring here is used as a generic concept, and is not limited to its purely geographical sense of contiguity.

Table 3.2. *Moran's I test for changes in regional sectoral concentration indices: EU-12 (1985–95)*

Sector	Standardised Moran's I test
Changes in regional specialisation index, L_i	1.602***
Changes in L_{ij} index for:	
Agricultural, forestry and fishery products	7.416*
Fuel and power products	1.309
Ferrous and non-ferrous ores and metals, other than radioactive	0.147
Non-metallic minerals and mineral products	0.706
Chemical products	4.304*
Metal products, machinery, equipment and electrical goods	3.468*
Transport equipment	−0.449
Food, beverages, tobacco	1.090
Textiles and clothing, leather and footwear	2.382**
Paper and printing products	1.258
Products of various industries	2.541**
Building and construction	7.014*
Recovery, repair, trade, lodging and catering services	3.672*
Transport and communication services	−0.359
Services of credit and insurance institutions	10.734*
Other market services	7.418*
Non-market services	10.642*

Notes: * significant at 1%.
** significant at 5%.
*** significant at 10%.

3.5 The effects of the new enlargement on the distribution of activity: from EU-15 to EU-27

One of the challenges facing the EU's regional policy is the accession of new countries to the Single Market and to the EMU. Specialisation patterns in many of these Eastern regions are quite similar to those in the less developed regions of the fifteen previous Member States. Boldrin and Canova (2003) note that initial conditions in the Eastern regions are approximately the same as those of the old newcomers, and that the policies are the same. The Cohesion Fund framework has not been erased. We can therefore suppose that integration would have the same effects as it had in the past on Spain, Portugal and Greece. But the same authors note that Eastern regions will enter a market that is larger and richer than it was in the mid-1980s, and also that their level of integration is higher.

Moreover, the accession of these countries is likely to have a marked effect on the geographical distribution of economic activity in the rest of

92   Mora, Vayá and Suriñach

the EU regions. Taking this into account, and after analysing the distribution of regional and sectoral concentration indices during the integration process of the 1980s, this section presents an analogous analysis for
the case of the Eastern regions. We computed the same indices as before
but this time for a sample of 180 regions (for EU-27), in order to test the
changes in distribution after considering Eastern economies.[17] It should
be noted that the lack of data prevents us from repeating the analysis
using seventeen sectors: only nine sectors are finally considered for the
sample of EU-27.

Table 3.3 depicts the values for sectoral concentration coefficients,
while Figure 3.3 shows the density function for the regional specialisation
coefficient (L_i) and for the sectoral regional concentration coefficients
(L_{ij}) for some of the nine sectors.[18] The same analysis, but only for the
sample of Eastern regions, is presented in Figure 3.4. Finally, in Table
3.4, the results of the Moran I test for these indices are summarised.

As we can see from Table 3.3, the Agriculture sector is the most
geographically concentrated; its degree of concentration when the Eastern regions are incorporated increases compared to the sample with only
EU-12 and EU-15 regions in 1995. The Fuel and power products sector
is also relatively concentrated through space. In contrast, the Services
sectors are clearly less concentrated. The inclusion of the Eastern
regions does not have a notable impact on the index analysed.

The overall regional specialisation index is analysed in Figures 3.3a
(for EU-27 regions) and 3.4a for Eastern regions only. Figure 3.3a1
shows the clear bimodality for EU-15 regions. Including the Eastern
regions, the heterogeneity is enhanced due to the width of dispersion of
the percentiles just above the average specialisation level. Figure 3.4
shows that, when considering Eastern regions only, there is an upper
cue with a significant mass of probability. So a considerable number of
Eastern regions are highly specialised in relation to the average. Specifically, as Figure 3.3a2 shows, Romanian regions (among the poorest
regions in the candidate countries), jointly with Prague and Ostravosko,
are the most specialised of the Eastern regions.[19] The opposite is the
case with some regions in Poland and Slovakia, plus Lithuania, Latvia
and Estonia. If all the EU-27 regions are considered, the most specialised regions are, together with Romanian regions, some regions

[17] A first empirical analysis about the detection of concentration or specialisation is done
for overall EU-25 regions in von Schütz and Stierle (2003).
[18] The results for all sectors could be provided by the authors upon request.
[19] In addition, it must be said that the global level of regional specialisation seems to be
higher in the case of Eastern regions than in the case of EU-12 regions.

Table 3.3. *Sectoral concentration coefficients* (L_j): *EU-15 and EU-27 (1995)*

Sector	EU-15	EU-27
Agricultural, forestry and fishery products	0.337	0.349
Fuel and power products	0.192	0.195
Manufactured products	0.122	0.121
Building and construction	0.116	0.118
Recovery, repair, trade, lodging and catering services	0.074	0.077
Transport and communication services	0.090	0.092
Services of credit and insurance institutions	0.151	0.155
Other market services	0.107	0.118
Non-market services	0.141	0.139

in Portugal (not Lisbon) and in Greece, some eastern regions in Germany, and some Finnish and Swedish regions; the opposite is true for the case of most of the UK, French and western Germany, some Italian regions and eastern Austria, and some regions in Poland and Slovakia.

In order to detect differences between sectors, we estimated kernel density functions for the nine sectors of activity considered. Comparing the distribution before and after including Eastern regions (Figures 3.3b to 3.3f), it can be seen that major changes are detected in the manufactured products sector. Slight movements also appear in the upper cue of the agricultural sector[20] and in the levels of specialisation just above the average for the construction sector. So, Figure 3.3d confirms that bimodality for the manufactured products sector could still be defended, but that there is also a concentration of probability around the average level. We would therefore need to examine the regional manufacturing data in more detail. Compensation of the two effects may cause similar concentration levels L_j for the manufacturing sectors, comparing the results of the two samples, EU-15 and EU-27 regions (Table 3.3).[21]

When considering the Eastern regions alone, Figure 3.4 shows high heterogeneity for all sectors. Only the Transport service sectors seem to be relatively homogenous. Agricultural and Fuel sectors show an above

[20] The Romanian regions plus Bulgaria are the most specialised in this sector (explaining part of their higher global level of specialisation detected). Considering the overall sample, most of the Greek regions, some Portuguese regions (as Alentejo and Centro), jointly with all the Romanian regions, show the highest levels of specialisation in this sector compared to the whole sample. In this sense, it is interesting to note that these regions also shows the highest levels of global specialisation and the lowest levels of GDP per capita, leading to the existence of a certain poverty trap.

[21] From this table we can see that rather similar results are obtained for most of the sectors considered.

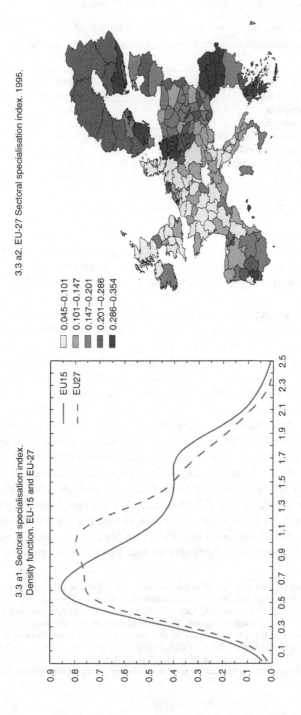

3.3 a2. EU-27 Sectoral specialisation index. 1995.

0.045–0.101
0.101–0.147
0.147–0.201
0.201–0.286
0.286–0.354

3.3 a1. Sectoral specialisation index.
Density function. EU-15 and EU-27

EU15
EU27

3.3 b1. Agricultural sector, L_{ij} index.
Density function. EU-15 and EU-27

3.3 b2. EU-27 Agricultural sector,
L_{ij} index. 1995.

3.3 c1. Fuel and power products, L_{ij} index.
Density function. EU-15 and EU-27

EU 15
EU 27

3.3 c2. EU-27 Fuel and power products,
L_{ij} index. 1995.

0.156–0.571
0.571–1
1–1.75
1.75–2.769
2.769–5.025

3.3d1. Manufactured products, L_{ij} index.
Density function. EU-15 and EU-27

— EU15
- - EU27

3.3d2. EU-27 Manufactured products,
L_{ij} index. 1995

0.206–1
1–1.5
1.5–1.844

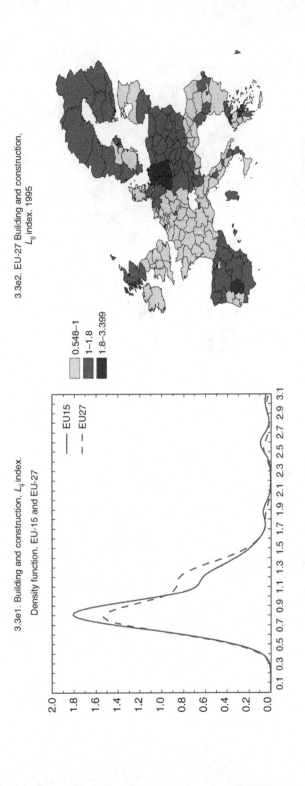

3.3e1. Building and construction, L_{ij} index.
Density function. EU-15 and EU-27

3.3e2. EU-27 Building and construction,
L_{ij} index. 1995

0.548–1
1–1.8
1.8–3.399

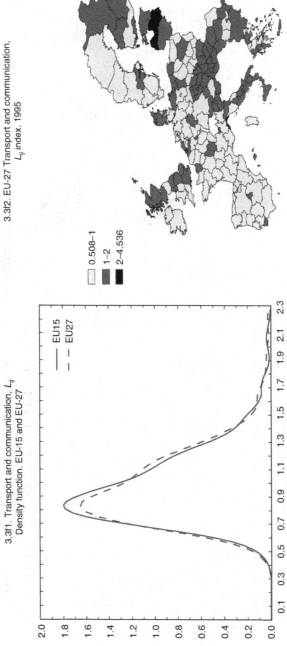

3.3f1. Transport and communication, L_{ij}
Density function. EU-15 and EU-27

EU15
EU27

3.3f2. EU-27 Transport and communication,
L_{ij} index. 1995

0.508–1
1–2
2–4.536

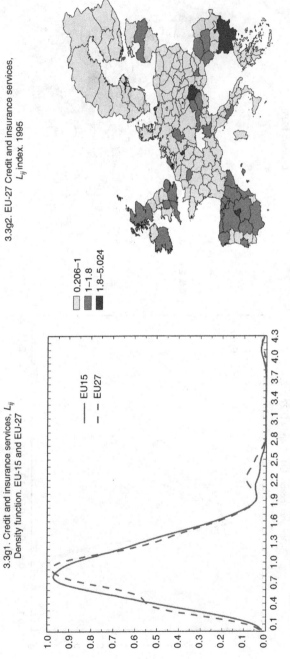

3.3g1. Credit and insurance services, L_{ij}
Density function. EU-15 and EU-27

3.3g2. EU-27 Credit and insurance services,
L_{ij} index. 1995

0.206–1
1–1.8
1.8–5.024

EU15
EU27

Figure 3.3. Distribution of specialisation indices: EU-15 and EU-27 (1995).

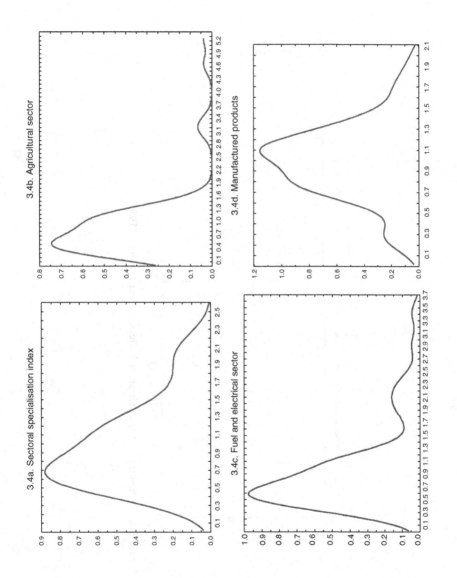

3.4a. Sectoral specialisation index

3.4b. Agricultural sector

3.4c. Fuel and electrical sector

3.4d. Manufactured products

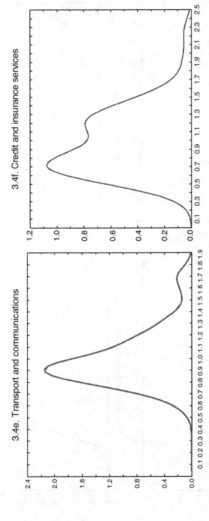

Figure 3.4. Distribution of specialisation indices: Eastern regions (1995).

Table 3.4. *Moran's I test for regional sectoral concentration indices: EU-27 (1995)*

Sector	Standardised Moran's I test
Regional specialisation index, L_i	19.096*
Regional sectoral concentration indices L_{ij} for:	
Agricultural, forestry and fishery products	19.927*
Fuel and power products	3.510*
Manufactured products	5.302*
Building and construction	13.280*
Recovery, repair, trade, lodging and catering services	6.525*
Transport and communication services	6.629*
Services of credit and insurance institutions	5.306*
Other market services	28.690*
Non-market services	10.159*

Notes: * significant at 1%.

average mass, indicating that some of the Eastern regions are clearly more specialised than others (Figures 3.4b and 3.4c). Meanwhile, the distribution of Manufactured products shows that the level of specialisation in a significant number of regions is considerably lower than average (Figure 3.4d). Additionally, some bimodality is detected for the regions in which specialisation is around average. Finally, bimodality is clearly shown for the case of credit and insurance services. Capital regions present a significant mass of probability in the levels of specialisation furthest from the average.

Finally, the spatial distribution of sectoral regional concentration coefficients for all sectors considered shows a highly significant positive spatial association between nearby regions (Table 3.4). So, the shorter the geographical distance between regions, the greater the similarity between their degree of overall specialisation and sectoral concentration indices (this is especially true in the case of agriculture, other market services, and the building and construction sectors).

3.6   Conclusions

Our findings go further than those previously reported in the literature. Whereas empirical evidence has focused on the evolution of concentration of national/regional activity, we identify the regions that alter the distribution, by estimating kernel density functions. In addition, spatial econometric tests allow us to detect whether changes in the distribution are spatially concentrated.

First, in the ten years after the mid-1980s enlargement significant changes are observed in some percentiles of the distribution of specialisation indices. These changes have not been uniform, and the estimation of kernel density functions and their comparison for the 1985–95 period highlights the role of specific regions in this process. Overall concentration indices hide partially relevant information; it may be that the changes observed in the specialisation indices are due to the involvement of only a few regions, and the rest of the regions stabilise their specialisation over the period. Secondly, we found that the changes in specialisation indices were spatially concentrated for some sectors (the changes in the indices show a positive spatial dependence scheme between nearby regions). Therefore, spatial distribution is relevant. The existence of externalities may account for the presence of clusters of regions with a similar pattern in the evolution of specialisation. Further analyses should aim to identify the factors that explain the partial tendency towards regional concentration.

But what can we learn from the previous enlargement? What lessons can be applied to an assessment of the more recent one? Most specialisation index distributions have increased in width since the mid-1980s enlargement. Thus, the changes in the distribution of regional activity seem to show that the entry of the Eastern regions has increased the gap in specialisation levels between old and new Member States. This reveals a European regional map where various groups of economies can be distinguished and in which there is now more heterogeneity. First, one group comprises the regions (basically those from long-standing Member States) showing a higher stability in their relative specialisation level. Secondly, a considerable number of regions that entered in the mid-1980s enlargement have increased their relative specialisation in labour-intensive industrial sectors and have introduced service sectors to a higher degree into their distribution of activity. Finally, Eastern regions may have enhanced the overall inequality of distribution of activity due to their higher relative specialisation level. Eastern regions are now compensating for their backwardness by taking the place of regions from the mid-1980s enlargement by specialising in labour-intensive sectors. Although additional sectoral information is not available, we have found a clear bimodality in the distribution of activity for Eastern regions for most of the sectors analysed. A higher decomposition of the manufacturing sector would allow us to define the sectors that show a more marked heterogeneity. So, further information is required to assess the changes due to the recent enlargement. Even so, the effects of the globalisation process may complicate the extrapolation of results to the consequences of new enlargement.

Last, only a conditional approach will identify the factors that economic theory (including new economic geography literature) sees as capable of explaining the evolution of changes in specialisation indices. The effects of the changes in specialisation indices on economic growth are not considered here (see Giannetti, 2002; and Mora et al., 2005 for analysis of this kind).

References

Aiginger, K., Böheim, M., Gugler, K., Peneder, M., Pfaffermayr, M. and Wolfmayr-Schnitzer, Y. 1999. 'Specialisation (and Geographic) Concentration of European Manufacturing'. DG Enterprise Working Paper, No. 1.

Altomonte, C. and Bonassi, C. 2002. 'Comparative Advantages or Economic Geography? An Assessment of EU Regional Disparities'. Paper presented at the 29th Annual Conference of the European Association for Research in Industrial Economics.

Altomonte, C. and Resmini, L. 1999. 'The Geography of Transition: Agglomeration Versus Dispersion of Firms Activity in the Countries of Central and Eastern Europe'. Paper presented at the European Workshop on 'Regional Development and Policy in Europe', Centre for European Integration Studies.

Amiti, M. 1999. 'Specialization Patterns in Europe'. *Weltwirtschaftliches Archiv*, vol. 134, pp. 573–593.

Anselin, L. 1988. *Spatial Econometrics: Methods and Models*. Dordrecht: Kluwer Academic Publishers.

Atkinson, A. 2002. 'Income Inequality in OECD Countries: Data and Explanations'. CESifo Working Paper, No. 881.

Ben-David, D. 1994. 'Convergence Clubs and Diverging Economies'. CEPR Discussion Paper, No. 922.

Boldrin, M. and Canova, F. 2003. 'Regional Policies and EU Enlargement'. CEPR Discussion Paper, No. 3744.

Brülhart, M. 1998. 'Trading Places: Industrial Specialisation in the European Union'. *Journal of Common Market Studies*, vol. 36, pp. 319–46.

Brülhart, M. and Torstensson, J. 1996. 'Regional Integration, Scale Economies and Industry Location'. *CEPR Discussion Paper*, No. 1435.

Brülhart, M. and Traeger, R. 2003. 'An Account of Geographic Concentration Patters in Europe'. *Regional Science and Urban Economics*, vol. 35, pp. 597–624.

Davis, D. and Weinstein, D. 1998. 'Market Access, Economic Geography and Comparative Advantage: An Empirical Assessment'. *Journal of International Economics*, vol. 59, pp. 1–23.

1999. 'Economic Geography and Regional Production Structure: An Empirical Investigation'. *European Economic Review*, vol. 43, pp. 379–407.

European Commission. 2003. 'European Competitiveness Report 2003'. Commission Staff Working Document SEC 1299, Commission of the European Communities, Brussels.

Giannetti, M. 2002. 'The Effects of Integration on Regional Disparities: Convergence, Divergence or Both?'. *European Economic Review*, vol. 46, pp. 539–67.

Haaland, J., Kind, H. and Midelfart-Knarvik, K. 1999. 'What Determines the Economic Geography of Europe?'. CEPR Discussion Paper, No. 2072.

Hallet, M. 2000. 'Regional specialisation and Concentration in the European Union' in Cuadrado-Roura, J. and Parellada, M. (eds.), *Regional Convergence in the European Union*, Berlin, Springer.

Hansen, N. 1990. 'Do Producer Services Induce Regional Economic Development?'. *Journal of Regional Science*, vol. 30, pp. 465–76.

Illeris, S. 1993. 'An Inductive Theory of Regional Development'. *Papers in Regional Science*, vol. 72, pp. 113–34.

Krieger-Boden, C. 2002. 'European Integration and the Division of Labour Between European Regions'. Paper presented at the 4th Annual Conference of the European Trade Study Group.

Krugman, P. 1991a. 'Increasing Returns and Economic Geography'. *Journal of Political Economy*, vol. 99, pp. 483–99.

1991b. *Geography and Trade*. Cambridge, MA: MIT Press.

1998. 'What's New About the New Economic Geography?'. *Oxford Review of Economic Policy*, vol. 14, pp. 7–17.

Krugman, P. and Venables, A. 1990. 'Integration and the Competitiveness of Peripheral Industry'. In Bliss, C. and Braga de Macedo, J. (eds.), *Unity with Diversity in the European Community*. Cambridge: Cambridge University Press.

1995. 'Globalization and the Inequality of Nations'. *Quarterly Journal of Economics*, vol. 110, pp. 857–80.

1996. 'Integration, Specialization and Adjustment'. *European Economic Review*, vol. 40, pp. 959–67.

Landesmann, M. 1995. 'The Pattern of East–West European Integration: Catching Up or Falling Behind?'. In Dobrinsky, R. and Landesmann, M. (eds.), *Transforming Economies and European Integration*. Aldershot: Edward Elgar.

2003. 'Structural Features of Economic Integration in an Enlarged Europe: Patterns of Catching-Up an Industrial Specialisation'. European Commission Economic Papers, No. 181.

Longhi, S., Nijkamp, P. and Traistaru, I. 2003. 'Economic Integration and Manufacturing location in EU Accession Countries'. Tinbergen Institute Discussion Paper, No. 093/3.

López-Bazo, E., Vayá, E., Mora, T. and Suriñach, J. 1999. 'Regional Economic Dynamics and Convergence in the European Union'. *Annals of Regional Science*, vol. 33, pp. 343–70.

Magrini, S. 1999. 'The Evolution of Income Disparities Among the Regions of the European Union'. *Regional Science and Urban Economics*, vol. 29, pp. 257–81.

Martin, P. and Ottaviano, P. 1999. 'Growing Locations: Industry Location in a Model of Endogenous Growth'. *European Economic Review*, vol. 43, pp. 281–302.

Midelfart-Knarvik, K., Overman, H. and Venables, A. 2000. 'Comparative Advantage and Economic Geography: Estimating the Location of Production in the EU'. CEPR Discussion Paper, No. 2618.

Molle, W. 1996. 'The Regional Economic Structure of the European Union: An Analysis of Long-Term Developments'. In Peschel, K. (ed.), *Regional Growth and Regional Policy Within the Framework of European Integration.* Heidelberg: Physica-Verlag.

Molle, W., van Holst, B. and Smit, H. 1980. *Regional Disparity and Economic Development in the European Community.* Farnborough: Saxon House.

Mora, T., Vayá, E. and Suriñach, J. 2005. 'Specialisation and Growth: The Detection of European Regional Convergence Clubs'. *Economics Letters,* vol. 86, pp. 181–85.

Moran, P. 1948. 'The Interpretation of Statistical Maps'. *Journal of the Royal Statistical Society Series B,* vol. 10, pp. 243–51.

Neven, D. 1990. 'EEC Integration Towards 1992: Some Distributional Aspects'. *Economic Policy,* vol. 10, pp. 14–62.

Ottaviano, G. and Puga, D. 1997. 'Agglomeration in the Global Economy: A Survey of the New Economic Geography'. *World Economy,* vol. 21, pp. 707–31.

Petrakos, G. 2000. 'The Spatial Impact of East–West Integration'. In Petrakos, G., Maier, G. and Gorzelak, G. (eds.), *Integration and Transition in Europe: The Economies Geography of Interaction.* London: Routledge.

Puga, D. 1999. 'The Rise and Fall of Regional Inequalities'. *European Economic Review,* vol. 43, pp. 303–34.

Puga, D. and Venables, A. 1996. 'The Spread of Industry: Spatial Agglomeration in Economic Development'. *Journal of the Japanese and International Economies,* vol. 10, pp. 440–64.

Quah, D. 1997. 'Empirics for Growth and Distribution: Stratification, Polarization and Convergence Clubs'. *Journal of Economic Growth,* vol. 2, pp. 27–59.

Resmini, L. 2002. 'Specialisation and Growth Prospects in Border Regions of Accession Countries'. Centre for European Integration Studies, ZEI Working Paper, B02-17.

Rodríguez-Pose, A. 1995. *Reestructuración socioeconómica y desequilibrios regionales en la Unión Europea.* Madrid: Instituto de Estudios Económicos.

Suarez-Villa, L. and Cuadrado-Roura, J. 1993. 'Regional Economic Integration and the evolution of Disparities'. *Papers in Regional Science,* vol. 72, pp. 369–87.

Vayá, E. and Suriñach, J. 2003. 'The Spatial Distribution of Labour Productivity in the European Regions: A Study in Spatial Econometrics'. In Fingleton, B. (ed.), *European Regional Growth.* Aldershot: Ashgate.

Venables, A. 1996. 'Equilibrium Locations of Vertically Linked Industries'. *International Economic Review,* vol. 37, pp. 341–59.

von Schütz, U. and Stierle, M. 2003. 'Convergence in an Enlarged EU? An Empirical Analysis of Regional Specialisation and Sectoral Concentration'. In Hausen, C., Resienk, M., Schürmann, N. and Stierle, M. (eds.), *Determinants of Growth and Business Cycles: Theory, Empirical Evidence and Policy Implications.* Berlin: Verlag Wissenschaft und Forschung.

Walz, U. 1999. *Dynamics of Regional Integration.* Heidelberg: Physica-Verlag.

4 Forecasting macroeconomic variables for the new Member States

Anindya Banerjee, Massimiliano Marcellino and Igor Masten

4.1 Introduction

The accession of ten countries to the European Union makes the forecasting of their key macroeconomic indicators such as GDP growth, inflation and interest rates an exercise of obvious importance. Because of the transition period, only short spans (denoted T) of reliable time series are available for each of these countries. This suggests the adoption of simple time series models as forecasting tools, because of their parsimonious specification and good performance (based on results available from studies for other countries).

However, despite the constraints on the time span of data, a large number of macroeconomic series of potential use in forecasting (for a given time span) are available for each country. This makes the recently proposed dynamic factor models a viable and alternative forecasting tool, where the limitations on estimation and forecasting implied by the short length of time series are compensated by extending the longitudinal dimensional (denoted N) of the data.

Dynamic factor models have been successfully applied in a number of papers to forecasting macroeconomic variables for the US and Euro area, including Stock and Watson (1999, 2002a, 2002b) and Marcellino, Stock and Watson (2001, 2003). Earlier applications of factor models include Geweke (1977), Sargent and Sims (1977), Engle and Watson (1981) and Stock and Watson (1991) who estimated small-N dynamic factor models in the time domain, where N denotes the number of variables in the data set on which information is available.

The primary justification for the use of factor models in large data sets (where N may exceed T) is their usefulness as a particularly efficient means of extracting information from a large number of data series, albeit of a short time span. Intuitively, the motivation underlying their use is that there are a few common non-observable economic factors that drive fluctuations in large cross-sections of macroeconomic time series.

Moreover, forecasts of key macroeconomic variables may be significantly improved, not least because, in a rapidly changing economy (subject to irregular shocks), especially in the economies of the new Member States, the ranking of variables as good leading indicators or forecasting devices for, say, inflation or GDP growth, is not at all clear *a priori*. Therefore, as described by Bernanke and Boivin (2003), factor models provide a methodology that allows us to remain "agnostic" about the structure of the economy, by employing as much information as possible in the construction of the forecasting exercise.

This methodology also permits the incorporation of data at different vintages, at different frequencies and different time spans, thereby providing a clearly specified and statistically rigorous but economical framework for the use of multiple data sets.

This chapter is a comparison of the relative performance of the two dominant forecasting approaches (time series models and dynamic factor models), within the empirically relevant framework of data from five new Member States. We start by discussing briefly the key aspects of the competing approaches in section 4.2. In this section we also describe the forecasting models and the criteria for forecast comparison. Section 4.3 describes the data for five of the new Member States, namely the Czech Republic, Hungary, Poland, Slovakia and Slovenia. Section 4.4 contains the results of the estimation and forecasting exercise using the data sets from the five countries and Euro area data compiled by Fagan, Henry and Mestre (2001). In this section, we evaluate and report on the relative performance of the competing methods, the role of Euro area information for forecasting, and the usefulness of robustifying techniques such as intercept corrections and second differencing. Section 4.5 concludes the chapter, and emphasises the uniqueness and importance of the issues discussed. To our knowledge, this chapter marks the first time that such methods have been used to model and forecast data from new Member States.

4.2   Methodology

In this section we briefly review the competing forecasting approaches we consider, and the criteria we use to evaluate their relative merits, see *e.g.* Marcellino, Stock and Watson (2003) or Artis, Banerjee and Marcellino (2005) for additional details.

All forecasting models are specified and estimated as a linear projection of an h-step-ahead variable, y_{t+h}^h, onto t-dated predictors, which at a minimum include lagged transformed values (denoted y_t) of x_t the series of interest. More precisely, the forecasting models all have the form:

$$y_{t+h}^h = \mu + \alpha(L)y_t + \beta(L)'Z_t + \varepsilon_{t+h}^h \qquad (1)$$

where $\alpha(L)$ is a scalar lag polynomial, $\beta(L)$ is a vector lag polynomial, μ is a constant, and Z_t is a vector of predictor variables. Due to the short sample available, the forecast horizon for all the reported empirical results in section 4.4 below is one quarter, so that $h = 1$ in (1).

The construction of y_{t+h}^h depends on whether the series is modelled as I (0), I(1) or I(2), where series integrated of order d, denoted I(d), are those for which the d-th difference (Δ^d) is stationary. Indicating by x the series of interest (usually in logarithms), in the I(0) case, $y_{t+h}^h = x_{t+h}$ and $y_t = x_t$. In the I(1) case, $y_{t+h}^h = \sum_{s=t+1}^{t+h} \Delta x_s$ so that $y_{t+h}^h = x_{t+h} - x_t$, while $y_t = x_t - x_{t-1}$. In words, the forecasts are for the growth in the series x between time period t and $t+h$. Finally, in the I(2) case, $y_{t+h}^h = \sum_{s=t+1}^{t+h} \Delta x_s - h\Delta x_t$ or $y_{t+h}^h = x_{t+h} - x_t - h\Delta x_t$, i.e. the difference of x between time periods t and $t+h$ and h times its growth between periods $t-1$ and t, and $y_t = \Delta^2 x_t$. This is a convenient formulation because, given that x_t and its lags are known when forecasting, the unknown component of y_{t+h}^h conditional on the available information is equal to x_{t+h} independently of the choice of the order of integration. This makes the mean square forecast error (MSE) from models for second-differenced variables directly comparable with, for example, that from models for first differences only. The MSE is computed as the average of the sum of squares of all the comparisons between the actual value of the variable and its forecast (under any of the methods given in section 4.2.1 below).

4.2.1   Forecasting models

The various forecasting models we compare differ in their choice of Z_t in equation (1). Let us list the forecasting models and briefly discuss their main characteristics.

Autoregressive forecast (ar_bic). Our benchmark forecast is a univariate autoregressive (AR) forecast based on (1) excluding Z_t. In common with the literature, we choose the lag length using an information criterion, the BIC, starting with a maximum of 6 lags.

Autoregressive forecast with second differencing (ar_bic_i2). Clements and Hendry (1999) showed that second differencing the variable of interest improves the forecasting performance of autoregressive models in the presence of structural breaks. This is an interesting option to be considered in the case of most of the new Member States, which have undergone several economic and institutional changes even after the fairly rapid transition to a market economy. This model corresponds to (1), excluding Z_t and treating the variable of interest as I(2).

Autoregressive forecast with intercept correction (ar_bic_ic). An alternative remedy in the presence of structural breaks over the forecasting period is to put the forecast back on track by adding past forecast errors to the forecast, e.g. Clements and Hendry (1999) and Artis and Marcellino (2001). They showed the usefulness of the simple addition of the h-step-ahead forecast error. Hence, the forecast is given by $\hat{y}_{t+h}^{h} + \varepsilon_t^{h}$, where $\hat{y}_{t+h}^{h}$ is the ar_bic forecast and ε_t^{h} is the forecast error made when forecasting y_t in period $t-h$. Since both second differencing and intercept correction increase the MSE when not needed, by adding a moving average component to the forecast error, they are not costless and should only be used if needed.

Autoregressive forecast with exogenous regressors (ar_ctr). We consider also AR models to which exogenous regressors are added in order to improve their predictive performance. For each of the variables we forecast, the exogenous regressor is its Euro area counterpart. For example, when forecasting inflation we choose the Euro area HICP inflation rate. The forecasts are produced with a model either with a fixed lag structure (three endogenous and exogenous lags) (ar_ctrfix) or with BIC selection (ar_ctr_bic). In addition, intercept-corrected versions of both forecasts are computed (ar_ctr_bic_ic and ar_ctrfix_ic respectively).

VAR forecasts (varf). Vector autoregressive (VAR) forecasts are constructed using equation (1) with chosen regressors Z_t. In particular, in the empirical analysis in section 4.4, Z_t includes lags of GDP growth, inflation and a short-term interest rate. Intercept corrected versions of the forecasts are also computed (varf_ic).

Factor-based forecasts. These forecasts are based on setting Z_t in (1) to be the estimated factors from a dynamic factor model due to Stock and Watson (2002b), to which we refer for additional details. Under some technical assumptions (restrictions on moments and stationarity conditions), the column space spanned by the dynamic factors f_t can be estimated consistently by the principal components of the $T \times T$ covariance matrix of the X's. The factors can be considered as an exhaustive summary of the information contained in a large data set.

It is also worth mentioning that the principal component based factor estimate remains consistent even in the presence of limited time variation in the parameters of the underlying factor model. Such a property can be very convenient for analysing the new Member States, whose economies are under rapid evolution.

We primarily consider three different factor-based forecasts. First, in addition to the current and lagged y_t, up to 4 factors and 3 lags of each of these factors are included in the model (fdiarlag_bic). Secondly, up to 12 factors are included, but not their lags (fdiar_bic). Thirdly, up to 12 factors appear as regressors in (1), but no current or lagged y_t is included (fdi_bic). For each of these three classes of factor-based forecasts the model selection is again based on BIC. The factors can be extracted from the unbalanced panel of available time series (prefix fac), where for some of the variables there are missing observations, or from the balanced panel (prefix fbp), and we consider them both. The former contains more variables than the latter, and therefore more information. The drawback is that missing observations have to be estimated in a first stage, which could introduce noise in the factor estimation.

In order to evaluate the forecasting role of each factor, for the unbalanced panel, we also consider forecasts using a fixed number of factors, from 1 to 4 (fdiar_01 to fdiar_04 and fdi_01 to fdi_04). For each of the 14 factor-based forecasts, we also consider the intercept corrected version (prefix ic).

Finally, to characterise the overall performance of factor models we also construct the pooled factor forecasts, denoted fac_pooled, by taking a simple average of all the factor-based forecasts. These pooled forecasts are then compared to the actual values of the series in the same way as for any other forecasting model. It is worth noting that the pooled factor forecasts have particular informative value. Since we consider many different versions of factor models it should not be surprising to find at least one model that forecasts better than simple linear models. The average performance of factor models in this respect tells us whether factor models are in general a better forecasting device or if their relative good performance is limited only to some special sub-models.

We consider factors extracted from country-specific data sets and also from the Euro area data set (see section 4.3 for a description of the variables included in each data set). Thus, in addition to considering only country-specific information we also construct factor-based forecasts from the updated data set used in the ECB's euro area wide model (Fagan, Henry and Mestre, 2005).

Euro area information is used in three ways. First, Euro area variables are used as exogenous regressors in the AR forecasts (ar_ctr models). Secondly, in the factor models, the forecast for each country is constructed using euro factors only, in the same way as described above for the country-specific factors. Finally, euro factors are combined with country-specific factors. Up to six of each of these is considered in the factor models without lags. In the models with lags we include up to three factors of both types with a maximum of two lags. Variable selection in the models, both with and without lags, is by the BIC criterion.

Additionally, in order to obtain comparable results for the unbalanced panel with a fixed number of factors, we add up to four euro factors to four country-specific factors (eu2_fac_fdiar_05 to eu2_fac_fdiar_08 and eu2_fac_fdi_05 to eu2_fac_fdi_08). We also consider their intercept corrected versions (prefix ic). These results are available upon request.

4.2.2   Forecast comparison

The forecast comparison is conducted in a simulated out-of-sample framework where all statistical calculations are done using a fully recursive methodology. The models are first estimated on data from 1994:1 to 2000:2 and 1-step-ahead forecasts are then computed. The estimation sample is then augmented by one quarter and the corresponding 1-step-ahead forecast is computed. The forecast period is 2000:3–2002:2, for a total of eight quarters, and the final estimation sample for one-quarter ahead forecasts is therefore 1994:1–2002:1. Every quarter (i.e. for every augmentation of the sample), all model estimation, standardisation of the data, calculation of the estimated factors etc., is repeated.

The forecasting performance of the various methods described is examined by comparing their simulated out-of-sample MSE relative to the benchmark autoregressive (AR) forecast (ar_bic). West (1996) standard errors are computed around the relative MSE in the empirical analysis of section 4.4.

We also consider pooling regressions where the actual values are regressed on the benchmark forecast and, in turn, on each of the competing forecasts. We report the coefficient of the latter, with robust standard errors. This coefficient should be equal to one for the benchmark forecast to be redundant, assuming that the two coefficients have to sum to one. Such a condition is also sufficient for the alternative forecast to MSE-encompass the benchmark forecast, under the additional hypothesis of unbiasedness of the former (see Marcellino, 2000).

4.3   The data

In the empirical application we consider five new Member States: the Czech Republic, Hungary, Poland, Slovakia and Slovenia. The three Baltic countries (and Cyprus and Malta) have been omitted at this stage due to data availability issues. The data are collected from OECD Main Economic Indicators, OECD Quarterly National Accounts, and IMF International Financial Statistics. We use data at a quarterly frequency because there are very few economic series available at a monthly frequency. Although for some countries many series are available from the beginning of 1992, the sample for estimation is set to 1994:1–2002:2 for all countries. The reason for this is direct comparability of results and the availability of a vast majority of series for all countries. National Accounts data for Poland and Hungary start only in 1995, but the missing observations are interpolated using the EM algorithm.

Altogether we have collected a panel with 52 series for the Czech Republic, 60 for Hungary, 56 for Poland, 47 for Slovakia and 38 for Slovenia. The data sets broadly contain output variables (GDP components, industrial production and sales); labour market variables (employment, unemployment, wages); prices (consumer, producer); monetary aggregates; interest rates (different maturities, lending and deposit rates); stock prices; exchange rates (effective and bilateral); imports, exports and net trade; survey data; and other miscellaneous series. A complete list of the variables (including those taken from the ECB's Euro area wide model that were used to extract euro factors) is available from us upon request.

Following Marcellino, Stock and Watson (2003), the data are pre-processed in three stages before being modelled with a factor representation. First, we pass all the series through a seasonal adjustment procedure as very few series are originally reported as seasonally adjusted. Seasonal adjustment is performed with the original X-11 ARIMA procedure. Secondly, the series are transformed to account for stochastic or deterministic trends, and logarithms are taken of all non-negative series that are not already in rates or percentage units. We apply the same transformations to all variables of the same type. The main choice is whether prices and nominal variables are I(1) or I(2). The I(1) case is our baseline model and all the results reported in section 4.4 apply to this choice. We have also recomputed all the results treating prices, wages, monetary aggregates and nominal exchange rates as I(2) variables. These results are briefly discussed in section 4.4.7.[1] Variables describing real economic activity are treated as I(1), whereas survey data are treated as I(0). All series were further standardised to have sample mean zero and unit sample variance.

Finally, the transformed seasonally adjusted series are screened for large outliers (outliers exceeding six times the interquartile range). Each outlying observation is recoded as missing data, and the EM algorithm is used to estimate the factor model for the resulting unbalanced panel.

Among the available variables, we have chosen to report forecasting results for GDP growth, inflation and the short-term interest rate (given by the Treasury bill rate where available, otherwise the lending rate).

[1] Full details are available from us upon request.

These are also the variables of central importance for policy-makers. Note, however, that the generality of the approach would easily allow us to extend the analysis to other variables of interest.

4.4   Forecasting results

Using the data sets described in section 4.3, we next conduct a forecast-comparison exercise. We include in the comparison all the models described in section 4.2. First, we present and discuss the results for each country, using country-specific information only, including factors computed from the country-specific data sets (Tables 4.1 to 4.5). We then evaluate the role of Euro area information by either incorporating control variables as described in section 4.2 or by using Euro area factors (detailed results available upon request). Finally, we summarise the results when nominal variables are treated as I(2).

4.4.1   The Czech Republic

The MSE of the competing methods relative to the benchmark AR model are reported in Table 4.1 for the Czech Republic. Four general comments can be made.

First, the factor models often outperform the other methods. The largest gain (67%) with respect to the benchmark AR model is for the interest rate variable (rtb3m). The corresponding number is slightly lower, although still impressive, for inflation (59%) and GDP growth (42%) for the best factor models for these variables. The poor performance of the pooled factor model is, however, surprising.

Secondly, using a fixed number of factors is often equivalent or better than BIC selection, and including an AR component in the forecasting model is usually beneficial.

Thirdly, there is no clear-cut ranking of the factors extracted from the unbalanced panel and the balanced panel. The former perform better for inflation, the latter for the interest rate, with comparable values for GDP growth. Though the additional information in the unbalanced panel can be useful for forecasting, when there are several missing observations the quality of the estimators based on interpolated data quickly deteriorates and this also has a negative impact on the factor estimators (see Angelini et al. (2003) for details).

Fourthly, to discuss the efficacy of methods to deal with structural breaks, we note that intercept correction is either helpful or not harmful when applied to the benchmark AR forecasts. It increases the MSE

Table 4.1. *Results for the Czech Republic, h = 1, I(1) prices and wages, country-specific factors*

Forecast method	gdp	(.)	cpi	(.)	rtb3m	(.)
ar_bic	1.00 (0.00)	(.)	1.00 (0.00)	(.)	1.00 (0.00)	(.)
ar_bic_i2	0.75 (0.27)	0.75 (0.22)	0.75 (0.27)	1.10 (0.56)	1.01 (0.46)	0.49 (0.49)
ar_bic_ic	1.47 (0.42)	0.23 (0.24)	0.88 (0.36)	0.58 (0.27)	1.03 (0.40)	0.47 (0.39)
varf	4.17 (5.14)	−0.59 (0.25)	1.08 (0.16)	0.08 (0.80)	5.56 (21.02)	0.07 (0.21)
varf_ic	6.12 (11.34)	−0.03 (0.12)	1.48 (0.49)	0.27 (0.17)	6.25 (19.78)	−0.01 (0.12)
a_fac_fdiarlag_bic	1.34 (0.56)	−0.60 (0.38)	0.41 (0.44)	0.80 (0.20)	2.22 (2.51)	0.30 (0.20)
a_fac_fdiar_bic	0.90 (0.09)	9.36 (3.43)	0.43 (0.40)	0.87 (0.15)	1.10 (0.84)	0.48 (0.17)
a_fac_fdi_bic	0.90 (0.09)	9.36 (3.43)	1.17 (0.30)	0.39 (0.15)	1.10 (0.84)	0.48 (0.17)
a_fbp_fdiarlag_bic	2.86 (3.57)	0.25 (0.16)	0.69 (0.39)	0.65 (0.17)	0.89 (0.48)	0.52 (0.08)
a_fbp_fdiar_bic	14.68 (119.39)	−0.04 (0.06)	0.69 (0.39)	0.65 (0.26)	0.89 (0.48)	0.52 (0.08)
a_fbp_fdi_bic	7.08 (34.29)	−0.03 (0.13)	0.74 (0.36)	0.69 (0.26)	0.89 (0.48)	0.52 (0.08)
a_fac_fdiar_01	0.86 (0.37)	0.84 (0.98)	1.35 (0.38)	0.27 (0.16)	1.10 (0.84)	0.48 (0.17)
a_fac_fdiar_02	0.58 (0.48)	0.68 (0.17)	0.52 (0.41)	0.75 (0.16)	0.78 (0.67)	0.56 (0.19)
a_fac_fdiar_03	0.68 (0.32)	1.34 (0.57)	0.43 (0.40)	0.87 (0.16)	0.79 (0.61)	0.54 (0.13)
a_fac_fdiar_04	1.63 (1.35)	0.20 (0.34)	0.44 (0.40)	0.93 (0.19)	0.33 (0.47)	0.73 (0.11)
a_fac_fdi_01	0.86 (0.37)	0.84 (0.98)	2.03 (0.87)	−0.05 (0.21)	1.10 (0.84)	0.48 (0.17)
a_fac_fdi_02	0.72 (0.33)	1.33 (0.74)	0.86 (0.34)	0.62 (0.32)	0.78 (0.67)	0.56 (0.19)
a_fac_fdi_03	0.68 (0.32)	1.34 (0.57)	0.68 (0.38)	0.74 (0.30)	0.79 (0.61)	0.54 (0.13)
a_fac_fdi_04	1.63 (1.35)	0.20 (0.34)	0.64 (0.35)	0.87 (0.34)	0.33 (0.47)	0.73 (0.11)
a_fac_ic_fdiarlag_bic	2.02 (1.34)	0.05 (0.31)	1.30 (0.64)	0.38 (0.19)	4.86 (13.20)	0.15 (0.17)
a_fac_ic_fdiar_bic	1.46 (0.42)	0.23 (0.24)	1.45 (0.80)	0.34 (0.20)	1.26 (0.73)	0.44 (0.15)
a_fac_ic_fdi_bic	1.46 (0.42)	0.23 (0.24)	0.68 (0.47)	0.68 (0.36)	1.26 (0.73)	0.44 (0.15)
a_fbp_ic_fdiarlag_bic	2.31 (1.91)	0.36 (0.10)	2.12 (1.37)	0.19 (0.17)	0.61 (0.51)	0.62 (0.15)
a_fbp_ic_fdiar_bic	35.13 (523.93)	−0.02 (0.03)	2.12 (1.37)	0.19 (0.17)	0.61 (0.51)	0.62 (0.15)
a_fbp_ic_fdi_bic	12.32 (59.11)	0.03 (0.07)	1.56 (0.91)	0.33 (0.18)	0.61 (0.51)	0.62 (0.15)
a_fac_ic_fdiar_01	1.66 (0.70)	0.15 (0.29)	0.64 (0.42)	0.69 (0.26)	1.26 (0.73)	0.44 (0.15)

a_fac_ic_fdiar_02	1.25 (0.59)	0.37 (0.30)	1.82 (1.14)	0.24 (0.20)	1.08 (0.74)	0.47 (0.26)
a_fac_ic_fdiar_03	1.54 (0.51)	0.23 (0.23)	1.46 (0.79)	0.34 (0.20)	1.15 (0.73)	0.45 (0.25)
a_fac_ic_fdiar_04	3.99 (4.95)	−0.05 (0.19)	1.53 (0.85)	0.31 (0.20)	0.60 (0.47)	0.71 (0.28)
a_fac_ic_fdi_01	1.66 (0.70)	0.15 (0.29)	0.77 (0.34)	0.60 (0.14)	1.26 (0.73)	0.44 (0.15)
a_fac_ic_fdi_02	1.50 (0.45)	0.21 (0.26)	1.10 (0.52)	0.46 (0.19)	1.08 (0.74)	0.47 (0.26)
a_fac_ic_fdi_03	1.54 (0.51)	0.23 (0.23)	1.14 (0.57)	0.45 (0.20)	1.15 (0.73)	0.45 (0.25)
a_fac_ic_fdi_04	3.99 (4.95)	−0.05 (0.19)	0.68 (0.46)	0.65 (0.22)	0.60 (0.47)	0.71 (0.28)
fac_pooled	1.76 (0.96)	0.03 (0.35)	0.97 (0.40)	0.52 (0.24)	0.51 (0.49)	0.66 (0.16)

RMSE for AR Model	0.005	0.006	0.389
MAE for AR model	0.005	0.005	0.304
MAE of best non-factor model	0.004	0.004	0.280
MAE of best factor model	0.004	0.003	0.191
MAE of fac_pooled	0.006	0.006	0.216

Notes: The initial estimation period is 1994:1–2000:2. The forecast period is 2000:3–2002:2. One-step-ahead forecasts. For each variable, the four columns report the MSE relative to the benchmark AR model, with West (1996) standard error in parentheses, and the coefficient of the forecast under analysis in a pooling regression with the benchmark forecast, with robust standard error in parentheses. We also report the root MSE and Mean Absolute Error (MAE) for the AR benchmark, and the MAE for the best non-factor model, factor model and pooled factor forecast. Prefix 'a' denotes use of country-specific factors only. See section 4.2.1 for details.

The forecasts in the rows of tables are (see section 4.2.1 for details):

ar_bic	AR model (BIC selection), benchmark
ar_bic_i2	AR model (BIC selection) for second-differenced variable
ar_bic_ic	AR model (BIC selection) with intercept correction
varf	VAR model
varf_ic	VAR model with intercept correction
fac_fdiarlag_bic	Factors from unbalanced panel (BIC selection), their lags, and AR terms

Model	Description
fac_fdiar_bic	Factors from unbalanced panel (BIC selection), and AR terms
fac_fdi_bic	Factors from unbalanced panel (BIC selection)
fbp_fdiarlag_bic	Factors from balanced panel (BIC selection), their lags, and AR terms
fbp_fdiar_bic	Factors from balanced panel (BIC selection), and AR terms
fbp_fdi_bic	Factors from balanced panel (BIC selection)
fac_fdiar_01	n factors from unbalanced panel, n = 1, 2, 3, 4, and AR terms
fac_fdiar_02	
fac_fdiar_03	
fac_fdiar_04	
fac_fdi_01	n factors from unbalanced panel, n = 1, 2, 3, 4
fac_fdi_02	
fac_fdi_03	
fac_fdi_04	
fac_ic_fdiarlag_bic	As factor models above, but with intercept correction
fac_ic_fdiar_bic	
fac_ic_fdi_bic	
fbp_ic_fdiarlag_bic	
fbp_ic_fdiar_bic	
fbp_ic_fdi_bic	
fac_ic_fdiar_01	
fac_ic_fdiar_02	
fac_ic_fdiar_03	
fac_ic_fdiar_04	
fac_ic_fdi_01	
fac_ic_fdi_02	
fac_ic_fdi_03	
fac_ic_fdi_04	
fac_pooled	Average of factor forecasts

of the VAR forecasts for all the three variables under analysis, while mixed results are obtained for the factor forecasts. Second differencing significantly improves the forecasting precision for GDP growth and inflation, while it leaves the results for the interest rate unaffected.

In more detail, for GDP growth the best model is fac_fdiar_02, with a relative MSE of 0.58. For inflation, the best model is fac_fdiarlag_bic with a relative MSE of 0.41. It is worth observing that this is the most general forecasting model, where the lag length of the autoregressive component and the choice of the number of factors and their lags are determined by the BIC criterion. For the interest rate, fac_fdi_04 is the best, namely a model with the first four estimated factors from the unbalanced panel as regressors. Any lags of the dependent variable included as regressors are eliminated by the BIC criterion as shown by the equality of the relative MSE between fac_fdi_04 and fac_fdiar_04. It yields a relative MSE of 0.33 (the second best is the same model with intercept correction, with a relative MSE of 0.60). There are several other factor models that perform well for all the three variables and systematically beat the AR.

Finally, when the forecasts from the best models are inserted in a pooling regression with the benchmark AR, their coefficients are not statistically different from one. As a consequence, there would be no significant gains from forecast pooling, which provides additional support for the best models. However, both the standard errors around the estimated coefficient in the pooling regressions and the West (1996) standard errors around the relative MSE are rather large, which suggests that the rankings reported above should be interpreted with care because most forecasting models are not statistically different from each other.

4.4.2 Hungary

The results for Hungary are reported in Table 4.2. The factor forecasts are not as good as for the Czech Republic. In particular, there are gains for GDP growth and, in a few cases, for the interest rate, but the AR forecast is the best for inflation. The gains for GDP growth are marginally higher than for the Czech Republic – about 47% for the best model. This may be mostly due to the substantially better performance of the AR benchmark for the Czech Republic, with an MSE of 0.005 for the Czech Republic versus 0.031 for Hungary. This may also account for the relatively better performance of the pooled factor forecast for GDP growth relative to the benchmark AR model when compared to the Czech Republic.

Table 4.2. *Results for Hungary, h = 1, I(1) prices and wages, country-specific factors*

Forecast method	gdp		cpi		rtb3m	
ar_bic	1.00 (0.00)	(.)	1.00 (0.00)	(.)	1.00 (0.00)	(.)
ar_bic_i2	2.25 (1.27)	−0.78 (0.29)	0.56 (0.27)	1.37 (0.47)	0.59 (0.46)	0.81 (0.34)
ar_bic_ic	2.31 (1.89)	−0.16 (0.23)	2.17 (2.90)	0.06 (0.32)	0.65 (0.49)	0.70 (0.32)
_varf	1.03 (0.14)	0.45 (0.17)	2.12 (2.48)	0.21 (0.19)	0.81 (0.22)	0.80 (0.35)
_varf_ic	1.56 (0.82)	−0.06 (0.49)	2.62 (2.35)	0.21 (0.16)	0.82 (0.39)	0.60 (0.21)
a_fac__fdiarlag_bic	0.88 (0.41)	0.58 (0.30)	2.56 (5.05)	0.18 (0.29)	0.93 (0.18)	0.67 (0.44)
a_fac__fdiar_bic	0.64 (0.35)	1.07 (0.45)	4.14 (8.20)	0.10 (0.12)	0.98 (0.18)	0.54 (0.37)
a_fac__fdi_bic	0.53 (0.44)	1.12 (0.34)	2.84 (1.98)	−0.15 (0.17)	0.98 (0.18)	0.54 (0.37)
a_fbp__fdiarlag_bic	1.22 (0.26)	−1.28 (0.89)	0.98 (0.49)	0.51 (0.31)	0.72 (0.35)	1.20 (0.75)
a_fbp__fdiar_bic	1.04 (0.22)	0.17 (1.55)	1.41 (0.59)	0.08 (0.41)	0.96 (0.19)	0.64 (0.62)
a_fbp__fdi_bic	0.83 (0.40)	1.05 (1.07)	1.41 (0.59)	0.08 (0.41)	0.96 (0.19)	0.64 (0.62)
a_fac__fdiar_01	1.25 (0.26)	−1.21 (0.35)	1.40 (0.31)	−0.26 (0.37)	0.89 (0.20)	0.67 (0.30)
a_fac__fdiar_02	1.20 (0.29)	−0.13 (0.79)	1.54 (0.45)	−0.26 (0.40)	0.93 (0.24)	0.61 (0.37)
a_fac__fdiar_03	0.55 (0.38)	1.33 (0.49)	2.34 (2.15)	0.01 (0.13)	0.99 (0.26)	0.51 (0.28)
a_fac__fdiar_04	0.72 (0.50)	0.73 (0.41)	1.80 (1.59)	0.20 (0.18)	1.22 (0.35)	0.32 (0.24)
a_fac__fdi_01	0.89 (0.40)	0.84 (1.16)	2.72 (1.93)	−0.13 (0.16)	0.89 (0.20)	0.67 (0.30)
a_fac__fdi_02	0.89 (0.50)	0.67 (0.73)	2.87 (2.06)	−0.15 (0.20)	0.93 (0.24)	0.61 (0.37)
a_fac__fdi_03	0.56 (0.47)	1.08 (0.37)	2.54 (2.45)	−0.05 (0.17)	0.99 (0.26)	0.51 (0.28)

a_fac_fdi_04	0.70 (0.50)	0.76 (0.43)	1.89 (1.68)	0.16 (0.17)	1.22 (0.35)	0.32 (0.24)
a_fac_ic_fdiarlag_bic	2.48 (2.28)	0.09 (0.14)	4.48 (9.61)	0.09 (0.17)	0.99 (0.52)	0.51 (0.28)
a_fac_ic_fdiar_bic	1.57 (0.61)	0.04 (0.36)	9.19 (52.11)	0.11 (0.10)	0.97 (0.50)	0.52 (0.28)
a_fac_ic_fdi_bic	1.42 (0.94)	0.30 (0.39)	3.67 (6.59)	-0.05 (0.27)	0.97 (0.50)	0.52 (0.28)
a_fbp_ic_fdiarlag_bic	2.62 (2.80)	-0.06 (0.25)	1.89 (1.01)	0.16 (0.18)	0.74 (0.53)	0.63 (0.27)
a_fbp_ic_fdiar_bic	2.37 (2.52)	0.03 (0.33)	2.48 (2.92)	-0.07 (0.32)	0.69 (0.41)	0.76 (0.27)
a_fbp_ic_fdi_bic	2.06 (2.07)	0.15 (0.37)	2.48 (2.92)	-0.07 (0.32)	0.69 (0.41)	0.76 (0.27)
a_fac_ic_fdiar_01	2.77 (3.37)	-0.03 (0.26)	1.96 (1.70)	0.01 (0.38)	0.65 (0.42)	0.76 (0.25)
a_fac_ic_fdiar_02	2.78 (3.56)	0.03 (0.29)	2.19 (2.08)	-0.07 (0.35)	0.72 (0.43)	0.70 (0.28)
a_fac_ic_fdiar_03	1.57 (0.79)	0.10 (0.32)	5.15 (13.87)	-0.17 (0.19)	1.18 (0.72)	0.41 (0.31)
a_fac_ic_fdiar_04	2.22 (1.59)	0.18 (0.21)	4.33 (9.54)	-0.15 (0.21)	1.68 (1.13)	0.26 (0.26)
a_fac_ic_fdi_01	2.22 (2.38)	0.14 (0.35)	3.54 (6.21)	-0.05 (0.28)	0.65 (0.42)	0.76 (0.25)
a_fac_ic_fdi_02	2.37 (2.65)	0.17 (0.32)	4.20 (8.93)	-0.10 (0.26)	0.72 (0.43)	0.70 (0.28)
a_fac_ic_fdi_03	1.71 (1.13)	0.25 (0.32)	5.62 (17.43)	-0.18 (0.18)	1.18 (0.72)	0.41 (0.31)
a_fac_ic_fdi_04	2.18 (1.57)	0.18 (0.22)	4.55 (10.93)	-0.16 (0.21)	1.68 (1.13)	0.26 (0.26)
fac_pooled	0.87 (0.53)	0.59 (0.38)	2.45 (2.10)	0.09 (0.22)	1.72 (0.87)	0.24 (0.21)

RMSE for AR Model	0.031	0.005	0.846
MAE for AR Model	0.025	0.004	0.624
MAE of best non-factor model	0.025	0.003	0.432
MAE of best factor model	0.019	0.004	0.474
MAE of fac_pooled	0.027	0.007	1.042

Notes: see notes to Table 4.1.

Using a fixed number of factors is often equivalent or better than BIC selection, especially for GDP growth. Intercept corrections are useful only for factor forecasts for the interest rate.

In more detail, for GDP growth the best model is fac_fdi_bic, with a relative MSE of 0.53. The best model for the Czech Republic, fac_fdiar_02, with a relative MSE of 1.20, can no longer beat the benchmark. For both inflation and interest rates, the best model is ar_bic_i2, with relative MSE of 0.56 and 0.59 respectively. The best factor model for the interest rate is fac_ic_fdiar_01 with relative MSE of 0.65, which is a close competitor to the non-factor models, but this is not the case for the inflation variable where factor-based forecasts are heavily dominated. The best model for interest rate for the Czech Republic, fac_fdiar_04, is not a strong competitor for Hungary.

Finally, as for the Czech Republic, when the forecasts from the best models are inserted in a pooling regression with the benchmark AR, their coefficients are not statistically different from one, but the related standard errors and those by West (1996) for the relative MSE are even larger than for the Czech Republic.

4.4.3   Poland

The results for Poland are reported in Table 4.3. For GDP growth and inflation, the findings are similar to those for the Czech Republic, with large average gains that reach 64% and 47% respectively for the best factor model. For the interest rate, the factors from the unbalanced panel are now the most useful, and some factor forecasts yield substantial gains. The pooled factor forecast shows gains of roughly 40% over the benchmark for GDP growth and inflation, while no gains are recorded for the interest rate. As in the case of the Czech Republic, the results indicate the overall usefulness of factor models as a general methodological approach to forecasting.

It is again confirmed that using a fixed number of factors is often equivalent or better than BIC selection, and no general conclusion can be drawn on including an AR component in the forecasting model. Intercept corrections are sometimes useful for forecasts for GDP growth.

In more detail, for GDP growth the best model is fac_fdiarlag_bic, with a relative MSE of 0.36. It should be noted, however, that the AR model with second differencing is a close competitor. The best model for the Czech Republic, fac_fdiar_02, can still beat the benchmark comfortably, with a relative MSE of 0.71. For inflation, the best model is fac_ic_fdi_bic, unbalanced panel, intercept correction and factor chosen by BIC criterion. For the interest rate, fac_fdi_04 is the best model, with a

Table 4.3. Results for Poland, h = 1, I(1) prices and wages, country-specific factors

Forecast method	gdp	(.)	cpi	(.)	rtb3m	(.)
ar_bic	1.00 (0.00)	(.)	1.00 (0.00)	(.)	1.00 (0.00)	(.)
ar_bic_i2	0.41 (0.52)	0.98 (0.34)	0.79 (0.25)	1.14 (0.84)	1.58 (1.02)	0.13 (0.40)
ar_bic_ic	0.87 (0.29)	0.55 (0.12)	1.88 (1.78)	0.06 (0.38)	3.00 (3.11)	-0.16 (0.23)
_varf	0.81 (0.28)	1.67 (1.21)	0.97 (0.15)	0.66 (0.73)	1.07 (0.26)	0.23 (1.00)
_varf_ic	0.47 (0.53)	0.72 (0.21)	1.75 (1.64)	0.04 (0.40)	2.30 (1.61)	-0.01 (0.35)
a_fac__fdiarlag_bic	0.36 (0.56)	1.37 (0.31)	1.62 (0.98)	0.11 (0.41)	2.10 (2.36)	0.23 (0.10)
a_fac__fdiar_bic	0.87 (0.49)	0.56 (0.23)	0.73 (0.27)	1.28 (0.63)	2.17 (2.56)	0.23 (0.10)
a_fac__fdi_bic	1.61 (0.55)	0.13 (0.31)	0.85 (0.61)	0.58 (0.36)	0.48 (0.21)	0.69 (0.14)
a_fbp__fdiarlag_bic	1.70 (0.85)	-0.80 (0.41)	0.96 (0.27)	0.74 (1.62)	2.10 (2.36)	0.23 (0.10)
a_fbp__fdiar_bic	1.81 (0.86)	-1.22 (0.41)	0.96 (0.27)	0.74 (1.62)	7.13 (41.14)	0.10 (0.03)
a_fbp__fdi_bic	1.81 (0.86)	-1.22 (0.41)	3.35 (2.03)	-0.08 (0.23)	0.68 (0.22)	0.61 (0.08)
a_fac__fdiar_01	0.85 (0.16)	2.66 (1.46)	0.87 (0.29)	1.15 (1.21)	2.30 (2.84)	0.21 (0.09)
a_fac__fdiar_02	0.71 (0.27)	2.29 (0.87)	0.88 (0.29)	1.10 (1.23)	2.31 (2.86)	0.21 (0.09)
a_fac__fdiar_03	0.80 (0.28)	1.30 (0.98)	0.90 (0.30)	0.94 (1.23)	2.90 (4.98)	0.17 (0.07)
a_fac__fdiar_04	0.74 (0.34)	1.23 (0.76)	1.24 (0.26)	-1.11 (0.81)	2.23 (3.65)	0.34 (0.14)
a_fac__fdi_01	0.85 (0.16)	2.66 (1.46)	1.47 (0.55)	-0.08 (0.31)	1.14 (0.54)	0.37 (0.42)
a_fac__fdi_02	0.71 (0.27)	2.29 (0.87)	1.43 (0.51)	-0.08 (0.32)	0.80 (0.29)	0.72 (0.34)
a_fac__fdi_03	0.70 (0.31)	2.16 (0.97)	1.38 (0.50)	-0.02 (0.36)	0.76 (0.26)	0.73 (0.27)
a_fac__fdi_04	0.69 (0.33)	2.59 (1.05)	1.13 (0.42)	0.28 (0.61)	0.48 (0.21)	0.69 (0.14)
a_fac_ic_fdiarlag_bic	0.50 (0.60)	0.73 (0.26)	4.67 (10.15)	-0.13 (0.23)	2.05 (1.29)	0.28 (0.14)
a_fac_ic_fdiar_bic	2.39 (1.93)	0.26 (0.09)	1.03 (0.66)	0.48 (0.37)	3.28 (4.22)	0.21 (0.10)
a_fac_ic_fdi_bic	2.96 (4.19)	0.24 (0.06)	0.53 (0.41)	0.74 (0.18)	0.90 (0.33)	0.53 (0.10)
a_fbp_ic_fdiarlag_bic	1.17 (0.74)	0.44 (0.22)	1.89 (1.67)	0.20 (0.35)	2.05 (1.29)	0.28 (0.14)
a_fbp_ic_fdiar_bic	0.87 (0.48)	0.56 (0.22)	1.89 (1.67)	0.20 (0.35)	12.20 (81.34)	0.11 (0.03)
a_fbp_ic_fdi_bic	0.87 (0.48)	0.56 (0.22)	5.79 (13.43)	-0.20 (0.18)	0.80 (0.33)	0.57 (0.14)
a_fac_ic_fdiar_01	0.86 (0.35)	0.56 (0.13)	1.79 (1.59)	0.18 (0.39)	2.40 (1.79)	0.26 (0.14)

Table 4.3. (cont.)

Forecast method	gdp	cpi	rtb3m
a_fac_ic_fdiar_02	0.70 (0.46)	0.61 (0.18)	1.77 (1.57)	0.18 (0.39)	2.35 (1.72)	0.25 (0.15)
a_fac_ic_fdiar_03	1.39 (0.30)	0.39 (0.08)	1.84 (1.65)	0.17 (0.38)	3.13 (2.77)	0.22 (0.11)
a_fac_ic_fdiar_04	1.17 (0.36)	0.45 (0.11)	2.62 (3.76)	-0.06 (0.24)	3.55 (5.54)	0.28 (0.06)
a_fac_ic_fdi_01	0.86 (0.35)	0.56 (0.13)	1.59 (1.17)	0.11 (0.40)	1.22 (0.55)	0.34 (0.34)
a_fac_ic_fdi_02	0.70 (0.46)	0.61 (0.18)	1.59 (1.23)	0.14 (0.42)	1.97 (1.03)	-0.07 (0.36)
a_fac_ic_fdi_03	0.88 (0.43)	0.54 (0.15)	1.53 (1.13)	0.17 (0.43)	2.14 (1.52)	-0.09 (0.30)
a_fac_ic_fdi_04	0.73 (0.46)	0.60 (0.17)	1.04 (0.61)	0.46 (0.57)	0.90 (0.33)	0.53 (0.10)
fac_pooled	0.57 (0.49)	0.83 (0.33)	0.63 (0.39)	1.27 (0.44)	1.03 (0.69)	0.49 (0.18)
RMSE for AR Model	0.006		0.009		0.705	
MAE for AR Model	0.005		0.008		0.692	
MAE of best non-factor model	0.004		0.006		0.692	
MAE of best factor model	0.003		0.006		0.491	
MAE of fac_pooled	0.004		0.006		0.519	

Notes: see notes to Table 4.1.

relative MSE of 0.48. The best model for the Czech Republic, fac_
fdiar_04, is much worse than the benchmark, with a relative MSE of 2.23.

Finally, as for the Czech Republic and Hungary, when the forecasts
from the best models are inserted in a pooling regression with the
benchmark AR, their coefficients are not statistically different from
one, but the related standard errors and those by West (1996) for the
relative MSE are fairly large.

4.4.4 Slovakia

The results for Slovakia are reported in Table 4.4. The performance of
factor forecasts for GDP growth is poor on average. The best model is
the VAR, with a relative MSE of 0.89. It is, however, possible to beat the
benchmark for both inflation and the interest rate using factor models,
with the best models being given by fac_ic_fdi_bic (relative MSE 0.41)
and fac_fdi_04 (relative MSE 0.44) respectively. Forecasting inflation is
also the only case where factor models as a whole produce improvement
in forecasting precision (relative MSE of fac_pooled is 0.91). The
best model for the interest rate shows no role for the lagged endogenous variable, while for inflation there are some gains after intercept
correction of the factor forecasts.

Since the best model for GDP growth is chosen using the BIC criterion, there is a role for its use. Including an AR component in the
forecasting model is not always efficacious.

4.4.5 Slovenia

The results for Slovenia are reported in Table 4.5. Overall, the results
are mixed, since for GDP growth the gain from using factor models is
comparable to Poland, while the best factor model for inflation has a
relative MSE of 1.02 and the benchmark AR model cannot be beaten for
forecasting interest rates. More generally, forecasts from the class of
factor models for inflation and interest rates are systematically beaten
by the benchmark AR model, their poor average performance confirmed
by looking at the pooled forecast where relative MSEs exceeding one can
be noted. For GDP growth, however, a number of factor models perform well, a result also reflected in a low value of the relative MSE for the
pooled forecast.

It is again confirmed that using a fixed number of factors is often
equivalent to BIC selection and, as for Slovakia, including an AR component in the forecasting model is not always convenient. Intercept
corrections are sometimes useful for GDP growth but not for the

Table 4.4. Results for Slovakia, h = 1, I(1) prices and wages, country-specific factors

Forecast method	gdp		cpi		rtb3m	
		(.)		(.)		(.)
ar_bic	1.00 (0.00)		1.00 (0.00)		1.00 (0.00)	
ar_bic_i2	1.90 (1.02)	0.08 (0.23)	1.06 (0.41)	0.46 (0.27)	2.42 (3.59)	0.05 (0.37)
ar_bic_ic	2.91 (2.99)	-0.31 (0.31)	0.69 (0.39)	0.60 (0.14)	3.56 (4.99)	-0.37 (0.19)
_varf	0.89 (0.25)	0.62 (0.26)	0.98 (0.29)	0.54 (0.60)	1.27 (0.53)	0.36 (0.22)
_varf_ic	2.31 (1.31)	0.05 (0.20)	1.08 (0.59)	0.48 (0.16)	3.14 (2.94)	-0.23 (0.25)
a_fac_fdiarlag_bic	6.56 (34.35)	-0.22 (0.01)	1.37 (0.68)	-0.04 (0.64)	1.23 (0.29)	0.30 (0.28)
a_fac_fdiar_bic	14.82 (128.32)	-0.17 (0.01)	1.37 (0.51)	-0.27 (0.25)	6.87 (35.51)	-0.21 (0.02)
a_fac_fdi_bic	27.31 (464.24)	-0.12 (0.00)	1.00 (0.00)	15.87 (48.55)	1.23 (0.29)	0.30 (0.28)
a_fbp_fdiarlag_bic	0.99 (0.11)	0.74 (2.17)	1.00 (0.13)	0.52 (0.88)	1.23 (0.29)	0.30 (0.28)
a_fbp_fdiar_bic	28.26 (645.52)	-0.11 (0.02)	1.00 (0.13)	0.52 (0.88)	1.23 (0.29)	0.30 (0.28)
a_fbp_fdi_bic	0.99 (0.11)	0.74 (2.17)	1.00 (0.13)	0.52 (0.88)	1.23 (0.29)	0.30 (0.28)
a_fac_fdiar_01	1.91 (0.73)	-0.63 (0.44)	0.99 (0.13)	0.58 (1.06)	1.16 (0.29)	0.37 (0.24)
a_fac_fdiar_02	4.12 (5.83)	-0.28 (0.11)	1.26 (0.50)	0.15 (0.41)	1.17 (0.30)	0.36 (0.24)
a_fac_fdiar_03	9.07 (41.41)	-0.26 (0.03)	1.05 (0.43)	0.46 (0.30)	1.18 (0.47)	0.40 (0.23)
a_fac_fdiar_04	8.22 (43.12)	-0.13 (0.11)	1.23 (0.47)	0.27 (0.35)	0.44 (0.35)	0.68 (0.11)
a_fac_fdi_01	1.91 (0.73)	-0.63 (0.44)	0.99 (0.13)	0.58 (1.06)	1.16 (0.29)	0.37 (0.24)
a_fac_fdi_02	2.26 (1.06)	-0.48 (0.23)	1.03 (0.18)	0.43 (0.44)	1.17 (0.30)	0.36 (0.24)
a_fac_fdi_03	3.42 (4.67)	-0.48 (0.10)	1.05 (0.18)	0.38 (0.40)	1.18 (0.47)	0.40 (0.23)
a_fac_fdi_04	5.74 (20.19)	-0.05 (0.17)	0.95 (0.17)	0.61 (0.37)	0.44 (0.35)	0.68 (0.11)

a_fac_ic_fdiarlag_bic	15.36 (120.43)	−0.10 (0.06)	1.73 (1.20)	0.34 (0.18)	2.44 (2.88)	−0.21 (0.22)
a_fac_ic_fdiar_bic	30.60 (317.51)	−0.09 (0.04)	1.22 (0.77)	0.44 (0.18)	15.69 (148.13)	−0.22 (0.02)
a_fac_ic_fdi_bic	55.23 (1174.48)	−0.07 (0.03)	0.41 (0.32)	0.81 (0.14)	2.44 (2.88)	−0.21 (0.22)
a_fbp_ic_fdiarlag_bic	2.66 (1.79)	0.09 (0.18)	0.63 (0.35)	0.64 (0.14)	2.44 (2.88)	−0.21 (0.22)
a_fbp_ic_fdiar_bic	62.29 (1946.59)	−0.07 (0.02)	0.63 (0.35)	0.64 (0.14)	2.44 (2.88)	−0.21 (0.22)
a_fbp_ic_fdi_bic	2.66 (1.79)	0.09 (0.18)	0.61 (0.36)	0.64 (0.14)	2.44 (2.88)	−0.21 (0.22)
a_fac_ic_fdiar_01	4.67 (6.69)	−0.09 (0.18)	1.61 (1.07)	0.65 (0.15)	2.46 (3.41)	−0.21 (0.22)
a_fac_ic_fdiar_02	7.05 (16.08)	−0.20 (0.12)	1.95 (1.24)	0.36 (0.15)	2.53 (3.51)	−0.23 (0.20)
a_fac_ic_fdiar_03	22.78 (247.73)	−0.09 (0.04)	1.82 (1.34)	0.34 (0.11)	2.23 (2.75)	−0.05 (0.34)
a_fac_ic_fdiar_04	17.66 (135.04)	−0.08 (0.05)	0.61 (0.36)	0.36 (0.12)	2.43 (3.79)	0.23 (0.27)
a_fac_ic_fdi_01	4.67 (6.69)	−0.09 (0.18)	1.01 (0.51)	0.65 (0.15)	2.46 (3.41)	−0.21 (0.22)
a_fac_ic_fdi_02	5.73 (9.85)	−0.09 (0.14)	1.10 (0.57)	0.50 (0.16)	2.53 (3.51)	−0.23 (0.20)
a_fac_ic_fdi_03	9.44 (36.28)	−0.10 (0.09)	1.01 (0.44)	0.47 (0.16)	2.23 (2.75)	−0.05 (0.34)
a_fac_ic_fdi_04	9.87 (45.93)	0.00 (0.07)		0.50 (0.12)	2.43 (3.79)	0.23 (0.27)
fac_pooled	17.35 (138.83)	−0.11 (0.05)	0.91 (0.42)	0.56 (0.27)	2.67 (3.16)	−0.15 (0.31)

RMSE for AR Model	0.004		0.010		0.502	
MAE for AR Model	0.003		0.009		0.402	
MAE of best non-factor model	0.003		0.005		0.458	
MAE of best factor model	0.003		0.007		0.310	
MAE of fac_pooled	0.013		0.007		0.679	

Notes: see notes to Table 4.1.

Table 4.5. *Results for Slovenia, h = 1, I(1) prices and wages, country-specific factors*

Forecast method	gdp		cpi		rtb3m	
		(.)		(.)		(.)
ar_bic	1.00 (0.00)	(.)	1.00 (0.00)	(.)	1.00 (0.00)	(.)
ar_bic_i2	0.92 (0.56)	0.54 (0.30)	2.07 (1.20)	-0.48 (0.32)	3.07 (3.29)	0.01 (0.14)
ar_bic_ic	0.79 (0.55)	0.59 (0.26)	2.16 (1.32)	-0.09 (0.34)	3.51 (3.30)	-0.03 (0.17)
_varf	2.07 (1.47)	-1.39 (0.21)	1.51 (0.56)	-0.62 (0.58)	5.11 (11.66)	-0.01 (0.24)
_varf_ic	1.69 (1.62)	0.29 (0.27)	3.66 (3.26)	-0.09 (0.21)	11.53 (42.22)	0.07 (0.09)
a_fac__fdiarlag_bic	1.39 (0.27)	-2.60 (1.44)	1.52 (0.64)	-0.50 (0.41)	2.70 (1.81)	-0.03 (0.24)
a_fac__fdiar_bic	1.39 (0.27)	-2.60 (1.44)	1.52 (0.64)	-0.50 (0.41)	2.84 (2.21)	-0.19 (0.21)
a_fac__fdi_bic	0.92 (0.31)	0.68 (0.79)	1.02 (0.04)	-3.78 (7.54)	2.84 (2.21)	-0.19 (0.21)
a_fbp__fdiarlag_bic	1.39 (0.27)	-2.60 (1.44)	1.02 (0.04)	-3.78 (7.54)	3.20 (2.14)	-0.18 (0.26)
a_fbp__fdiar_bic	1.39 (0.27)	-2.60 (1.44)	1.26 (0.76)	0.31 (0.42)	3.15 (2.44)	-0.30 (0.22)
a_fbp__fdi_bic	1.17 (0.37)	0.22 (0.61)	1.21 (0.75)	0.36 (0.40)	3.15 (2.44)	-0.30 (0.22)
a_fac__fdiar_01	1.46 (0.32)	-2.27 (1.32)	1.19 (0.26)	-0.49 (1.07)	2.84 (2.21)	-0.19 (0.21)
a_fac__fdiar_02	1.33 (0.26)	-0.77 (0.82)	1.23 (0.61)	0.20 (0.59)	2.72 (1.98)	-0.22 (0.23)
a_fac__fdiar_03	1.38 (0.31)	-0.92 (0.76)	1.28 (0.67)	0.20 (0.53)	4.56 (8.18)	-0.28 (0.15)
a_fac__fdiar_04	1.14 (0.32)	0.23 (0.59)	1.14 (0.42)	0.20 (0.79)	6.16 (19.81)	-0.28 (0.07)
a_fac__fdi_01	0.53 (0.26)	1.45 (0.38)	1.03 (0.07)	-1.68 (3.81)	2.84 (2.21)	-0.19 (0.21)
a_fac__fdi_02	0.46 (0.27)	1.33 (0.30)	1.03 (0.07)	-1.03 (3.91)	2.72 (1.98)	-0.22 (0.23)
a_fac__fdi_03	0.44 (0.27)	1.44 (0.32)	1.16 (0.24)	-0.25 (1.09)	2.91 (2.42)	-0.25 (0.23)
a_fac__fdi_04	0.54 (0.26)	1.30 (0.25)	1.14 (0.42)	0.20 (0.79)	2.57 (2.08)	-0.27 (0.22)

a_fac_ic_fdiarlag_bic	0.97 (0.77)	0.51 (0.35)	4.54 (6.31)	−0.06 (0.20)	5.94 (9.53)	−0.29 (0.18)
a_fac_ic_fdiar_bic	0.97 (0.77)	0.51 (0.35)	4.54 (6.31)	−0.06 (0.20)	6.66 (9.77)	−0.26 (0.15)
a_fac_ic_fdi_bic	1.57 (0.49)	0.39 (0.08)	2.16 (1.31)	−0.08 (0.34)	6.66 (9.77)	−0.26 (0.15)
a_fbp_ic_fdiarlag_bic	0.97 (0.77)	0.51 (0.35)	2.16 (1.31)	−0.08 (0.34)	6.32 (12.72)	−0.32 (0.14)
a_fbp_ic_fdiar_bic	0.97 (0.77)	0.51 (0.35)	2.66 (2.73)	−0.04 (0.22)	6.68 (12.68)	−0.37 (0.14)
a_fbp_ic_fdi_bic	1.55 (0.99)	0.40 (0.10)	2.57 (2.50)	0.09 (0.22)	6.68 (12.68)	−0.37 (0.14)
a_fac_ic_fdiar_01	0.98 (0.79)	0.51 (0.34)	3.05 (2.76)	−0.10 (0.26)	6.66 (9.77)	−0.26 (0.15)
a_fac_ic_fdiar_02	0.50 (0.35)	0.77 (0.22)	4.24 (6.43)	−0.01 (0.20)	6.53 (9.79)	−0.27 (0.15)
a_fac_ic_fdiar_03	0.55 (0.37)	0.72 (0.21)	4.40 (6.96)	−0.02 (0.19)	10.37 (40.95)	−0.27 (0.06)
a_fac_ic_fdiar_04	0.45 (0.27)	0.68 (0.13)	3.47 (4.00)	−0.02 (0.22)	14.82 (101.06)	−0.20 (0.04)
a_fac_ic_fdi_01	0.89 (0.46)	0.53 (0.13)	2.27 (1.51)	−0.12 (0.33)	6.66 (9.77)	−0.26 (0.15)
a_fac_ic_fdi_02	0.57 (0.28)	0.60 (0.08)	2.25 (1.48)	−0.13 (0.34)	6.53 (9.79)	−0.27 (0.15)
a_fac_ic_fdi_03	0.46 (0.28)	0.64 (0.09)	2.69 (2.33)	0.01 (0.27)	7.42 (11.48)	−0.34 (0.09)
a_fac_ic_fdi_04	0.47 (0.29)	0.65 (0.10)	3.47 (4.00)	−0.02 (0.22)	6.91 (10.67)	−0.38 (0.08)
fac_pooled	0.67 (0.30)	0.83 (0.30)	1.67 (0.88)	−0.04 (0.41)	5.46 (15.52)	−0.17 (0.10)
RMSE for AR Model	0.006		0.005		0.606	
MAE for AR Model	0.005		0.004		0.517	
MAE of best non-factor model	0.003		0.005		0.729	
MAE of best factor model	0.003		0.004		0.853	
MAE of fac_pooled	0.003		0.005		1.158	

Notes: see notes to Table 4.1.

remaining two variables. Moreover, forecasting results with factors from balanced and unbalanced panels are virtually identical as the difference between the two panels is only in one series. For this reason there is very small difference between balanced and unbalanced factors estimates.

In more detail, for GDP growth the best model is fac_fdi_03, with a relative MSE of 0.44. Both for inflation and for the interest rate, no model beats the benchmark, with the best performing factor model (fac_fdi_bic) providing a relative MSE of 1.02 for inflation, while for the interest rate the relative MSEs are considerably higher.

4.4.6   *The role of Euro area information*

So far, the factors to be used as regressors in the forecasting models are extracted from the country-specific data sets, and no Euro area information has been incorporated. Yet, as mentioned before, because of the increasing integration with Europe, in particular with the creation of the Euro area, it could be that Euro area information is also relevant for forecasting macroeconomic variables for the new Member States. To evaluate whether this is the case, we use Euro area information in two ways. The detailed tables and results are available from us upon request. First, we include Euro area variables in the AR models as described in section 4.2.1. Secondly, we extract factors from the Euro area data set as described in section 4.3, and use them for forecasting either instead of or in combination with the country-specific factors. To save space, we only comment on the results where country-specific and Euro area data are combined, those when only Euro area data are used are qualitatively similar.

Three kinds of questions can be asked. First, does the best performing model come from the class that includes Euro area information? Secondly, how do AR models with Euro area variables compare with the ones without such information present? Thirdly, how are factor models affected in their forecasting performance by incorporating Euro area variables?

The answer to the first question is that, for Hungarian GDP growth, and interest rate and Slovenian GDP growth, the best forecasting models include Euro area information.

In answer to the second question, and related to the first, the performance of the class of autoregressive models is helped in some instances by the incorporation of Euro area information. For example, for Hungary, for forecasting GDP growth the best non-factor model overall is an AR model with Euro area GDP growth as a control variable. Substantial gains also occur for Hungary for the interest rate series, where an intercept corrected AR model with Euro area interest rate as a control variable with a relative MSE of 0.43 becomes the best non-factor model (and the best model overall). The same model is the best non-factor model for Slovakia in forecasting inflation. The reverse phenomenon, however, occurs, for example for Czech GDP growth where the best non-factor model that does not incorporate Euro area information has a relative MSE of 0.75 compared with a relative MSE of 1.24 for a model which does.

Thus, evaluating the performance of factor models in particular with Euro area information, it may be noted that the role of such information appears to be limited, although alternative ways of combining Euro area information into country-specific data sets may yet yield different conclusions.[2] This finding is not surprising in the light of the findings of Artis et al. (2006) who highlight a decrease in business cycle synchronisation between the Euro area and the new Member States, mostly attributable to the process of convergence and thus, in principle, specific to the period studied.

Our finding also matches closely the results reported by Darvas and Szapáry (2004) who undertook an analysis of the synchronisation of business cycles between the EMU and the eight new EU members from Central and Eastern Europe. In contrast to the GDP and industrial production data usually analysed, they extended their analysis to the major expenditure and sectoral components of GDP and used several measures of synchronisation. The main findings of their paper were that Hungary, Poland and Slovenia had achieved a high degree of synchronisation with the EMU for GDP, industrial production and exports, but not for consumption and services. The remaining countries had achieved less or no synchronisation. Recalling that it is for Hungary and Slovenia (for GDP growth) that Euro area information is useful in forecasting, it is natural to assign a key role to synchronisation. This also leads us to conclude in favour of the hypothesis that the role of Euro area information is greatest in the countries for which synchronisation of the variables with the EMU is high. We do not identify a role for Euro area information for Poland – the remaining country for which Darvas and Szapáry (2004) found synchronisation – mainly because factor models with Euro area information are strong overall performers for GDP

---

[2] It is possible that, in the single-equation models, better forecasting results using Euro area information may be found by a more general selection of leading indicators. Thus, we may investigate, for example, if inflation in a given new Member State is determined not by inflation in the Euro area but by GDP growth in the Euro area. This is less true when factors are extracted from Euro area data and used for forecasting, since in this case a large amount of information, taking account of such possibilities, is implicitly utilised.

growth (relative MSE of 0.57 for the pooled factor forecast) and thus hard to beat.

4.4.7   I(2) prices, wages and money

Since there is uncertainty in the literature about whether prices, wages and money are integrated of order 1 or 2, and the sample sizes are too small for reliable testing of this hypothesis, we prefer to evaluate the robustness of our analysis by repeating it under the assumption of $I(2)$ nominal variables. Note that, since the choice of order of integration of the nominal variables affects the computation of all the factors, we can expect differences not only for forecasting inflation but also for GDP growth and short-term interest rate.

Overall, the second differencing of nominal variables does not lead to a significant improvement in forecasting precision.

4.5   Conclusions

In this chapter, we have evaluated the relative performance of factor models and more traditional small-scale time series methods for forecasting macroeconomic variables for five new Member States. Since these countries are characterised by short time series, simple methods can be expected to perform comparatively well. On the other hand, the availability of large sets of macroeconomic indicators suggests that factor methods may also be suitable.

The results can be summarised as follows. Concentrating first on models with country-specific information, a factor model yields the best forecasts for GDP growth for four of the five countries in the sample, namely the Czech Republic, Hungary, Poland and Slovenia. The gains range from 42% for the Czech Republic to 64% for Poland. A VAR is the best forecasting model for Slovakia. For inflation, in the case of Hungary an AR model with second differencing is the best model, while factor models are preferred for the Czech Republic, Poland and Slovakia. For Slovenia, a factor model marginally under-performs the benchmark AR model. For the short-term interest rate, factor models work best for the Czech Republic, Poland and Slovakia. An AR model with second differencing is the best model for Hungary, while for Slovenia the benchmark AR model dominates all others. Thus, out of the fifteen time series (three variables for each of the five countries), factor models provide the best forecasts in ten cases. When Euro area information is allowed, this count drops to eight (or nine) out of fifteen cases, with the best forecasting models for Slovenian GDP growth (only marginally) and for Hungarian interest rates switching to non-factor models. The best forecasting model for Hungary for GDP growth remains a factor model, but is one that incorporates Euro area information.

In order to consider the overall performance of factor models for each of the variables studied, instead of looking only at the best model, the behaviour of the pooled factor forecast (fac_pooled) can be taken to be a good guide. For example, reflective of the results reported above, fac_-pooled has relative MSEs of 2.45 and 1.72 (Table 4.2) for Hungarian inflation and interest rate (while the corresponding figures are 0.97 and 0.51 for the Czech Republic (Table 4.1)). For Poland, a country for which performance of the factor models are on par with the Czech Republic, the relative MSEs are given by 0.57, 0.63 and 1.03 for GDP growth, inflation and interest rate respectively (Table 4.3). Similar patterns may be discerned by considering Tables 4.4 and 4.5, where the good performance of a specific factor model is often matched by low numbers for the relative MSE of the fac_pooled forecast while the converse is true in cases where factor models perform poorly.

Four other general results emerge from the analysis. First, in samples as short as ours it may be better to use a fixed model rather than selection using the BIC criterion. Secondly, adding an AR component to the factor model is usually beneficial. Thirdly, the pooled factor forecasts in general yield smaller gains with respect to the benchmark than the best factor forecasts, indicating that careful model selection is important. Finally, intercept corrections and second differencing (as forecast-robustifying devices against structural breaks) may yield gains in some cases but should be used with care.

With factor models dominating roughly two-thirds of the time, we think it appropriate to conclude that overall the results are supportive of a careful use of factor models for forecasting macroeconomic variables for the new Member States. Interesting directions for future research in this context are mostly related to the collection of better data sets, with longer, cleaner and higher frequency time series, and detailed simulation studies to investigate the efficacy of factor methods in panels of data with short T and relatively larger N.

References

Angelini, E., Henry, J. and Marcellino, M. 2003. 'Interpolation and Backdating with a Large Information Set'. ECB Working Paper, No. 252.

Artis, M., Banerjee, A. and Marcellino, M. 2005. 'Factor Forecasts for the UK'. *Journal of Forecasting*, vol. 24, pp. 279–98.

134   *Banerjee, Marcellino and Masten*

Artis, M. and Marcellino, M. 2001. 'Fiscal Forecasting: The Track Record of IMF, OECD and EC'. *Econometrics Journal*, vol. 4, pp. 20–36.

Artis, M., Marcellino, M. and Proietti, T. 2006. 'The Cyclical Experience of the New Member States'. Chapter 5, this volume.

Bai, J. and Ng, S. 2003. 'Confidence Intervals for Diffusion Index Forecasts with a Large Number of Predictors'. *Mimeo*.

Bernanke, B. and Boivin, J. 2003. 'Monetary Policy in a data-Rich Environment'. *Journal of Monetary Economics*, vol. 50, pp. 525–46.

Clements, M. and Hendry, D. 1999. *Forecasting Non-Stationary Economic Time Series*. Cambridge, MA: MIT Press.

Darvas, Z. and Szapáry, G. 2004. 'Business-Cycle Synchronisation in the Enlarged EU: Co-movements in the New and Old Members'. Magyar Nemzeti Bank Working Paper, No. 1.

Engle, R. and Watson, M. 1981. 'A One-Factor Multivariate Time Series Model of Metropolitan Wage Rates'. *Journal of the American Statistical Association*, vol. 76, pp. 774–81.

Fagan, G., Henry, J. and Mestre, R. 2005. 'An area-wide model (AWM) for the Euro Area'. *Economic Modelling*, vol. 22, pp. 39–59.

Geweke, J. 1977. 'The Dynamic Factor Analysis of Economic Time Series'. In Aigner, D. and Goldberger, A. (eds.), *Latent Variables in Socio-Economic Models*. Amsterdam: North Holland.

Marcellino, M. 2000. 'Forecast Bias and RMSE Encompassing'. *Oxford Bulletin of Economics and Statistics*, vol. 62, pp. 533–42.

Marcellino, M., Stock, J. and Watson, M. 2001. 'A Dynamic Factor Analysis of the Euro Area'. Mimeo.

2003. 'Macroeconomic Forecasting in the Euro Area: Country Specific Versus Euro Wide Information'. *European Economic Review*, vol. 47, pp. 1–18.

Sargent, T. and Sims, C. 1977. 'Business Cycle Modelling Without Pretending to Have Too Much A-Priori Economic Theory'. In Sims, C. (ed.), *New Methods in Business Cycle Research*. Minneapolis: Federal Reserve Bank of Minneapolis.

Stock, J. and Watson, M. 1991. 'A Probability Model of the Coincident Economic Indicators'. In Lahiri, K. and Moore, G. (eds.), *Leading Economic Indicators: New Approaches and Forecasting Records*. New York: Cambridge University Press.

1998. 'Diffusion Indexes'. NBER Working Paper, No. 6702.

1999. 'Forecasting Inflation'. *Journal of Monetary Economics*, vol. 44, pp. 293–335.

2002a. 'Forecasting Using Principal Components from a Large Number of Predictors'. *Journal of the American Statistical Association*, vol. 97, pp. 1167–79.

2002b. 'Macroeconomic Forecasting Using Diffusion Indexes'. *Journal of Business and Economic Statistics*, vol. 20, pp. 147–62.

West, K. 1996. 'Asymptotic Inference About Predictive Ability'. *Econometrica*, vol. 64, pp. 1067–84.

5 The cyclical experience of the new Member States

Michael Artis, Massimiliano Marcellino and Tommaso Proietti

5.1 Introduction

In this chapter we study the business cycle in the new Member States, focusing on the degree of cyclical concordance both within this group of countries, which turns out to be in general lower than that between the existing EU countries, and with respect to the Euro area, which is also generally low when GDP data are used, slightly higher with industrial production. Traditional optimal currency area criteria would say that these results cast doubt on the wisdom of adopting the euro in the near future for most of these countries; but other criteria such as the extent of trade and the probable non-availability of a well-established stabilisation regime outside monetary union membership point in the opposite direction.

The structure of this chapter is as follows. In the next section, we discuss the relevance of the topic under examination, briefly referring to some previous studies. The novel contribution of the present chapter stems from its use, in combination with new filtering techniques, of a flexible algorithm for dating the business cycle. These are discussed in section 5.3 of the chapter, full technical detail on the dating algorithm being postponed to the Appendix to this chapter. In section 5.4, we present the results of applying these techniques to the data sets available for the new Member States. Three concepts of the cycle are distinguished – the classical cycle, the growth cycle and the deviation cycle – and results for each are presented in turn. In section 5.4.4 we compare our results with those available in two other recent papers, finding a high (but not complete) degree of similarity in the principal substantive results obtained. In section 5.5, we bring together some conclusions. The Appendix to this chapter provides full technical detail on the dating algorithm.

5.2 The salience of the topic

The task of this chapter is to identify the business cycle experience of the new Member States (or, more accurately, the Central and Eastern

European components thereof), with particular emphasis on the extent to which the business cycles of the different countries are similar to each other and similar to the cyclical experiences of the Western European members of the European Union and its EMU. Study of this topic is not novel, and a number of papers exist which have a similar substantive orientation to ours;[1] in section 5.4.4 of this chapter we compare our results with those obtained in the two most recent papers of this type, by Babetskii (2004) and by Darvas and Szapáry (2004).

Whilst the study of business cycles and their coherence is of interest in itself, a commonly cited motivation for studies of the business cycles in the new Member States derives from Optimal Currency Area (OCA) theory. The traditional form of this theory stresses that in joining a monetary union a country abandons the use of an independent monetary policy which could be addressed to the idiosyncratic shocks which hit that country and must accept instead the monetary policy that the union's central bank pursues. The concentration in these studies on whether shocks and cycles are similar between possible monetary union partners is justified by the premise that a high degree of similarity would make the loss of an independent policy small and to that extent would help justify participation in the union. Hence the OCA 'null' is in effect the assumption that a country can, on its own and with an independent currency and monetary policy, prosecute an effective stabilisation policy. But this is in fact a hotly contested assumption in application to our set of countries, where a lack of credibility in the context of markets of highly mobile capital seems to render an independent currency and monetary policy as much a source of shocks as a means of stabilisation. Experience suggests that quite a high price has to be paid for an independent currency in the circumstances in which the countries with which we are concerned find themselves. Recent papers by Frankel (2005) and by de Grauwe and Schnabel (2005) make this point. These authors are not alone in suggesting that the potential for currency instability as an outsider is in effect a new form of justification for participation in a monetary union.

This does not mean that study of the business cycle experience of these countries is beside the point, however. Aside from its intrinsic scientific interest, it is easy to see that a number of potential findings could have a salience for policy formation. First, it may prove to be the case that for some countries a high degree of business cycle sympathy will be found between them and the leading countries of the EMU; if so,

[1] Earlier studies include Boone and Maurel (1998, 1999), Buiter and Grafe (2001), Fidrmuc (2004) and Korhonen (2001, 2003).

the gain to these countries from joining the union seems particularly clear, for by joining they will be able to acquire a stabilising monetary policy they probably would not be able to exercise otherwise. More likely perhaps – as we shall see, this is the case in general – business cycle sympathy may be found to be rather low: in this case, if the OCA null is in any case not confirmed, the countries concerned will likely not lose anything, so to speak, 'on the stabilisation account', from joining the monetary union. In any event, it is of particular interest to know what the pattern of business cycle sympathy *between* the new Member States has been: for, in the event this is for example high, it could be a predictor of 'solidarity' behaviour at the political level. It is one thing if all the new Member States are 'in the same boat', another if their fortunes are quite different. Finally, it is important to note that the new Member States are not all in the same position regarding either their business cycle affiliations or the applicability of the 'OCA null'.

There is, unfortunately, at least one more qualification to be made regarding the usefulness of business cycle studies of the new Member States. This is simply the point that these countries have undergone a rather exceptional experience in the recent past; they have all experienced the transition from a centrally planned to a market-oriented economy marked by an initial phase of output loss ('the transition recession'). This makes the useable period of observations short and itself exceptional, as it features a period of ongoing structural change. To draw strong conclusions about the likely future cyclical propensities of these economies from their experience in this period is correspondingly hazardous.

Nevertheless and relative to previous studies, we believe that the work reported in this chapter has certain advantages. In particular, the study of cycles has enjoyed a renaissance in recent years, and we are able to capitalise on this by employing the latest techniques here; and we have more useful data available to us than had many earlier authors.

5.3   Our approach

At the broadest level, the business cycle has been characterised as an oscillatory movement in general economic activity. The literature has distinguished, more sharply, between the 'classical cycle', the 'growth rate cycle' and the 'deviation cycle'. The classical cycle is the measure of the cycle associated with the pioneering work of the NBER in business cycle dating; it is distinguished by an absolute decline in economic activity following a peak and an absolute rise following a trough. To distinguish cycles from blips, it is customary to insist on some measure of duration of the recession (following the peak) and of the expansion (following the trough), as is clarified later in this section. Classical cycles are comparatively rare in growing economies (as will be seen to be the case for the new Member State economies examined here), so that attention is more often focused on the deviation cycle or the growth cycle. The deviation cycle is identified as a cycle in the detrended series of economic activity, whilst the growth rate cycle is a cycle in the rate of economic growth. In the next section we deploy measures of all these concepts of the cycle.

Recent advances in business cycle theory (see, for example, Harding and Pagan (2001, 2003a, 2003b); Baxter and King (1999)) have incorporated three factors of concern to us here.

First, the contribution of Baxter and King (1999) has led investigators to the widespread use of band-pass filters. In order to study the deviation cycle some form of detrending needs to be adopted and the band-pass filters in general have come to be seen as superior to the low-pass filters employed in much previous work and to be less vulnerable to some of the criticisms of low-pass filters that can be found in the contributions of, for example, Cogley and Nason (1995), King and Rebelo (1993) and Harvey and Jäger (1993). In the work reported on below, we have occasion to use a particular form of band-pass filter, one based on the combination of two HP-filters (see Hodrick and Prescott (1997) for the original HP-filter).

Secondly, in examining business cycle similarities across countries, we make use of a measure of (corrected) concordance. This measure is suited for application to cycles which have been distinguished only by their phase, thus resulting in a [0,1] series for which a measure of cross-correlation may seem less appropriate. The concordance measure, uncorrected, is based simply on the proportion of observations in which two different countries' cycles have been in the same phase, and the correction allows for the fact that the null of independence may not be represented by 50%. This measure has evolved from a first use in Artis *et al.* (1997) through Harding and Pagan (2001) to the form in which we use it here (Artis *et al.*, 2003).

Third, where it is desired to date cycles, recent experience has illuminated the choice between deterministic algorithms to identify patterns in the data, and Markov switching models which may be used to estimate the probability that a particular observation belongs to a particular phase of the cycle. The former approach is associated with the classical NBER tradition and was set out in univariate form by Bry and Boschan (1971); it was revived more recently by Harding and Pagan (2001). The latter was associated with Hamilton's work, and the two approaches have been compared in Hamilton (2003) and Harding and Pagan (2003a; 2003b).

The approach we use here combines elements of each of the two alternatives. As in Artis *et al.* (2004b), we employ a probabilistic dating algorithm, as in the Markov switching approach, but where the probability of being in a certain regime is computed non-parametrically based on a particular pattern recognition scheme, as in the deterministic approach. This algorithm allows more flexibility than the traditional deterministic methods but estimation is simpler than in the standard Markov switching approach, which is an important advantage in the analysis of short time series such as those available for the new Member States.

For the sake of exposition, we briefly illustrate the dating algorithm with reference to the quarterly case. Additional details can be found in Artis *et al.* (2004b) and the technical Appendix to this chapter. Despite the apparent complexity of the algorithm, its implementation requires less than seventy lines of Ox code.

At any time t, the economy can be in either of two mutually exclusive states or *phases*: expansion (E_t) or recession (R_t). A peak terminates an expansion, whereas a trough terminates a recession. For the imposition of minimum duration constraints and to enforce the alternation of peaks and troughs, it is useful to distinguish turning points within the two basic states, by posing:

$$E_t \equiv \begin{cases} EC_t & \text{Expansion Continuation} \\ P_t & \text{Peak} \end{cases}$$

$$R_t \equiv \begin{cases} RC_t & \text{Recession Continuation} \\ T_t & \text{Trough} \end{cases}$$

From EC_t we can make a transition to P_{t+1} or continue the expansion ($EC_t \to EC_{t+1}$), but not vice versa, since only $P_t \to RC_{t+1}$ is admissible. Analogously, from RC_t we can visit either RC_{t+1} or T_{t+1}, but from T_t we move to EC_{t+1} with probability 1.

Denoting by $p_{EP} = P(P_{t+1} | EC_t)$ the probability of making a transition to a peak within an expansionary pattern, $p_{EE} = P(EC_{t+1} | EC_t) = 1 - p_{EP}$, and analogously $p_{RT} = P(T_{t+1} | RC_t)$, $p_{RR} = P(RC_{t+1} | RC_t) = 1 - p_{RT}$, we define a first order Markov chain (MC) with four states, denoted S_t, with transition matrix:

	EC_{t+1}	P_{t+1}	RC_{t+1}	T_{t+1}
EC_t	p_{EE}	p_{EP}	0	0
P_t	0	0	1	0
RC_t	0	0	p_{RR}	p_{RT}
T_t	1	0	0	0

The dating rules impose ties on the minimum duration of a phase, which amounts to two quarters, and this is automatically enforced in the quarterly case by our four-states characterisation, and on the minimum duration of a full cycle, which amounts to five quarters. The minimum duration constraints are important for the characterisation of the chain: that imposed on the full cycle duration determines the order of the MC, whereas that imposed on the length of the phases determines the number of admissible states. Further detail may be found in the Appendix to this chapter.

5.4   Application and results

As the reports prepared by the European Commission highlight, the progress made by accession countries in the direction of statistical harmonisation with the EU has been substantial.[2] The quarterly national accounts macro aggregates are produced at a very high level of compliance with the European System of Accounts (ESA-95) methodology. However, they are available for a very short time span, typically starting in the early 1990s. Therefore, whilst our primary focus is on the quarterly gross domestic product (GDP) series at constant prices, which is the most used summary measure of aggregate economic activity, we also compare the results with those obtained in Artis *et al.* (2004a) using the monthly industrial production index (IPI) (total industry). The data sources are the OECD (Main Economic Indicators) and Eurostat. The series are available for different sample periods, as is illustrated in Table 5.1, and in general refer to eight of the ten enlargement countries, excluding Cyprus and Malta.

5.4.1   Classical cycles

Figure 5.1 reports the dating of the classical cycles for the new Member States and the Euro area. It turns out that Poland, Hungary and Slovakia are in expansion for the entire period under investigation. The cyclical experience of the Euro area, with a trough in 1993:1, appears to be rather different from that of the new Member States.

Lithuania and Estonia experienced a common downturn during the years 1998–9, connected with the contemporaneous Russian economic crisis. The amplitude of this recessionary episode has also the same size, the output loss being around 3%, and the steepness is similar, since the

---

[2] The reports are available at http://europa.eu.int/comm/enlargement/report2002/index. htm. Chapter 12 of the individual country documents report on statistical harmonisation.

Table 5.1. *Data availability for the new Member States*

	GDP (quarterly)		IPI (monthly)	
Country	Start	End	Start	End
Czech Republic (CZE)	1994.q1	2003.q3	1990.m01	2003.m12
Slovakia (SVK)	1993.q1	2003.q3	1989.m01	2003.m12
Poland (POL)	1995.q1	2003.q3	1985.m01	2003.m12
Hungary (HUN)	1995.q1	2003.q3	1980.m01	2003.m12
Slovenia (SVN)	1992.q1	2003.q3	1980.m01	2003.m12
Estonia (EST)	1993.q1	2003.q3	1995.m01	2003.m12
Latvia (LVA)	1995.q1	2003.q3	1980.m01	2003.m12
Lithuania (LTU)	1995.q1	2003.q3	1996.m01	2003.m12

recession lasted between four and five quarters. The fluctuations in the Latvian GDP series around the same period do not qualify for a major recession, as the absolute fall in output concerns only two quarters with very limited amplitude.

For the Czech Republic, a recession is found starting in the third quarter of 1996 and ending in 1998, that is not found in industrial production. The output loss associated with this recession is about 3%.

For comparison purposes, in Figure 5.2, we report the classical dating for the same sample period and countries based on industrial production series (see Artis *et al.* (2004a) for details). Some interesting results emerge. In particular, the downturn in 1998–9 is now common to all the new Member States, with some differences in the exact dates, and it also emerges for the Euro area, though with a very limited output loss. A second milder recessionary episode is also identified in the first part of the sample for the Czech Republic, Slovakia, Slovenia and Latvia, but in this case the period in question differs substantially across the countries. Overall, the evidence of cyclical synchronisation remains rather weak both across countries and with the Euro area.

Artis *et al.* (2004a), using the sample available for industrial production (reported in Table 5.1), find that certain characteristics of the post-transition business cycle of the new Member States are not dissimilar from those of some EU countries and the Euro area. In particular, the proportion of time spent in expansion is around 0.75, a shade less than the the value for the Euro area, which amounts to 0.81. The average duration of the downturns is slightly less than one year, which is longer than the Euro area (7.3 months), but is comparable to Italy (11.2 months); the dispersion around the average is not negligible, however, and it must be stressed that duration is longer for the Baltic States. The

142 *Artis, Marcellino and Proietti*

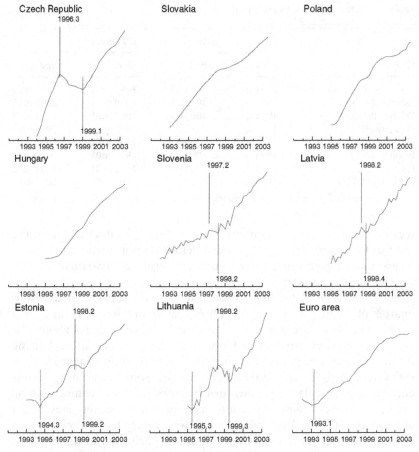

Figure 5.1. Quarterly seasonally adjusted GDP: classical cycle turning points.

main difference lies with the amplitude of the downturns: the percentage of output lost on average in recession is much larger for the new Member States than for the Euro area.

Artis *et al.* (2004a) also compute the standardised concordance index proposed in Artis *et al.* (2003), as a formal measure of cyclical concordance, and find that, among the countries under analysis, only Poland has significant concordance with the Euro area. Across new Member States, the cyclical concordance is statistically significant only for five out of twenty-one pairs of countries, namely, Slovenia and the Czech Republic, Slovenia and Slovakia, Estonia and the Czech Republic, Estonia and

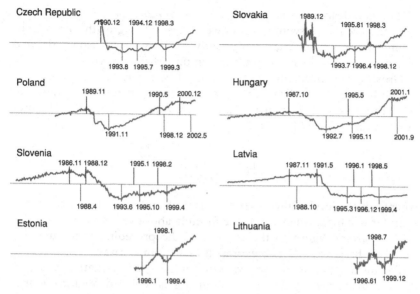

Figure 5.2. Industrial production: classical cycle turning points.

Slovakia, and Estonia and Slovenia. Though these results should be interpreted with care because of the small sample available, they are in line with the reported descriptive evidence based on GDP data of low synchronisation of the classical business cycles of new Member States across themselves and with the Euro area.

We do not report on classical business cycle concordance based on GDP for two related reasons: first and foremost, the pervasive growth which characterised the post-transition period renders classical business cycle concordance and synchronisation less likely and perhaps less relevant from an interpretative standpoint; the second reason is related to the limited extent of the available sample, for which too few recessionary episodes are found. As is clear from Figure 5.1, classical business cycle synchronisation is perfect for Slovakia, Poland and Hungary, but this evidence has little or no value.

5.4.2 Growth rate cycles

In this subsection and the next, we turn our attention to the measurement of two alternative definitions of the business cycle that are potentially more valuable, especially for the assessment of cyclical concordance, in a situation characterised by pervasive growth and a sustained catching-up process.

The first deals with the notion of a *growth rate cycle* and is concerned with the cyclical upswings and downswings in the growth rate of economic activity at a given, usually yearly, horizon. A recession is defined as a prolonged and sustained decline in underlying growth.

Growth rate chronologies are produced by the Economic Cycle Research Institute (http://www.businesscycle.com), that adopts a measure of underlying growth with an annual horizon, constructed as follows (Layton and Moore, 1989):

$$q_t = \left[\frac{y_t}{\sum_{j=1}^{s} y_{t-j}/s} \right]^{2s/(s+1)}$$

where y_t is the level of the series and s is the number of observations in a year; for instance, when $s = 4$, the formula above yields the ratio of the latest quarter's figure to the average of the preceding four quarters, raised to the power 4/2.5 to express it as an annual rate.

The turning points in q_t are the same as $\Delta_s \ln y_t$. As a matter of fact, if the arithmetic average in the denominator is replaced by a geometric one, it is immediately apparent that the logarithm of q_t is a weighted moving average of $s - 1$ consecutive growth rates, $\Delta \ln y_t$, with linearly decreasing weights:

$$\ln q_t = w(L)\Delta\ln y_t, \quad \omega(L) = \frac{2s}{s+1} \sum_{j=0}^{s-2} (s-j)L^j.$$

Recalling that the yearly growth rate $\Delta_s \ln y_t$ is an average of s growth rates with uniform weights,

$$\Delta_s\ln y_t = S(L)\Delta\ln y_t, \quad S(L) = 1 + L + L^2 + \cdots + L^{s-1},$$

the use of q_t or the latter for quarterly data does not make much difference, so we apply our dating algorithm to $\Delta_4 \ln y_t$.

Table 5.2 reports the pairwise correlation coefficient between the GDP yearly growth rates for the eight countries, a selection of countries belonging to the Euro area (namely Austria, representing a relatively small economy in the Euro Area, Germany, Italy) and the Euro area itself. The empirical evidence is clear-cut: correlation is fairly high within the Euro area, within the Baltic countries and between Hungary, Poland and the Euro area.

Growth cycle chronologies are displayed in Figure 5.3 for the new Member States and in Figure 5.4 for the Euro area (EA) and its selected Member States. Table 5.3 reports the pairwise standardised concordance indices. The location of the turning point and the values of the

Table 5.2. *Correlation between yearly growth rates,* $\Delta_4 \ln y_t$

	CZE	SVK	POL	HUN	SVN	EST	LVA	LIT	A	D	I	EA
CZE	1.00	0.36	-0.26	-0.57	0.12	-0.15	-0.09	-0.01	-0.31	-0.01	0.09	-0.23
SVK	0.36	1.00	0.30	-0.58	-0.45	0.04	0.25	0.63	-0.24	-0.16	0.01	-0.32
POL	-0.26	0.30	1.00	0.12	-0.35	0.22	0.05	0.02	0.46	0.46	0.28	0.44
HUN	-0.57	-0.58	0.12	1.00	0.23	0.32	0.32	-0.11	0.58	0.68	0.62	0.75
SVN	0.12	-0.45	-0.35	0.23	1.00	0.23	0.24	0.13	0.02	0.06	0.07	0.05
EST	-0.15	0.04	0.22	0.32	0.23	1.00	0.82	0.67	-0.00	-0.01	0.19	0.06
LVA	-0.09	0.25	0.05	0.32	0.24	0.82	1.00	0.68	-0.07	0.11	0.45	0.07
LIT	-0.01	0.63	0.02	-0.11	0.13	0.67	0.68	1.00	-0.27	-0.35	-0.05	-0.37
A	-0.31	-0.24	0.46	0.58	0.02	-0.00	-0.07	-0.27	1.00	0.77	0.62	0.82
D	-0.01	-0.16	0.46	0.68	0.06	-0.01	0.11	-0.35	0.77	1.00	0.80	0.94
I	0.09	0.01	0.28	0.62	0.07	0.19	0.45	-0.05	0.62	0.80	1.00	0.85
EA	-0.23	-0.32	0.44	0.75	0.05	0.06	0.07	-0.37	0.82	0.94	0.85	1.00

indices confirm the high degree of concordance of the growth rate cycle in the Euro area: both Germany and Italy contribute to the emergence of a growth-rate cycle recession at the end of 2002, whereas for Austria growth peaked two quarters before; more generally, peaks and troughs are almost coincident. The same cannot be said with respect to the eight new Member States, which undergo rather different business cycle experiences, as Figure 5.3 clearly shows. Nevertheless, at the end of the sample, a recessionary pattern, concordant with that experienced in the Euro area, emerges for five countries. The standardised concordance index is significant only within the Euro area and between Hungary and the Euro Area.

5.4.3 Deviation cycles

It might be argued that the deviation cycle is the notion of the business cycle that is most useful for our investigation, in that it considers the fluctuations relative to a measure of tendency, thereby providing a way to assess business cycle stance that abstracts from catching-up dynamics.

As is well known, the choice of detrending technique that is used to isolate the deviation cycle can be a controversial matter. We have chosen to extract the cycle by using the band-pass version of the so-called Hodrick and Prescott filter, which attempts to isolate the fluctuations with a periodicity between 1.25 and 8 years.

The filter is easily obtained from the difference of two low-pass filters, the first being the HP trend filter with smoothness parameter,

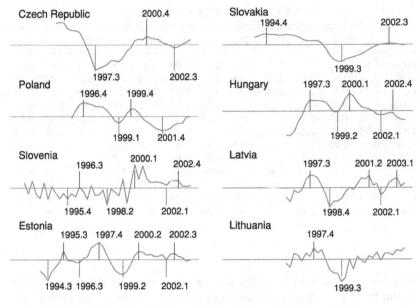

Figure 5.3. Quarterly seasonally adjusted GDP: growth rate cycle turning points.

λ_1, corresponding to the cut-off frequency, $\omega_l = 2\pi/(1.25s)$, where s is the number of observations in a year; this reduces the amplitude of high-frequency components, with a period less than $1.25s$ years, for example 5 quarters or 15 months. The second is the HP-filter for trend extraction with smoothness parameter λ_2 corresponding to $\omega_u = 2\pi/(8s)$ (period of 8 years), which aims at retaining the components with a period greater than 8 years. The smoothness parameter is related to the cut-off frequency via the equation $\lambda = [2(1 - \cos \omega)]^{-2}$.[3] Hence, for quarterly data ($s = 4$), $\lambda_1 = 0.52$ and $\lambda_2 = 667$ (notice that the latter is smaller than the value suggested by Hodrick and Prescott for quarterly data, which is 1,600).[4]

---

[3] See Pollock (1999) and Gómez (2000) for further details.
[4] It is a matter of debate whether we should concentrate our analysis and dating efforts on the band-pass component rather than on the high-pass one (that is, in our case, the HP cycle corresponding to λ_2); the latter is affected by high frequency variation, which greatly interferes with the dating process, so that the dating procedure would nevertheless need to go through a preliminary stage where turning points are identified on the band-pass series. Then, a local search on the high-pass series around the provisional turning points would be required. However, we have decided to adopt the first solution.

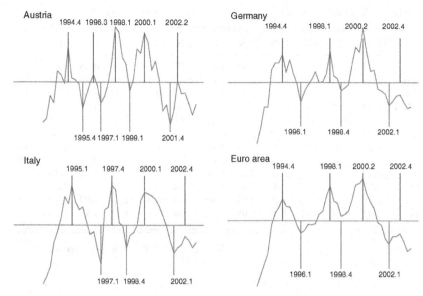

Figure 5.4. Quarterly seasonally adjusted GDP: growth rate cycle turning points.

The choice of the second cut-off frequency is arbitrary,[5] but we follow the convention used by Baxter and King (1999). As a matter of fact, the HP band-pass filter could be viewed as a finite sample implementation of the Baxter and King ideal filter. With respect to the approximation proposed by these authors, it provides estimates for the first and final three years that obviously rely on asymmetric filters and it does not suffer from the Gibbs phenomenon (see Artis *et al.*, 2004b).

The dating is carried out as described in section 5.3: by cumulating the HP band-pass component and applying the Markov chain dating algorithm, we identify the points at which the deviation cycle crosses zero (the duration restrictions are enforced at this stage); subsequently, the maximum (peak) or the minimum (trough) are located between two crossings.

Figure 5.5 displays the HP band-pass deviation cycles extracted for the acceding countries (excluding Hungary) and the Euro area. The three countries for which no classical cycles were found, Slovakia,

---

[5] According to the Burns and Mitchell definition, "in duration business cycles vary from more than one year to ten or twelve years" (Burns and Mitchell, 1946, p. 3).

Table 5.3. *Real GDP – Growth rate cycle – Standardised Concordance Index*

	CZE	SVK	POL	HUN	SVN	EST	LVA	LIT	A	D	I	EA
CZE	–	-0.31	-0.29	-1.52	-0.82	-1.06	-0.78	-1.43	-0.19	0.35	0.67	0.35
SVK	-0.31	–	-0.68	-0.57	0.67	-0.09	0.52	1.24	0.59	0.20	0.73	0.20
POL	-0.29	-0.68	–	1.47	-1.38	0.02	0.77	0.59	1.32	0.67	0.56	0.67
HUN	-1.52	-0.57	1.47	–	-1.65	2.16	2.29	1.13	2.06	**2.40**	1.79	**2.40**
SVN	-0.82	0.67	-1.38	-1.65	–	0.00	-1.11	1.13	-0.84	-1.05	-0.88	-1.05
EST	-1.06	-0.09	0.02	2.16	0.00	–	1.45	1.07	0.66	1.62	1.66	1.62
LVA	-0.78	0.52	0.77	2.29	-1.11	1.45	–	1.09	0.73	1.99	1.43	1.99
LIT	-1.43	1.24	0.59	1.13	1.13	1.07	1.09	–	-0.05	-0.10	-0.37	-0.10
A	-0.19	0.59	1.32	2.06	-0.84	0.66	0.73	-0.05	–	**3.12**	**2.84**	**3.12**
D	0.35	0.20	0.67	2.40	-1.05	1.62	1.99	-0.10	**3.12**	–	**3.08**	**4.13**
I	0.67	0.73	0.56	1.79	-0.88	1.66	1.43	-0.37	**2.84**	**3.08**	–	**3.08**
EA	0.35	0.20	0.67	2.40	-1.05	1.62	1.99	-0.10	**3.12**	**4.13**	**3.08**	–

Note: Computed on available data points from 1993 to 2003. Values greater than 2.33 (99th percentile of a standard normal variate) in bold.

Poland and Latvia, now present clear cyclical patterns, which are also very similar in the case of Slovakia and Latvia.

The amplitude of the output gap is larger for Estonia and Lithuania, whose cyclical pattern is comparable and close to that for Latvia. The amplitude of the gap for the other countries is in general larger than for the Euro area, a fact confirmed by the analysis of the industrial production series. Average steepness is instead comparably sized.

For the Czech Republic, one major recessionary episode is found, with the trough in 1999:1, in line with the previous finding using GDP level data and in common with several other new Member States.

Tables 5.4 and 5.5 report, respectively, the pairwise correlation co-efficients and the standardised concordance index (the values in bold are significant at the 1% level). Although the sample sizes available do not allow any firm conclusion to be drawn, the highest concordance with the Euro area deviation cycle is found for Hungary, followed by Poland, but the null hypothesis of no cyclical synchronisation cannot be rejected for any country except Hungary (with respect to Austria and Germany). Artis *et al.* (2004a) report results when using industrial pro-duction data that yield somewhat more extensive evidence of significant cross-correlations and concordance.

Finally, in general the highest degree of synchronisation across the new Member States is among the Baltic States, a finding that is also robust to the use of industrial production series.

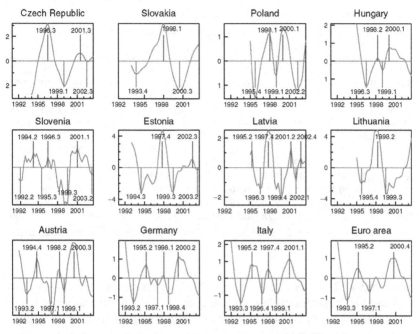

Figure 5.5. Quarterly seasonally adjusted GDP: HP band-pass deviation cycles.

5.4.4 Comparison with recent studies

To set these results in context, we now briefly refer to the findings of two recent studies of the same topic, these being the papers by Babetskii (2004) and Darvas and Szapáry (2004). Babetskii's (2004) paper takes the route of looking for (a)symmetries in shock-experience as opposed to business cycle experience, following the example of Bayoumi and Eichengreen (1993) in employing the SVAR approach of Blanchard and Quah (1989). The methodology produces estimates of demand and supply shocks and by applying a Kalman filter a time-varying estimate of the degree of (a)symmetry between countries in their stochastic experience can be obtained. In all cases, the degree of asymmetry of *demand* shocks between members of the group of Central and Eastern European countries (CEECs) and the European Union is shown to have decreased over time, though for supply shocks this is not the case. As other observers have done, Babetskii notes that the share of trade of the CEECs conducted with the European Union has risen over time (with the exception of Estonia) and is generally high. Given the 'endogeneity'

Table 5.4. *Correlation between HP band-pass cycles*

	CZE	SVK	POL	HUN	SVN	EST	LVA	LIT	A	D	I	EA
CZE	1.00	0.19	-0.35	-0.38	0.37	-0.01	-0.07	-0.21	-0.30	0.16	0.28	-0.02
SVK	0.19	1.00	-0.07	-0.55	-0.38	0.48	0.49	0.83	-0.60	-0.44	-0.20	-0.51
POL	-0.35	-0.07	1.00	0.25	-0.04	0.27	0.24	0.22	0.41	0.28	0.11	0.28
HUN	-0.38	-0.55	0.25	1.00	0.25	0.00	0.21	-0.19	0.70	0.70	0.66	0.78
SVN	0.37	-0.38	-0.04	0.25	1.00	0.06	0.13	-0.26	0.11	0.30	0.18	0.14
EST	-0.01	0.48	0.27	0.00	0.06	1.00	0.83	0.74	-0.27	-0.23	-0.04	-0.22
LVA	-0.07	0.49	0.24	0.21	0.13	0.83	1.00	0.70	-0.13	0.07	0.35	0.01
LIT	-0.21	0.83	0.22	-0.19	-0.26	0.74	0.70	1.00	-0.39	-0.47	-0.25	-0.50
A	-0.30	-0.60	0.41	0.70	0.11	-0.27	-0.13	-0.39	1.00	0.77	0.64	0.84
D	0.16	-0.44	0.28	0.70	0.30	-0.23	0.07	0.47	0.77	1.00	0.89	0.96
I	0.28	-0.20	0.11	0.66	0.18	-0.04	0.35	-0.25	0.64	0.89	1.00	0.90
EA	-0.02	-0.51	0.28	0.78	0.14	-0.22	0.01	-0.50	0.84	0.96	0.90	1.00

argument of Frankel and Rose (1997), it is tempting to consider that existing low business cycle or shock correlations will give way to higher ones through time. But of course the CEECs might constitute a special case, so the argument needs to be grounded in their experience to date. For this purpose Babetskii (2004) enquires whether bilateral trade intensities can be linked to the corresponding bilateral shock symmetries. A positive answer is arrived at for demand shocks, in line with the endogeneity argument. But no such result can be found for supply shocks.

The study of Darvas and Szapáry (2004) supplies extensive analysis of synchronisation between the CEECs and the EMU, referring both to GDP and industrial production with extensions to the major expenditure categories of imports, exports, consumption and investment. The authors attempt to comment also on trends in the degree of synchronisation, though the short period for which the data are available suggests caution in making such comparisons. The authors use both low-pass HP-detrending and Baxter–King band-pass procedures to identify cycles. Their principal conclusion is that only Hungary, Poland and Slovenia show evidence of much synchronisation with countries in the West. Our results also suggest that Hungary in particular exhibits synchronisation with the West, and some individual countries of the EU; our results also identify Poland as second in rank in this respect, though our evidence for Slovenia is less strong than appears in the Darvas–Szapáry study. The general result that – with the exceptions noted – synchronisation is weak or absent is much the same as in our case.

Table 5.5. *Gross domestic product – HP band-pass deviation cycles Standardised Concordance Index*

	CZE	SVK	POL	HUN	SVN	EST	LVA	LIT	A	D	I	EA
CZE	–	0.19	0.09	-1.11	**2.50**	-0.01	-0.31	-0.32	0.18	0.34	1.10	-0.19
SVK	0.19	–	0.57	-0.81	-0.95	1.45	0.91	1.31	-1.52	-0.93	-0.35	-1.51
POL	0.09	0.57	–	1.96	0.42	-0.67	-0.12	1.40	1.19	0.94	0.39	-0.34
HUN	-1.11	-0.81	1.96	–	-1.16	-0.12	0.84	0.05	**2.82**	**2.69**	2.21	2.00
SVN	**2.50**	-0.95	0.42	-1.16	–	0.05	-0.26	1.20	0.15	-0.47	0.21	-0.72
EST	-0.01	1.45	-0.67	-0.12	0.05	–	2.22	1.19	-0.99	-0.81	0.65	-0.92
LVA	-0.31	0.91	-0.12	0.84	-0.26	2.22	–	1.23	0.54	0.83	**2.40**	0.65
LIT	-0.32	1.31	1.40	0.05	1.20	1.19	1.23	–	0.47	-1.11	-0.22	-1.31
A	0.18	-1.52	1.19	**2.82**	0.15	-0.99	0.54	0.47	–	**3.80**	**3.15**	**3.35**
D	0.34	-0.93	0.94	**2.69**	-0.47	-0.81	0.83	-1.11	**3.80**	–	**3.37**	**3.50**
I	1.10	-0.35	0.39	2.21	0.21	0.65	**2.40**	-0.22	**3.15**	**3.37**	–	**3.28**
EA	-0.19	-1.51	-0.34	2.00	-0.72	-0.92	0.65	-1.31	**3.35**	**3.50**	**3.28**	–

Note: Values greater than 2.33 (99th percentile of a standard normal variate) in bold.

5.5 Conclusions

In this chapter, we have analysed the evolution of the business cycle in the accession countries, considering three different definitions of the cycle. Because of the pervasive growth in the post-transition period, the deviation cycle (where the turning points are characterised by changes relative to *trend*) represents the most promising and appropriate version of the business cycle. For this definition of the cycle we find that the degree of concordance *within* the group of accession countries is not in general as large as that between them and the existing EU countries (the Baltic countries constitute an exception). Between the new Member States and the Euro area the indications of synchronisation are generally low when GDP data are used, and slightly higher with industrial production. Hungary, and to a lesser extent Poland, supply exceptions to the generalisation. These results are similar to those evident in other recent work. We obtain similar results for the classical cycle, though this is plainly a less useful concept of the cycle to use in the context supplied by the post-transition economic experience of these countries.

The process of European integration has already experienced four waves of accessions, the first in 1973 (Denmark, Ireland and the United Kingdom), the second in 1981 (Greece), the third in 1986 (Spain and Portugal) and the fourth in 1995 (Austria, Finland and Sweden). The issue that emerges quite naturally is whether the degree of business cycle synchronisation was similar at the time of these earlier accessions as it is now for the most recent enlargement to the East.

152   *Artis, Marcellino and Proietti*

Artis *et al.* (2004a) make such a comparison, finding that business cycle concordance was generally higher in those previous episodes, and that only Poland, Hungary and Slovenia comply with the same level of cyclical synchronisation.

By traditional OCA criteria, these results are not in favour of an early adoption of the euro, but the very high levels of trade with EU countries (Buiter and Grafe, 2001) and the fact that an effective stabilisation policy does not seem to be available for most of these countries outside monetary union, point in the opposite direction.

References

Alesina, A. and Barro, R. 2002. 'Currency Unions' *Quarterly Journal of Economics*, vol. 117, pp. 409–436.
Artis, M., Kontolemis, Z. and Osborn, D. 1997. 'Business Cycles for the G-7 and European Countries'. *Journal of Business*, vol. 70, pp. 249–79.
Artis, M., Marcellino, M. and Proietti, T. 2003. 'Dating the Euro Area Business Cycle'. CEPR Discussion Paper, No. 3696.
    2004a. 'Characterising the Business Cycle for the Accession Countries'. CEPR Discussion Paper, No. 4457.
    2004b. 'Dating Business Cycles: A Methodological Contribution with an Application to the Euro Area'. *Oxford Bulletin of Economics and Statistics*, vol. 66, pp. 537–65.
Babetskii, I. 2004. 'EU Enlargement and Endogeneity of some OCA Criteria: Evidence from the CEECs'. Czech National Bank Working Paper, No. 2.
Baxter, M. and King, R. 1999. 'Measuring Business Cycles: Approximate Band-Pass Filters for Economic Time Series'. *Review of Economics and Statistics*, vol. 81, pp. 575–93.
Bayoumi, T. and Eichengreen, B. 1993. 'Shocking Aspects of European Monetary Integration'. In Torres, F. and Giavazzi, F. (eds.), *Adjustment and Growth in the European Monetary Union*. Cambridge: Cambridge University Press and CEPR.
Blanchard, O. and Quah, D. 1989. 'The Dynamic Effects of Aggregate Demand and Supply Disturbances'. *American Economic Review*, vol. 79, pp. 655–73.
Boone, L. and Maurel, M. 1998. 'Economic Convergence of the CEECs with the EU'. CEPR Discussion Paper, No. 2018.
    1999. 'An Optimal Currency Area Perspective of the EU Enlargement of the CEECs'. CEPR Discussion Paper, No. 2119.
Bry, G. and Boschan, C. 1971. *Cyclical Analysis of Time Series: Selected Procedures and Computer Programs*. New York: National Bureau of Economic Research.
Buiter, B. and Grafe, C. 2001. 'Central Banking and the Choice of Currency Regime in Accession Countries'. SUERF Studies, No. 11 (Vienna: Société Universitaire de Recherches Financières).
Burns, A. and Mitchell, W. 1946. *Measuring Business Cycles*. New York: National Bureau of Economic Research.

Cogley, T. and Nason, J. 1995. 'Effects of the Hodrick–Prescott Filter on Trend and Difference Stationary Time Series: Implications for Business Cycle Research'. *Journal of Economic Dynamics and Control*, vol. 19, pp. 253–78.

Darvas, Z. and Szapáry, G. 2004. 'Business Cycle Synchronization in the Enlarged EU: Comovements in the (Soon-to-be) New and Old Members'. Magyar Nemzeti Bank Working Paper, No. 1.

De Grauwe, P. and Schnabel, F. 2005. 'Exchange Rate Regimes and Macroeconomic Stability in Central and Eastern Europe'. In Schadler, S. (ed.), *Euro Adoption in Central and Eastern Europe: Opportunities and Challenges*. Washington: IMF.

Doornik, J. 2001. *Ox: An Object-Oriented Matrix Programming Language*. London: Timberlake Consultants Press.

Fidrmuc, J. 2004. 'The Endogeneity of the Optimum Currency Area: Criteria, IntraIndustry Trade, and EU Enlargement'. *Contemporary Economic Policy*, vol. 22, pp. 1–12.

Frankel, J. and Rose, A. 1997. 'Is EMU More Justifiable Ex Post than Ex Ante?.' *European Economic Review*, vol. 41, pp. 753–60.

Frankel, J. 2005. 'Real Convergence and Euro Adoption in Central and Eastern Europe: Trade and Business Cycle Correlations as Endogenous Criteria for Joining EMU'. In Schadler, S. (ed.), *Euro Adoption in Central and Eastern Europe: Opportunities and Challenges*. Washington: IMF.

Gómez, V. 2001. 'The Use of Butterworth Filters for Trend and Cycle Estimation in Economic Time Series'. *Journal of Business and Economic Statistics*, vol. 19, pp. 365–73.

Hamilton, J. 2003. 'Comment on "A Comparison of Two Business Cycle Dating Methods"'. *Journal of Economic Dynamics and Control*, vol. 27, pp. 1691–3.

Harding, D. and Pagan, A. 2001. 'Extracting, Analysing and Using Cyclical Information'. Mimeo.

2003a. 'A Comparison of Two Business Cycle Dating Methods'. *Journal of Economic Dynamics and Control*, vol. 27, pp. 1681–90.

2003b. 'Rejoinder to James Hamilton'. *Journal of Economic Dynamics and Control*, vol. 27, pp. 1695–98.

Harvey, A. and Jäger, A. 1993. 'Detrending, Stylized Facts and the Business Cycle'. *Journal of Applied Econometrics*, vol. 8, pp. 231–47.

Hodrick R. and Prescott, E. 1997. 'Postwar US Business Cycles: An Empirical Investigation'. *Journal of Money, Credit and Banking*, vol. 29, pp. 1–16.

King, R. and Rebelo, S. 1993. 'Low Frequency Filtering and Real Business Cycles'. *Journal of Economic Dynamics and Control*, vol. 17, pp. 207–33.

Korhonen, I. 2001. 'Some Empirical Tests on the Integration of Economic Activity Between the Euro Area and the Accession Countries'. BOFIT Discussion Paper, No. 9.

2003. 'Some Empirical Tests on the Integration of Economic Activity Between the Euro Area and the Accession Countries: A Note'. *Economics of Transition*, vol. 11, pp. 177–96.

Layton, A. and Moore, G. 1989. 'Leading Indicators for the Service sector'. *Journal of Business and Economic Statistics*, vol. 3, pp. 379–86.

Lundbergh, S. and Teräsvirta, T. 2002. 'Forecasting with Smooth Transition Autoregressive Models'. In Clements, M. and Hendry, D. (eds.), *A Companion to Economic Forecasting*. Oxford: Blackwell.

Mundell, R. 1961. 'A Theory of Optimum Currency Areas'. *American Economic Review*, vol. 51, pp. 657–65.

Pollock, D. 1999. *Handbook of Time Series Analysis, Signal Processing and Dynamics*. London: Academic Press.

Appendix: the dating algorithm

Recall, from section 5.3 above, that the dating rules impose ties on the minimum duration of a phase, which amounts to two quarters, and this is automatically enforced in the quarterly case by our four states characterisation, and on the minimum duration of a full cycle, which amounts to five quarters. The minimum duration constraints are important for the characterisation of the chain: that imposed on the full cycle duration determines the order of the Markov Chain (MC), whereas that imposed on the length of the phases determines the number of admissible states.

The tie on the full cycle yields a fifth order MC that can be converted to a first order one by combining elements of the original chain, S_t. The states of the derived MC are defined by appropriately combining the original ones into

$$S_t^* = \{S_{t-4}, S_{t-3}, S_{t-2}, S_{t-1}, S_t\}$$

The ties, however, reduce the number of states to 24. These are listed in Table 5.6: the first column labels the states and the second spells out how they are formed by combining the elementary states of the original MC.

The last two columns indicate the states to which a transition is admissible (two at most) and the associated transition probability. The transition matrix is thus immediately derived from the above table. It should be noted that all the states ending with a peak or a trough must visit certain states with probability one.

The two parameters p_{EP} and p_{RT} uniquely specify the Markov chain. These can be estimated by maximum likelihood techniques from an observed time series in a model-based framework, if it is assumed that the latter is a realisation of a stochastic process that is dependent upon the state of the economy as represented by the chain. This idea is at the foundation of the class of Markov switching models, that postulate that the growth rate and/or the innovation variance and/or the transmission mechanism vary according to recessions and expansions.

Table 5.6. *Description of the Markov chain generated by the quarterly dating rules*

States S_t^*	$S_t^* = \{S_{t-4}, S_{t-3}, S_{t-2}, S_{t-1}, S_t\}$					States S_{t+1}^* that can be visited			
	S_{t-4}	S_{t-3}	S_{t-2}	S_{t-1}	S_t	S_{t+1}^*	Trans. Prob.	S_{t+1}^*	Trans. Prob.
S_1^*	P	RC	RC	RC	RC	S_{17}^*	p_{RR}	S_{18}^*	p_{RT}
S_2^*	P	RC	RC	RC	T	S_{19}^*	1		
S_3^*	P	RC	RC	T	EC	S_{20}^*	p_{EE}	S_{21}^*	p_{EP}
S_4^*	P	RC	T	EC	EC	S_{22}^*	p_{EE}	S_{23}^*	p_{EP}
S_5^*	T	EC	EC	EC	EC	S_9^*	p_{EE}	S_{10}^*	p_{EP}
S_6^*	T	EC	EC	EC	P	S_{11}^*	1		
S_7^*	T	EC	EC	P	RC	S_{12}^*	p_{RR}	S_{13}^*	p_{RT}
S_8^*	T	EC	P	RC	RC	S_{14}^*	p_{RR}	S_{15}^*	p_{RT}
S_9^*	EC	EC	EC	EC	EC	S_9^*	p_{EE}	S_{10}^*	p_{EP}
S_{10}^*	EC	EC	EC	EC	P	S_{11}^*	1		
S_{11}^*	EC	EC	EC	P	RC	S_{12}^*	p_{RR}	S_{13}^*	p_{RT}
S_{12}^*	EC	EC	P	RC	RC	S_{14}^*	p_{RR}	S_{15}^*	p_{RT}
S_{13}^*	EC	EC	P	RC	T	S_{16}^*	1		
S_{14}^*	EC	P	RC	RC	RC	S_1^*	p_{RR}	S_2^*	p_{RT}
S_{15}^*	EC	P	RC	RC	T	S_3^*	1		
S_{16}^*	EC	P	RC	T	EC	S_4^*	1		
S_{17}^*	RC	RC	RC	RC	RC	S_{17}^*	p_{RR}	S_{18}^*	p_{RT}
S_{18}^*	RC	RC	RC	RC	T	S_{19}^*	1		
S_{19}^*	RC	RC	RC	T	EC	S_{20}^*	p_{EE}	S_{21}^*	p_{EP}
S_{20}^*	RC	RC	T	EC	EC	S_{22}^*	p_{EE}	S_{23}^*	p_{EP}
S_{21}^*	RC	RC	T	EC	P	S_{24}^*	1		
S_{22}^*	RC	T	EC	EC	EC	S_5^*	p_{EE}	S_6^*	p_{EP}
S_{23}^*	RC	T	EC	EC	P	S_7^*	1		
S_{24}^*	RC	T	EC	P	RC	S_8^*	1		

As mentioned above, we consider the alternative strategy of scoring the two parameters according to patterns in the series, y_t. There are several ways of doing so, with different degrees of complexity, but we will concentrate on the BBQ rule by Harding and Pagan (2001). Other, simpler, popular rules are the calculus and Okun's rule.

According to the BBQ dating rule, we define an expansion termination sequence, ETS_t, and a recession terminating sequence, RTS_t, respectively as:

$$ETS_t = \{(\Delta y_{t+1} < 0) \cap (\Delta_2 y_{t+2} < 0)\}$$
$$RTS_t = \{(\Delta y_{t+1} > 0) \cap (\Delta_2 y_{t+2} > 0)\} \tag{1}$$

The former defines a candidate point for a peak, which terminates the expansion, whereas the latter defines a candidate for a trough.

Table 5.7. *Joint probability distribution of possible events*

	ETS_t	$\overline{ETS}_t$	Marginal
RTS_t	0	$P_t^{(RTS)}$	$P_t^{(RTS)}$
$\overline{RTS}_t$	$P_t^{(ETS)}$	$1 - P_t^{(ETS)} - P_t^{(RTS)}$	$1 - P_t^{(RTS)}$
Marginal	$P_t^{(ETS)}$	$1 - P_t^{(ETS)}$	1

The joint distribution of the sequences $\{ETS_t, RTS_t, t = 1, \ldots T\}$ depends on the stochastic process generating the available series and is usually analytically intractable due to the presence of serial correlation and the mutually non-exclusive nature of the termination sequences. As regards the latter, denoting by $\overline{ETS}_t$ the complementary event of ETS_t, $\overline{RTS}_t$ that of RTS_t and defining $P_t^{(ETS)} = P(ETS_t)$. $P_t^{(RTS)} = P(RTS_t)$. at time t the joint probability distribution of the possible events is provided by Table 5.7, from which it can be seen that ETS_t and RTS_t cannot both be true at the same time.

Serial correlation complicates the computation of $P_t^{(ETS)}$ and $P_t^{(RTS)}$, since the terminating sequences are not independent of their past; furthermore, it must be stressed that the BBQ rule induces autocorrelation itself, that is even if $\Delta y_t \sim NID (\mu, \sigma^2)$, e.g. y_t is a random walk, $\{ETS_t, RTS_t, t = 1, \ldots T\}$ will be autocorrelated. Therefore, it seems that the only way to go about the characterisation of a business cycle for a particular stochastic process is stochastic simulation.

Let us return to the non-parametric scoring of the transition probabilities according to the available time series. If at time t the chain S_t^* is in any of the expansionary states for which a transition to a peak is possible and an expansion terminating sequence occurs at time $t+1$, i.e. ETS_{t+1} is true, then we move to a new state t the chain S_{t+1}^*, such that $S_{t+1} = P_{t+1}$ and the previous four elementary states are common to the last four in S_t^*.

It is useful at this point to classify the states of S_t^* by defining the sets:

$S_{EP} = \{S_3^*, S_4^*, S_5^*, S_9^*, S_{19}^*, S_{20}^*, S_{22}^*\}$ defines the set of states featuring an expansionary state at time t ($S_t = EC_t$) and that are available for a transition to a peak.

$S_P = \{S_6^*, S_{10}^*, S_{21}^*, S_{23}\}$ defines the set of states featuring a peak at time t ($S_t = P_t$).

$S_{RT} = \{S_1^*, S_7^*, S_8^*, S_{11}^*, S_{12}^*, S_{14}^*, S_{17}^*\}$ defines the set of states featuring a recessionary state at time t ($S_t = RC_t$).

$S_T = \{S_2^*, S_{13}^*, S_{15}^*, S_{18}^*\}$ defines the set of states featuring a trough at time t ($S_t = T_t$).

The set of expansionary states, S_E, is the union of S_{EP}, S_P and S_{16}^*, in symbols:

$$S_E = S_{EP} \cup S_P \cup S_{16}^*$$

The set of recessionary states, S_R, is the union of S_{RT}, S_T and S_{24}^*, in symbols:

$$S_R = S_{RT} \cup S_T \cup S_{24}^*$$

The scoring rules are then formalised in the following algorithm:

If $\{S_t^* = s_{EP}, s_{EP} \in S_{EP}\}$ and ETS_{t+1} is true, then $\{S_{t+1}^* = s_P, s_P \in S_P\}$. Hence, the transition probability p_{EP} is computed as:

$$
\begin{aligned}
p_{EP} &= P(\{S_t^* = s_{EP}, s_{EP} \in S_{EP}\} \cap ETS_{t+1}) \\
&= I(ETS_{t+1}) \sum_{s_{EP} \in S_{EP}} P(S_t^* = s_{EP}),
\end{aligned}
\tag{2}
$$

where $I(\cdot)$ is the indicator function. Else, if ETS_{t+1} is false, then the expansion is continued, that is $S_{t+1}^* = s_{EP}$, $s_{EP} \in S_{EP}$; the associated transition probability is $p_{EE} = 1 - p_{EP}$.

Else, if $\{S_t^* = s_{RT}, s_{RT} \in S_{RT}\}$ and RTS_{t+1} is true, then $\{S_{t+1}^* = s_T, s_T \in S_T\}$. Hence, the transition probability p_{RT} is computed as:

$$
\begin{aligned}
p_{RT} &= P(\{S_t^* = s_{RT}, s_{RT} \in S_{RT}\} \cap RTS_{t+1}) \\
&= I(RTS_{t+1}) \sum_{s_{RT} \in S_{RT}} P(S_t^* = s_{RT}),
\end{aligned}
\tag{3}
$$

Else, if RTS_{t+1} is false, then the recession is continued, that is $S_{t+1}^* = s_{RT}$, $s_{RT} \in S_{RT}$; the associated transition probability is $p_{RR} = 1 - p_{RT}$.

The case when ETS_{t+1} and RTS_{t+1} are both false is implicitly covered by the above dating rule. Probabilistic dating based on a maintained stochastic process replaces the indicator function, $I(\cdot)$, with the probability of the terminating sequences, $P_{t+1}^{(ETS)}, P_{t+1}^{(RTS)}.$

Let now $\mathcal{F}_t$ denote the collection of $I(ETS_j)$, $I(RTS_j)$, $j = 1, 2, \ldots t$, and let $P(S_t^* \mid \mathcal{F}_t)$ denote the probability of being in any particular state at time t conditional on this information set. Assuming that this probability is known, we can compute recursively the probability of the chain at subsequent times by the following filter:

1 Given the availability of $P(S_t^* \mid \mathcal{F}_t)$ at time t, let us denote by π_t^* the $m \times 1$ vector containing them, with $m = 24$ in the quarterly case. Define the two $m \times 1$ selection vectors v_{EP}, with ones corresponding to the elements of S_{EP} and zero otherwise, and v_{RT}, with ones corresponding to the elements of S_{RT} and zero otherwise.

2 Compute the transition probabilities of the chain according to (2) and (3), that is $p_{EP} = I(ETS_{t+1})v'_{EP}\pi^*_t$, $p_{RT} = I(RTS_{t+1})v'_{RT}\pi^*_t$, $p_{EE} = 1 - p_{EP}$, $p_{RR} = 1 - p_{RT}$ and insert them in the transition matrix of the chain, hereby denoted by T.

3 Compute the probabilities $P(S^*_{t+1}|\mathcal{F}_{t+1})$ belonging to the vector π^*_{t+1} as

$$\pi^*_{t+1} = T'\pi^*_t$$

The algorithm is initialised by assigning values to π^*_t: if one knows that at the beginning of the sample we are in expansion, $\pi^*_t \propto v_E$, where v_E is the selection vector corresponding to S_E, whereas if we know that the system was in recession, $\pi^*_1 \propto v_R$, where v_R selects the elements of S_R. Otherwise, we can learn from the first observations about the initial probability vector, and in the case these are ambiguous use a uniform prior, which amounts to setting the elements of π^*_1 equal to $1/m$.

Finally, the algorithm recursively produces $P(S^*_t|\mathcal{F}_t)$, for all $t = 1, \ldots, T$, and hence, marginalising previous states $S_{t-j}, j = 1, 2, 3, 4$, the probabilities of each elementary event, $P(S_t|\mathcal{F}_t)$, and $P(E_t|\mathcal{F}_t) = P(EC_t|\mathcal{F}_t) + P(P_t|\mathcal{F}_t)$, $P(R_t|\mathcal{F}_t) = P(RC_t|\mathcal{F}_t) + P(T_t|\mathcal{F}_t)$, can be obtained. For instance,

$$P(E_t|\mathcal{F}_t) = \sum_{s_E \in S_E} P(S^*_t = s_E).$$

6 Demand and supply shocks in the new Member States

Raúl Ramos and Jordi Suriñach[*]

6.1 Introduction

Most studies of the possible effects of the European monetary unification process that use the Optimum Currency Areas (OCA) approach conclude that the success of European Economic and Monetary Union (when benefits outweigh costs) will depend on the capacity of European economies to give more flexibility to markets – both labour and goods and services markets – and on the degree of symmetry of future shocks (see Ramos et al., 1999). In the context of enlargement, much of the academic debate (Lättemäe, 2003) has also focused on the analysis of business cycle synchronicity.[1] Specifically, though new Member States are expected to gain in the long run from joining the euro, the loss of monetary policy may create problems in the near term. In fact, the costs of participating in monetary union depend to a certain extent on the similarity between business cycles in the Euro area and in the new Member States. Only a few studies have considered this issue. One of the reasons for this may lie in the shortage and instability of economic data for the new Member States. In fact, as Fidrmuc (2001) states, some of these studies review periods of seven years or less, meaning that only one business cycle is covered by the available data, when in fact for the results to be reliable, the time period needed to establish this synchronisation would have to be longer.[2]

In a previous study, Ramos and Suriñach (2004) analysed whether the recent economic evolution of these countries and the expected

[*] The authors wish to thank three anonymous referees, the members of the European Forecasting Network and the staff of the DG ECFIN of the European Commission for their helpful comments and suggestions. The usual disclaimer applies. Financial support is gratefully acknowledged from CICYT SEJ 2005–04348 project.
[1] A second aspect also treated in the literature is the analysis of capital flows (mainly foreign direct investment) and currency crisis in the new Member States (see, for example, Begg et al., 2003; Eichengreen, 2003 or Eichengreen et al., 2003). These aspects are partially considered in Chapter 9 of this volume.
[2] An extensive review of this literature can be found in Fidrmuc and Korhonen (2003).

160   Ramos and Suriñach

Table 6.1. *Share of the industrial sector as a percentage of total GDP (average 1998–2002)*

Country	GDP$_m$/GDP[b]
Euro area	28.85%
New Member States[a]	32.38%
Cyprus	–
Czech Republic	40.55%
Estonia	29.05%
Hungary	30.26%
Latvia	26.44%
Lithuania	31.64%
Poland	33.58%
Slovakia	30.14%
Slovenia	37.40%

Notes: [a] a weighted average of country data using the share of industrial GDP for the base year 2000.
[b] GDP_m = manufacturing GDP.
Source: World Development Indicators.

developments in the coming years put them in a better or worse position to join the euro. Of course, this was only a partial analysis of the problems that new Member States face on their road to the monetary union,[3] but the results were interesting; they concluded that, in terms of business cycle synchronicity, the situation has worsened in the recent years.

This chapter extends this previous research, providing empirical evidence on the evolution of the degree of symmetry of shocks experienced by new Member States by using a larger and more recent data set and more sophisticated econometric techniques. Specifically, we will focus on the manufacturing sector. It is already known that in current EU Member States it was this sector that felt the effects of the Single Market programme most, due to its greater openness (European Commission, 1990). Moreover, the share of manufacturing in the total GDP is relatively high in all new Member States (Table 6.1).

The rest of the chapter is structured in three sections: section 6.2 briefly summarises the literature on the topic; section 6.3 presents the results of estimating demand and supply shocks for new Member States

[3] A more general analysis involving topics such as fiscal imbalances, the need to monitor banking systems in new Member States, implications for labour markets or ECB design after accession can be found in Eichengreen (2003) and Eichengreen and Ghironi (2003).

and of analysing the evolution of shock symmetry between new Member States and the euro; and section 6.4 summarises the main findings of the chapter.

6.2   Asymmetric shocks and the Optimum Currency Areas approach

The starting point for considering the benefits and costs of joining the euro for new Member States is the Theory of Optimum Currency Areas.[4] The seminal contribution of Mundell (1961), followed by McKinnon (1963) and Kenen (1969), among others, set the stage for future research. These initial studies were part of the intense debate during the 1960s and early 1970s about fixed versus flexible exchange rates. Their objective was to identify the criteria that determine whether a country should join a currency area or not. The strategy consisted in identifying the main benefits and costs that membership of a currency area would entail for an individual country. If for every participant, benefits outweigh costs, then the currency area is said to be optimal. The intensification of the European monetary integration process has brought up to date the main ideas of these contributions, which are now applied to the analysis of the potential benefits and risks of monetary union. Indeed, while there is a certain consensus on the positive economic effects of monetary union, especially at a microeconomic level (De Grauwe, 1997) – which can be summarised as direct and indirect benefits of transaction cost reduction, less uncertainty, and more transparency in price determination mechanisms – there is no agreement on its potential costs.

Obviously, the main cost of joining a currency area is the loss of monetary policy instruments at national level (e.g. the exchange rate) as stabilisation mechanisms against macroeconomic disturbances that affect only one country in the area or affect countries in different ways. Macroeconomic disturbances of this kind (known as 'asymmetric shocks') cannot be dealt with by a common monetary policy, and so alternative adjustment mechanisms are needed to achieve macroeconomic stabilisation.

Taking the contributions of the 1960s as a starting point, several modern-day studies have tried to identify empirically the main adjustment mechanisms other than the exchange rate used in Euro area countries. The analysis of other currency areas (mainly, the United States and Canada) has shown the importance of factor mobility, fiscal federalism

[4] See also Chapter 5 of this volume.

and wage and price flexibility. However, the peculiarities of the new Member States make it difficult to apply this approach. In fact, one difference between more recent studies and the traditional view is the interest in the effect of asymmetric shocks once the currency area is established.

This is the usual approach in the various studies that have considered the situation of the new Member States. The idea is that cyclical synchronicity is a positive indicator for monetary union, since it suggests that the single monetary policy will be broadly appropriate for all union members. To our knowledge, apart from the study by Ramos and Suriñach (2004) mentioned above, the most recent works in this area are by Fidrmuc and Korhonen (2003) and Horvath and Ratfai (2004).

Fidrmuc and Korhonen (2003) assess the correlation of supply and demand shocks during the 1990s. Their findings suggest that, for some new Member States (Hungary and Estonia), 'joining the Euro area fairly quickly would not imply large welfare losses because of asymmetric business cycles'. As for other countries (i.e. Lithuania and Slovakia), 'early membership in the monetary union could prove to be detrimental for them'.

The main innovation of Horvath and Ratfai's (2004) study was the consideration of seasonal effects (ignored in previous work) when estimating demand and supply shocks. Their results were much more pessimistic compared to those obtained by previous authors.

Summarising, there is a certain consensus that shocks between old and new EU Member States have been idiosyncratic, with very few exceptions. However, the sample considered in the two studies quoted includes only quarterly information up to 2000. Will the picture change when more recent data are included? Will the recent economic downturn worsen or improve the situation of the new Member States? Both issues will be considered in the next section.

6.3   Empirical analysis

6.3.1   Some descriptive statistics

As mentioned above, the objective of this chapter is to provide new evidence on the degree of shock symmetry in the manufacturing sector between the new Member States and the Euro area.

With this aim in mind, we will use monthly data on industrial production indices and producer price indices obtained from the OECD's Main Economic Indicators, the IMF's International Financial Statistics, the Eurostat short-term statistics data set and a range of national sources.

Table 6.2. *Data availability for the new Member States*

Monthly data	Industrial production index	Industrial producer prices
New Member States[a]	1992:1–2003:12	1992:1–2003:12
Cyprus	1990:1–2003:12	1990:1–2003:12
Czech Republic	1992:1–2003:12	1993:1–2003:12
Estonia	1994:1–2003:12	1994:1–2003:12
Hungary	1990:1–2003:12	1990:1–2003:12
Latvia	1996:1–2003:12	1993:12–2003:12
Lithuania	1997:1–2003:12	1992:1–2003:12
Poland	1990:1–2003:12	1990:1–2003:12
Slovakia	1992:1–2003:12	1993:1–2003:12
Slovenia	1991:12–2003:12	1991:12–2003:12

Notes: [a] a weighted average of country data produced using the share of industrial GDP for the base year 2000.
Source: OECD Main Economic Indicators, Eurostat Short-Term Indicators, IMF International Financial Indicators and national sources.

The time period considered for the analysis here starts in 1990 (or at the moment data became available) and ends in December 2003. The countries considered are: Cyprus, the Czech Republic, Estonia, Hungary, Latvia, Lithuania, Poland, Slovakia and Slovenia[5] (Table 6.2).

In order to provide a benchmark for the results obtained, the situation of European countries before the start-up of the EMU is also considered. Specifically, we will use monthly data from 1982 to 1998 on industrial production indices and producer price indices obtained from the OECD's Main Economic Indicators, the IMF's International Financial Statistics and the Eurostat short-term statistics data set (see Table 6.3).

In both cases, data have been previously deseasonalised and outliers corrected using Tramo/Seats.

We first examine some descriptive statistics on industrial production growth and producer price inflation in the EU countries and the new Member States. As shown in Table 6.4, average inflation and growth during the period considered was significantly higher in the new Member States than in the Euro area (with the sole exception of Latvia). The variability of both inflation and growth was also significantly higher (again, the only exception is Latvia). Excluding Greece, the differences between the new Member States and the EU countries (as an aggregate)

[5] Malta has not been included in the analysis due to data restrictions.

164   *Ramos and Suriñach*

Table 6.3. *Data considered for European countries*

Monthly data	Industrial production index	Industrial producer prices
Euro area	1982:1–1998:12	1982:1–1998:12
Austria	1982:1–1998:12	1982:1–1998:12
Belgium	1982:1–1998:12	1982:1–1998:12
Denmark	1982:1–1998:12	1982:1–1998:12
Finland	1982:1–1998:12	1982:1–1998:12
France	1982:1–1998:12	1982:1–1998:12
Germany	1982:1–1998:12	1982:1–1998:12
Greece	1982:1–1998:12	1982:1–1998:12
Ireland	1982:1–1998:12	1982:1–1998:12
Italy	1982:1–1998:12	1982:1–1998:12
Luxembourg	1982:1–1998:12	1982:1–1998:12
Netherlands	1982:1–1998:12	1982:1–1998:12
Portugal	1982:1–1998:12	1990:1–1998:12
Spain	1982:1–1998:12	1982:1–1998:12
Sweden	1982:1–1998:12	1982:1–1998:12
United Kingdom	1982:1–1998:12	1982:1–1998:12

Source: OECD Main Economic Indicators, Eurostat Short-Term Indicators and IMF International Financial Indicators.

Table 6.4. *Descriptive statistics for the new Member States and the Euro area (1992–2003)*

	Industrial production		Producer prices	
Year-on-year growth rates	Average	St. Dev.	Average	St. Dev.
Euro area	1.87	2.70	1.31	2.39
New Member States[a]	5.44	4.13	5.44	4.14
Cyprus	2.95	5.71	2.72	3.17
Czech Republic	3.93	6.29	2.12	2.44
Estonia	8.05	7.86	2.10	2.98
Hungary	11.32	9.24	7.21	4.14
Latvia	2.87	7.61	0.23	2.18
Lithuania	7.51	12.27	2.46	10.22
Poland	5.21	5.45	4.33	2.89
Slovakia	5.14	6.44	5.77	3.55
Slovenia	2.62	3.21	5.41	2.74

Notes: [a] a weighted average of country data produced using the share of industrial GDP for the base year 2000.
Source: OECD Main Economic Indicators, Eurostat Short-Term Indicators, IMF International Financial Indicators and national sources.

Table 6.5. *Descriptive statistics for the old Member States and the Euro area (1982–98)*

Year-on-year growth rates	Industrial production		Producer prices	
	Average	St. Dev.	Average	St. Dev.
Euro area	2.06	3.10	2.31	2.79
Austria	3.38	3.94	0.37	2.42
Belgium	2.02	4.06	0.70	5.05
Denmark	3.30	7.87	1.55	3.47
Finland	3.72	5.55	1.77	3.06
France	1.56	3.34	1.75	3.96
Germany	1.87	3.94	1.09	1.51
Greece	0.85	4.76	12.39	6.11
Ireland	9.78	7.04	2.11	3.04
Italy	1.83	4.56	4.36	3.38
Luxembourg	2.97	6.73	0.83	4.33
Netherlands	1.96	4.92	1.15	1.88
Portugal	3.41	5.36	2.10	3.49
Spain	2.30	4.39	3.96	4.15
Sweden	2.39	6.19	3.73	4.20
United Kingdom	2.04	3.33	3.79	2.04

Source: OECD Main Economic Indicators, Eurostat Short-Term Indicators and IMF International Financial Indicators

are considerably higher than between EU countries and Euro area aggregates between 1982 and 1998 (Table 6.5).

The plot of the values of the correlation coefficients between the Euro area and the new Member States (Figure 6.1) in terms of the year-on-year growth rates of industrial production and producer prices is similar to that of the correlations between the Euro area and the EU countries (Figure 6.2). These results indicate that there are considerable differences in the business cycles between the new Member States and EU countries.[6] However, these differences can arise either from differences in shocks that they have experienced, or from differences in the responses to these shocks. The above correlation analysis cannot discriminate between the two aspects. For example, in some countries, lower correlations may be due to a greater discipline in terms of monetary policy (a self-imposed restriction on adjustment mechanisms) rather than an increase in asymmetric shocks. This issue is considered in the following section.

---

[6] Similar results are shown in Chapter 5 using a different methodology.

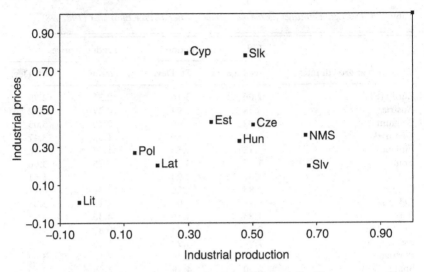

Figure 6.1. Correlation coefficients between the Euro area and the new Member States for the year-on-year growth rates of industrial production and producer prices (all available observations).

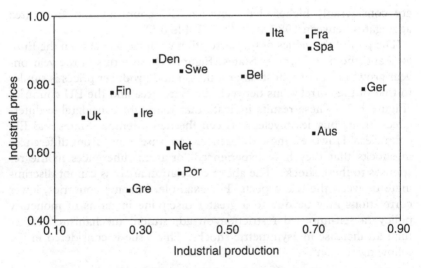

Figure 6.2. Correlation coefficients between the Euro area and the old Member States for the year-on-year growth rates of industrial production and producer prices (1982–98).

6.3.2 Demand and supply shocks: the Bayoumi and Eichengreen (1992) model

There have been several attempts to distinguish disturbances from other components of observed output movements (see, for example, Caporale (1993) or Stockman (1998)). However, in this context, the methodology proposed by Bayoumi and Eichengreen (1992, 1996), extending the work by Blanchard and Quah (1989), has become the standard. The main assumption of their model is that there are two kinds of shocks: shocks that affect the demand curve (for example, due to monetary or fiscal policy changes) and shocks that affect the supply curve (for example, technological changes). From the model, it is also clear that demand and supply shocks have different effects on output and prices. In fact, this implies that, while supply shocks have permanent effects on the level of output, demand shocks have only temporary effects, while both have permanent effects on the level of prices.

These assumptions can be easily introduced in a structural bivariate VAR on output and prices to obtain the series of demand and supply shocks. The starting point of the model is the following:

$$
\begin{bmatrix} \Delta Y_t \\ \Delta P_t \end{bmatrix} = \sum_{i=0}^{\infty} \begin{bmatrix} a_{11i} & a_{12i} \\ a_{21i} & a_{22i} \end{bmatrix} \cdot \begin{bmatrix} \varepsilon_{dt} \\ \varepsilon_{st} \end{bmatrix},
\tag{1}
$$

where ΔY_t and ΔP_t represent, respectively, changes in the logarithm of output and prices at time t, ε_{dt} and ε_{st} represent supply and demand shocks, and a_{kji} represents each of the elements of the impulse response function to shocks.

The identification restriction is based on the previously stated assumption about the effects of the shocks. As output data is in first differences, this implies that the cumulative effects of demand shocks on output must be zero:

$$
\sum_{i=0}^{\infty} a_{11i} = 0
\tag{2}
$$

The model defined by equations (1) and (2) also implies that the bivariate endogenous vector can be explained by lagged values of every variable. If B_i represents the value of model coefficients, the model to be estimated is the following:

$$
\begin{bmatrix} \Delta Y_t \\ \Delta P_t \end{bmatrix} = B_1 \cdot \begin{bmatrix} \Delta Y_{t-1} \\ \Delta P_{t-1} \end{bmatrix} + B_2 \cdot \begin{bmatrix} \Delta Y_{t-2} \\ \Delta P_{t-2} \end{bmatrix} + \cdots + \begin{bmatrix} e_{yt} \\ e_{pt} \end{bmatrix},
\tag{3}
$$

where e_{yt} and e_{pt} are the residuals of each VAR equation. Equation (3) can also be expressed as:

$$\begin{bmatrix} \Delta Y_t \\ \Delta P_t \end{bmatrix} = (I - B(L))^{-1} \cdot \begin{bmatrix} e_{yt} \\ e_{pt} \end{bmatrix} = (I + B(L) + B(L)^2 + \ldots) \cdot \begin{bmatrix} e_{yt} \\ e_{pt} \end{bmatrix}, \quad (4)$$

and in an equivalent manner:

$$\begin{bmatrix} \Delta Y_t \\ \Delta P_t \end{bmatrix} = \sum_{i=0}^{\infty} \begin{bmatrix} d_{11i} & d_{12i} \\ d_{21i} & d_{22i} \end{bmatrix} \cdot \begin{bmatrix} e_{yt} \\ e_{pt} \end{bmatrix} \quad (5)$$

Putting together equations (1) and (5):

$$\sum_{i=0}^{\infty} \begin{bmatrix} d_{11i} & d_{12i} \\ d_{21i} & d_{22i} \end{bmatrix} \cdot \begin{bmatrix} e_{yt} \\ e_{pt} \end{bmatrix} = \sum_{i=0}^{\infty} L^i \cdot \begin{bmatrix} a_{11i} & a_{12i} \\ a_{21i} & a_{22i} \end{bmatrix} \cdot \begin{bmatrix} \varepsilon_{dt} \\ \varepsilon_{st} \end{bmatrix}, \quad (6)$$

a matrix, denoted by c, can be found that relates demand and supply shocks with the residuals from the VAR model.

$$\begin{bmatrix} e_{yt} \\ e_{pt} \end{bmatrix} = \left[\sum_{i=0}^{\infty} \begin{bmatrix} d_{11i} & d_{12i} \\ d_{21i} & d_{22i} \end{bmatrix}^{-1} \cdot \sum_{i=0}^{\infty} L^i \cdot \begin{bmatrix} a_{11i} & a_{12i} \\ a_{21i} & a_{22i} \end{bmatrix} \right] \cdot \begin{bmatrix} \varepsilon_{dt} \\ \varepsilon_{st} \end{bmatrix} = c. \begin{bmatrix} \varepsilon_{dt} \\ \varepsilon_{st} \end{bmatrix} \quad (7)$$

From (7) it seems clear that in the 2×2 model considered, four restrictions are needed to define uniquely the four elements of matrix c. Two of these restrictions are simple normalisations that define the variances of shocks ε_{dt} and ε_{st}. The usual convention in VAR models is to impose the two variances equal to one, which, together with the assumption of orthogonality, define the third restriction $c'c = \Sigma$, *where Σ is the covariance matrix of the residuals e_y and e_p. The final restriction that permits matrix c to be uniquely defined comes from economic theory and has been defined above in equation (2). In terms of the model, introducing (2) in (7), it follows that:*

$$\sum_{i=0}^{\infty} \begin{bmatrix} d_{11i} & d_{12i} \\ d_{21i} & d_{22i} \end{bmatrix} \cdot \begin{bmatrix} c_{11} & c_{12} \\ c_{21} & c_{22} \end{bmatrix} = \begin{bmatrix} 0 & . \\ . & . \end{bmatrix}, \quad (8)$$

and the resolution of this system permits us to estimate the series of demand and supply shocks from residuals of the estimated VAR.

Once the series of structural shocks have been obtained, the most common way to evaluate degrees of symmetry is by calculating the correlation coefficients between the series of shocks (previously obtained using one of the available methodologies). If the values of these coefficients are high, the countries under study would be expected to have experienced relatively symmetrical disturbances.

We estimated this VAR model using monthly data on industrial production and producer prices monthly series from 1990:1 (or at the moment data came available) to 2003:12 for the new Member States considered and the Euro area. Prior to this, we analysed the order of integrability of the output and price series for the considered countries and found that each series considered has a unit root. The VAR models were estimated in first differences since the null hypothesis of non-cointegration could not be rejected using the Johansen test. As for the number of lags included in the models, we kept a homogenous identification scheme for every country. The number of lags chosen was four, as this was the optimal number in most cases according to the Schwartz information criteria. The results were also satisfactory in terms of adjustment and residual diagnostic tests and the signs of the variables were as expected.

As in the previous section, and in order to obtain a benchmark for the situation of the new Member States, we applied a similar approach for EU countries for the period 1982:1 to 1998:4. The results were also satisfactory from the econometric point of view.

Table 6.6 shows the values of the correlation coefficients measuring the relationship between demand shocks in the Euro area with the rest of countries for the whole period considered, while Table 6.7 provides the same information for supply shocks.

In terms of demand shocks, the values of the correlations with the Euro area are positive but very low. In fact, the value for the correlation between the Euro area and the new Member States demand shocks is 0.2, a value substantially below those observed for the current members of the Euro area in the years before they adopted the euro (Ramos *et al.*, 2003). Although correlations between new Member States' demand shocks are not very high, in some cases the values are higher than those with the Euro area (e.g. between Hungary and Poland).

In terms of supply shocks, the results are similar to those found for demand shocks. Correlations are quite low, with the sole exceptions of Cyprus and Lithuania, and there is even one country with a negative value (Latvia). As before, the highest correlation between new Member States is that between Hungary and Poland.

The values of the correlation coefficients between the series of demand and supply shocks of the Euro area and the new Member States are plotted in Figure 6.3. As in Fidrmuc and Korhonen (2003), the comparison between Figures 6.1 and 6.3 shows that demand and supply

Table 6.6. *Correlations between demand shocks series (1990[a]–2002)*

	New Member States	Cyprus	Czech Republic	Estonia	Hungary	Latvia	Lithuania	Poland	Slovakia	Slovenia
Euro area	0.20	0.18	0.11	0.06	0.07	0.17	0.10	0.02	0.15	0.13
New Member States		0.10	0.58	0.38	0.44	0.17	0.09	0.55	0.31	0.22
Cyprus			0.09	-0.01	-0.01	0.05	0.05	0.01	0.14	0.09
Czech Republic				0.18	0.14	0.11	0.02	0.18	0.20	0.17
Estonia					0.32	0.26	0.16	0.29	0.21	0.13
Hungary						0.05	0.06	0.41	0.09	0.03
Latvia							0.18	0.05	0.05	0.04
Lithuania								-0.01	0.16	-0.02
Poland									0.13	0.11
Slovakia										0.15

Notes: [a] First observation available.

Table 6.7. *Correlations between supply shocks series (1990[a]–2002)*

	New Member States	Cyprus	Czech Republic	Estonia	Hungary	Latvia	Lithuania	Poland	Slovak R.	Slovenia
Euro area	0.00	0.33	0.14	0.07	0.05	−0.04	0.22	0.05	0.15	0.00
New Member States		0.03	−0.05	0.02	−0.01	0.07	−0.04	−0.04	−0.04	0.03
Cyprus			0.10	0.04	0.12	0.07	0.17	0.04	0.08	−0.06
Czech Republic				0.14	0.13	0.06	0.21	0.09	0.05	−0.03
Estonia					0.15	0.02	0.01	0.16	0.20	0.03
Hungary						−0.08	0.01	0.30	0.09	0.04
Latvia							0.09	−0.02	0.04	−0.06
Lithuania								0.03	0.10	−0.02
Poland									0.17	0.05
Slovakia										0.00

Notes: [a] First observation available.

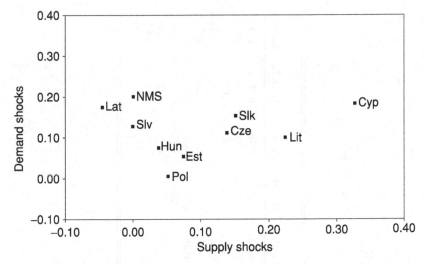

Figure 6.3. Correlation coefficients between the Euro area and the new Member States for demand and supply shocks (all available observations).

shocks are less strongly correlated than industrial production growth and producer price inflation. This result indicates that macroeconomic policies to deal with asymmetric shocks in the new Member States have been able to stabilise the business cycle. However, it clearly indicates that joining the monetary union may be costly for some of them that rely on the exchange rate adjustment channel.

If we compare the values of the correlation coefficients for demand and supply shocks between the Euro area and the new Member States with those for EU countries before adopting the euro (Table 6.8), we see that they are clearly lower than the Euro area members but not very different from non-Euro area members (especially for demand shocks). The results for supply shocks are much more pessimistic. The comparison between Figures 6.3 and 6.4 provides a clear view of the differences between the two sets of countries.

However, one additional aspect to be considered when comparing economic developments of these countries with those in the Euro area is that, during the period under study, the economies of the new Member States were involved in a transformation process that led to a high number of structural changes. For this reason, one way to take into account possible changes in the relationships between the new

Table 6.8. *Correlations between demand and supply shocks in the old Member States (1982–98)*

Correlations with the Euro area	Demand shocks	Supply shocks
Austria	0.33	0.18
Belgium	0.24	0.26
Denmark	0.18	0.29
Finland	0.14	0.09
France	0.42	0.39
Germany	0.57	0.64
Greece	0.04	0.08
Ireland	0.09	0.30
Italy	0.25	0.48
Luxembourg	0.19	0.12
Netherlands	0.26	0.35
Portugal[a]	0.17	0.29
Spain	0.34	0.34
Sweden	0.10	0.46
United Kingdom	0.10	0.37

Notes: [a] 1990–1998.

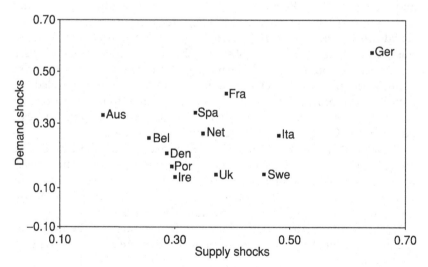

Figure 6.4. Correlation coefficients between the Euro area and the old Member States for demand and supply shocks (all available observations).

Table 6.9. *Correlations between shocks by sub-periods (new Member States)*

	Demand shocks		Supply shocks	
Correlations with the Euro area	1990–1997	1998–2003	1990–1997	1998–2003
New Member States	0.17	0.30	0.03	−0.02
Cyprus	0.12	0.27	0.18	0.42
Czech Republic	0.11	0.12	0.04	0.22
Estonia	0.12	−0.01	0.07	0.06
Hungary	0.11	0.00	0.00	0.10
Latvia	0.22	0.18	0.04	−0.09
Lithuania	0.25	0.08	−0.11	0.32
Poland	−0.03	0.18	0.06	0.03
Slovakia	0.18	0.13	0.05	0.30
Slovenia	0.21	0.03	−0.01	−0.02

Member States and the Euro area consists in splitting the sample into a number of sub-periods.[7]

When looking at the values of the correlation coefficients between different sub-periods (Table 6.9), the most interesting result is that, in terms of demand shocks, correlations have increased for the aggregate and for Cyprus and Poland, and have decreased for the rest (with the sole exception of the Czech Republic). It seems that the economic slowdown has increased the heterogeneity of demand shocks. In contrast, the correlations in terms of supply shocks have clearly increased for a number of countries. This result shows that in more recent years asymmetric shocks are related to factors that can be controlled by national governments (demand) while those related to non-controllable factors (such as transition effects) tended to decrease (supply). This can be interpreted as good news for the new Member States.

Table 6.10 shows the results of a similar exercise for the case of EU countries before the adoption of the euro. As we can see, in most cases the correlations in the first sub-period (1982–90) are lower than in the second sub-period (1991–8), and in nearly all cases they are clearly higher than the values found for the new Member States.

However, the method used to analyse the evolution of the degree of symmetry of shocks (which consisted of splitting the available data into

---

[7] Instead of splitting the sample when calculating correlations, VAR models were also estimated for the two sub-periods. The results were quite similar and are available from the authors on request.

Table 6.10. *Correlations between shocks by sub-periods (old Member States)*

	Demand shocks		Supply shocks	
Correlations with the Euro area	1982–1990	1991–1998	1982–1990	1991–1998
Austria	0.23	0.47	0.15	0.22
Belgium	0.22	0.27	0.23	0.32
Denmark	0.21	0.14	0.23	0.42
Finland	0.13	0.19	0.07	0.14
France	0.44	0.40	0.42	0.29
Germany	0.58	0.56	0.68	0.60
Greece	0.02	0.08	0.03	0.14
Ireland	0.03	0.22	0.42	0.14
Italy	0.11	0.56	0.49	0.44
Luxembourg	0.20	0.18	0.14	0.09
Netherlands	0.26	0.30	0.38	0.30
Portugal[a]	–	–	0.06	0.38
Spain	0.19	0.53	0.28	0.53
Sweden	0.14	0.04	0.48	0.39
United Kingdom	0.12	0.07	0.34	0.42

Notes: [a] 1990–1998.

two different sub-periods) may not be totally accurate: the number of different periods and the break points are, in fact, unknown. Nor does this approach take into consideration the fact that the European economic and monetary unification process is dynamic and gradual. To include these two issues in our analysis, in 6.3.3 we propose a time-varying coefficient model based on state-space models and estimated using the Kalman filter.

6.3.3   A dynamic analysis of the degree of shock symmetry in the new Member States

Time-varying coefficient models allow us to include in the model the possibility of changing relationships between the variables under consideration. Haldane and Hall (1991) were the first to use this kind of model; they applied a state-space model to assess the extent to which movements in the pound were associated with movements in the US dollar or in the deutschmark. A similar model can be used to analyse the evolution of the degree of symmetry of shocks experienced by new Member States. To our knowledge, this method was first used in the context of the European Monetary Unification process by Boone (1997) to analyse the degree of symmetry of demand and supply shocks for the entire economy, and was modified by Ramos *et al.* (2003) for the analysis of the industrial sector. The model used was the following:

$$(X - Z)_t = a_t + b_t.(Y - Z)_t + \varepsilon_t; \tag{9}$$

$$a_t = a_{t-1} + \eta_{1t} \tag{10}$$

$$b_t = b_{t-1} + \eta_{2t} \tag{11}$$

where Z_t represents the series of shocks in the Euro area, X_t the series of shocks in the country considered, and Y_t the shocks in the rest of the world (which is proxied by shocks in the United States). The parameters a_t and b_t are time-varying coefficients which allow us to assess the dynamic evolution of asymmetries. ε_t, η_{1t} and η_{2t} are uncorrelated random terms that follow a normal distribution with zero mean and known variance.

Coefficient a_t is a time-varying parameter which approximates all those factors that have a systemic influence on both variables. The introduction of this variable also eliminates the adverse effects of the possible omission of relevant variables in the relationships considered, especially factors affecting the long-run levels of both variables. The value of coefficient a_t summarises, then, the differences in the averages of the two variables and can be interpreted as an indicator of 'autonomous' convergence between the countries considered.

As for b_t, if $E\{lim_{t\to\infty} b_t\} = 0$ (meaning that b_t takes values starting from 1 in the first years of the period and ending with values near 0), then the evolution of country X has approached the area of influence of country Z in terms of shocks. If, on the contrary, $E\{lim_{t\to\infty} b_t\} = 1$, then X has approached the influence area of Y (the rest of the world). In other words, in the first case shocks experienced by X and Z have tended to be more symmetrical while in the second case shocks have tended to be more asymmetrical.

Boone's results, after estimating this model for the whole economy using the Kalman filter, provide evidence of a convergence in terms of supply shocks for the core countries, and also for the peripheral countries except for Greece and the UK. As for demand shocks, he finds that the distinction between core and peripheral countries is very slight, though the convergence process seems to have stopped in the mid-1980s.

Ramos *et al.* (2003) conclude that demand shocks experienced by European countries were more symmetrical during the first half of the

1990s, while supply shocks have been more symmetrical since the mid-1980s, probably as a consequence of the Single European Act and the Single Market Programme.

The model by Ramos *et al.* (2003), also used here, differs from Boone's (1997) in two aspects. First, we analyse the degree of symmetry between shocks for the manufacturing sector, not the entire economy. Secondly, given that by definition a shock cannot be anticipated, the series of shocks estimated following Bayoumi and Eichengreen's (1992) method have zero mean. As a result, we must include the parameter a_t in the specification in order to approximate the behaviour of factors affecting the long-run level of the variables, as they have zero mean. Hence, in the proposed model we have imposed the restriction $a_t = 0$.[8] Furthermore, we assume that $a_t = 0$ considerably simplifies the estimation process of the model using the Kalman filter.[9]

Thus, the model considered can be expressed by two equations instead of three:

$$(X - Z)_t = b_t.(Y - Z)_t + \varepsilon_t \qquad (12)$$

$$b_t = b_{t-1} + \eta_t \qquad (13)$$

where, as before, Z_t represents the series of shocks in the Euro area, X_t the series of shocks in the country considered, and Y_t the shocks in the rest of the world (which is proxied by shocks in the United States). The parameter b_t is a time-varying coefficient which allows us to assess the dynamic evolution of asymmetries, and ε_t and η_t are uncorrelated random terms that follow a normal distribution with zero mean and known variance.

As stated above, these equations can be easily estimated for every country considered using the Kalman filter once the model is interpreted as a state-space representation: equation (12) can be understood as the measurement equation and equation (13) as the transition equation.

To obtain estimates of the dynamic measures of the evolution of the degree of shock symmetry, we must first estimate the values of the unknown hyperparameters and solve the problem of the initialisation of the Kalman filter. As for the estimation of the hyperparameters

[8] Hall *et al.* (1992) use similar reasons to impose this assumption in order to analyse the relationships between European countries in terms of inflation evolution.
[9] This reduces the number of hyperparameters to be estimated and the treatment of initial values, so one would expect the estimates obtained to be more robust than in the previous specification.

of the model, the only unknown values are those of the covariance matrix of the perturbations in equations (12) and (13); the rest of the hyperparameters are given by the model specification.

The unknown values of the hyperparameters were estimated by maximum likelihood. We used prediction error decomposition (Harvey, 1981, 1984) to estimate the expression of the system's likelihood function. Next, this function was maximised with respect to the estimated hyperparameters using the numerical optimisation procedure proposed by Broyden–Fletcher–Goldfarb–Shanno (BFGS). As for the treatment of the initial values of b_t, we applied the method proposed by Harvey and Phillips (1979) which consists in initialising the filter with very high values of the variance of the estimation error. This – after applying sequentially the Kalman filter equation – produces a convergence process that reduces error, giving accurate estimates of the state vector.

It is important to point out, nevertheless, that the main criticism of the application of the state-space models in economics is related to the possible sensitivity of the results to the maximum likelihood procedure considered and the treatment of the initial values. We therefore applied a sensitivity analysis to the results following Hackl and Westlund (1996), finding no substantial alterations in the results.

Figure 6.5 shows the results for demand and supply shock symmetry (the evolution of b_t) between new Member States with respect to the Euro area, as opposed to the rest of the world (the United States).[10]

With the sole exception of Lithuania, the dynamic analysis of demand shocks shows that new Member States showed strong evidence towards convergence to the Euro area in terms of shocks during the second half of the 1990s, though this convergence seems to have ceased during the last years of the period under study. The results are not surprising since demand shocks are related to differences in national macroeconomic policies, differences which have narrowed due to preparation for joining the European Union, but which could have widened in order to face the global economic downturn of recent years.

As for supply shocks, the results also show a trend towards convergence in reference to the Euro area during practically the entire period, but especially towards the end. The convergence process in terms of shock symmetry also accelerated in the last years, possibly due to structural reforms related to accession to the European Union.

---

[10] As usual in the literature, a smoothing algorithm has been applied after the application of the Kalman filtering (see Harvey, 1989).

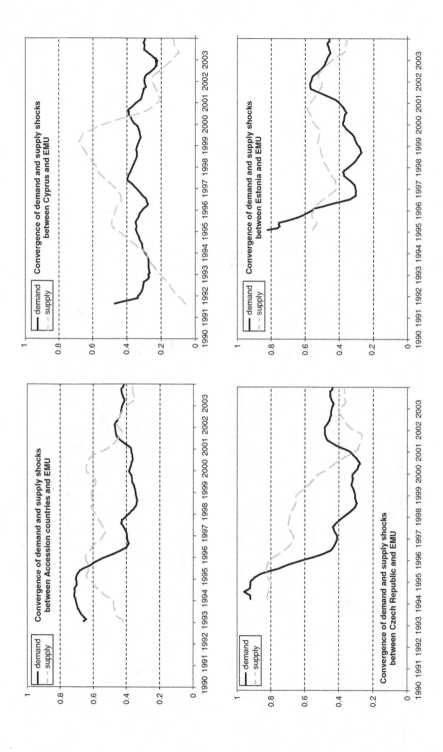

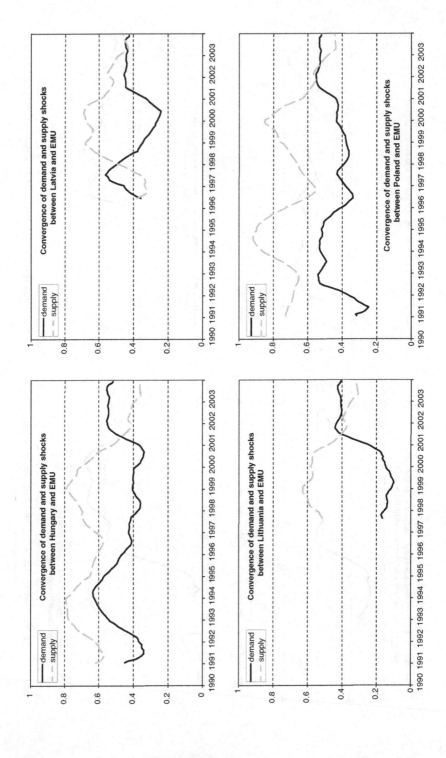

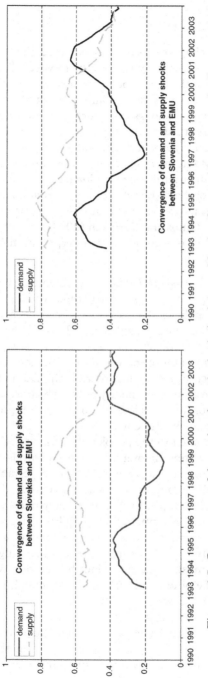

Figure 6.5. Convergence of demand and supply shocks in the new Member States with respect to the Euro area in relative terms of the rest of the world.

6.4   Conclusions

The objective of this chapter was to assess whether the recent economic evolution of the new Member States and their expected development in the coming years place them in a better or a worse position to join the euro. Like previous studies (Fidrmuc and Korhonen, 2003; Lättemäe, 2003), we found that the shocks are more asymmetrical in candidate countries than in current Euro area members, and that the situation has worsened during recent years for demand shocks but not for supply shocks. While the first finding may be related to a less strict coordination of economic policies in order to face the global economic recession of the last few years, the second may be related to the structural reforms carried out in these countries to prepare their entry to the European Union.

To conclude, as in Ramos and Suriñach (2004), we note certain issues that should be taken into account when interpreting the above results from a policy point of view:

• First, according to Lucas' (1976) critique, changes in economic policy could lead to changes in economic structure, which makes it difficult to analyse ex ante policies, based on ex post data. Moreover, in the context of OCA literature, Frankel and Rose (1996) claimed that OCA criteria may be endogenous. According to these authors, monetary union will lead to more trade and this will increase the degree of business cycle synchronicity. Also, there is the fact that, once established, there will be a single monetary policy which would increase the degree of integration of participating countries. Ex post correlations would be higher than ex ante correlations.

• A second issue is related to the problem of 'sufficiency' (Artis, 2003). The main findings of this chapter rely on cross-correlations of shocks, but 'there is nothing in the relevant theory to establish what is a 'satisfactory value' for a cross-correlation. This is the problem of sufficiency' (Artis, 2003, p. 25). We have compared the values of the correlations of the new Member States with Euro area aggregates with the values of these correlations for non-monetary union countries and with the values between EU countries before adopting the euro. We have seen that, in most cases, the values for the new Member States were lower than the others, but are they low enough to indicate that most shocks have been asymmetrical?

• And, last but not least, it is important to stress again that the analysis in this chapter is a partial analysis. We have focused on the role of asymmetric shocks in the manufacturing sector in the light of the probable accession to the monetary union of the new Member States.

However, these economies also face other problems on the road to the monetary union. One of the most important problems is the probability of financial crisis under large capital inflows, but, as we noted above, if the new Member States continue to internationalise their banking systems and efficient monitoring mechanisms are implemented, the danger of banking problems of this type should be considerably reduced (Eichengreen and Ghironi, 2003).

In any case, taking into account that, on average, the correlations are still far away from the values of the Euro area countries, the flexibility of real sector and labour markets will be essential prerequisites for countries aiming to join the euro.

References

Artis, M. 2003. 'Analysis of European and UK Business Cycles and Shocks'. HM Treasury, available at http://www.hm-treasury.gov.uk.

Bayoumi, T. and Eichengreen, B. 1992. 'Shocking Aspects of European Monetary Unification'. NBER Working Paper, No. 3949.

1996. 'Operationalizing the Theory of Optimum Currency Areas'. CEPR Discussion Paper, No. 1484.

Begg, D., Eichengreen, B., Halpern, L., von Hagen, J. and Wyplosz, C. 2003. 'Sustainable Regimes of Capital Movements in Accession Countries'. CEPR Policy Paper, No. 10.

Blanchard, O. and Quah, D. 1989. 'The Dynamic Effects of Aggregate Demand and Supply Disturbances'. *American Economic Review*, vol. 79, pp. 655–73.

Boone, L. 1997. 'Symétrie des chocs en Union Européenne: Un analyse dynamique'. *Economie Internationale*, vol. 70, pp. 7–34.

Caporale, G. 1993. 'Is Europe an Optimum Currency Area? Symmetric Versus Asymmetric Shocks in the EC'. *National Institute Economic Review*, vol. 144, pp. 95–103.

De Grauwe, P. 1997. *The Economics of Monetary Integration*. Oxford: Oxford University Press.

Eichengreen, B. 2003. *Capital Flows and Crises*. Boston: MIT Press.

Eichengreen, B. and Ghironi, F. 2003. 'EMU and Enlargement'. In Buti, M. and Sapir, A. (ed.), *EMU and Economic Policy in Europe: The Challenge of the Early Years*. Cheltenham: Edward Elgar.

European Commission. 1990. 'One Market, One Money'. *European Economy*, vol. 44.

Fidrmuc, J. 2001. 'The Endogeneity of the Optimum Currency Area: Criteria, Intraindustry Trade and EMU Enlargement' Katholieke Universiteit Leuven, Centre for Transition Economics Discussion Paper, No. 106.

Fidrmuc, J. and Korhonen, I. 2003. 'Similarity of Supply and Demand Shocks Between the Euro Area and the CEECs'. *Economic Systems*, vol. 27, pp. 313–34.

184   Ramos and Suriñach

Frankel, J. and Rose, A. 1996. 'The Endogeneity of the Optimum Currency Area Criteria'. NBER Working Paper, No. 5700.

Hackl, P. and Westlund, A. 1996. 'Demand for International Telecommunication: Time-Varying Price Elasticity'. *Journal of Econometrics*, vol. 70, pp. 243–60.

Haldane, A. and Hall, S. 1991. 'The Sterling's Relationship with the Dollar and the Deutschmark: 1976–89'. *Economic Journal*, vol. 101, pp. 436–43.

Hall, S., Robertson, D. and Wickens, M. 1992. 'Measuring Convergence of the EC Economies'. *Manchester School of Economic and Social Studies*, vol. 60, pp. 99–111.

Harvey, A. 1981. *The Econometric Analysis of Time Series*. Oxford: Deddington.

1984. 'Dynamic Models, the Prediction Error Decomposition and State Space Models'. In Hendry, D. and Wallis, K. (eds.), *Econometrics and Quantitative Economics*. Oxford: Basil Blackwell.

1989. *Forecasting, Structural Time Series Models and the Kalman Filter*. Cambridge: Cambridge University Press.

Harvey, A. and Phillips, G. 1979. 'Maximum Likelihood Estimation of Regression Models with Autoregressive-Moving Average Disturbances'. *Biometrika*, vol. 66, pp. 49–58.

Horvath, J. and Rátfai, A. 2004. 'Supply and Demand Shocks in Accession Countries to the Economic and Monetary Union'. *Journal of Comparative Economics*, vol. 32, pp. 202–11.

Kenen, P. 1969. 'The Theory of Optimum Currency Areas: An Eclectic View'. In Mundell, R. and Swoboda, A. (eds.), *Monetary Problems of the International Economy*. Chicago: Chicago University Press.

Lättemäe, R. 2003. 'EMU Accession Issues in Baltic Countries'. Ezoneplus Working Paper, No. 17A.

Lucas, R. 1976. 'Econometric Policy Evaluation: A Critique'. *Journal of Monetary Economics*, Supplementary Series, No. 1, pp. 19–46.

McKinnon, R. 1963. 'Optimum Currency Areas'. *American Economic Review*, vol. 53, pp. 717–24.

Mundell, R. 1961. 'A Theory of Optimum Currency Areas'. *American Economic Review*, vol. 51, pp. 657–65.

Ramos, R., Clar, M. and Suriñach, J. 1999. 'Specialisation in Europe and Asymmetric Shocks: Potential Risks of EMU'. In Fischer, J. and Nijkamp, K. (eds.), *Spatial Dynamics of European Integration. Regional and Policy Issues at the Turn of the Millennium*. Berlin: Springer-Verlag.

2003. 'A Dynamic Analysis of Asymmetric Shocks in EU Manufacturing'. *Applied Economics*, vol. 35, pp. 881–92.

Ramos, R. and Suriñach, J. 2004. 'Shocking Aspects of European Enlargement'. *Eastern European Economics*, vol. 42, pp. 36–57.

Stockman, A. 1988. 'Sectoral and National Aggregate Disturbances to Industrial Output in Seven European Countries'. *Journal of Monetary Economics*, vol. 21, pp. 387–409.

7 Monetary transmission in the new Member States

*Raúl Ramos and Jordi Suriñach**

7.1 Introduction

The analysis of the monetary transmission mechanism aims to describe the channels through which monetary policy decisions are transmitted to the economy and affect policy objectives. Knowledge of the monetary transmission mechanism underpins the effective conduct of monetary policy; it allows not only selection of an adequate set of policy instruments, but also their implementation in a timely way.

There is a broad range of empirical evidence on the effects and the transmission of monetary policy for the United States, the Euro area and for most EU countries (see Ganev *et al.*, 2002; Ehrmann *et al.*, 2003; or Goodhart, 2003) using three different, well-defined methodologies:

- First, the approach known as the 'narrative method'. Following Ganev *et al.* (2002), this method consists of identifying policy shocks, developing a counterfactual (i.e. what would have happened to the outcome variables in the absence of the shock) comparing the actual with the counterfactual, and then drawing conclusions.
- Secondly, the use of structural VAR models or small- (or large-) scale macroeconomic models to analyse and quantify the existence of different effects of monetary policy on output and prices. The comparison of the responses to a monetary shock with those obtained for other countries may shed light on the existence of different transmission channels.
- Last, the use of micro data in order to analyse how the effects of the monetary policy arise. Asymmetries in the transmission of monetary policy are usually related to the characteristics of the mechanisms through which monetary policy influences the real economy and how agents (financial and non-financial firms, households etc.) behave.

* The authors wish to thank three anonymous referees, the members of the European Forecasting Network and the staff of the DG ECFIN at the European Commission for their helpful comments and suggestions. The usual disclaimer applies. Financial support is gratefully acknowledged from CICYT SEJ 2005–04348/ECON.

This chapter applies the second approach. Specifically, we aim to shed light on monetary transmission in the new Member States, comparing their transmission mechanisms with those in the Euro area using structural VAR models. Unfortunately, due to data restrictions, in this chapter we will not include Malta and Cyprus in the analysis.

The analysis of the monetary transmission in the new Member States is especially relevant because, after joining the EU, these states are expected to join the Euro area. In this context, it is important to note that asymmetries in the transmission of monetary policy in a monetary union may destabilise the business cycle, and put countries out of phase with one another in a way that cannot be corrected by deficit-constrained fiscal policies. The effect would be to delay convergence (Hughes-Hallet and Piscitelli, 1999; Kieler and Saarenhimo, 1998).

An additional aspect that makes this analysis interesting is the fact that the monetary history of the new Member States has been characterised by a wide spectrum of exchange rate regimes constantly evolving over time (Lavrac, 2003). In 2004, three countries have an inflation-targeting regime (the Czech Republic, Hungary and Poland); one has a managed floating regime (Slovakia); three countries have joined ERM-II after accession (Estonia, Lithuania and Slovenia); while one has a fixed peg to the SDR (Latvia).

It is also worth mentioning that the use of monetary policy (and the way it has been used) has not been independent from the exchange rate system adopted. The new Member States that rely on fixed exchange rates, particularly on hard pegs like currency boards, have their hands tied as far as monetary policy is concerned. On the other hand, the new Member States that opted for floating exchange rate regimes, particularly free floaters with inflation targeting, remain independent in terms of their monetary policies, with those relying on intermediate regimes, such as managed floating, somewhere in between.

For this reason, as Rusek (2001) highlights, exchange rate dynamics in the new Member States reflects not only the domestic monetary conditions, but also, to a significant degree, the capital flows, reflecting changing expectations of a future economic performance. In fact, according to Rusek (2001, p. 85), 'the conditions of transition economies cast doubts on the stability of the relationship between monetary aggregates on one side and the price level, nominal output and nominal exchange rates on the other. Whether monetary policy has an impact and plays the role under these circumstances is, therefore, an empirical question which can only be answered by data.'

In fact, due to the continuous changes experienced by these economies, the analysis of the role of monetary policy and its transmission is not an easy task. As Golinelli and Rovelli (2002) highlight, in official policy reports of some central banks during the past decade, one often encounters statements implying that 'monetary aggregates behaved unpredictably', 'the relation between money and growth was unpredictable' or 'changes in interest rates did not significantly affect in a negative way domestic demand'.[1]

Another point to take into account is that the size and sophistication of money and financial markets, and the composition and quality of bank portfolios, have improved considerably in the course of transition in the new Member States, while the productive sector has been subject to considerable restructuring (Golinelli and Rovelli, 2002). As a result, the channels of transmission are likely to have evolved somewhat, although, again, this is mainly an empirical question. Those authors obtained evidence of stability in the relationships analysed.

The rest of the chapter is structured in three sections: section 7.2 briefly summarises the literature considering monetary transmission in the new Member States; section 7.3 presents our empirical evidence on the role of monetary policy in the new Member States; and, finally, section 7.4 summarises the main findings.

7.2   Review of the empirical literature on monetary transmission in the new Member States

The objective of this section is to summarise the available evidence on monetary transmission in the new Member States.

In this context, one aspect that should be taken into account is the relationship between the exchange rate system and the level of capital controls of the country in question and the degree of monetary independence. The evolution of the different exchange rate systems in these countries is shown in Table 7.1.

Taking this into account, instead of looking at the evidence available for individual countries, we will present it in four different groups.

The first group is the Czech Republic, Hungary and Poland, three countries which have adopted a direct inflation targeting approach to guide their monetary policy (although in Hungary more than one nominal anchor is considered). Poland has a free floating exchange rate system, while the Czech Republic has a managed floating exchange rate system, and Hungary has a fixed peg, but with ±15% bands. In the three

---

[1] In this context, it is not surprising that, at the start of the transition period, many of the new Member States have not chosen to exercise an active, independent monetary policy, and instead have adopted a fixed exchange rate policy.

Table 7.1. *Official exchange rate regimes since 1994*

	Czech Republic	Estonia	Hungary	Latvia	Lithuania	Poland	Slovakia	Slovenia
1	1994–1996 Basket Peg 65% DEM, 35% USD Band ±0.5%	1992–2004 Currency board ECU/euro	1994–1996 Crawling peg 70% ECU, 30% USD Band ±2.25%	1994– Fixed Peg SDR[a] Band ±1%	1994–2002 Currency board USD	1994–1995 Crawling peg 45% USD, 35% DEM, 10% GBP, % FF, 5% SF Band ±1%	1994–1996 Basket peg 60% DEM, 40% USD Band ±1,5%	1994–2004 Managed floating
2	1996–1997 Basket Peg 65% DEM, 35% USD Band ±7.5%	2004– ERM-II	1997–1999 Crawling peg 70% DEM, 30% USD Band ±2.25%		2002–2004 Currency board euro	1995–1998 Crawling peg 45% USD, 35% DEM, 10% GBP, % FF, 5% SF Band ±7%	1997–1998 Basket peg 60% DEM, 40% USD Band ±7%	2004– ERM-II
3	1997–2001 Managed floating		2000–2001 Crawling peg 100% euro Band ±15%		2004– ERM-II	1998–1999 Crawling peg 45% USD, 35% DEM, 10% GBP, % FF, 5% SF Band ±10%	1998– Managed floating	
4	2001–2002 Free floating		2001– Fixed Peg euro Band ±15%			1999–2000 Crawling peg 45% USD, 55% EUR Band ±7%		
5	2002– Managed floating					2000– Free floating		

Notes: [a] SDR is a basket of currencies, including the USD, the euro, the yen and the pound sterling.

Source: Data compiled from Frömmel and Schobert (2003) and IMF, Annual Report on Exchange Rate Arrangements and Exchange Restrictions, various issues.

countries, we should expect a high degree of autonomy in the conduct of monetary policy.

The second group is formed by Slovakia alone. This country uses the exchange rate as a nominal anchor for monetary policy, and its exchange rate system is a managed floating one. It is worth mentioning that in Slovakia various indicators are monitored in order to conduct the monetary policy. In this case, the ability to use discretionary monetary policy would be similar to the previous case, although slightly more limited.

The third group comprises Estonia, Lithuania and Slovenia, countries that joined ERM-II after accession. In fact, before acceding, Estonia and Lithuania introduced a currency board in order to obtain price stability by eliminating the (money-supply-related) domestic sources of inflation, while Slovenia opted for managed floating. In the former two countries, there was no active monetary policy under the currency board arrangement. This means that exogenous changes in interest rates or money supply did not arise from monetary policy. In fact, once the currency board is in place, fluctuations in the nominal exchange rate become external shocks to which the system adjusts automatically.

Lastly, the situation in Latvia is different, as this country adopted a fixed peg with the SDR. However, under this exchange rate arrangement, the role of monetary policy is also very limited.

Figure 7.1 summarises the interactions between the exchange rate system, capital controls and monetary independence in these countries.

There are only a few works that have considered the role of monetary transmission mechanisms in the new Member States. The most relevant ones in this context are Golinelli and Rovelli (2002), Ganev *et al.* (2002), Korhonen (2002), Lavrac (2003) and Coricelli *et al.* (2003).

Generally speaking, a common result in these works is that there is no evidence of a clear monetary transmission mechanism in the new Member States. Most of the studies find some link between market interest rates (those influenced or set by central banks) and commercial banks' deposit and lending rates. However, this link is usually very weak. In fact, most studies generally do not find a significant relationship between monetary variables and inflation or GDP, although the role of the interest rate and exchange rate channels has been highlighted for most of the countries considered.

In particular, the evidence available for the Czech Republic and Poland shows that monetary transmission may be quite similar to that found in other Euro-area countries operating through both the interest rate and the exchange rate channels. The evidence for Hungary also highlights the role of both channels, although the exchange rate seems to be more important in relative terms.

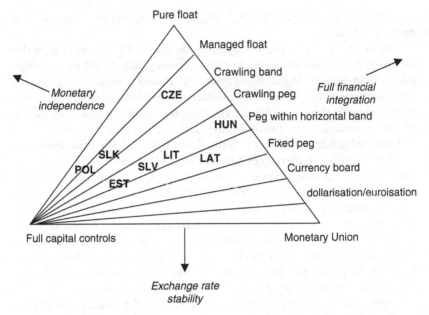

Figure 7.1. The exchange rate system, capital controls and monetary policy independence (adapted from Dean, 2003).

In Slovakia and Slovenia, there is clear evidence of an exchange rate channel, while it seems that the interest rate channel of monetary policy remains blocked. In this context, the monetary authorities should pursue further de-indexation of the financial contracts and be ready to use interest rates to defend the currency and fight inflation. For example, Festi (2001) defends the use of open market policy instruments by the Slovenian central bank. Indeed, he stresses that this would allow a permanent flow of money between commercial banks and the central bank that would permit the sending of signals to the money market. In fact, shifting to a balanced conduct of monetary policy that also relies on the interest rate channel in a de-indexed economy environment would contribute to preparing the financial sector for the ECB policy-operating environment, where monetary policy is implemented and transmitted primarily through interest rates (Suardi, 2001), and only to a minor extent through the exchange rate (Angeloni *et al.*, 2003b).

The results for Estonia show evidence of the interest rate and credit channels, but not of the exchange rate channel. In Lithuania, the interest rate and exchange rate channels have been effective in the transmission of monetary policy. According to Vetlov (2001), the reasons for the existence of an exchange rate channel for Lithuania but not for Estonia are the presence in Lithuania of the dollar as the anchor currency and the relatively high level of trade between Lithuania and Russia.

Lastly, the evidence for Latvia is not as clear. Babich (2001) suggests that the monetary transmission in Latvia works through the interest rate and credit channels but not through the exchange rate channel. However, Ganev *et al.* (2002) provide evidence in favour of the interest rate and exchange rate channels (although these results are probably due to the instability of the Latvian equations in their model).

In section 7.3, we will use structural VAR models in order to analyse the role of monetary policy in the new Member States using a homogeneous approach and a common database.

7.3   Empirical evidence

7.3.1   Methodology and data

In this section, different VAR models will be used in order to assess the dynamics of the relationships between output, prices, interest rates, money and the exchange rate in the framework of the monetary transmission literature. As in Morsink and Bayoumi (2001), we choose this methodology in preference to the alternatives mentioned above, because it allows us to place minimal restrictions on how monetary shocks affect the economy. In fact, it explicitly recognises the simultaneity between monetary policy and macroeconomic developments (reaction function) as well as the dependence of economic variables on monetary policy. Moreover, as Garbuza (2003, p. 26) highlights, 'it is the most widely used tool in the literature for the analysis of monetary transmission mechanisms', so the results obtained can be easily compared with the ones obtained by other authors for different countries.

As regards the data, it is important to take into account the structural changes in the new Member States and the fact that the quality of the data at the beginning of the transition period for some countries is not comparable to that in Euro-area countries. For these reasons, the period considered for the analysis here starts in 1993 (or 1995) and the countries considered are the following: the Czech Republic, Estonia, Hungary, Latvia, Lithuania, Poland, Slovakia and Slovenia.[2] The calculations in this section use quarterly or monthly data obtained from the OECD's Main Economic Indicators, the IMF's International Financial Statistics

---

[2] As mentioned above, Malta and Cyprus are not included in the analysis, due to data restrictions.

and the European Central Bank data set and different national sources. Table 7.2 provides detailed information on the data set considered. All data have been previously deseasonalised and outliers corrected using Tramo/Seats.

7.3.2   *Monetary transmission in the Euro area*

The basic specification   In order to analyse the peculiarities of the monetary transmission in the new Member States, we first specify and estimate a benchmark VAR model to assess the effects of a monetary policy shock in the Euro area.

The specified VAR model for the Euro area, following Peersman and Smets (2003), is the following:

$$
\begin{bmatrix} y_t^{EA} \\ p_t^{EA} \\ m_t^{EA} \\ s_t^{EA} \\ x_t^{EA} \end{bmatrix} = A(L). \begin{bmatrix} y_{t-1}^{EA} \\ p_{t-1}^{EA} \\ m_{t-1}^{EA} \\ s_{t-1}^{EA} \\ x_{t-1}^{EA} \end{bmatrix} + B. \begin{bmatrix} cp_t^{W} \\ y_t^{US} \\ s_t^{US} \end{bmatrix} + U_t^{EA} \tag{1}
$$

where y_t^{EA} denotes Euro area real GDP, p_t^{EA} consumer prices, m_t^{EA} broad money, s_t^{EA} the short-term interest rate and x_t^{EA} the real effective exchange rate. cp_t^{W} is a world commodity price index, y_t^{US} the US real GDP and s_t^{US} the short-term interest rate in the US.[3,4]

The inclusion of cp_t^{W}, y_t^{US} and s_t^{US} helps to solve the so-called 'price puzzle'.[5] The effect of these exogenous variables on the Euro area endogenous variables is assumed to be contemporaneous. By treating these variables as exogenous, it is implicitly assumed that there is no feedback from the Euro area variables to the world and US variables.

The monetary policy shock is identified through a standard Cholesky decomposition with the variables ordered as in (1). The underlying assumption is that policy shocks have no contemporaneous impact on output, prices and money, but may have a contemporaneous effect immediately. However, the interest rate does not respond contemporaneously

---

[3] As in Peersman and Smets (2003), monetary aggregates are included in the specification due to the prominence assigned to them by a number of central banks included in the study.

[4] When appropriate, different dummy variables have been included in order to control for 'known' structural breaks.

[5] The empirical finding in the literature is that prices rise following an interest rate tightening (see, for example, Sims, 1992).

Table 7.2. *Data availability for the Euro area and the new Member States*

Quarterly Data	Real GDP	Consumer prices	Short-term interest rate	Money	Real effective exchange rate	Surplus/deficit	Private final consumption expenditure	Gross fixed capital formation	Net exports of goods and services
Main source	OECD Quarterly National Accounts	OECD Main Economic Indicators	IMF International Financial Statistics	IMF International Financial Statistics	OECD Main Economic Indicators	IMF International Financial Statistics	OECD Quarterly National Accounts		
Euro area	1985:1–2003:2	1985:1–2003:2	1985:1–2003:2	1985:1–2003:2	1985:1–2003:2	–	1985:1–2003:2	1985:1–2003:2	1985:1–2003:2
Czech Republic	1994:1–2003:2	1991:1–2003:2	1993:1–2003:2	1992:1–2003:2	1993:1–2003:2	1993:1–2003:2	1994:1–2003:2	1994:1–2003:2	1994:1–2003:2
Estonia	1993:1–2003:2	1991:1–2003:2	1993:2–2003:2	1993:1–2003:2	1996:1–2003:2	–	1993:1–2003:2	1993:1–2003:2	1993:1–2003:2
Hungary	1995:1–2003:2	1985:1–2003:2	1985:1–2003:2	1990:4–2003:2	1985:1–2003:2	1997:1–2003:2	2000:1–2003:2	1995:1–2003:2	1995:1–2003:2
Latvia	1991:1–2003:2	1992:3–2003:2	1993:3–2003:2	1993:1–2003:2	1996:1–2003:2	1996:1–2003:2	1995:1–2003:2	1995:1–2003:2	1995:1–2003:2
Lithuania	1995:1–2003:2	1991:1–2003:2	1993:1–2003:2	1993:1–2003:2	1993:3–2003:2	1999:1–2003:2	1993:1–2003:2	1993:1–2003:2	1993:1–2003:2
Poland	1995:1–2003:2	1995:1–2003:2	1989:4–2003:2	1996:4–2003:2	1985:1–2003:2	1996:1–2003:2	1995:1–2003:2	1995:1–2003:2	1995:1–2003:2
Slovakia	1993:1–2003:2	1991:1–2003:2	1993:1–2003:2	1990:1–2003:2	1990:1–2003:2	2001:1–2003:2	1993:1–2003:2	1993:1–2003:2	1993:1–2003:2
Slovenia	1992:1–2003:2	1991:1–2003:2	1991:4–2003:2	1992:1–2003:2	1992:1–2003:2	1993:1–2003:2	1999:1–2003:2	1999:1–2003:2	1999:1–2003:2

Monthly Data	Industrial production index	Consumer prices	Short-term interest rate	Money	Real effective exchange rate	Deficit/deficit
Main source	*OECD MEI/IMF IFS*	*OECD Main Economic Indicators*	*IMF International Financial Statistics*	*IMF International Financial Statistics*	*OECD Main Economic Indicators*	*IMF International Financial Statistics*
Euro area	1990:1–2003:6	1990:1–2003:6	1990:1–2003:6	1990:1–2003:6	1990:1–2003:6	–
Czech Republic	1992:1–2003:6	1993:1–2003:6	1993:1–2003:6	1993:1–2003:6	1996:1–2003:6	1993:1–2003:6
Estonia	1994:1–2003:6	1992:1–2003:6	1993:2–2003:6	1992:6–2003:6	1990:1–2003:6	–
Hungary	1990:1–2003:6	1990:1–2003:6	1990:1–2003:6	1990:3–2003:6	1990:1–2003:6	1997:1–2003:2
Latvia	1996:1–2003:6	1992:1–2003:6	1993:7–2003:6	1993:6–2003:6	1996:1–2003:6	1996:1–2003:2
Lithuania	1997:1–2003:6	1992:5–2003:6	1992:12–2003:6	1993:1–2003:6	1993:7–2003:6	1999:1–2003:2
Poland	1990:1–2003:6	1990:1–2003:6	1990:1–2003:6	1990:1–2003:6	1990:1–2003:6	1997:1–2003:2
Slovakia	1992:1–2003:6	1993:1–2003:6	1993:1–2003:6	1993:1–2003:6	1990:1–2003:6	–
Slovenia	1991:1–2003:6	1992:1–2003:6	1993:1–2003:6	1991:12–2003:6	1992:1–2003:6	1993:1–2003:2

to changes in the effective exchange rate.[6] We think this assumption is valid, since the Euro area (as a whole) is a large and relatively closed economy (Peersman and Smets, 2003).[7]

The model has been estimated in levels[8] using quarterly data, which implicitly allows for cointegrating relationships among the variables under consideration (Ramaswamy and Slok, 1998). We stress that this specification is necessarily simple in order to allow comparisons with those of the new Member States. As stated above, the information available for the new Member States for most macroeconomic series dates back only to the early 1990s; as the time period considered is quite short, an explicit analysis of the long-run behaviour of the variables considered is not possible. The lag order of the VAR model is determined using the Schwarz criterion and is usually between order one and three when using different samples.

Extensions of the basic specification   In this section, we specify three different VAR models that would provide empirical evidence on the influence of a monetary policy shock on other macroeconomic variables that have not been included in the basic model. In particular, we consider the effects of a monetary policy shock on various components of GDP: private consumption, gross fixed capital formation and net trade of goods and services.

The impact of a monetary shock on GDP components is interesting from the point of view of policy analysis. The analysis of the reactions of consumption, investment and net exports across different countries provides useful information for identifying the most relevant transmission channels and, also, which agents are more affected by expansionary or contractionary monetary policies.

---

[6] The economics behind this identification scheme have been widely analysed in the literature on VARs and monetary policy. See, for example, Sims (1992).

[7] Apart from this recursive identification strategy, there are other alternative identification schemes to identify monetary policy shocks (see, for example, Ramaswamy and Slok, 1998). For example, we could allow for a contemporaneous interaction between the short-term interest rate and the exchange rate using a structural VAR model (as in Sims and Zha, 1998 or Peersman and Smets, 2003), or we could combine short and long restrictions as in Galí (1992) or Gerlach and Smets (1995). We tested some of these alternative identification schemes and the results were quite similar to the ones shown here, although in some cases there were problems of convergence when estimating the structural decomposition, probably due to the small number of observations available. These results are available from the authors on request.

[8] We also estimated a VAR model including GDP year-on-year growth rate, the inflation rate, the monetary aggregate year-on-year growth rate, the interest rate and the real effective exchange rate year-on-year growth rate. The results were quite similar to those obtained with the variables in levels and are available from the authors on request.

With this aim, three different alternatives are considered:

- First, GDP is replaced in model (1) by the variable of interest (for example, consumption or investment) applying the same ordering as before in the Cholesky decomposition.
- Secondly, the variable of interest is subtracted from total GDP and is placed second in model (1).[9] As before, the Cholesky decomposition is applied using this ordering.
- Thirdly, model (1) is augmented with the macroeconomic variable of interest (for example, consumption or investment).[10] With this ordering, when applying the Cholesky decomposition, we assume that the macroeconomic variable of interest does not affect the block of endogenous variables in each of the models.

The three strategies yielded very similar results. Here we present the results using the second strategy, since it permits interactions between the GDP component considered and the others. As before, the models are estimated in levels,[11] and the lag length is determined using the Schwarz criterion.

Results   The results of the impulse response functions of the VAR models for the Euro area, using data from 1985:1 to 2003:2, are shown in Figure 7.2.[12,13] Specifically, the first part of the figure summarises the effects of a one-standard deviation monetary policy shock[14] on real GDP, consumer prices, the real effective exchange rate and the short-term interest rate. The second part shows the impact of the monetary policy shock for each of the components of the GDP (consumption, investment and net exports) calculated using different augmented VAR models.[15]

---

[9] See Morsink and Bayoumi (2001).
[10] A similar approach can be found in Peersman and Smets (2001) and Mojon and Peersman (2001).
[11] See footnote 7 above.
[12] As a previous step to the estimation of the VAR models, we analysed the degree of integrability of the different variables using the Dickey-Fuller and Augmented Dickey-Fuller tests. In most cases, the hypothesis of I(0) is rejected in favour of I(1). The results are available from the authors on request.
[13] The stability of the results has been checked using different samples. The obtained impulse response functions were quite similar and are available from the authors on request.
[14] The standard deviation of monetary policy shocks has usually been used to simulate the effects of monetary policy as it represents the 'average' monetary policy shock in the country considered for the given period. Of course, other alternatives exist, but this approach has become the 'standard' in the VAR literature. One criticism pointed out by Bagliano and Favero (1998) is that the standard deviation of monetary policy shocks depends on the specification used. However, as they acknowledge, the impulse response functions estimated using different definitions are not substantially different from each other.
[15] The responses of the other variables in the models are not shown as they are quite similar to those shown in the first part of the figures, but are available from the authors on request.

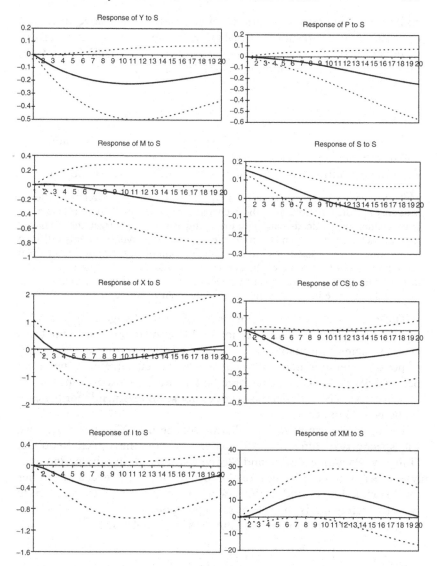

Figure 7.2. Impulse-response functions for the Euro area (1985:1–2003:2).

The impulse response patterns in this figure are broadly in line with standard results in the literature (Adao *et al.*, 2003). Specifically, after an unexpected increase in the short-term interest rate, there is a real appreciation of the exchange rate, and a temporary reduction of output, prices and money. The response patterns of consumption and investment are quite similar to the response of real GDP. However, the effect on investment is considerably higher than the response of real GDP. In contrast, the response of consumption is weaker and slower.

7.3.3   Monetary transmission in the new Member States

The VAR models   In the extensive mid-1990s literature on measuring monetary policy shocks using VAR models, the exchange rate was usually omitted from the analysis. As Smets (1997) points out:

> while the neglect of the exchange rate may be justified for a large relatively closed economy like the United States, the exchange rate plays a prominent role in more open economies. Indeed many countries find it useful to target the exchange rate. In such a regime, domestic monetary policy shocks will be mainly reflected in exchange rate innovations. More generally, monetary authorities in open economies may offset some of the contemporaneous exchange rate shocks they face because the shocks significantly affect the economy, again suggesting a role for a exchange rate in the measurement of the policy stance.

The point here is that the inclusion of the exchange rate in a VAR model complicates the identification problem. As in the case of the Euro area, it seems reasonable to assume that the interest rate does not respond contemporaneously to changes in the effective exchange rate, because we are dealing with large and relatively closed economies.[16] However, this kind of assumption does not seem reasonable for the case of the new Member States.

Taking into account the peculiarities of the new Member States, we will specify two different VAR models: one for the Czech Republic, Hungary, Poland, Slovakia and Slovenia where, during the period analysed, there was a certain degree of monetary independence, and another for Estonia, Latvia and Lithuania where the adopted exchange rate system severely limits the role of monetary policy.

The model for the first set of countries is the following:

$$
\begin{bmatrix} y_t^A \\ p_t^A \\ x_t^A \\ m_t^A \\ s_t^A \end{bmatrix} = A(L) \cdot \begin{bmatrix} y_{t-1}^A \\ p_{t-1}^A \\ x_{t-1}^A \\ m_{t-1}^A \\ s_{t-1}^A \end{bmatrix} + B \cdot \begin{bmatrix} y_t^{EA} \\ p_t^{EA} \\ s_t^{EA} \end{bmatrix} + U_t^A \tag{2}
$$

---

[16] Morsink and Bayoumi (2001) apply a similar reasoning for the case of Japan.

where, y_t^A denotes real GDP, p_t^A consumer prices, x_t^A the real effective exchange rate, m_t^A the quantity of money, and s_t^A the short-term interest rate for the considered new Member State. As before, y_t^{EA} is the real GDP in the Euro area, p_t^{EA} is the level of prices in the Euro area, and s_t^{EA} is the short-term interest rate in the Euro area.[17]

The model for the second set of countries is the following:

$$
\begin{bmatrix} s_t^{EA} \\ y_t^A \\ p_t^A \\ m_t^A \\ s_t^A \end{bmatrix} = A(L) \cdot \begin{bmatrix} s_{t-1}^{EA} \\ y_{t-1}^A \\ p_{t-1}^A \\ m_{t-1}^A \\ s_{t-1}^A \end{bmatrix} + B \cdot \begin{bmatrix} x_t^A \\ y_t^{EA} \\ p_t^{EA} \end{bmatrix} + U_t^A
\tag{3}
$$

where s_t^{EA} denotes the short-term interest rate in the Euro area,[18] y_t^A real GDP, p_t^A consumer prices, m_t^A the quantity of money and s_t^A the short-term interest rate for the country considered. As before, x_t^A is the real effective exchange rate for the considered new Member State, y_t^{EA} is the real GDP in the Euro area, and p_t^{EA} is the level of prices in the Euro area.

For the Czech Republic, Hungary, Poland, Slovakia and Slovenia, the monetary policy shock is identified through a standard Cholesky decomposition with the variables ordered as in (2).[19] This means that there is a contemporaneous impact of all the endogenous variables on the monetary policy variables. On the other hand, there is no immediate impact of a monetary policy shock on the other variables (Mojon and Peersman, 2003).

For Estonia, Latvia and Lithuania, the monetary policy shock is identified through a standard Cholesky decomposition with the variables ordered as in (3). This approach is similar to that applied for Estonia in

[17] Instead of including y_t^{EA}, p_t^{EA} and s_t^{EA}, we have also included the corresponding variables for the United States, y_t^{US}, p_t^{US} and s_t^{US}. The results were quite similar to the ones shown here and are available from the authors on request.

[18] It is worth mentioning that the introduction of the Euro-area interest rate in these models as an endogenous variable could be controversial as it is clear that the economic and monetary conditions of these countries have had little (or no) influence on its evolution. However, due to their exchange rate systems, macroeconomic variables in the new Member States have clearly reacted to Euro-area monetary conditions. In a VAR framework, the only possibility to analyse the reaction of these variables through impulse response functions is by including the Euro-area interest rate as an endogenous variable. In any case, the ordering of the variables in the Cholesky decomposition mitigates the problem.

[19] Garbuza (2003) applies a similar approach for the case of Poland.

the structural model by Pikkani (2001) and Lättemäe and Pikkani (2001).[20]

In both cases, as before, and in order to consider the effects of a monetary policy shock on various components of GDP (private consumption, gross fixed capital formation and net trade of goods and services), models (2) and (3) are augmented with the macroeconomic variable of interest using a strategy similar to that applied for the Euro area. The different VAR models for the new Member States are estimated in levels[21] using quarterly data from 1993:1 (or 1995:1) up to 2002:2.[22,23] The lag length is determined using the Schwarz criterion (usually between one and three).

Results   The results of the impulse response functions of the VAR models for the new Member States are shown in Figures 7.3 to 7.10. As in Figure 7.3, the first part summarises the effects of a one-standard deviation monetary policy shock on real GDP, consumer prices, the real effective exchange rate and the short-term interest rate, while the second part shows the impact of the monetary policy shock for each of the components of the GDP (consumption, investment and net exports).

Following Morsink and Bayoumi (2001), and to gain an idea of the share of fluctuations in output and prices caused by different shocks, the table at the bottom of each figure shows the results of calculating variance decomposition at forecast horizons of one to four years. The

---

[20] The different specification for these countries is related to the discussion in the previous section about the different exchange rate systems. Of course, other differences between countries such as the financial (Carlino and DeFina, 1998a, 1998b, 1999) or the legal structure (Cecchetti, 1999) could play an important role in explaining differences in the transmission of monetary policy, and are not explicitly considered in this chapter. However, it is worth mentioning that, although the degree of financial development is surely relevant in the two steps of monetary transmission (from policy variables to market interest rates, loans etc., and from financial conditions to real activity), some authors have stressed that it would be more relevant for the first step than for the second (see Cecchetti, 1999). Moreover, other authors such as Carlino and DeFina (1998a, 1999) have found evidence that the effects of the banking system are clearly interrelated with other variables such as the average size of firms or the predominance of more interest-rate-sensitive sectors such as manufacturing or building. Further research would focus on these two aspects.

[21] We have also estimated a VAR model including all variables except interest rates as year-on-year growth rates. The results were quite similar to those obtained with the variables in levels and are available from the authors on request.

[22] See footnote 14 above.

[23] All the models have also been estimated on monthly data (see Table 7.2) where total GDP is replaced by industrial production. Unless indicated, the results obtained are similar to the ones shown here and are available from the authors on request.

second column of each sub-table gives the forecast error of the variable for each forecast horizon.[24] A higher relative influence of each kind of shock could be interpreted as evidence of a higher relevance of the associated transmission channel: the interest rate channel or the exchange rate channel.

In most cases, the impulse response functions observed are broadly in line with the results found for the Euro area, in that an unexpected increase in the short-term interest rate, followed by a real appreciation of the exchange rate, temporarily reduces output and prices. However, it is worth mentioning that confidence bands around the estimates of the responses to the monetary policy shock are very high, probably due to the short time period considered. For this reason, as we highlight in section 7.4, the results should be treated with some caution; in some cases, differences across countries are likely to be non-significant.

In the Czech Republic (Figure 7.3), the response of GDP and prices is very low and, in the case of prices, is only negative eight quarters after the initial shock. The reactions of consumption and investment are very similar to those observed for overall GDP. As regards the results of the variance decomposition of output and prices, the relative contribution of interest rates in explaining the variance of output and prices is very high (more than 50% after two years of the initial shock) while the relative contribution of the exchange rate is also relevant in the case of prices (around 20%). These results can be interpreted as evidence of the importance of both these transmission channels in this country.

In Hungary (Figure 7.4), the reaction of both real GDP and prices is faster than in the Euro area (only three or four quarters after the shock). However, the effects are not as persistent as in the Czech Republic. In contrast with the results of previous authors, the variance decomposition of output and prices shows that the interest rate is the major transmission channel, with a relative contribution of around 30% after two years of the initial shock for both output and prices.

The results for Poland are shown in Figure 7.5. Due to the high uncertainty surrounding the estimates of the impulse response function, we re-estimated the model using monthly data. The results (available on request) indicate that the patterns observed for the impulse response functions are quite close to those observed for the Euro area, with the sole exception that the response of real GDP is much faster than in the

---

[24] As indicated by Morsink and Bayoumi (2001), the source of the forecast error is the variation in the current and future values of the innovations to each variable in the VAR model.

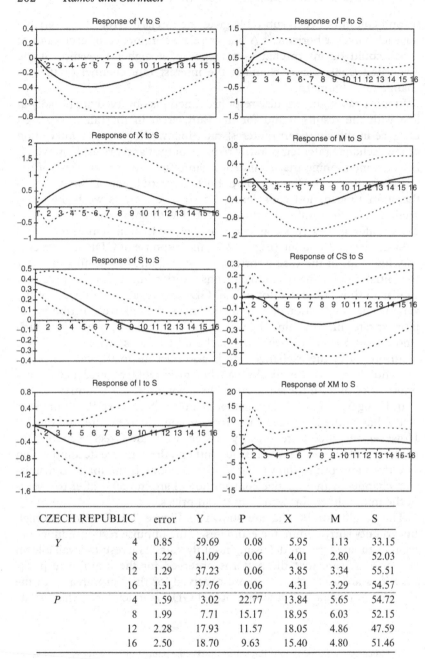

CZECH REPUBLIC	error	Y	P	X	M	S
Y	4	0.85	59.69	0.08	5.95	1.13	33.15
	8	1.22	41.09	0.06	4.01	2.80	52.03
	12	1.29	37.23	0.06	3.85	3.34	55.51
	16	1.31	37.76	0.06	4.31	3.29	54.57
P	4	1.59	3.02	22.77	13.84	5.65	54.72
	8	1.99	7.71	15.17	18.95	6.03	52.15
	12	2.28	17.93	11.57	18.05	4.86	47.59
	16	2.50	18.70	9.63	15.40	4.80	51.46

Figure 7.3. Impulse-response functions for the Czech Republic (1994:1–2003:2).

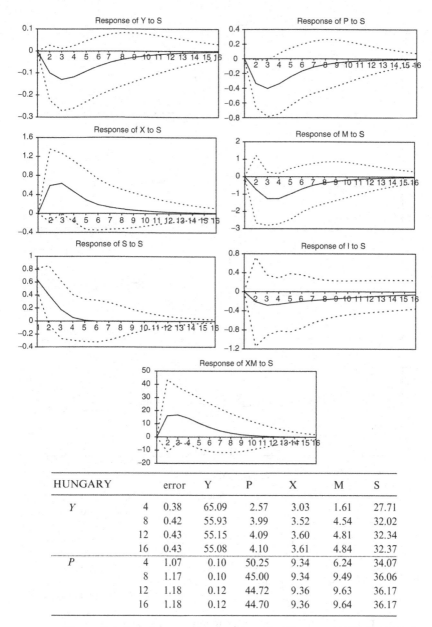

HUNGARY	error	Y	P	X	M	S
Y	4	0.38	65.09	2.57	3.03	1.61	27.71
	8	0.42	55.93	3.99	3.52	4.54	32.02
	12	0.43	55.15	4.09	3.60	4.81	32.34
	16	0.43	55.08	4.10	3.61	4.84	32.37
P	4	1.07	0.10	50.25	9.34	6.24	34.07
	8	1.17	0.10	45.00	9.34	9.49	36.06
	12	1.18	0.12	44.72	9.36	9.63	36.17
	16	1.18	0.12	44.70	9.36	9.64	36.17

Figure 7.4. Impulse-response functions for Hungary (1985:4–2003:2).

204   *Ramos and Suriñach*

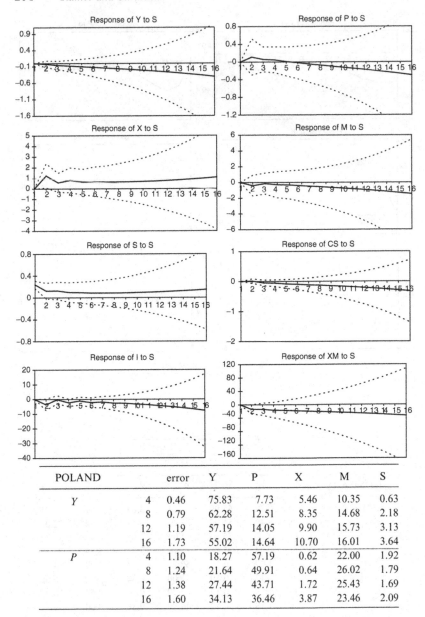

POLAND		error	Y	P	X	M	S
Y	4	0.46	75.83	7.73	5.46	10.35	0.63
	8	0.79	62.28	12.51	8.35	14.68	2.18
	12	1.19	57.19	14.05	9.90	15.73	3.13
	16	1.73	55.02	14.64	10.70	16.01	3.64
P	4	1.10	18.27	57.19	0.62	22.00	1.92
	8	1.24	21.64	49.91	0.64	26.02	1.79
	12	1.38	27.44	43.71	1.72	25.43	1.69
	16	1.60	34.13	36.46	3.87	23.46	2.09

Figure 7.5. Impulse-response functions for Poland (1996:4–2003:2).

Euro area. The results of the variance decomposition highlight the relevance of the interest rate channel (directly and through money) in the transmission of monetary policy while the exchange rate channel does not seem to be very important. This finding may be related to the strategy of Poland's central bank before adopting an inflation-targeting regime.

The results for Slovakia (Figure 7.6) are different from those mentioned above: the reaction of real GDP is the opposite of what would be expected after a contractionary monetary policy shock. The reason for this movement is the impact of the shock on the exchange rate and the effects on consumption and investment, which, surprisingly, increase after the shock. The results are better behaved when the model is estimated using monthly data,[25] but the 'exchange rate puzzle' still persists. A possible explanation may be the high level of foreign direct investment during this period in the country considered, a kind of investment which is related not only to domestic monetary conditions but also to global economic developments. As regards the transmission channels, as in Kuijs (2002) or Ganev et al. (2002), the results from the model suggest that the most important transmission channel is the exchange rate channel, while the impact of broad money changes and interest rates changes seems to be modest.

The results for Slovenia (Figure 7.7) are quite similar to those for Slovakia: the responses of GDP and the exchange rate to a monetary shock are the opposite of those expected. As mentioned above, and according to Caprirolo and Lavrac (2003), the main characteristic of monetary policy in Slovenia has been the monetary authorities' preference for using non-market arrangements to price monetary policy instruments, including capital controls, in order to minimise the costs of implementing monetary policies. This has resulted in a policy framework that is vulnerable to exchange rate shocks, as the interest rate channel of monetary policy remains blocked. The results of the variance decomposition confirm this: the relative contribution of interest rates to output and prices is below 1%, while the role of the exchange rate is clearly important (more than 25% in both cases after two years).

In Estonia (Figure 7.8), the reaction of GDP and prices to a monetary shock is very fast, although the magnitude of these effects is small and they are short-lived. This result is in line with those reported by Pikkani (2001) and Lättemäe and Pikkani (2001). There is no clear evidence of the presence of a well-defined interest rate or exchange rate channel.

---

[25] This aspect has also been highlighted by Kutan and Brada (2000).

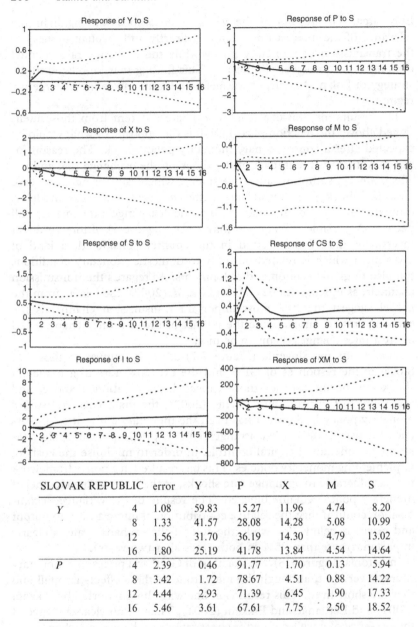

SLOVAK REPUBLIC	error	Y	P	X	M	S
Y	4	1.08	59.83	15.27	11.96	4.74	8.20
	8	1.33	41.57	28.08	14.28	5.08	10.99
	12	1.56	31.70	36.19	14.30	4.79	13.02
	16	1.80	25.19	41.78	13.84	4.54	14.64
P	4	2.39	0.46	91.77	1.70	0.13	5.94
	8	3.42	1.72	78.67	4.51	0.88	14.22
	12	4.44	2.93	71.39	6.45	1.90	17.33
	16	5.46	3.61	67.61	7.75	2.50	18.52

Figure 7.6. Impulse-response functions for Slovakia (1993:1–2003:2).

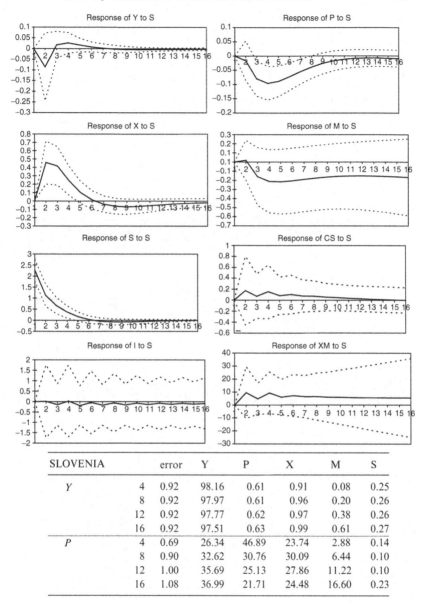

SLOVENIA		error	Y	P	X	M	S
Y	4	0.92	98.16	0.61	0.91	0.08	0.25
	8	0.92	97.97	0.61	0.96	0.20	0.26
	12	0.92	97.77	0.62	0.97	0.38	0.26
	16	0.92	97.51	0.63	0.99	0.61	0.27
P	4	0.69	26.34	46.89	23.74	2.88	0.14
	8	0.90	32.62	30.76	30.09	6.44	0.10
	12	1.00	35.69	25.13	27.86	11.22	0.10
	16	1.08	36.99	21.71	24.48	16.60	0.23

Figure 7.7. Impulse-response functions for Slovenia (1993:1–2003:2).

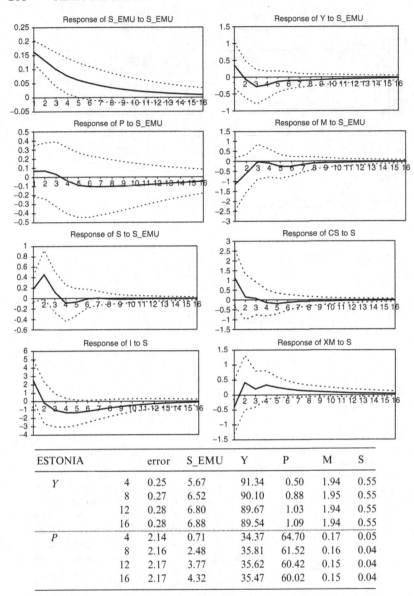

ESTONIA		error	S_EMU	Y	P	M	S
Y	4	0.25	5.67	91.34	0.50	1.94	0.55
	8	0.27	6.52	90.10	0.88	1.95	0.55
	12	0.28	6.80	89.67	1.03	1.94	0.55
	16	0.28	6.88	89.54	1.09	1.94	0.55
P	4	2.14	0.71	34.37	64.70	0.17	0.05
	8	2.16	2.48	35.81	61.52	0.16	0.04
	12	2.17	3.77	35.62	60.42	0.15	0.04
	16	2.17	4.32	35.47	60.02	0.15	0.04

Figure 7.8. Impulse-response functions for Estonia (1996:1–2003:2).

The results for Latvia (Figure 7.9) show a clear response of prices to a monetary shock but monetary policy does not seem to have clear effects on output. In fact, the reaction of the domestic interest rate, in the opposite direction to the Euro-area monetary policy shock, may explain the positive reaction of consumption and investment and, as a result, of real GDP. The results of the variance decomposition provide support for the view that monetary transmission in Latvia works through interest rate and credit channels.

As in Vetlov (2001), the results for Lithuania (Figure 7.10) show clear effects of monetary policy on output, but less clear effects on prices. In fact, the response of prices is the opposite of that expected, but is probably not significantly different from zero. As regards GDP components, investment is much more sensitive than consumption to the interest rate shock, as in the Euro area. As regards the transmission channels, the 'direct' interest rate channel seems to have been effective during the period considered.

Summarising, we conclude that monetary policy has been effective in fighting inflation or in stabilising output in nearly all the new Member States considered due to the importance of the interest rate channel – in some cases in combination with the exchange rate channel. The only exceptions are Slovakia and Slovenia (Figures 7.6 and 7.7).

Extension of the basic results

THE INTERACTIONS BETWEEN MONETARY AND FISCAL POLICY There is extensive literature on the interaction between fiscal and monetary policy, from the theoretical perspective (Chari and Kehoe, 1999). However, this issue is not addressed in this section. Specifically, the objective of the chapter is to test empirically whether the interaction between fiscal and monetary policies is relevant for the new Member States.[26,27] In fact, in the past, decisions to loosen fiscal policy have been accompanied by a tightening in monetary policy to fight inflation. In some countries, most notably in Poland but also in Hungary, this mix of monetary and fiscal policies led to a large inflow of foreign speculative portfolio that reduced the availability of domestic credit and investment. Moreover, as Ganev et al. (2002) highlight, 'during transition, the institutions which are important for the effectiveness of monetary policy are underdeveloped

---

[26] This issue will be analysed in more detailed in chapter 8 in the context of the sustainability of fiscal deficits.

[27] One disadvantage of this empirical approach is that it does not provide any insight into the economics behind this interaction. Further research will devote more attention to this issue.

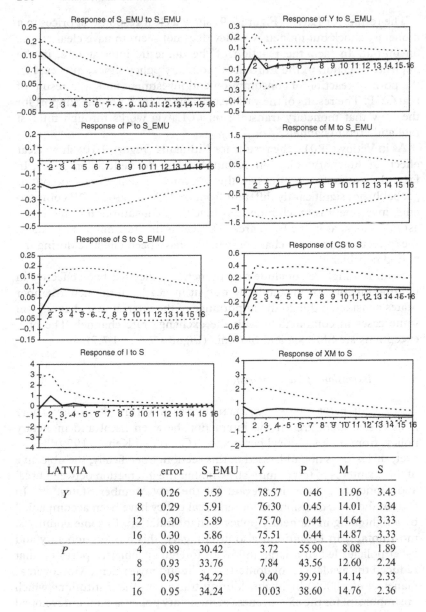

LATVIA		error	S_EMU	Y	P	M	S
Y	4	0.26	5.59	78.57	0.46	11.96	3.43
	8	0.29	5.91	76.30	0.45	14.01	3.34
	12	0.30	5.89	75.70	0.44	14.64	3.33
	16	0.30	5.86	75.51	0.44	14.87	3.33
P	4	0.89	30.42	3.72	55.90	8.08	1.89
	8	0.93	33.76	7.84	43.56	12.60	2.24
	12	0.95	34.22	9.40	39.91	14.14	2.33
	16	0.95	34.24	10.03	38.60	14.76	2.36

Figure 7.9. Impulse-response functions for Latvia (1996:1–2003:2).

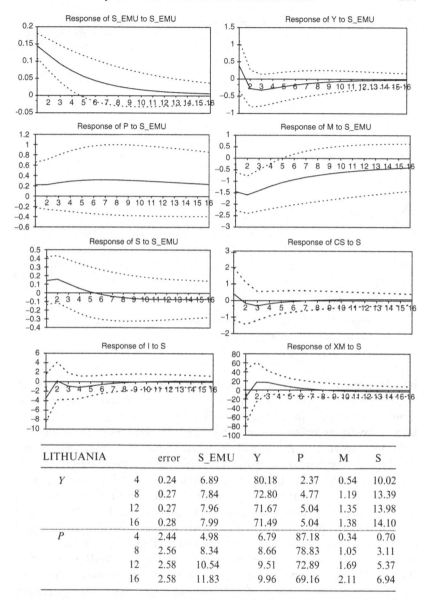

LITHUANIA		error	S_EMU	Y	P	M	S
Y	4	0.24	6.89	80.18	2.37	0.54	10.02
	8	0.27	7.84	72.80	4.77	1.19	13.39
	12	0.27	7.96	71.67	5.04	1.35	13.98
	16	0.28	7.99	71.49	5.04	1.38	14.10
P	4	2.44	4.98	6.79	87.18	0.34	0.70
	8	2.56	8.34	8.66	78.83	1.05	3.11
	12	2.58	10.54	9.51	72.89	1.69	5.37
	16	2.58	11.83	9.96	69.16	2.11	6.94

Figure 7.10. Impulse-response functions for Lithuania (1995: 1–2003:2).

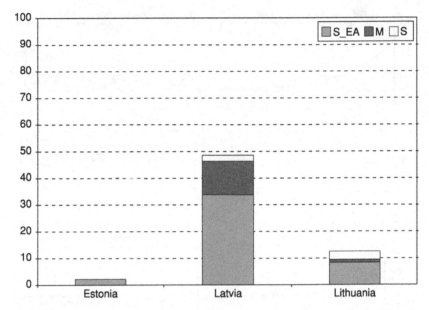

Figure 7.11. Variance decomposition of prices two years after the shock (Estonia, Latvia and Lithuania).

by definition, while processes hampering monetary transmission (budget deficits, bad loans) may be very strong or even dominant at times. This environment may even force the monetary authority itself into inconsistent actions, decreasing their effectiveness even further.'

In order to analyse the role of the interactions between monetary and fiscal policy in monetary transmission,[28] we have re-estimated model (3) for Hungary and Poland, introducing their fiscal deficit as an exogenous variable. In this regard, the procedure is similar to that applied by Morsink and Bayoumi (2001) in their analysis of the role of broad money on private demand in the Japanese economy. Including fiscal deficit as an exogenous variable generates a VAR identical to the original, except that it blocks off any responses within the VAR which pass through the deficit; hence, comparisons of the responses of the two models provide a measure of the importance of interactions between fiscal and monetary policy.[29] The impulse response functions of prices to

---

[28] The effects of conditioning for fiscal deficit have also been considered for the rest of the countries analysed (when possible taking into account data restrictions). The results were quite similar to the ones shown in the previous subsection.

a monetary shock in these countries using this alternative VAR model (available from the authors on request) show that, for both countries, interactions between fiscal and monetary policy have negatively affected the efficiency of the latter to fight inflation. This issue is especially relevant in the context of a monetary union. Using a two-country sticky-prices model to analyse the interactions between fiscal and monetary policy, the results of Lombardo and Sutherland (2004) show that there are welfare gains from fiscal policy cooperation in a monetary union. It is worth recalling that the independence of the central bank is necessary for the effective implementation of monetary policy – not only because it is a legal prerequisite to joining the monetary union, but for economic reasons as well.

EVIDENCE ON THE CORRELATION OF MONETARY SHOCKS BETWEEN NEW MEMBER STATES AND THE EURO AREA An additional aspect that may be of interest in this context is the analysis of the correlation of monetary shocks between the new Member States and the Euro area, and in particular for the countries that have had a higher degree of monetary independence. As previously analysed in Chapters 5 and 6, business cycle and shock symmetry is usually seen as a positive indicator in the context of a currency area. Table 7.3 shows the values of the correlation coefficient of monetary shocks between the Czech Republic, Hungary, Poland, Slovakia and Slovenia and the Euro area for the period 1993–2003 and for two sub-periods: before and after the introduction of the euro.

Table 7.3. *Correlation of monetary shocks between selected new Member States and the Euro area*

Country	Sample	Full period	Up to 1998	1999–2003
Czech Republic	1994:2–2003:2	0.29	0.32	0.48
Hungary	1997:1–2003:2	−0.17	−0.23	−0.18
Poland	1997:1–2003:2	0.31	0.45	0.32
Slovakia	1993:2–2003:2	0.01	0.23	−0.10
Slovenia	1993:1–2003:2	−0.13	−0.23	−0.09

[29] In 1999, together with the national central banks of the countries of the Euro area, the ECB launched a major research project to study the transmission of monetary policy. Twenty-three papers were produced: six of them were macroeconomic studies of both the entire Euro area economy and the constituent countries; seven of them studied firm-level investment behaviour; and the other ten analysed bank-level balance sheets and income statements. For more details, see Angeloni *et al.* (2003b).

For all the observations available, the values of the correlation coefficient are positive and significant only for the Czech Republic and Poland, while the values for Hungary, Slovakia and Slovenia are negative. When looking at the results by sub-periods, in the most recent years, the situation has only improved for the Czech Republic, which, on the basis of this partial approach, seems to be the country in the best position to join the Euro area.

7.4   Conclusions

The objective of this chapter was to compare the mechanisms of monetary transmission in the new Member States with those existing in the Euro area. The evidence obtained using VAR models suggests that monetary policy has been effective in the fight against inflation or in stabilising output in most of these new Member States, due to the major role of the interest rate channel and, in some cases, in combination with the exchange rate channel. The only exceptions are Slovakia and Slovenia.

One important conclusion is that, from the perspective of the monetary transmission channels, entry into ERM-II soon after accession is a clear option. In fact, this was the option chosen by Estonia, Lithuania and Slovenia. However, although the new Member States should join ERM-II for a minimum period of two years as a prerequisite to joining the Euro area, the timing of entry and the length of their participation should be determined on a case-by-case basis since the participation of countries with different policy objectives may complicate its functioning. As Solbes (2004) highlights, 'the ERM-II mechanism should not be seen as a mere waiting room for the adoption of the euro... It can help countries to achieve real and nominal convergence.'

Another issue that has been addressed is the role of the interactions between fiscal and monetary policies in Hungary and Poland. The results obtained using VAR models and conditioning for fiscal deficits show that fiscal policy has negatively affected the efficiency of the monetary policy to control inflation. It is worth recalling that the independence of the central bank is necessary for an effective conduct of monetary policy – not only because it is a legal prerequisite to accession to the monetary union, but also for economic reasons.

The chapter has also provided evidence of the correlation of monetary shocks between the new Member States and the Euro area, specifically for those countries with a higher degree of monetary independence. Correlation between monetary shocks is usually seen as a positive indicator in the context of a currency area. From this partial perspective, the countries in the best position to join the Euro area appear to be the Czech Republic and Poland.

However, certain issues should be taken into account when interpreting our results. First, since the lack of data available limited the time period of the study, confidence bands around the estimates of the responses to the monetary policy shock are very high (indeed, in some cases, differences across countries are likely to be non-significant). Moreover, one of the problems with cross-country comparisons is that the size of the estimated monetary policy shocks differs across countries. Even if we imposed the same initial disturbance, the problem would not be solved, as we would have to assume that the estimated parameters of the model are invariant to the specification of the policy rule, and then the Lucas critique would apply (Mojon and Peersman, 2001).

In any case, it seems that monetary policy can play an important role as a stabilisation tool for these countries, a tool that would be lost as soon as they join the Euro area. For this reason, more attention should be focused on the analysis of transmission channels of the monetary union using micro data on banks and firms.

To our knowledge, the only study that has analysed this issue in this context is by Brada et al. (2003). They investigate empirically the role of bank lending in monetary transmission mechanism in the Czech Republic using bank-level data for 1994–2001. Their results show that changes in monetary policy indicators have counter-intuitive results. In fact, in terms of the bank-lending hypothesis, monetary policy does not appear to have a significant effect on the supply of bank loans. For these authors, the findings suggest that Czech policy-makers cannot influence aggregate demand through shifts in loan supply and, as a result, it seems that the bank-lending channel has a limited role in designing monetary policy strategies. This result, in agreement with earlier studies using macro data (and this one), clearly provides additional information to broaden our knowledge of how monetary policy works. This kind of research should be extended to the rest of the new Member States in the near future; the experience for current Euro area members in the context of the Eurosystem Monetary Transmission Network should provide an excellent guideline (see Angeloni et al., 2003b; Chatelain et al., 2003; and Ehrmann et al., 2003, for case studies).[30]

---

[30] The results for consumption are not shown because the time series for this variable starts in 2000:1.

References

Adao, B., Alves, N. and Correia, I. 2003. 'The Conduct of Monetary Policy: A Critical Review'. *Banco de Portugal Economic Bulletin*, vol. 9, pp. 83–94.

Angeloni, I., Kashyap, A., Mojon, B. and Terlizzese, D. 2003a. 'The Output Composition Puzzle: A Difference in the Monetary Transmission Mechanism in the Euro Area and US'. *Journal of Money Credit and Banking*, vol. 35, pp. 1265–306.

2003b. 'Monetary Transmission in the Euro Area: Does the Interest Rate Channel Explain All?'. NBER Working Paper, No. 9984.

Babich, V. 2001. 'Monetary Transmission in Latvia'. *Baltic Economic Trends*, vol. 2, pp. 16–27.

Bagliano, F. and Favero, C. 1998. 'Measuring Monetary Policy with VAR Models: An Evaluation'. *European Economic Review*, vol. 42, pp. 1069–112.

Brada, J., Denizer, C., Kutan, A. and Yigit, T. 2003. 'Is There a Bank Lending Channel in Transition Economies? Evidence from Czech Banks' Balance Sheets'. Mimeo.

Caprirolo, G. and Lavrac, V. 2003. 'Monetary and Exchange Rate Policy in Slovenia'. Ezoneplus Working Paper, No. 17G, available at http://www.ezoneplus.org.

Carlino, G. and DeFina, R. 1998a. 'The Differential Regional Effects of Monetary Policy'. *Review of Economics and Statistics*, vol. 80, pp. 572–87.

1998b. 'Monetary Policy and the US States and Regions: Some Implications for European Monetary Union'. Federal Reserve Bank of Philadelphia Working Paper, No. 98–17.

1999. 'The Differential Regional Effects of Monetary Policy: Evidence from the US States'. *Journal of Regional Science*, vol. 39, pp. 339–58.

Cecchetti, S. 1999. 'Legal Structure, Financial Structure, and the Monetary Policy Transmission Mechanism'. *Economic Policy Review*, vol. 5, pp. 9–28.

Chari, V. and Kehoe, P. 1999. 'Optimal Fiscal and Monetary Policy'. In Taylor, J. and Woodford, M. (eds.), *Handbook of Macroeconomics*, vol. 1C, North-Holland: Elsevier Science.

Chatelain, J., Generale, A., Hernando, I., von Kalckreuth, U. and Vermeulen, P. 2003. 'New Findings on Firm Investment and Monetary Transmission in the Euro Area'. *Oxford Review of Economic Policy*, vol. 19, pp. 73–83.

Coricelli, F., Jazbec, B. and Masten, I. 2003. 'Exchange Rate Pass-Through in Candidate Countries'. CEPR Discussion Paper, No. 3894.

Dean, J. 2003. 'Exchange Rate Regimes in Central and Eastern European Transition Economies'. Mimeo.

Ehrmann, M., Gambacorta, L., Martinez-Pagés, J., Sevestre, P. and Worms, A. 2003. 'The Effects of Monetary Policy in the Euro Area'. *Oxford Review of Economic Policy*, vol. 19, pp. 58–72.

Festi, M. 2001. 'Monetary Policy Instruments in Slovenia'. *Eastern European Economics*, vol. 39, pp. 64–86.

Fidrmuc, J. and Korhonen, I. 2004. 'The Euro Goes East: Implications of the 2000–2002 Economic Slowdown for Synchronisation of Business Cycles

Between the Euro and CEECs'. *Comparative Economic Studies*, vol. 6, pp. 45–62.

Frömmel, M. and Schobert, F. 2003. 'Nominal Anchors in EU Acceding Countries – Recent Experiences'. Universität Hannover Discussion Paper, No. 267.

Galí, J. 1992. 'How Well Does the IS-LM Model Fit Postwar US Data'. *Quarterly Journal of Economics*, vol. 107, pp. 709–38.

Ganev, G., Molnar, K., Rybinski, K. and Wozniak, P. 2002. 'Transmission of Monetary Policy in Central and Eastern Europe'. CASE reports, No. 52.

Garbuza, Y. 2003. 'The Transmission Mechanism of Monetary Policy: Investigating the Exchange Rate Channel for Central and Eastern European Countries (Case of Poland)'. Mimeo.

Gerlach, S. and Smets, F. 1995. 'The Monetary Transmission Mechanism: Evidence from the G-7 Countries'. CEPR Discussion Paper, No. 1219.

Golinelli, R. and Rovelli, R. 2002. 'Monetary Policy Transmission, Interest Rate Rules and Inflation Targeting in Three Transition Countries'. Ezoneplus Working Paper, No. 10.

Goodhart, M. 2003. 'EMU and the Monetary Transmission Mechanism'. HM Treasury.

Hughes-Hallet, A. and Piscitelli, L. 1999. 'EMU in Reality: The Effect of a Common Monetary Policy on Economies with Different Transmission Mechanisms'. *Empirica*, vol. 26, pp. 337–58.

Kieler, M. and Saarenhimo, T. 1998. 'Differences in Monetary Policy Transmission? A Case Not Closed'. DG ECFIN European Economy Economic Papers, No. 132.

Korhonen, I. 2002. 'Selected Aspects of Monetary Integration'. *Focus on Transition*, vol. 1, pp. 101–7.

Kuijs, L. 2002. 'Monetary Policy Transmission Mechanisms and Inflation in the Slovak Republic'. IMF Working Paper, No. 02/80.

Kutan, A. and Brada, J. 2000. 'The Evolution of Monetary Policy in Transition Economies'. *Federal Reserve Bank of St. Louis*, March/April 2000 issue, pp. 31–40.

Lättemäe, R. and Pikkani, R. 2001. 'The Monetary Transmission Mechanism in Estonia'. *Baltic Economic Trends*, vol. 2, pp. 7–15.

Lavrac, V. 2003. 'Final Report: Monetary and Fiscal Policy'. Ezoneplus Working Paper, No. 17, available at http://www.ezoneplus.org.

Lombardo, G. and Sutherland, A. 2004. 'Monetary and Fiscal Interactions in Open Economies'. *Journal of Macroeconomics*, vol. 26, pp. 319–47.

Mishkin, F. 2000. 'Inflation Targeting in Emerging Market Countries'. *American Economic Review*, vol. 90, pp. 105–9.

Mojon, B. and Peersman, G. 2003. 'A VAR Description of the Effects of Monetary Policy in the Individual Countries of the Euro Area'. In Angeloni, I., Kashyap, A. and Mojon, B. (eds.), *Monetary Policy Transmission in the Euro Area*, Cambridge University Press.

Morsink, J. and Bayoumi, T. 2001. 'A Peek Inside the Black Box: The Monetary Transmission in Japan'. *IMF Staff Papers*, vol. 48, pp. 22–57.

Peersman, G. and Smets, F. 2003. 'The Monetary Transmission Mechanism in the Euro Area: More Evidence from VAR Analysis'. In Angeloni, I.,

Kashyap, A. and Mojon, B. (eds.), *Monetary Policy Transmission in the Euro Area*, Cambridge University Press.

Pikkani, R. 2001. 'Monetary Transmission Mechanism in Estonia – Empirical Model'. Eesti Pank Working Paper, No. 5.

Ramaswamy, R. and Slok, T. 1998. 'The Real Effects of Monetary Policy in the European Union: What Are The Differences?'. IMF Staff Papers vol. 45, pp. 374–96.

Rusek, A.2001. 'The Role and Impact of Monetary Policy in CEFTA Countries'. *International Advances in Economic Research*, vol. 7, pp. 83–90.

Siklos, P. and Abel, I. 2001. 'Is Hungary ready for Inflation Targeting?'. Mimeo, available at http://papers.ssrn.com/sol3/papers.cfm?abstract_id=285712.

Sims, C.1992. 'Interpreting the Time Series Facts: The Effects of Monetary Policy'. *European Economic Review*, vol. 36, pp. 975–1011.

Sims, C. and Zha, T. 1998. 'Does Monetary Policy Generate Recessions?'. Federal Reserve Bank of Atlanta Working Paper, No. 98–12.

Smets. F. 1997. 'Measuring Monetary Policy Shocks in France, Germany and Italy: The Role of the Exchange Rate'. BIS Working paper, No. 42.

Solbes, P. 2004. 'Euro Adoption in the Accession Countries Opportunities and Challenges'. Mimeo, speech delivered at Prague Conference on 'Euro Adoption in the Accession Countries', 2 February, 2004.

Suardi, M. 2001. 'EMU and Asymmetries in Monetary Policy Transmission'. DG ECFIN European Economy Economic Paper, No. 157.

Vetlov, I. 2001. 'Aspects of Monetary Policy and the Monetary Transmission Mechanism in Lithuania'. *Baltic Economic Trends*, vol. 2, pp. 28–36.

8 Promoting fiscal restraint in three Central European Member States

Emilio Rossi and Zbyszko Tabernacki

8.1 Introduction

In reviewing key policy challenges facing the governments of the ten new Member States, one can identify two major challenges:[1]

- the need for fiscal restraint in the run-up to membership in the Economic and Monetary Union;
- the role of monetary and fiscal policies and the independence of the central bank.

The developments in the area of public finance and the need to reduce budget deficits sharply in the next several years constitute by far the biggest challenge for accession countries. This challenge is of particular importance for the largest economies in the group, as, in their case, the build-up in government spending over the last several years has resulted in a public finance position that is not sustainable in the longer term. Moreover, their fiscal situation threatens to prevent the economies not only from meeting the Maastricht criteria, but also from reaching their growth potential. In this chapter, we expand our analysis of the fiscal position of the accession countries and discuss likely scenarios of developments. In order to keep the study manageable, while providing a comprehensive review of the issues involved, we concentrate on analysing the situation prevalent in the three largest new EU member economies: Poland, the Czech Republic and Hungary (hereinafter referred to as the CE-3). These three economies accounted for 78% of the GDP of all accession countries in 2002 and were (with the exception of Malta) by far the furthest from meeting the Maastricht criterion for fiscal budget deficit levels. After a background discussion in section 8.2, we review, in section 8.3, the developments in the fiscal position of the

---

[1] The present chapter is drawn from a large exercise of simulations of alternative scenarios of fiscal policy run in 2003. While some numbers referring to 2003 and 2004 may turn out to be different by the time of the publication of this book, most of the considerations regarding the impact of fiscal policies planned in the CE-3 Member States remain valid.

CE-3 countries in the last few years, providing detailed discussions on the 2002 and 2003 budgets. In section 8.4, we review the pre-accession economic programmes adopted by the three governments, placing special emphasis on the public-finance aspects of the programmes. Subsequently, in section 8.5, we outline several scenarios of developments in the public-finance positions of the CE-3 countries for the years 2004–6.

It is important to note that, while difficulties in keeping deficits under control are common for all three economies, the underlying causes of these problems and the suggested solutions may well vary among the countries. These specific differences are discussed in detail in this chapter.

8.2   Background

The fiscal balances of the CE-3 have deteriorated considerably over the last two years. The reasons for the widening of state and consolidated budget deficits have differed among the countries. Some of the excessive increases in expenditures stemmed from outlays related to the implementation of pension, healthcare and educational reforms. In addition, the economic slowdown across the region that hit in late 2001, 2002 and 2003 kept tax revenues below expectations and resulted in short-term liquidity problems. Finally, the governments in Hungary and the Czech Republic introduced extensive fiscal packages to stimulate their struggling economies through large-scale investment and current spending programmes.

In addition to short-term factors worsening deficits in the region, regional budgets are also suffering from the effects of past short-term decisions taken without proper assessment of their long-term consequences. This applies in particular to Poland and Hungary, where the previous and current governments competed in offering entitlements to large portions of the population without taking into account the impact of future demands on public funds. In Poland, these took the form of indexation of wages and retirement and disability payments. In Hungary, the entitlements were part of a pre- and post-election spending spree that resulted in a one-off 52% rise in the wages of public sector employees. In the Czech Republic, the lack of proper supervision of the banking system in the early 1990s and the indirect method of dealing with the 'bad loan' problems still haunts the national government.

In many cases, decisions to increase fiscal spending from already high levels were made with the full understanding that the resulting build-up of deficits and, in consequence, of net public debt would put meeting the Maastricht criterion - a public finance deficit no larger than 3.0% of

GDP in the course of the next several years - out of reach. The argument used by some of the policy-makers in the region (some of whom continue to support this view) is that, while reductions in the budget deficits should ultimately be undertaken to meet the criterion, this process should not ignore the developments in the real economy. In brief, if the movement towards greater fiscal restraint threatened to bring about a significant slowdown in economic growth, such a restrictive policy should be reviewed and adjusted as appropriate. Notably, the governments of the CE-3 stated recently that, while accession to the EMU and the adoption of the euro in the shortest time possible would be desirable, their policies with respect to budgets would be more balanced and would take into account a variety of factors.

Such an approach could, however, bring unwanted results. The policy of increasing government spending purportedly to prop up growth in the economy may well serve to hide the fact that most of the monies spent are used ineffectively and on programmes that, in the end, do not achieve the desired results. The evidence suggests that most of the increase in spending has not necessarily been directed towards investment, but rather ended up expanding already excessive entitlement programmes. In addition, it is likely that such policies may in almost all cases, amid an environment in which fighting inflation remains the top priority of local central bankers, lead to unnecessarily high interest rates. This, in turn, actually serves to depress domestic private investment.

Although the fiscal positions of the accession countries have clearly been affected by an economic slowdown that can be at least partially linked to the weakness of the global economy, the widening of the budget deficits was due mostly to excessive spending rather than to an unanticipated shortfall in budgetary revenues. In many of the largest accession countries, the large share of fixed costs in the budget, mostly related to social spending, limits room for manoeuvring by the governments. Sometimes, the only hope left is for much stronger growth that would boost tax revenues and close the budget gap. Moreover, the willingness of national governments to reduce deficits is countered by the need to maintain at least the appearance of an intact social safety net to avoid defeat at the polls at the hands of a disenchanted electorate.

8.3   The weak point of medium-term budgetary planning

In addition to attempting to use fiscal policy as a tool to prop up growth in struggling economies as well as please the electorate with increased social spending, one of the major inherent weaknesses of public finance planning in Central Europe is its short-term perspective. While the so-called medium-term economic plans are being published, the truth is that budgets have been and, in some cases, still are prepared just for the following year. Such an approach makes it very difficult for policy-makers to assess the long-term effects of their budgeting decisions. In addition, it also makes the influence of political and social interest groups on the budget planning process that much more important. The governments refer to these as 'social considerations' in designing the budget. The belief is quite widespread that stricter reductions are not necessary in the short term as it will be up to the next government in power to take care of the fiscal consequences of current actions.

Some attempts at providing a more extended view of the budgetary policy-making process have been undertaken, but only quite recently. For example, in the Czech Republic the new Act on Budgetary Rules requires individual ministries and extra-budgetary funds to present three-year projections of expenditures. Each new draft law is now also to be accompanied by an assessment of its impact on the budget in a perspective of three years. This is, however, an exception to the rule. For example, the first serious attempt at capping expenditure levels proposed by the former Polish finance minister Marek Belka during the preparation of the 2002 draft budget was flatly rejected by his successor as an unnecessary constraint. Under this concept, dubbed 'inflation plus 1%' and envisaged to anchor public finances in periods of slow growth, the government does not target a specific amount for the state budget deficit, but rather concentrates on restricting growth in expenditures. The deficit is treated as a residual, and fluctuates depending on the collection of budget revenues. This system could have proven particularly useful in the short term to stabilise the expenditure side of the budget. In the long term, however, major expenditure cuts might still be needed to bring the deficits down to considerably lower levels.

The high share of fixed (legally mandated) expenditures in total budgetary spending is another constraint for policy-makers. As a result of past policy decisions and adopted laws, this share has been steadily increasing over the last several years. To use the example of the Czech Republic, the cumulative rate of growth in socially related spending (pensions, disability payments and public-sector wages) far exceeded that for other categories of expenditures (see Table 8.1) and contributed to a steady rise of those expenditures in the total.

This structure of expenditures is not very different for Poland and Hungary. It also implies that, short of freezing these fixed expenditures in real terms, or cutting them outright through drastic reforms of enti-tlement programmes (both of which are planned for the next several

Table 8.1. *Dynamics of public expenditure in the Czech Republic 1995–2001*

	Expenditure growth 1995–2001 in %	Weight in total expenditures 2001
Total general government expenditure	54.5	100.0
Of which: Social security and health care	95.1	33.9
Health care	58.8	15.9
Education	28.8	10.1
Defence services	29.0	8.8
Transportation and communication	59.4	8.0
Housing and community services	47.6	6.5
General public services	5.0	5.9
Other economic affairs and services	83.5	5.9
Recreational and cultural services	70.6	2.5
Agriculture, forestry, fisheries	112.4	2.4

Source: Pre-Accession Economic Program, August 2003, the Czech Republic.

years), the only area of public spending where the governments still enjoy some flexibility are expenditures incurred by the governmental departments and agencies. In these cases, with budget revenues dependent on tax collections that, in turn, reflect the pace of economic growth, the safest way to reduce expenditures gradually and without a dampening of economic growth is the implementation of a system of medium-term expenditure ceilings. Such ceilings, usually applied for periods of between three and five years, set the maximum amounts of spending for all levels of expenditures that are relatively fixed and can be predicted. These ceilings apply to spending by all branches of the government including off-budgetary funds. The ceilings can then be reviewed every three to five years, and the spending levels monitored regularly to determine the availability of funds within the preset budget.

The British experience could be considered a good guideline in the application of such maximum spending targets. In 1998, the UK government announced a new process for the planning and controlling of future public expenditures. Beginning with the 1999–2000 budget, the country's public spending has been regulated by the Total Managed Expenditure (TME) system. The TME included two major components, Annually Managed Expenditure (AME) and Departmental Expenditure Limits (DEL). Public expenditures were divided roughly equally in value terms between AME and DEL. The AME was home to a small number of large programmes, whose expenditures are demand-led, volatile and large in relation to the department. As such, the programmes under the AME are unsuited to planning in strict three-year forecasts. Such programmes include: social security, housing subsidies, EU funding for the Common Agricultural Policy, public service pensions and the lottery. The AME projections were reviewed semi-annually.

The DEL consisted of the bulk of the expenditure programmes managed by individual ministries and departments. The government, abandoning annual spending reviews of these programmes, initiated a Comprehensive Spending Review (CSR) in which strict, multi-year spending limits for each department were set for 1999–2000, 2000–1 and 2001–2. Another CSR was held in 2002, establishing limits for 2003–4, 2004–5 and 2005–6. The spending teams of the Treasury's Public Service Directorate, in consultation with individual departments, draw up the three-year limits. Spending limits for each department are strict, with increases only in exceptional cases, drawing additional funds from the DEL reserve only after a review from the Treasury. Departments are, however, allowed to carry over any unused funds from one year to the next. Within the limit, each department is allowed to allocate its own resources and chart its own decisions.

Departmental spending is clearly delineated between current and capital spending, with DELs separated between resource and capital. The capital DEL includes spending on fixed assets, making loans and buying shares. The resource DEL then encompasses the rest of spending, including the operating costs of the departments, the purchasing of services, grants and subsidies to the private sector, and non-cash items such as depreciation. In return for flexibility within departments for resource allocation, the departments had to sign three-year performance contracts, or Public Service Agreements, with specific output and result targets. The new TME was designed to free departments from the bureaucracy of annual budgets and to focus on strategic planning and results.

8.4   Public finance in the pre-accession economic programmes

The absence of a transparent medium-term budget plan and clear planning guidelines makes forecasting budget deficits in the CE-3 very difficult. While, in all cases, the budget deficit level of 3.0% of GDP is a generally accepted target for the medium term, it is almost impossible to follow the progress in nominal convergence to this target. With a complete lack of a legally or even organisationally defined schedule, the only source of information on the government's medium-term plans with respect to public finances is information included in the

Pre-Accession Economic Programme filed on an annual basis by candidate country governments with the European Commission. An updated set of these reports was filed with the Commission in August 2003. The picture transpiring from these plans is not very promising. Moreover, the reports and conclusions included therein in no way require the governments to undertake specific actions. Rather, they should be viewed as a general framework for nominal convergence with the criteria set by the EU. The experience of 2003–4 teaches us that the commitment of the CE-3 governments to stick to the published guidelines is illusory. The assumptions and the results vary substantially between the annual documents. Therefore, there is no guarantee that the plan would not be changed again. Nevertheless, these reports warrant a closer look.

With the exception of Hungary, where the government is planning to undertake a massive reduction in government spending to bring the deficit down from 9.2% of GDP in 2002 to just under 3.0% of GDP in 2006, the other two countries seem to take a much more liberal approach to budget expenditure management. As such, the target date for meeting the 3.0% of GDP level has been seriously postponed from the original plans, to 2007 in Poland and 2008 or even 2009 in the Czech Republic.

The Polish government now seems resigned to the fact that the public finance deficit is likely to grow substantially in 2004 before accelerating economic growth permits a reduction in the gap in the subsequent years. Calculated according to the ESA-95 methodology, the public finance gap is set to rise from close to 4.1% in 2003 to 5.0% in 2004 before declining gradually to 4.0% in 2005 and below 3.4% in 2006. While the rise in 2004 reflects the unwillingness of the government to face reality and cut expenditures, the forecast for the subsequent years is even more questionable, mostly due to two factors. First, the assumed growth of 5.0% in both 2004 and 2005 and 5.6% in 2006 exceeds even the most optimistic consensus forecasts. Secondly, the first year of planned reduction falls in 2005, an election year. It is therefore hard to imagine that the government's resolve to cut expenditures will be strong enough to outweigh political considerations. The plan provides little information in terms of identification of areas where cuts or realignments will be introduced. This type of information will not be available until the full medium-term economic programme is announced in September 2005.

Even without the detailed programme at hand, it is safe to assume that the government will attempt to identify several categories of expenditures where rationalisation of spending and the introduction of even

Table 8.2. *Poland, fiscal developments (central government budget, percentage of GDP)*

	2002	2003	2004	2005	2006
Budget revenues	42.1	43.1	42.9	42.2	42.1
Budget expenditures	45.9	47.2	47.9	46.2	45.5
Deficit (ESA-95)	-3.8	-4.1	-5.0	-4.0	-3.4
Deficit (current Polish methodology)	-6.0	-6.1	-5.8	-4.8	-4.0

Source: Ministry of Finance, Pre-Accession Economic Program of Poland, August 2003.

small adjustment to existing regulations could result in major savings for the government.

First and foremost, large savings are potentially available within the inefficient social security scheme for the farmers (KRUS). Currently, farmers are not required to contribute to the programme, while they receive regular retirement benefits. The introduction of a system of nominal farmers' contributions could reduce the expenditures by as much as 12 billion zlotys.

Similar to the situation in the Czech Republic, Poland features one of the most developed systems of disability payments, which is, due to obvious abuses, one of the most expensive in Europe. The determination of possible areas of savings within the system would require close co-operation between several branches of the government, but is likely to be met with strong opposition on the part of the current beneficiaries of the system.

On the expenditure side, the programme might suggest implementation of tighter controls over spending in special funds and independent agencies of the state treasury as well as organisational changes in the state administration of funds. Among others, nine of the twenty special funds could be incorporated into the state budget. These represent accounts maintained outside the government budget that allow budgetary units to offer payments of bonuses to employees. The total amount of those funds is estimated at 4.6 billion zlotys in 2003. Most of these funds are at the disposal of the Ministry of Finance (29.1% of total funds), the Ministry of Treasury (27.7%), the Interior Ministry (21.9%) and the Ministry of Education (9.9%).

In its review of the current situation of public finances in the Czech Republic, contained in the pre-accession programme, the government openly admits that the situation has deteriorated to such a degree that the lack of any sensible reform in the near future creates a risk of the general budget deficit reaching 8–9% of GDP during 2004–6.

Table 8.3. *Czech Republic, fiscal deficits (ESA-95, general government, percentage of GDP)*

	2002	2003	2004	2005	2006
General government deficit	−6.7	−7.6	−5.9	−4.8	−4.0
Central government deficit	−6.7	−7.3	−5.3	−4.3	−3.6
Local government deficit	0.1	−0.2	−0.5	−0.4	−0.4
Social security funds	−0.1	−0.1	0.0	0.0	0.0

Source: Pre-Accession Economic Program, August 2003.

This is mostly due to a persistent tendency for expenditures to grow in real terms. In addition to the staggering costs of the *Ceska konsolidacni agentura* (CKA), the increases in general expenditure levels are mostly due to growing social expenditures. Social security and the so-called social assistance expenditures have been the fastest growing category of spending. For example, during 1999–2001, total budget expenditures rose cumulatively by 54.5%, while those on social security and social care almost doubled in the same period. This expenditure essentially crowded out all remaining types of expenditure. In addition, the government resorted to discretionary spending starting in 1999 to prop up the economy coming out of a bout of post-transition recession.

In light of the above problems, the Czech government has adopted a medium-term fiscal framework based on the baseline macroeconomic forecast that assumes a gradual acceleration of economic growth in the years 2003–6. It is also assumed that the budget in 2003 will not exceed 7.6% of GDP, and that the trend towards a growing deficit will be reversed starting in 2004. The framework also assumes that the public finance deficit will be reduced to 4.0% of GDP by 2006 and below 3.0% not later than in 2008.

Proposed fiscal reforms are very gradual compared to those suggested in Hungary and even Poland. The reform is to consist of a combination of measures on both the revenue and the expenditure sides of the general government budgets including a reform of the pension system (such as moving away from the pay-as-you-go system supposed to take effect in 2004 and the reduction of the possibility of early retirement), as well as cutting sickness benefits.

With a stated goal of joining the EMU at the earliest possible date, the fulfilment of convergence criteria, including that of the budget deficit and public-debt-to-GDP ratios are high on the Hungarian government's agenda. The government forecasts indicate that, following the

Table 8.4. *Hungary, fiscal developments (general government, percentage of GDP)*

	2002	2003	2004	2005	2006
Budget revenues*	44.5	43.0	44.5	44–44.5	43.5
Budget expenditures*	53.7	47.8	48.3	47.0	46.0
Deficit	-9.2	-4.8	-3.8	-2.8	-2.5
* of which: EU transfers	0.2	0.4	0.5–1.0	1.0	1.0

Source: Pre-Accession Economic Program of Hungary, August 2003.

4.8% of GDP budget deficit in 2003, the deficit would then be cut by 1 percentage point of GDP in each of the subsequent two years, thus dropping to 2.8% of GDP in 2005. It will then be reduced to 2.5% in 2006. The programme rests on the assumption that the reduction during 2003, from 9.2% of GDP to 4.8% of GDP, indeed materialises. This in turn will require meeting the 3.5% GDP growth target, as well as the continuation of better-than-expected tax collection, in particular with respect to VAT and corporate and simplified enterprise taxes. The plan also assumes that the trend of budget deficit underperformance on the part of the local governments would hold in 2003, reducing the impact of this category on the general budget deficit. In light of the risk inherent in such an optimistic forecast, the Hungarian government is ready to admit that an overshooting of the 2003 target is likely. The excessive spending might be combined with an unexpected reduction in tax revenues not only in 2003, but also in 2004. According to the plan, if the deficit in 2004 runs the risk of exceeding the target, expenditures will be cut to implement necessary corrections.

In the period 2003–6, the overall public-debt-to-GDP ratio is expected to fluctuate between 54% of GDP and 57–8%. The risk of the public debt exceeding 60% of GDP is rather remote, even under the most unfavourable circumstances. The real key to the viability of the plan will be its implementation in 2004. As the government admits, previous commitments render it impossible to reduce the growth in budget expenditures below the aggregate growth in the economy. The reduction in the deficit will therefore depend almost exclusively on increased revenue collection.

Starting in 2004, the government will initiate the process of a three-year framework budget act by the parliament. Arguably, the most important aspect of budget management, expenditure controls are covered with the minimum amount of detail in the pre-accession programme. The government assumes that, due to previous commitments, the expenditures of the general government will increase considerably. The reduction in the deficit will, however, necessitate a reduction in the growth in expenditures, which in turn will require a change in their structure.

8.5   Scenarios

Given the past experiences with fiscal laxity in Central Europe, one needs to view the macroeconomic growth assumptions and the resulting forecasts of budgetary performance presented in the pre-accession programmes and the already published or soon-to-be-published medium-term economic programmes with scepticism. Growth figures, although plausible under the most favourable sets of circumstances, are usually adjusted upwards to fit a politically acceptable spending plan in terms of the budget-deficit-to-GDP and public-debt-to-GDP ratios. The budget figures themselves also incorporate a number of rather broad assumptions on the revenue side to present a smooth process of nominal convergence with the EU's criteria. As a result, the baseline figures presented in the programmes should be viewed as the optimistic scenarios of developments, where a chance of an actual undershooting is rather minimal, and even further restricted by the ability of the government to find 'socially justifiable' methods of spending the excess funds available.

The range of possible negative outcomes in terms of the deficit-to-GDP ratio is considerably skewed towards the early years of the forecast period. This results from the widespread perceptions among the political elites that only the final-year target is set firmly, while the interim annual targets could be adjusted upwards by increasing expenditures to satisfy social demands and positioning themselves in preparation for parliamentary elections. Even though a later adjustment would have to be considerably more radical on the expenditure side, and may actually involve a sharp rise in taxes, the governing elites are willing to accept short-term risk for political gain.

Among the government baseline scenarios presented below, the Hungarian approach is clearly the most radical in terms of timing and severity of expenditure cuts in the first several years. It is also the plan that brings the deficit to target levels of below 3.0% of GDP in the shortest. On the other hand, the Czech government's baseline seems overly pessimistic with respect to growth prospects for the Czech economy. This does not change the opinion, however, that the fiscal problems in this country are by far the most severe.

While the government scenario could be described as relatively optimistic, at least three other scenarios can be developed. The results of the scenarios on the budget bottom line and the associated assumptions are presented in the tables below. Below we provide a brief review of the results.

8.5.1   The 'official' scenario

This scenario reflects the official government outlook as of mid-2003 of the most likely growth path for the relevant economies. These forecasts usually assume that:

- The actual accession to the EU in May 2004 does not result in a dramatic change in the development of key macroeconomic parameters, but will only enhance the trends already present during the pre-accession period.
- Growth within the EU is expected to be quite weak in 2003 and 2004, followed by a substantial acceleration in 2005–6, with the majority of risks still on the downside. Growth in the EU accelerates from near zero in 2003 to slightly above trend 2.8–3.0% by 2005. Commodity markets are assumed to stabilise with the price of oil not exceeding US$24 dollar per barrel.
- Gradual acceleration of growth takes place in 2004–6, with growth oscillating between 2% and 4% in the Czech Republic, 3.5–5.0% in Hungary and 5.0–5.6% in Poland.
- Growth in household consumption is conditional upon stable growth in real wages. Moderation in wage increases provides for a sufficient lag in growth of average wages relative to labour productivity growth.
- Investment starts growing faster following the accession, due to the transfer of modern technologies and the creation of new, more . modern export capacities. The contribution of net trade should be neutral over the next several years.
- The external sectors stabilise with current accounts remaining manageable in the years 2003–6.

The official scenario produces a decline in ESA-95 calculated budget deficit in the years 2004–6 in Hungary. The public deficits in Poland and the Czech Republic increase temporarily in 2004, but then decline in the later years, due in part to austerity measures, but mostly due to an acceleration of economic growth in the period. The adjustment is much more gradual in the Czech case.

8.5.2   The baseline scenario

This scenario reflects our current assessment of the economic outlook for the CE-3 economies and our view of the most likely scenario of fiscal adjustments in the coming years. This scenario is *de facto* roughly based on similar assumptions as those used by the government scenario, but is stripped of the overly optimistic assumption as to the governments' ability to reduce deficit spending in the current political and social environment. It also reflects the different growth trends that are assumed in our forecasts. In Hungary we assume that the budgets of local governments will be balanced in 2003 and beyond, despite past evidence of excessive spending that leads to higher deficits that are reported in the last months of the year and as such cannot be properly incorporated in the baseline general government budget projection. Additional spending on wages for teachers and the effects of the one-off increase on the wages of public sector employees are also included. The cumulative difference in the deficit in Hungary relative to the government baseline scenario is equal to 0.4% of GDP in 2003 and 0.5–1.0% of GDP in 2004–5.

In the case of Poland, we assume that the budget deficit in 2003 will be implemented in line with the original budget law. However, several expenditure items will not be included in the official numbers, and as a result will have to be treated as additional expenditures in 2004. The assumed public sector deficit is closer to 5.5% of GDP under the ESA-95 methodology, and significantly exceeds 6.5% under the old system of reporting. This is a major loosening of fiscal policy when compared with 2003 and could have negative consequences on the outlook for the remaining years of the forecast period. Starting in 2005, our 'baseline scenario' assumes considerably lower rates of growth in the economy. Slower growth in household consumption and corporate profits bring lower tax revenues. The need to co-finance EU transfers and a political commitment to support inefficient social programmes further widen the deficits in 2004–5. Deficits in the later years move into line with the forecast, but growth still fails to reach the projected 5.6% annual rate, staying instead in the 4.0–4.5% range.

In the Czech Republic, the realistic scenario is actually the closest to the official government approach with slightly stronger than assumed economic growth matched by higher spending in the earlier years. In general, we believe that the Czech official programme is the most conservative and closest to reality.

8.5.3   The 'expansion/austerity' scenario

This hypothetical scenario follows in general the growth pattern for the three economies developed under the baseline scenario. This time, we assume, however, that the need to boost growth in the next two years (mostly due to political considerations related to upcoming parliamentary elections), results in higher spending in the initial period of the forecast. Specifically, the governments are successful in implementing the revenue side measures, such as planned reductions in personal and corporate income taxes, (a) while failing to implement on time medium-term expenditure frameworks for all categories of flexible budget spending, (b) while failing to pass through the respective parliaments' measures aimed at reforming the excessive social spending on pension benefits, sickness benefits, and (c) while wage growth in the public sector continues to exceed planned limits due to the opposition on the part of trade unions.

The resulting overshooting of the deficit, when compared with the official scenario, is then 'corrected' in the years 2005–6. This is achieved through the application of very restrictive spending policies that effectively freeze most of the expenditure categories in nominal terms at the previous year's levels. This scenario has an unwelcome effect of dampening growth potential in the later years of the forecast. It also results in the practice of artificial reductions in spending or even a need to increase taxes temporarily to meet the deficit and public debt criteria. Another negative effect of such an approach would involve elements of creative accounting aimed at reducing the transparency of government spending and delaying the necessary spending to future years in order to meet certain targets and criteria. The application of such a short-term approach to public deficits will only cumulate the problems, by postponing the actual reform into the future. Under this scenario, real economic convergence is delayed. Growth in the private sector is constrained by more aggressive monetary tightening at the least opportune of times. Finally, the financial markets punish the country's government by pushing up the yields on the government's domestic currency and foreign currency denominated debt.

8.5.4   The 'fiscal prudence' scenario

This most desirable approach to fiscal management is also the least likely in terms of implementation. It requires a disciplined approach to reforms and political will to implement changes in legislation to reduce mandatory spending. This approach effectively freezes most of the social spending, such as pension and disability benefits at the levels of the current year, leads to a reduction in the number of recipients of some of these benefits, implements cuts in the public sector workforce of up to 10–15% of the current levels. In addition, such a prudent, albeit not necessarily politically viable, approach would result in setting up a system of medium-term limits on expenditures that can be managed on the central government level and an almost complete elimination of other categories of expenditures by the incorporation of off-budgetary funds into the main budget, a programme of annual savings on the ministerial level with respect to variable expenditures. Application of a combination of increased taxes on VAT and excise taxes is matched with a more liberal application of tax cuts for individuals and businesses.

Appendix A: The results of fiscal scenarios for the CE-3 economies

Table 8.5. *Poland, fiscal scenarios (according to ESA-95 methodology)*

	2003	2004	2005	2006
Official Scenario				
GDP (annual growth in %)	3.0	5.0	5.0	5.6
General budget revenues (% of GDP)	43.1	42.9	42.2	42.1
General budget expenditures (% of GDP)	47.2	47.9	46.2	45.5
General budget balance (% of GDP)	−4.1	−5.0	−4.0	−3.4
Baseline Scenario				
GDP (annual growth in %)	3.0	3.9	4.3	4.0
General budget revenues (% of GDP)	43.2	43.4	43.1	43.0
General budget expenditures (% of GDP)	47.3	48.9	47.6	47.0
General budget balance (% of GDP)	−4.1	−5.5	−4.5	−4.0
Expansion/Austerity Scenario				
GDP (annual growth in %)	3.0	3.9	4.3	3.8
General budget revenues (% of GDP)	43.2	43.3	43.1	43.2
General budget expenditures (% of GDP)	47.3	49.2	47.9	47.0
General budget balance (% of GDP)	−4.1	−5.8	−4.8	−3.8
Fiscal Prudence Scenario				
GDP (annual growth in %)	3.0	3.9	4.4	4.2
General budget revenues (% of GDP)	43.2	43.2	43.0	42.9
General budget expenditures (% of GDP)	47.3	48.3	47.5	46.7
General budget balance (% of GDP)	−4.1	−5.1	−4.5	−3.8

Table 8.6. *Czech Republic, fiscal scenarios (according to ESA-95 methodology)*

	2003	2004	2005	2006
Official Scenario				
GDP (annual growth in %)	2.4	2.8	3.2	3.6
General budget revenues (% of GDP)	42.4	43.8	43.4	42.8
General budget expenditures (% of GDP)	50.0	49.7	48.2	46.8
General budget balance (% of GDP)	−7.6	−5.9	−4.8	−4.0
Baseline Scenario				
GDP (annual growth in %)	2.5	3.5	4.1	4.4
General budget revenues (% of GDP)	42.1	43.5	43.1	42.5
General budget expenditures (% of GDP)	50.4	49.3	47.7	46.5
General budget balance (% of GDP)	−8.3	−5.8	−4.6	−4.0
Expansion/Austerity Scenario				
GDP (annual growth in %)	2.5	3.5	4.1	3.8
General budget revenues (% of GDP)	42.1	43.5	43.0	42.6
General budget expenditures (% of GDP)	50.4	49.6	47.8	46.4
General budget balance (% of GDP)	−8.3	−6.1	−4.8	−3.8
Fiscal Prudence Scenario				
GDP (annual growth in %)	2.5	3.5	4.1	4.4
General budget revenues (% of GDP)	42.1	43.5	43.1	42.5
General budget expenditures (% of GDP)	50.1	48.9	47.6	46.3
General budget balance (% of GDP)	−8.0	−5.4	−4.5	−3.8

Appendix B: Country case studies

Poland

Public finances and the implementation of a lax fiscal policy have been the weakest elements of Poland's economic policy mix since the mid-1990s. Following the early years of so-called 'shock therapy', the boom years of 1994–7 coincided with the implementation of rather loose fiscal policy under the leadership of then Deputy Prime Minister and Minister of Finance, Grzegorz Kolodko. Despite registering annual growth rates in excess of 6.0%, the Polish SLD–PSL coalition government failed to reduce markedly the absolute scale of the budget deficit, boasting instead about gradually reducing the deficit as a percentage of GDP. That led to overheating of the economy and widened the current account deficit to a degree that necessitated a radical cooling-off programme implemented by the central bank with the use of high real interest rates.

In the years immediately following the parliamentary election that brought to power the centre–right AWS–UW coalition and the return to the finance ministry of the author of the original shock therapy, Leszek Balcerowicz, again ushered in some degree of fiscal prudence to Poland's

Table 8.7. *Hungary, fiscal scenarios (according to ESA-95 methodology)*

	2003	2004	2005	2006
Official Scenario				
GDP (annual growth in %)	3.5	3.5	4.0–4.5	4.5–5.0
General budget revenues (% of GDP)	43.0	44.5	44–44.5	43.5
General budget expenditures (% of GDP)	47.8	48.3	47.0	46.0
General budget balance (% of GDP)	−4.8	−3.8	−2.8	−2.5
Baseline Scenario				
GDP (annual growth in %)	3.2	3.9	4.0	4.0
General budget revenues (% of GDP)	43.1	43.8	43.5	42.8
General budget expenditures (% of GDP)	48.3	48.2	47.5	46.6
General budget balance (% of GDP)	−5.2	−4.4	−4.0	−3.8
Expansion/Austerity Scenario				
GDP (annual growth in %)	3.2	3.9	4.0	3.6
General budget revenues (% of GDP)	43.0	43.4	43.0	43.5
General budget expenditures (% of GDP)	48.4	48.5	47.4	47.3
General budget balance (% of GDP)	−5.4	−5.1	−4.4	−3.8
Fiscal Prudence Scenario				
GDP (annual growth in %)	3.2	3.9	4.1	4.0
General budget revenues (% of GDP)	43.1	43.4	43.2	43.0
General budget expenditures (% of GDP)	48.3	47.7	46.4	46.0
General budget balance (% of GDP)	−5.2	−4.3	−3.2	−3.0

economic policies. The general government deficit was reduced to 2.1% of GDP by 2000 and seemed destined to remain under control in the near future. Unfortunately, after the departure of the UW from the ruling coalition, the plummeting popularity of the AWS government and its labour union roots led to a spending spree and the passage of a number of laws that have proven seriously detrimental to the health of Poland's public finances for the years to come. A young, Western-educated Minister of Finance, Jaroslaw Bauc, brought in to determine the extent of the damage done, concluded that, in the absence of a whole series of reforms, the public sector deficit might loom as large as 11% of GDP by 2003. While his predictions were later determined to be overly pessimistic, the reality caught up with the policy-makers, forcing a more serious reconsideration of the situation.

Following a disastrous fiscal performance in 2001, when the radical shortfall in revenues, combined with minimal cuts in expenditures, resulted in a major widening of the deficit, the 2002 budget in its version presented by the Finance Minister, Marek Belka, who represented the newly elected SLD–UP government, was a major step in taking control of developments in Poland's government finances. Given only six weeks to present a comprehensive budget draft for 2002, Belka put together a document intended to establish a basis for reforming public finances over the next several years. The document was based on very realistic, even conservative, assumptions. Its only major weakness was the fact that it did not transparently address the issue of budget obligations inherited from past years. In particular, the document did not present a solution for dealing with the amounts owed by the Social Security Fund (ZUS) to the private pension funds, estimated at around 6 billion zlotys. Otherwise, the budget was a much needed step in the right direction that temporarily calmed investors' concerns about the government's control over public finances.

Under this budget plan, the level of the budget deficit was to be determined by the government's success in collecting budget revenues. For 2002, Minister Belka assumed that, following the implementation of changes to tax regulations he proposed, budget revenues would reach 143.97 billion zlotys, allowing the budget deficit to remain under 40 billion zlotys, or 5.3% of GDP, according to the Polish methodology. The size of the budget deficit could not be changed unless a revision to the budget was passed by the parliament. Any shortfall in budget revenues was to be matched by a corresponding reduction in expenditures. The data on budget performance in 2002 were very encouraging. According to these data, the budget deficit, at 39,412 million zlotys, fell somewhat short of the annual target of a 40 billion zloty deficit. This positive result was mainly due to a better-than-expected collection of corporate income taxes (108.3% of the annual target) and revenues from other budgetary agencies, mostly increased customs tariffs. Most budget expenditures met the targets set earlier. Financing of public debt was less than expected, at 96.1% of the plan for the domestic portion of the debt, and 95.9% for the external debt.

Instead of building on Belka's plan and moving ahead with further restructuring of expenditures, his successor as Minister of Finance and former holder of this post, Grzegorz Kolodko, prepared the 2003 budget in record time in the late summer of 2002. The document's format, although named 'a budget of stabilisation and development', followed roughly the same assumptions as the budget for 2002, although the rule of limiting expenditures was dropped. The revenues were estimated at 155.7 billion zlotys and expenditures at 194.4 billion zlotys, 8.5% and 6.3%, respectively, more than in 2002 in nominal terms, despite very low inflation. The budget deficit was planned at 38.7 billion zlotys, marginally less than the actual deficit reported for 2002. However, a number of actual spending items were not included in the expenditure count, remaining instead below the line. The government also assumed that privatisation revenues, at 9 billion zlotys, would substantially exceed the collections from that source in the preceding year.

According to preliminary data from the Ministry of Finance, Poland's central government budget deficit reached 61.5% of the annual plan after the first six months of 2003. The deficit amounted to 23.8 billion zlotys. Revenues came in at 71.9 billion zlotys (46.2% of the annual plan) and expenditures at 95.7 billion zlotys (49.2% of the plan). Despite the higher deficit, the budget implementation in 2003 has been proceeding according to schedule. State spending remains in check, while inflows of revenues have slowed, mostly due to lower inflows from corporate and personal income taxes. On the other hand, revenues from indirect taxes reached 46.3% of the total annual target. Also in June, the budget received a full transfer of the profit from the National Bank of Poland in the amount of 4.6 billion zlotys. Privatisation has so far generated only 1.168 billion zlotys, only 3 million zlotys more than in the first five months of the year (15.8% of the annual plan).

While the 2003 budget seems on target, although much higher in terms of percentage of GDP than might have been the case were expenditure controls put in place, the future of Poland's public finances is by no means secure. There are several reasons for this. First and foremost, the current ruling coalition, nearing an all-time low in terms of popularity and facing another parliamentary vote in 2005, is not willing to reduce spending in the most socially sensitive categories. These include, among others, the inefficient social security scheme for farmers (KRUS) (currently farmers are not required to contribute to the programme, while they receive regular retirement benefits), a number of off-budgetary government agencies and funds, as well as a disability payments system that is, due to obvious abuses, one of the most expensive in Europe, if not the world. Secondly, the need to boost growth following two years of mediocre performance makes it that much more difficult to increase taxes. So far, the Ministry of Finance has scrapped the previous plan to reduce personal income tax rates and proceeded with increases in VAT and excise tax rates, actions that are necessary to align Polish tax regulations with the EU norms. Finally, weaker than expected revenues from privatisation of state property mean that a larger portion of the deficit needs to be financed by the issuance of government securities, at a higher cost, as yields rise.

The situation calls for radical measures. However, these have not been forthcoming. Quite to the contrary, the final format of the budget for 2003 became a point of disagreement between then-Finance Minister, Kolodko, and the new Deputy Prime Minister, Jerzy Hausner, that led to the resignation of the former earlier in 2003.

Kolodko spent his last two months in office presenting the outline of his plan of reform of public finances to all the parties. The updated version of his programme, although still not very progressive, incorporated a number of substantial changes to the original assumptions, and was given a fairly lukewarm reception by employers, trade unions, taxpayers, opposition parties and, most importantly, members of the cabinet. This version of the programme differed in some crucial points from the original plan. Kolodko lowered his GDP growth forecast from 3.5% to 3.0%. Furthermore, he adjusted his programme to incorporate some of the ideas promoted by Hausner. These adjustments included, notably, a reduction in the corporate income tax rate from 27% to 19%, effective in 2004. Even in light of the compromise offered by Kolodko, however, Hausner continued to criticise the package, claiming that it still kept the tax burden 'too high'. Specifically, he questioned the need to introduce a 19% tax on capital gains in 2004, the effects of liquidation of all tax breaks and exemptions, and the lack of clearly defined tax-free income allowances for the poor. Hausner also questioned the Ministry of Finance's resolve in dealing with the rising debt of government funds and agencies, such as the Labour Fund. What Hausner did not discuss was the impact his proposals, if implemented, would have on the budget's bottom line. According to rough estimates, Kolodko's adjusted plan still included 'a financing gap' of close to 12 billion zlotys to be covered partially through a release of the zloty revaluation reserve, a move that was not going to be approved by the current management of the National Bank of Poland. Kolodko also removed from the budget 10 billion zlotys in past-due transfers owed to private pension funds by the Social Security Fund (ZUS), arguing that privatisation revenues would finance the shortfall in 2004. As a result, the budget showed a deficit of only 38.7 billion zlotys or 3.9% of GDP (4.6% using the EU's ESA-95 methodology).

The Ministry of Finance presented the first draft of the 2004 budget prepared by Deputy Prime Minister, Jerzy Hausner, and Minister of Finance, Andrzej Raczko, on 22 July 2003. This draft was then discussed and approved by the cabinet two days later and sent to the parliament for discussion and eventual approval in September. The document, presented for the first time in accordance with the EU's ESA-95 methodology, shows a budget deficit of 45.5 billion zlotys, on revenues of 152.7 billion zlotys and expenditures of 198.2 billion zlotys. In developing the budget assumptions, Minister Raczko introduced a number of major amendments to the original draft designed by his predecessor, Grzegorz Kolodko. First and foremost, the new draft assumes economic growth at 4.5–5.0% in 2004. Raczko also assumes moderately slower growth in private and public consumption and investment. The average annual exchange rate for the zloty is now estimated at 4.25 against the euro, compared to 4.15 in the last assessment. More importantly, the Finance Ministry removed from budget revenues the 9 billion zlotys from the liquidation of the revaluation reserve at the National Bank of Poland (NBP) that Kolodko insisted be included despite vocal opposition from the NBP. The official revenue estimates call for 150.0 billion zlotys in almost guaranteed inflows, with the remaining 2.7 billion zlotys expected to accrue due to 'more efficient collection of taxes'. On the expenditure side, Minister Raczko drastically reduced the spending levels that were requested by individual ministers (by almost 17 billion zlotys). On the other hand, 12 billion zlotys due in transfers to private pension funds are still not included in expenditures, in accordance with ESA-95, and will have to be financed by a combination of privatisation receipts and debt issuance. Although the Ministry of Finance wants to raise the ceiling for foreign debt issuance to 15 million zlotys (US$3.5 billion) in 2004, a substantial portion of these transfers will have to be financed by additional debt issuance on the domestic market. In summary, the new draft is clearly more transparent than the 'virtual budget' suggested by Kolodko, but it still offers a major loosening of fiscal policy in 2004. If implemented, the budget gap in 2004 would bring the total public debt to above 55% of GDP, dangerously close to the 60% limit set in the constitution.

Czech Republic

The fiscal situation in the Czech Republic has to a large extent been affected negatively by the failed efforts to restructure the banking sector during the 1990s. In the end, the government decided to transfer the non-performing loans from commercial banks to the *Konsolidacni banka*, a loan restructuring agency. This permitted a serious clean-up of bank loan portfolios, but also left the budget with the financial burden of an agency that was likely to generate massive losses for a number of years that would have to be covered through budget subsidies. In their assessments of the situation of public finances over the years, both the World Bank and the OECD have warned the Czech government about the country's large budget deficits. They acknowledged early on, however, that the large projected consolidated deficit for 2001 was due to the high costs of bank restructuring, which should have peaked in 2001 and started to decline in years to come. The clean-up of the *Investicni a Postovi Banka* bank alone, which was placed into forced administration and sold in 2000 with government guarantees, boosted expenditures significantly in 2001. According to the Ministry of Finance, the cost of bailing out the financial sector was supposed to weigh on government finances until 2004 or 2005. But international financial institutions have also pointed to several additional areas where fiscal restructuring was necessary to bring budgets under control. Pensions represented one of the most significant problems in mandatory spending. Other areas for suggested reform included healthcare, education, housing and transportation. It was ascertained that, if budget deficits were not brought under control over the next several years, macroeconomic balance could be threatened, particularly once privatisation revenues run out.

A January 2001 agreement between the largest Czech political parties, CSSD and ODS, called for a gradual reduction in state budget deficits over the next few years, with a deficit of 10 billion koruna in 2002 and a balanced budget by 2003. However, the CSSD was counting the bank restructuring losses from *Ceska konsolidacni agentura* (formerly *Konsolidacni banka*) below the line. When these expenses are included, the overall budget deficit is boosted considerably. Even discounting bank bailout expenses, budget deficits were higher than planned in 2001. The state budget deficit reached 67.7 billion koruna (3.1% of GDP), considerably more than the deficit that was finally approved of 49 billion koruna. Revenues reached 626.22 billion koruna, while expenditures totalled 693.92 billion koruna. The then-Finance Minister, Jiri Rusnok, stated that the privatisation of fourteen firms brought in revenues of 164 billion koruna for the National Property Fund in 2001. The proceeds from some of those sales did not arrive until 2002, however. Other privatisation projects that were supposed to be completed in 2001 but faced delays included the telecommunications firm, Cesky Telecom, and the CEZ utility company, together with six electricity distributors. According to the Finance Ministry, the consolidated budget deficit for 2001 reached 52.2 billion koruna (2.4% of GDP). The deficit would have been considerably higher if it were not for income from extra-budgetary accounts. With privatisation revenues excluded, the consolidated budget deficit jumped to 5.3% of GDP.

The Czech Republic's 2002 budget bill envisaged a deficit of 46.2 billion koruna, with revenues of 690.4 billion and expenditures of 736.6 billion koruna. Mandatory costs were projected to make up 52% of total budget expenditures, or 16.6% of GDP. In the absence of pension reform, 29.7% of the total state budget was set to go to pensions. Although the budget target was widely expected to be exceeded given the cabinet's lax fiscal approach, the state budget ended 2002 with an unexpectedly low preliminary deficit of 45.72 billion koruna (2.8% of GDP). Revenues reached 705.04 billion koruna in 2002, while expenditures totalled 750.76 billion koruna. According to Finance Minister, Bohuslav Sobotka, the better-than-expected results were achieved primarily because of an improvement in tax revenues, mainly from corporations. The deficit would have been considerably higher if privatisation revenues and income from the repayment of Russia's Soviet-era debt had been excluded, however. Of the total proceeds from the sale of Transgas, 20.6 billion koruna were transferred to the state budget in 2002, in addition to 17.2 billion koruna from Russia's debt repayment. Extraordinary revenues totalled 53.5 billion koruna in 2002. Excluding those one-off revenues, the deficit reached 99.2 billion koruna (4.4% of GDP).

The Finance Ministry's initial draft state budget for 2003 counted on a deficit of 157.3 billion koruna. Of that amount, 60 billion koruna were to be used to cover debts relating to bank restructuring. While expenditures were projected to rise on mandatory items, such as pensions and social insurance, revenue totals were expected to fall as one-off revenue flows such as privatisation income ceased to be included in the budget. The government approved its draft budget for 2003, with a gap of 111.3 billion koruna, which was 46 billion koruna less than in the Finance Ministry's original proposal. That included expenditures of 795.4 billion koruna and revenues of 684.1 billion koruna. The budget planned for GDP growth of 3.3%, inflation at 2.0% and average unemployment of 9.9%. In order to reduce the deficit, the government made spending cuts of about 3.5 billion koruna, including 1.5 billion koruna at the Defence Ministry alone. The main reason for the lower deficit, however, was the delay in paying for losses from the bank bailout agency, *Ceska konsolidacni agentura* (CKA). The government decided that it would cover only losses for 2001 in 2003, totalling 18.6 billion koruna. Funds for covering damage from the August floods were expected to total 17 billion koruna. The implementation of the Czech state budget deficit proceeded roughly according to the plan reaching 62.1 billion cumulatively in the first seven months of 2003, or around 56% of the annual deficit target of 111.3 billion koruna. Revenues totalled 394.7 billion koruna, while expenditures amounted to 456.9 billion.

Fiscal reform remains the key policy concern for the Czech Republic. If the government does not take serious reform measures, the budget deficit will continue to rise, endangering long-term growth. Deputy Finance Minister, Eduard Janota, recently speculated that, unless radical changes were implemented, the state budget gap for 2004 could not be smaller than 140 billion koruna, while growing demands for public sector wage hikes may push the deficit even higher. In a meeting in May 2003, ruling coalition representatives agreed to reduce the public finance deficit to 4.0% of GDP by 2006 - down from an estimated 6.7%

in 2003 - representing savings of 92 billion koruna over the next three years. The approved deficit target represented an improvement over the 2002 coalition agreement, which stipulated that the public finance deficit would be cut to 4.9–5.4% of GDP by 2006. Last December, Finance Minister, Bohuslav Sobotka, had offered two versions of public finance reform: one that would reduce the deficit to 4.9% of GDP by 2006 and a more radical scenario that would cut the deficit to 3.7% of GDP. Even with Sobotka's more radical plan, the cuts would not be as deep as recommended by non-governmental economic experts and the central bank. Within the government, one of the junior ruling parties, the Freedom Union, would like to bring the deficit to 3.1% of GDP by 2006.

After repeated delays, the Czech cabinet finally approved its preliminary blueprint for public finance reform in June 2003. According to the plan, the corporate income tax will be cut gradually from 31% to 24% over the next three years. In order to compensate for the negative effects such a step will have on budget revenues, excise duties on cigarettes and alcohol will be raised. The government also agreed that it will not impose a uniform VAT rate, although most services and some goods will soon be taxed at the higher rate of 22%. While the real estate transfer tax will be cut from 5% to 3%, the coalition does not intend to introduce an inheritance tax. The retirement age will be raised to 63, and other aspects of pension reform will be approved in the future. Moreover, sickness benefits will be cut.

Excluding privatisation revenues and losses connected with bank restructuring, the state budget gap is expected to reach 83 billion koruna in 2004, down from 92 billion koruna in the previous year. While the parliament met to begin discussions on certain aspects of the legislation on 22 July, the government must submit its draft state budget for 2004 to the lower house by the end of September. The cabinet has not yet discussed its plans for budget cuts for individual ministries, an issue that is sure to be a struggle. In June, Finance Minister, Bohuslav Sobotka, surprised other cabinet ministers when he proposed spending cuts that were more radical than expected, negatively affecting farmers, police, scientists and the army. Critics pointed out that the reforms approved by the cabinet did not go far enough since they failed to include much-needed changes in the pension and social welfare systems. Moreover, the cabinet's plan to cut corporate income tax to 24% by 2006 is widely seen as insufficient, particularly given that the rate is being slashed to 18–19% in the other three Visegrad countries. On the other hand, the discussions on public finance reform have been met with protests from the labour unions, while the Defence Minister, Jaroslav Tvrdik, resigned in May in protest at proposed budget cuts in the army. Prime Minister Vladimir Spidla pointed out that the reforms are inevitable and would be even more severe if the current coalition was replaced by the opposition Civic Democratic Party, which is now the most popular in the country. Although the parliament approved the bills in the first reading on 24 July, their final approval in the autumn currently appears highly uncertain.

Public finance reform still requires the final approval of the parliament, which will certainly be complicated, given the leftist slant of some representatives of the Social Democrats (CSSD), the dominant party in the ruling coalition. Some CSSD members would prefer higher taxes to decreases in spending, arguing that radical budget cuts would make it difficult for the party to fulfil its pre-election promises, particularly in the area of social policy. In that light, the 2004 state budget law will be extremely difficult to approve and could mark a breaking point for the ruling coalition. Even if the government's proposals are eventually approved by the parliament and signed by the president, the public finance deficit is unlikely to fall below 3% of GDP until 2008, at the earliest.

Hungary

In 2000, Hungary adopted a two-year budget cycle. Hence, the government proposed and the Hungarian parliament passed budgets for both 2001 and 2002 in autumn 2000. Despite these good intentions, the government had to modify both budgets, increasing budgetary expenditures in both years. The government initially argued that better-than-expected tax revenues had made it possible to increase spending without expanding the fiscal deficit. The first revision of the two-year budget was announced in August 2001. The Hungarian government decided to spend an additional 284.6 billion forint in 2001 and 200.0 billion forint in 2002. The additional expenditures for 2001 included 47.1 billion forint for increased subsidies for pharmaceuticals, 67.1 billion forint to increase various pensions, and 25 billion forint to accelerate construction under the *Szechenyi* infrastructure programme. The 200 billion forint boost in 2002 was to be spent primarily on infrastructure projects. The government also planned to spend an additional 100 billion forint on highway construction. In addition, substantial sums were designated for mortgage interest rate subsidies. The government had been providing subsidised credits at interest rates of 8%; and these were to be reduced to 6% in 2002. These changes resulted in a 2.9% increase in expenditures in the consolidated budget in 2001, financed by an additional 3.1% increase in revenues. The officially reported figure of the public sector budget deficit was 3.3% of

GDP in 2001, below the revised budget target of 3.4%. However, the Hungarian budget accounting system did not correspond to EU standards, according to which the Hungarian 2001 deficit was as high as 5% of GDP. On paper, the 2002 budget looked fairly good, although most observers believed it would be looser once off-budget expenditures were incorporated into the picture. The consolidated fiscal balance was budgeted to rise to 505 billion forint, from 493 billion in 2001, a very modest nominal increase. However, after eight months of the year, the consolidated fiscal deficit expanded to 756 billion forint. A further revision to the 2002 budget expanded the deficit to over 1.2 trillion forint; but even this assumption was proven wrong.

Hungary's cash-based consolidated budget deficit totalled 1.62 trillion forint in 2002 (9.6% of GDP, or 9.2% of GDP according to ESA-95 methodology), more than triple the 445 billion forint deficit reported for 2001. In December 2002 alone, the deficit amounted to a shocking 615.8 billion forint. In addition, the deficit was not only much larger than the original annual target of 505 billion forint, but also larger than the revised figure of 1.22 trillion forint set in the final revision to the 2002 budget, which was approved in December. The widening of the deficit was entirely due to excessive spending. In fact, revenues exceeded the initial target by 3.1%.

Hungary's fiscal performance in the first four months of 2003 was very disappointing. The cumulative general government budget deficit for the first four months totalled 400.4 billion forint, up from 316.1 billion forint for the same period of 2002. As a result, the deficit reached 48.1% of the full year target. In April alone, the budget deficit exceeded the market consensus, reaching 118.2 billion forint, compared with 74.3 billion forint a year earlier. While budget expenditures are usually front-loaded in the first quarter of the year, the pattern for this year is rather worrisome, as the increase in the deficit has clearly been due to increased spending, rather than lower revenues. In May, growth in the deficit slowed considerably, with the cumulative total reaching 408.7 billion forint, but then exploded by 192.4 billion forint in June. This brought the cumulative deficit to a stunning 601.1 billion forint, or 72% of the annual target after just six months of the year. More importantly, the preliminary figures do not include the deficits in the budgets of local governments that are added to the final annual budget figure in December. The general government budget was also in deficit because of a larger deficit in the social security fund that offset the surplus in the state budget. The government recently revised its budget deficit target for the year to 4.8% of GDP, but even this figure looks quite unrealistic in light of the performance to date.

9 Current account dynamics in the new Member States

Paolo Zanghieri *

9.1 Introduction

The twelve Central and Eastern European countries, which either joined the European Union (EU) in May 2004 or are scheduled to do so as early as 2007,[1] often show high current account deficits, which are sometimes close or even beyond those values which common sense and past experience associate with a high probability of a balance-of-payment crisis. A natural question therefore arises: are these deficits sustainable or do some countries require policy action? A related question is how the current account is likely to evolve in the medium term, i.e. up to 2007. The aim of this chapter is to provide a tentative answer, by means of a normative analysis based on econometric estimation of the determinants of the current accounts to be used for a projection of external balances. The role of capital inflows, and in particular of foreign direct investment (FDI), is stressed.

The chapter is structured as follows. In section 9.2 the basic accounting identities, and some stylised facts about external balances in CEECs, are presented. Section 9.3 deals with the importance of the current account as a factor responsible for currency crises. A quick review of the standard methodologies used for current account assessment is presented in section 9.4. Section 9.5 summarises some empirical studies of the current account. In section 9.6, panel estimation of current account dynamics is performed; the results are then employed to simulate the future path of foreign debt accumulation, given some assumptions on growth and fiscal policy. Section 9.7 is devoted to a discussion

* This article was written when the author was an economist at the CEPII, Centre d'Etudes Prostectives et d'Infomations Internationales, – 9 rue Georges Pitard, 75015 Paris. The author wishes to thank, without implications, Lionel Fontagnè, Agnés Benassy-Queré, Mike Artis and Debora Revoltella for useful comments and suggestions.
[1] I will analyse eight of the ten countries which joined the EU in 2004, i.e. the Czech Republic, Estonia, Hungary, Latvia, Lithuania, Poland, Slovakia and Slovenia, and Bulgaria and Romania, whose scheduled accession date is 2007. We omit Cyprus and Malta due to their small size and peculiar economic structure.

of two important policy issues, namely the saving rate in new EU members and the adoption of the euro. Section 9.8 concludes.

9.2   Basic identities and some stylised facts

Some macroeconomic identities show that the current account can be seen as the difference between savings and investment. The current account is the balance between export and import of goods and services plus the interest income from the stock of net foreign assets:

$$CA_t = X_t - M_t + r_t B_t \qquad (1)$$

where X is export, M import, B the stock of net foreign assets and r the interest rate. The basic GDP identity can be rewritten as:

$$X_t - M_t = Y_t - C_t - G_t - I_t \qquad (2)$$

where Y is GDP, C and G private and government consumption, and I investment. Therefore, the equation for the current account can be rewritten as:

$$CA_t = Y_t + r_t B_t - C_t - G_t - I_t \qquad (3)$$

Defining saving (S) as the difference between available resources (GDP and revenue from net foreign assets) and non-capital expenditure, we have:

$$CA_t = S_t - I_t \qquad (4)$$

Table 9.1 shows non-overlapping three-year averages of the savings, investment and current account ratios to GDP in the CEECs, together with data for 2003.

The Czech Republic showed a significant current account deficit during the second half of the 1990s, as the rapid transformation of the industrial sector required a strong import of capital goods. A significant drop in total savings (due mainly to government deficit) is responsible for its deterioration in the last years. A quick reduction of the deficit can be observed in Hungary, where a strong recovery in savings reduced the gap by more than a half between 1994 and 2002, while the investment ratio remained broadly constant: a sizeable drop in (public) saving is responsible for the worsening of the deficit in 2003. The strong increase in investment at the end of the 1990s is responsible for the rapid deterioration of the current account in Poland, where a drop in savings in the last three years can also be observed: the current account gap shrank in 2003 due to a fall in investment. The external deficit

Table 9.1. *Saving, investment and current account to GDP ratios*

	1994–6	1997–9	2000–2	2003
Czech Republic				
Saving	26.98	25.24	21.60	20.52
Investment	30.90	29.17	27.45	26.73
Current account	−3.92	−3.93	−5.85	−6.21
Hungary				
Saving	14.14	19.45	20.36	13.32
Investment	20.53	23.26	23.36	22.30
Current account	−6.39	−3.81	−3.00	−8.98
Poland				
Saving	18.89	19.23	17.03	16.10
Investment	19.10	24.70	21.32	18.29
Current account	−0.21	−5.47	−4.29	−2.19
Slovakia				
Saving	27.30	25.97	22.95	24.68
Investment	28.04	33.59	30.19	25.79
Current account	−0.74	−7.62	−7.24	−1.11
Slovenia				
Saving	22.45	23.57	23.83	23.54
Investment	21.32	25.12	24.16	23.90
Current account	1.13	−1.55	−0.33	−0.36
Estonia				
Saving	19.54	18.82	18.73	15.22
Investment	26.46	27.52	26.80	28.42
Current account	−6.92	−8.70	−8.07	−13.2
Latvia				
Saving	16.01	14.91	18.56	15.57
Investment	16.13	23.74	26.61	24.16
Current account	−0.12	−8.83	−8.05	−8.59
Lithuania				
Saving	15.18	12.39	15.37	14.55
Investment	22.34	23.56	20.43	21.40
Current account	−7.16	−11.17	−5.06	−6.85
Bulgaria				
Saving	14.07	12.49	11.99	10.80
Investment	14.19	13.04	17.36	19.57
Current account	−0.12	−0.55	−5.37	−8.77
Romania				
Saving	16.93	13.47	16.60	16.62
Investment	21.54	19.02	20.83	22.52
Current account	−4.61	−5.55	−4.23	−5.90

widened considerably in the Slovak Republic after 1997, pushed both by an increase in investment (which slowed down in the last years) and by a smooth decline in total savings. Finally, Slovenia has virtually no current account deficit.

Turning to the Baltic states, we observe that Estonia's external deficit has always been at 'dangerous levels' and has recently dropped to around 13% of GDP as a consequence of one-off factors but also strong domestic demand. Lithuania shows a strong deterioration during the 1997–9 period due to a sustained fall in savings. The gap has narrowed in the most recent period due to an increase in savings (mainly public) and a dip in the investment ratio; however, the pick-up in domestic demand is likely to widen the deficit, as witnessed by data for 2003. Finally, the big surge in investment is mainly responsible for the rapid and persistent widening of the deficit in Latvia. Given the strength of domestic demand, such a deficit is not likely to shrink in the near future.

Bulgaria suffered a quick deterioration of its external balance between 2000 and 2002, as a consequence of rapid economic development following the 1996–7 banking crisis; the investment boom has been matched by a marked deterioration in total savings, which can be explained to a large extent by expansionary fiscal policies. By contrast, Romania shows a broadly stable deficit.

All in all, we can conclude this brief analysis by saying that current account positions in the new EU members do not show a homogeneous pattern either in terms of the level of the deficit or in terms of its dynamics and driving forces.

9.3   How important is the current account?

The importance of current account imbalances as a warning signal of currency crisis is recognised by most of the recent theoretical and empirical literature. It has not been so in the past.

One of the most important policy implications of the intertemporal models of current accounts is that, as long as deficits are created by increasing investment, these should not be a cause for concern, as the build-up of external debt will be repaid easily thanks to increased growth. Government deficit is the only important variable that should be kept in check. Such a view of the current account deficit has been named Lawson's Doctrine, after the former British Chancellor of the Exchequer, Nigel Lawson, who first proposed it in the 1980s. However, the sequence of debt and balance-of-payments crisis that has occurred in the last twenty years showed that such a theory is seriously flawed.[2] Anecdotal evidence shows that a widening (even though not necessarily

---

[2] See Reisen (1998) and Edwards (2002) for a thorough discussion of the pitfalls of the Lawson Doctrine.

large) of the current account deficit is almost always present before an exchange rate crisis (see, for example, Corsetti, Pesenti and Roubini (1999) and Radelet and Sachs (2000) on the Asian Crisis). The importance of the current account is witnessed by its widespread use in early-warning indicators of currency crises.[3]

Article 3A of the Maastricht Treaty includes 'a sustainable balance of payments' among the guiding principles that EU countries must follow in setting their economic policies. The situation and development of the balance of payments on current accounts is included as an additional criterion in assessing a country's readiness to join the Economic and Monetary Union.

These provisions are rather vague. However, a look at the various reports on new EU members (see, for example, European Commission, 2002b) shows that external balances are one of the most closely watched variables.

9.4   Methodologies for assessing sustainability

Following Frenkel and Razin (1997), two different, but interrelated, concepts can be distinguished: a country's solvency and current accounts sustainability.

An economy is said to be solvent if the present discounted value of future surpluses in the balance of trade and services is equal to current external indebtedness. Such a definition is obviously difficult to apply as it relies on future events or policy decisions. This leads to the definition of sustainability. A current account deficit is sustainable if the continuation of the existing government policy stance and private sector behaviour is not going to entail a drastic policy shift (such as a fiscal contraction) or lead to a currency or balance-of-payments crisis. Of course, such a definition needs to be complemented by a benchmark level for the current account. Moreover, in order to assess the sustainability of the deficit, the source of it must be taken into account. A deficit created by a reduction in savings is clearly more worrying than one created by a surge in investment, which increases future growth and ability to repay.

In order to have an assessment of current account sustainability, a benchmark value is needed. The International Monetary Fund has over the years developed a methodology to arrive at a quantitative measure of sustainability, based on several macroeconomic indicators,[4] which at the

---

[3] Recent surveys of these models can be found in Edison (2003) and Abiad (2003).

[4] A more detailed description of this methodology can be found in Isard *et al.* (2001).

same time provides an indication of exchange rate misalignment. Such an approach is closely linked to the Fundamental Equilibrium Exchange Rate (FEER) (see, for example, Williamson, 1994) approach. It consists of determining first the current account position that would exist in the long run given the current level of the exchange rate once the temporary effects of past levels of activity have been absorbed by the economy, or, in other words, when the economy is operating at a 'normal level' of capacity utilisation. This 'underlying' measure of the current account is then compared with a measure of 'sustainable' balance, which would be financed by nominal capital flows assuming that the country under investigation and its trade and financial partners have low inflation and operate at a reasonable rate of capacity utilisation. The next steps imply finding a level of the effective real exchange rate that equates the two definitions of balance described above, and therefore derives the necessary adjustment.[5] However, this methodology requires heroic assumptions to be made about the steady-state values of the main economic variables, and, given the peculiar conditions of the countries under analysis, is probably not very reliable.

Another widely used methodology which assumes that the economy is at the steady state is the one developed by Milesi-Ferretti and Razin (1996). It is a simple, but theoretically consistent, accounting framework in which the current stock of external debt is assumed to be the optimal one. The benchmark level for the current account is therefore the one which stabilises the debt, given some simple assumption about growth and real interest and exchange rates. Such a method can be easily extended to incorporate non-debt financing capital inflows such as FDI (see Doisy and Hervè, 2003). While its simplicity is appealing, such a methodology is probably not very useful for the analysis of the new EU members, as the two basic assumption underlying it are probably not met: first of all, it is very likely that the effect of the 'big bang' experienced by these economies roughly ten years ago will be felt for a while. Secondly, as shown by Table 9.2, the overall debt level of these countries is, with the notable exception of Bulgaria, not very high. Therefore, given their investment needs and growth prospects, a further increase in external debt need not trigger any crisis,[6] and consequently its observed level of debt is not the optimal one.[7]

---

[5] See for details Isard et al. (2001) and Williamson (1994).
[6] Moreover, as pointed out by Reinhart et al. (2003), it is difficult to identify a clear-cut relationship between the level of external debt and the occurrence of a crisis.
[7] Zanghieri (2004) provides a detailed description of this method and an application to the new EU members.

Table 9.2. *External debt to GDP ratios*

	1995–8	1999–2002
Czech Republic	33.84	41.03
Hungary	63.27	61.07
Poland	35.62	37.42
Slovakia	36.37	59.66
Slovenia	27.33	33.51
Estonia	23.73	49.75
Latvia	22.31	63.92
Lithuania	17.64	41.02
Bulgaria	93.44	76.72
Romania	23.39	27.68

Another way of testing for sustainability, borrowed from the public finance literature, is to check whether the current accounts follow a stationary process. This would mean that in the long run the intertemporal budget constraint linking savings and investment is respected. Coakley *et al.* (1996) apply this concept to OECD countries and link their findings to the Feldstein–Horioka puzzle.[8] Such an approach is not feasible here due to the short time span considered.

A simpler, and probably more trivial, definition of sustainability is the following: a current account position is sustainable as long as foreign investors are willing to finance it. In light of the recent financial crises in emerging markets, it should be added that the quality of the sources of financing matters a lot: a high percentage of short-term debt increases the probability of sudden capital outflows leading to a crisis. It is almost unanimously recognised that foreign direct investment is by far the surest form of external financing. Thus a very simple way to check for sustainability is to see how much of the deficit is financed by FDI. Table 9.3 shows the difference between net FDI flows and the current account deficit (as a percentage of GDP) for the last five available years. We can see that, seen from this angle, external sustainability does not seem to be an issue for most of the countries. In contrast, the situation of Estonia and Hungary has worsened rapidly. Whether inflows can be kept at this level in the medium run is obviously a key policy question.[9]

---

[8] See also Coakley *et al.* (2004) for a more sophisticated approach.

[9] A much more positive view can be found in Boeri and Brucker (2002), who claim that EU entry might double FDI inflows. Empirical analyses on FDI in these countries can be found in Bevan and Estrin (2000) Garibaldi *et al.* (2002), Buch *et al.* (2001) and Kinoshita and Campos (2003).

Table 9.3. *Difference between net FDI flows and current account balance as percentage of GDP*

	1999	2000	2001	2002	2003
Czech Republic	12.47	7.78	3.89	5.87	−3.41
Hungary	1.91	1.75	2.11	−2.36	−3.94
Poland	−0.51	3.89	0.29	5.00	−1.23
Slovakia	−1.21	10.14	NA	NA	NA
Slovenia	−3.07	−2.45	5.40	5.91	4.61
Estonia	1.06	4.86	6.84	−4.28	−1.75
Latvia	−3.01	1.17	−7.06	−3.70	−5.56
Lithuania	−4.21	−0.69	−1.06	−0.15	−5.88
Bulgaria	1.07	2.81	−0.14	1.10	−1.64
Romania	−0.73	−0.83	−2.62	−0.90	−2.66

9.5   Modelling the current account

From a theoretical point of view, the standard reference for current account analysis is the intertemporal approach developed in the last twenty years or so and synthesised by Obstfeld and Rogoff (1995, 1996) and Razin (1995).

On the empirical front, Chinn and Prasad (2003) provide a comprehensive analysis of the medium-term determinants of the current account, employing a panel of eighty-nine industrial and developing countries over the 1977–95 period, through panel and cross-section techniques. Their aim is not to discriminate among the competing theoretical models, but rather to provide a set of stylised facts upon which a theory can be built. Their main findings are that government budget balance, initial foreign asset position and indicators of financial deepening are positively correlated with current accounts. Demographic variables such as the dependency ratio have a strong, negative impact on the current accounts. Terms of trade volatility (used as proxy of macroeconomic uncertainty) is positively correlated to the external balances in developing countries. Agents may tend to save more in order to smooth consumption in the face of volatile income flows, and the ability of a country to run a large current accounts deficit can be hampered by high terms of trade volatility making international investors unwilling to put money into its economy. Other variables such as openess to trade and measures of capital controls do not seem to have significant effects. They also find no evidence in favour of the stage-of-development hypothesis, i.e. that countries whose per capita GDP is closer to that of industrialised countries run lower external deficits. A similar approach is taken by Calderon *et al.* (2002), who use a more sophisticated methodology. Bussière *et al.* (2004) apply a similar methodology (complemented by a theoretical model) to study the current account dynamics in old and new EU members.

9.6   A simple econometric model

9.6.1   The model

This section presents the results of an econometric study of the determinants of current accounts position for the ten countries analysed. The data used are described in Appendix A to this chapter.

Following Alesina *et al.* (1999), the long-term and short-term determinants of the current account are modelled separately. In the first step, the short-term dynamics are modelled by panel regression, using more volatile variables. Then the residuals are averaged across time in order to derive country fixed effects, roughly representing the share of current account variability not explained by short-term determinants. These fixed effects are then used in a cross-section regression where less volatile variables are employed as dependent variables. Appendix B to this chapter provides more details on the procedure.

The results are presented in Table 9.4.[10] We can observe that the coefficient on government budget balance is positive and highly significant. Its size is broadly in line with that of the studies on current accounts mentioned above and some panel analysis of savings behaviour, such as Edwards (1995) on developing economies and Schrooten and Stephan (2002) on transition economies. A percentage point deterioration in government budget brings about nearly a 0.4 point deterioration in the deficit, as public dissavings are not fully compensated by higher private savings. The negative correlation between real per capita income and the current account is at odds with the catching-up theory, but can be seen as a proof of consumption-smoothing behaviour. It is also consistent with analogous studies on current accounts in developing countries. Increases in income, which are thought to be very persistent or permanent, lead to a reduction in savings and therefore a drop in the external balance. It can also be associated with the fact that growth reduces the borrowing constraints agents face, as shown for developing countries by Lane and Milesi-Ferretti (2001), in their estimation of the determinants of the change in net foreign asset position.

---

[10] Data availability restricted the estimation to the 1992–2002 period.

Table 9.4. *Short-term determinants of the current account*

Dependent variable: current account to GDP ratio	
Current account (lagged)	0.35
t-stat	7.66
Budget balance	0.36
t-stat	2.47
Real per capita GDP	−0.02
t-stat	−2.18
Financial deepening	0.08
t-stat	3.99
Trade openness	−0.04
t-stat	−3.49
R squared	0.64
Number of observations	107

Notes: Financial deepening is the ratio between M2 and GDP; trade openness is the sum of import and export divided by GDP.

As shown by Chinn and Prasad (2003) and Blanchard and Giavazzi (2003), the negative relationship does not hold for developed countries, and therefore it is safe to say that the result found for the CEECs will change over time with the catching-up process. However, given the time horizon considered (up to 2007), it is reasonable to assume that the sign of the parameter will not change.

The measure of financial deepening (i.e. the ratio of M2 to GDP) has been widely used in growth regressions and in studies on savings. Edwards (1995) finds that this variable is positively correlated with savings, as a deeper and more sophisticated financial system would provide incentives to people to save more. However, this variable might be seen as a measure of the borrowing constraints faced by private agents, and therefore be associated with lower savings (see Blanchard and Giavazzi, 2003). Moreover, it is important to recall that this estimation does not disentangle the effects of the explanatory variables on savings and investment, and that the effects of financial deepening on the latter are ambiguous. In any case, the results seem to suggest that financial deepening, measured in this way, influences the current account mainly via savings: a deeper, more sophisticated financial system would encourage private savings. The development of financial intermediation is likely to ease investment, with negative effects on the external balances:[11] a more detailed discussion on the link between

---

[11] Actually, the ratio of net domestic credit to GDP was tried as an explanatory variable, but it turned out to be non-significant.

Table 9.5. *Long-term determinants of the current account*

Dependent variable: average of first-step regression residuals	
Old dependency ratio	−0.12
t-stat	−3.04
External debt to GDP ratio	0.04
t-stat	2.61
R squared	0.46
Number of observations	10

Notes: Old dependency ratio is the ration between people above 65 and people aged between 15 and 65.

current accounts and financial deepening is developed in the next sub-section.

The coefficient on the trade openness index is in line with what is traditionally found in the literature. According to Milesi-Ferretti and Razin (1998, 2000) a higher degree of openness would enhance a country's ability to pay off the external debt, and would therefore reduce the external borrowing constraints, allowing for a higher deficit.

Turning to the cross-section regression for the long-run determinants (Table 9.5), only the old dependency ratio, defined as the percentage of population aged more than 65 years to the population between 15 and 65, and external debt to GDP ratio turned out to be significant.[12] The sign of the dependency ratio is the one indicated by standard life-cycle theory in that an older population has less savings. The positive link with external debt can be interpreted as the foreign asset position being a constraint limiting the size of the deficit.

Catching-up will tend to reduce external imbalances over time, but, at the same time, the easing of the borrowing constraint faced by economic agents will counterbalance this trend. Economic policy will therefore have to be very cautious: moreover, in the short run, the sizeable 'twin deficits' effects strengthens the case for disciplined fiscal policy, especially for those countries willing to join the ERM-II mechanism quickly in order to adopt the euro as soon as possible. In the long run, further pressures on the current account are likely, as in most of the countries considered old dependency ratios are set to rise rapidly.

The simple econometric model just described can be used to project the future path for external debt. Conclusions on sustainability can be

[12] I also tried a young dependency ratio, total population and per capita income (in PPP terms) relative to the EU-15 average. None of these variables turned out to be significant.

derived from this projection, given some assumption on the behaviour of exogenous variables and on capital flows.

9.6.2   Projections

As stated in section 9.3, a current account balance is said to be sustainable if, given the projected path of some key macroeconomic variables, it stabilises the stock of external debt at the current level. The simple econometric model just developed can then be used in order to have a rough idea of the future development of these countries' stocks of external debt up to 2007. To this end, a forecast growth path and an estimate of the future fiscal policy stance are needed, together with further assumptions on financial deepening, as well as assumptions on net inflows of foreign capital.

Before turning to the assumptions made and the results obtained, two warnings are essential. First of all, it is important to recall that the econometric model is very simple and the panel methodology forces an averaging out of countries characterised by a high heterogeneity. Secondly, such a model can give a hint about the sustainable level of current accounts only if we retain the definition of sustainable as the level stabilising foreign debt.

The forecasts for real GDP and trade openness are obtained from the forecasts made by the European Commission and available on the AMECO database. Future values of the government deficit have been obtained by the European Commission forecast and by Global Insight up to 2006. A scenario of gradual reduction of government deficit was employed for the remaining year. Projecting financial deepening and, above all, the impacts of the development of the financial system on the external balances is much more difficult. If, on the one hand, the regression shows that the ratio of M2 over GDP has a positive effect on the external balance, hinting at this aggregate having a stronger effect on savings rather than investment, the same conclusion probably does not hold true if other, broader, monetary aggregates are considered.[13] With the development of a sounder banking system, the opportunities for investment are bound to increase. At the same time, stronger banks will be more capable of borrowing abroad, thereby worsening external imbalances. The ratio of M2 to GDP is projected to grow at the average rate of the last four years.

---

[13] Using M3 instead was not feasible due to the lack of homogeneous data.

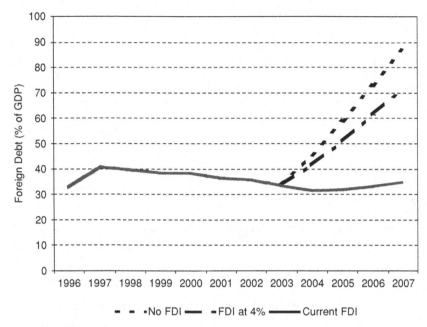

Figure 9.1. Czech Republic, actual and projected external debt (as % of GDP).

In order to forecast the trajectory of debt, we assume that FDI is the only non-debt-creating foreign source of capital. Therefore, net foreign debt evolves according to:

$$D_{t+1} = D_t - CA_t - FDI_t \qquad (5)$$

where all the variables are expressed as a ratio to GDP, and FDI is net FDI flows.

We derived the debt path under three different assumptions on future FDI flows: equal to the 2000–3 average, fixed at 4% of GDP and equal to zero. The results are reported in Figures 9.1 to 9.10.

According to the simulations, external debt is going to increase in most of the countries regardless of the assumptions made on FDI flows.[14] As noted above, the results should be viewed as showing a trend.

---

[14] The odd results for the Czech Republic and Slovakia are driven by the massive inflows of FDI recorded in the last years, which are unlikely to be maintained in the medium term.

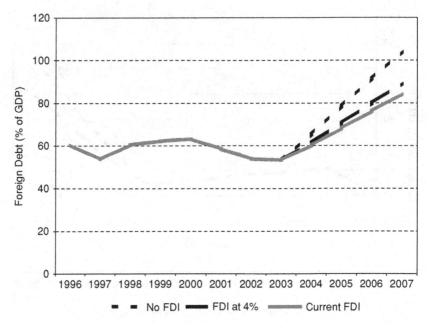

Figure 9.2. Hungary, actual and projected external debt (as % of GDP).

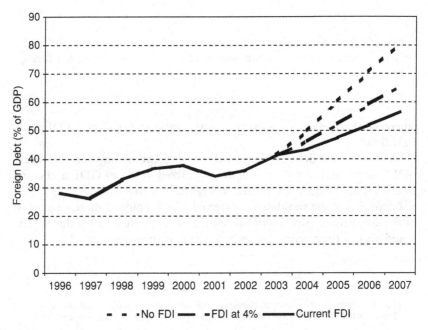

Figure 9.3. Poland, actual and projected external debt (as % of GDP).

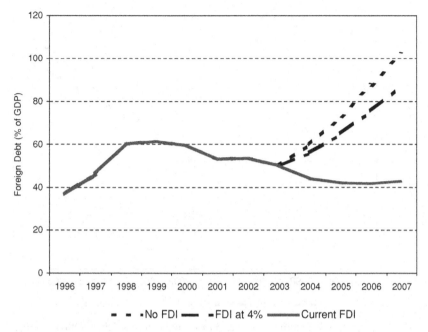

Figure 9.4. Slovakia, actual and projected external debt (as % of GDP).

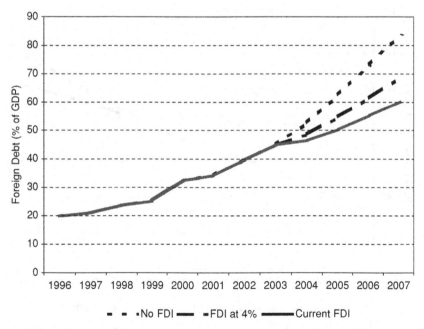

Figure 9.5. Slovenia, actual and projected external debt (as % of GDP).

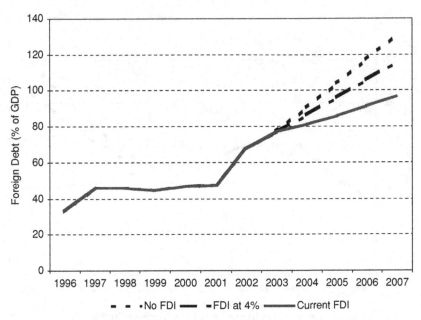

Figure 9.6. Estonia, actual and projected external debt (as % of GDP).

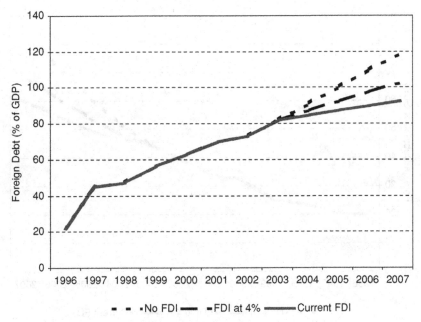

Figure 9.7. Latvia, actual and projected external debt (as % of GDP).

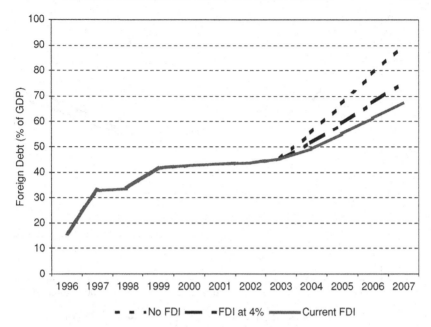

Figure 9.8. Lithuania, actual and projected external debt (as % of GDP).

The main implications of this simple simulation exercise are twofold. First, widening deficits are a natural product of the transition process, that can be seen as an idiosyncratic productivity shock (see Glick and Rogoff (1995) for the consequences of country-specific versus world-wide productivity shocks on the current accounts), and therefore the usual criteria used to assess sustainability ought to be amended in order to allow for the peculiar situation of these countries.

Secondly, new Member States have committed themselves to a quick reduction of their budgets deficits. According to the simulations, these measures (provided that they are really implemented and yield the expected outcome) would not suffice to avoid a deterioration of the external imbalances. Moreover, keeping FDI inflows at the observed level would not be enough to stabilise debt in most cases.

The implication for countries willing to join ERM-II as soon as possible is that, if the government is keen on targeting the current accounts by means of the fiscal policy only, it will be obliged to take much harsher measures, with possibly negative consequences on growth.

Moreover, this outlook is not exempt from large downside risks. Whereas the assumption of sustained growth for the near future seems

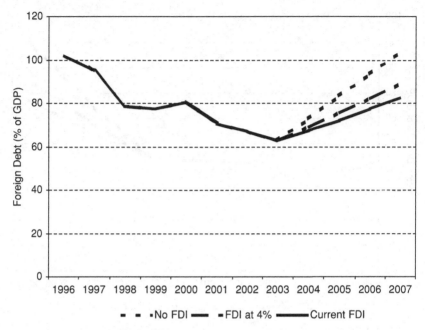

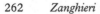

Figure 9.9. Bulgaria, actual and projected external debt (as % of GDP).

to be highly realistic, the simulation rests heavily upon the continuation of disciplined fiscal policies, enabling the domestic saving rate not to diverge too much from the investment rate. Moreover, the assumption of FDI being the only source of foreign capital that does not create debt might become more and more questionable over time. The end of the privatisation process is likely to reduce FDI inflows, and the development of the financial system will stimulate the surge of other forms of financing, such as portfolio investment or bank loans. If, on the one side, they will not contribute to the external debt, they nevertheless are much more volatile and might make these countries much more exposed to the risk of reversals and a balance-of-payments crisis.

9.7   Policy issues

9.7.1   Increasing the saving rate?

The prospect of a large and possibly widening deficit naturally raises questions about the current level of the savings rate and the possible options to increase it.

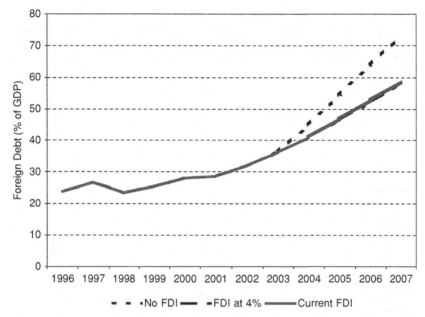

Figure 9.10. Romania, actual and projected external debt (as % of GDP).

Table 9.6 shows the figures for the countries under analysis and for two other European countries, Portugal (a natural benchmark for the CEECs) and Germany. The averages over the 1993–7 and 1998–2002 period are reported. As series on personal savings are not available for most of the new EU members, they are derived by subtracting the government budget balance from total savings. This is, admittedly, quite a crude approximation, but is widely used in the empirical literature (see Loyaza *et al.*, 2000).

We can see that both total and private savings rate are mostly in line with those of current EU Members, and in many cases they have increased in the second sub-period. Schrooten and Stephan (2002) carry out an econometric analysis of the determinants of savings in these countries, using data ranging from 1990 to 1999. They find that the driving forces are basically the same as in Western countries: income level and growth have a positive influence, as well as better institutions, whereas lower barriers to international borrowing lower savings. Public savings partially crowd out private ones. The obvious policy implication is that promoting growth will have a beneficial effect on private savings.

Table 9.6. *Total and private saving ratios*

	1993–7	1994–2002
Czech Republic		
Total saving	26.9	23.3
Private saving	24.1	23.8
Hungary		
Total saving	14.1	19.9
Private saving	15.8	23.0
Poland		
Total saving	17.1	17.9
Private saving	20.8	21.1
Slovakia		
Total saving	26.6	24.2
Private saving	26.8	25.6
Slovenia		
Total saving	22.4	23.8
Private saving	22.4	24.0
Estonia		
Total saving	20.0	19.4
Private saving	25.4	23.3
Latvia		
Total saving	18.8	17.6
Private saving	21.1	20.8
Lithuania		
Total saving	14.7	14.0
Private saving	15.4	16.6
Bulgaria		
Total saving	11.8	11.7
Private saving	16.6	16.3
Romania		
Total saving	15.8	15.0
Private saving	20.2	18.5
Portugal		
Total saving	20.3	19.1
Private saving	22.4	18.5
Germany		
Total saving	21.7	20.7
Private saving	21.1	20.1

Concerning government savings, they could be used by government as a (limited) insurance against too wide external deficits and the related risks. A larger surplus or a smaller deficit would act as a buffer and probably increase market confidence. Of course, one can question the feasibility of even tighter fiscal policies, over and above the quite successful programmes of fiscal restraint carried out by the CEECs in recent years. As pointed out by Sapir *et al.* (2003), fiscal consolidation might at some point clash with real convergence targets, in that the overall poor level of public capital, which is critical in order to make long-term growth sustainable, needs a strong investment effort by the government. Coricelli and Ercolani (2002) make a somewhat similar argument: they find that almost all the budget deficit in the new EU members is structural. Moreover, investment expenditure is much higher than in existing EU members. This should warn against the application to these countries of the Maastricht deficit criteria as they might risk hampering the development of badly needed infrastructure.

9.7.2   Early adoption of the euro: is it wise?

Another obvious implication is that the CEECs will need substantial capital inflows, in a period in which some hard decisions about the choice of the exchange rate regime will be taken. At the same time, abiding by the *acquis communautaire* implies the complete scrapping of the system of capital controls some countries still have in place.

Recent episodes of crisis show that full capital account liberalisation, a large current account deficit and the 'wrong' exchange rate regime can create a lethal mix leading to a painful financial crisis. Concerning the CEECs, it is known that full EMU membership will be attained at some point: the most pressing problems therefore relate to the interim period. The whole issue boils down to a single question: which regime should be adopted before the adoption of the euro?

Almost all the debate has been centred on the consequences of the marked real appreciation trend shown by these countries (due to the Balassa–Samuelson effect) and how to accommodate it within the premises of the Maastricht Treaty. According to Begg *et al.* (2003), unilateral euroisation would be by far the best option, as it would isolate the new EU members from turbulence in the years preceding EMU membership, solving almost automatically the problems related to large financial inflows, provided that the requirements of a high fiscal responsibility, price stability and a sound banking system are met.

Buiter and Grafe (2002) suggest that the current EC Treaty should be amended in order to allow the CEECs to euroise at a negotiated parity as soon as possible. Moreover, as the Balassa–Samuelson effect would generate an inflation rate well above that of current EMU members once the exchange rate is fixed, a different (and somehow looser) inflation criterion should be envisaged for new EU members.

However, these studies seem to concentrate overly on the pure Balassa–Samuelson effect, and overlook the impact of the massive capital flows the CEECs are receiving.

Capital scarcity in these countries translates into a high marginal productivity of capital, which normally attracts foreign capital. Monetary authorities are faced with a dilemma: if they set nominal rates in order to have a real rate which mirrors the high productivity, foreign capital will pour into their economies, leading to a large deficit and an appreciating real exchange rate. By contrast, if monetary authorities try to dampen these flows by means of interest rates much below the marginal productivity of capital, they are likely to depress private savings. The consequent gap with respect to investment would translate into a current account deficit.[15]

Such a phenomenon would occur regardless of the exchange rate regime chosen. If monetary authorities aim at keeping a fixed exchange rate regime, they will try to fight exchange rate appreciation by sterilising incoming capital flows. The increase in the supply of domestic currency will lead to a drop in the interest rate, which would depress savings and stimulate investment, leading to a current account deficit. Moreover, an increase in money supply would translate into higher inflation. Under a flexible exchange rate regime, the exchange rate appreciation would harm external competitiveness, worsening the trade balance and therefore the current account.

However, the choice of the exchange rate regime is critical, even though no regime would insulate a capital-importing country from the risk of a balance-of-payments crisis.

With a long-lasting fixed exchange rate regime, agents might tend to borrow heavily in the foreign currency, making the costs of adjusting the exchange rate very high, as devaluation would entail massive defaults and, possibly, a banking crisis. Moreover, setting the parity in an environment of an appreciating real exchange rate is very difficult. Moreover, with such a regime, any reduction of external imbalances would have to be made by reducing prices and wages or by compressing domestic demand. None of these options is probably very viable and meaningful. A flexible exchange rate would act as a partial disincentive to having large foreign exchange open positions, making the whole system less vulnerable. In this case, however, the mismatching of banks' assets and liabilities can become sizeable, and large swings in the exchange rate can cause problems with non-performing loans.

---

[15] Lipschitz *et al.* (2002) present a similar argument in a more formalised way.

Given that no regime is free from potentially serious drawbacks, the quality of the financial system in the new EU members plays a critical role. Calvo and Mishkin (2003) argue that, in order to have successful macro-economic policies in emerging economies, the development of good fiscal, financial and monetary institutions is even more important than the choice of the exchange rate regime. As shown by almost all the recent examples of exchange rate crisis, weak institutions amplify the effects of external shocks or greatly reduce the ability of the economic authorities to react to them. The recent surveys on the subject (see, for example, chapter 10 below and the regular reports produced by the European Commission and the European Bank for Reconstruction and Development) show that the level of adequacy of financial institutions is quite diverse.

Given the speed of transition, it is likely that the new EU members will continue to have relevant external imbalances well after their adoption of the euro. Moreover, as emphasised by Blanchard and Giavazzi (2003), the single currency, by reducing transaction costs and eliminating the currency risk, is likely to deliver a more efficient allocation of savings and investment across countries, possibly widening the external imbalances according to the differences in capital intensity and growth prospects. The observed increased variance between the current account positions in the EU Member States is cited as evidence of this process. They conclude that this is a natural phenomenon and that benign neglect is the most appropriate form of policy response. However, their conclusion is probably too optimistic: a widening deficit might also originate from a less-than-optimal intertemporal allocation of resources which could translate into a persistent slowdown in long-term growth, exacerbating the deficit problem.

9.8   Conclusions

The objective of this chapter was to analyse the new EU members' external balances, in order to shed some light on their future prospects and their medium-term sustainability. The estimates given should be taken with caution as they derive from highly stylised models of the economies.

The main conclusions that can be drawn are the following:

- During the catching-up process, imbalances are likely to remain large for a while. This is to some extent a natural outcome, but given the absence of any restriction on capital flows and the lessons drawn from recent balance-of-payments crises, current account deficits must be carefully monitored. In particular, it is crucial to consider whether the main driving force is the dynamic of savings or investment. On the savings side, fiscal policy could play an important role, avoiding large budget deficits, even though the task is not at all straightforward given the need for public investment these countries have.

- The size of FDI flows is critical in order to maintain debt dynamics in check. Therefore, an important challenge for these countries is to guarantee that external deficits continue to be financed by relatively sure sources such as FDI. As privatisation has ended or is close to the end in most of the countries, microeconomic reforms securing the interest of foreign investors are essential. However, it is likely that over time FDI will be replaced by more volatile sources of flows. This would necessitate particular attention to the state of the financial system.

- Concerning accession to the EMU, the relevant size of external imbalances (and therefore of the capital inflows financing it) should be taken into account in the design of the transition path leading to the adoption of the euro. A tentative conclusion is that countries still using a flexible exchange rate regime should maintain it as long as convergence has (among other things) reduced the size of the deficit. This must be complemented by strong and credible commitments to keep inflation in check and to an improvement in financial institutions in order to have monetary policies transmitted to the real sector in the most powerful way. Adopting a fixed exchange rate agreement and choosing the wrong parity would shift the burden of the adjustment to domestic demand, a devaluation being impossible (in the case of euroisation) or extremely difficult or painful, in the case of a pegged rate or a currency board.[16] The correction of imbalances would then entail a compression in demand or a marked reduction in nominal wages. On the other hand, countries already using various forms of fixed exchange rate arrangements may find shifting to a flexible exchange rate too costly, in terms of turbulence in the financial system. Their economic authorities will have to pay even more attention to checking current account imbalances, using demand policies, and at the same time guaranteeing that deficits are financed in a relatively safe way, and managed by sound financial institutions.

References

Abiad, A. 2003. 'Early Warning Systems: A Survey and a Regime-Switching Approach'. IMF Working Paper, No. 32.

Alesina, A., Hausmann, R., Hommes, R. and Stein, E. 1999. 'Budget Institutions and Fiscal Performances in Latin America'. *Journal of Development Economics*, vol. 59, pp. 253–73.

[16] See Edwards and Levy Yeyati (2003).

Begg, D., Eichengreen, B., Halpern, L., von Hagen, J. and Wyplosz, C. 2003. 'Sustainable Regimes of Capital Movements in Accession Countries'. CEPR Policy Paper, No. 10.

Bevan, A. and Estrin, S. 2000. 'The Determinants of Foreign Direct Investment in Transition Economies'. CEPR Discussion Paper, No. 2638.

Blanchard, O. and Giavazzi, F. 2003. 'Current Account Deficits in the Euro Area: The End of the Feldstein–Horioka Puzzle?'. *Brookings Papers on Economic Activity*, vol. 2, pp. 147–86.

Boeri, T. and Brücker, H. 2002. 'Eastern Enlargement and EU-Labour Markets: Perceptions, Challenges and Oppertunities'. *World Economics*, March 2002.

Buch, C., Kokta, R. and Piazolo, D. 2001. 'Does the East Get What Would Otherwise Flow to the South? FDI Diversion in Europe'. Kiel Institute of World Economics Working Paper, No. 1061.

Buiter, W. and Grafe, C. 2002. 'Anchor, Float or Abandon Ship: Exchange Rate Regimes for New EU Members'. CEPR Discussion Paper, No. 3184.

Bussière, M., Fratzscher, M. and Müller, G. 2004. 'Current Account Dynamics in OECD and EU Acceding Countries – An Intertemporal Approach'. ECB Working Paper, No. 311.

Calderon, C., Chong, A. and Loayza, N. 2002. 'Determinants of Current Account Deficits in Developing Countries'. *Contributions to Macroeconomics*, vol. 2, Article 2.

Calvo, G. and Mishkin, F. 2003. 'The Mirage of Exchange Rate Regimes for Emerging Market Economies'. NBER Working Paper, No. 9808.

Chinn, M. and Prasad, E. 2003. 'Medium-Term Determinants of Current Accounts in Industrial and Developing Countries: An Empirical Exploration'. *Journal of International Economics*, vol. 59, pp. 47–76.

Coakley, J., Fuertes, A. and Spagnolo, F. 2004. 'Is the Feldstein–Horioka Puzzle History?'. *Manchester School*, vol. 72, pp. 569–90.

Coakley, J., Kulasi, F. and Smith, R. 1996. 'Current Account Solvency and the Feldstein–Horioka Puzzle'. *Economic Journal*, vol. 106, pp. 620–7.

Coricelli, Fabrizio and Ercolani, Valerio. 2002. 'Cyclical and Structural Deficits on the Road to Accession: Fiscal Rules for an Enlarged European Union'. CEPR Discussion Paper No.3672.

Corsetti, G., Pesenti, P. and Roubini, N. 1999. 'Paper Tigers? A Model of the Asian Crisis'. *European Economic Review*, vol. 43, pp. 1211–36.

Doisy, H. and Hervé, K. 2003. 'Les implications des déficits courants des PECO'. *Economie Internationale*, No. 95, pp. 59–88.

Edison, H. 2003. 'Do Indicators of Financial Crisis Work? An Evaluation of an Early Warning System'. *International Journal of Finance and Economics*, vol. 8, pp. 11–53.

Edwards, S. 1995. 'Why Are Savings Rates So Different Across Countries? An International Comparative Analysis'. NBER Working Paper, No. 5097.

2002. 'Does the Current Account Matter?'. NBER Working Paper, No. 8275.

Edwards, S. and Levy Yeyati, E. 2003. 'Flexible Exchange Rates as Shock Absorbers'. NBER Working Paper, No. 9867.

European Commission. 2002a. 'Public Finances in EMU'.

270   *Zanghieri*

2002b. 'Update of the Report on Macroeconomic and Financial Sector Stability Developments in Candidate Countries'. Enlargement Paper, No. 11.

European Forecasting Network. 2004. 'Spring 2004 Economic Outlook Report'. Available at http://www.efn.uni-bocconi.it.

Frenkel, J. and Razin, A. 1997. *Fiscal Policy and Growth in the World Economy.* Cambridge, MA: MIT Press.

Garibaldi, P., Mora, N., Sahay, R. and Zettelmeyer, J. 2002. 'What Moves Capital to Transition Economies?'. IMF Working Paper, No. 02/64.

Glick, R. and Rogoff, K. 1995. 'Global Versus Country-Specific Productivity Shocks and the Current Account'. *Journal of Monetary Economics*, vol. 35, pp. 159–92.

Halpern, L. and Wyplosz, C. 2002. 'Economic Transformation and Real Exchange Rates in the 2000s: The Balassa Samuelson Connection'. *Mimeo*, University of Leuven.

Isard, P., Faruqee, H., Kincaid, G. and Fetherson, M. 2001. 'Methodology for Current Account and Exchange Rate Assessment'. IMF Occasional Paper, No. 209.

Kinoshita, Y. and Campos, N. 2003. 'Why Does FDI Go Where It Goes? New Evidence from the Transition Economies'. CEPR Discussion Paper, No. 3984.

Lane, P. and Milesi-Ferretti, G. 2001. 'Long Term Capital Movements'. NBER Macroeconomics Annuals 2001.

Lipschitz, L., Lane, T. and Mourmouras, A. 2002. 'Capital Flows to Transition Economies: Master or Servant?'. IMF Working Paper, No. 02/11.

Loyaza, N., Lopez, H., Schmidt-Hebbel, K. and Servén, L. 2000. 'Saving in the World: Stylised Facts'. Saving Across the World Project, Washington DC: World Bank.

Milesi-Ferretti, G. and Razin, A. 1996. 'Sustainability of Persistent Current Account Deficits'. NBER Working Paper, No. 5467.

1998. 'Sharp Reductions in Current Account Deficits: An Empirical Analysis'. *European Economic Review*, vol. 42, pp. 897–908.

2000. 'Current Account Reversal and Currency Crises: Empirical Regularities'. In Krugman, P. (ed.), *Currency Crises*. Chicago: University of Chicago Press.

Nickell, S. 1981. 'Biases in Dynamic Models with Fixed Effects'. *Econometrica*, vol. 49, pp. 1417–26.

Obstfeld, M. and Rogoff, K. 1995. 'The Intertemporal Approach to the Current Account'. In Froot, C. and Rogoff, K. (eds.), *Handbook of International Economics*, vol. 3. Amsterdam: North-Holland.

1996. 'Foundations of International Economics'. Cambridge, MA: MIT Press.

Radelet, S. and Sachs, J. 2000. 'The Onset of the East Asian Financial Crisis'. In Krugman, P. (ed.), *Currency Crises*, Chicago: Chicago University Press.

Razin, A. 1995. 'The Dynamic-Optimizing Approach to the Current Account: Theory and Evidence'. In Kenen, P. (ed.), *Understanding Interdependence; The Macroeconomics of the Open Economy*. Princeton, NJ: Princeton University Press, pp. 169–98.

Reinhart, C., Rogoff, K. and Savastano, M. 2003. 'Debt Intolerance'. NBER Working Paper, No. 9908.

Reisen, H. 1998. 'Sustainable and Excessive Current Account Deficits'. OECD Development Centre, Technical Paper, No. 132.

Schrooten, M. and Stephan, S. 2002. 'Back on Track? Savings Puzzles in EU–Accession Countries'. DIW Discussion Paper, No. 306.

Sapir, A., Aghion, P., Bertola, G., Hellwig, M., Pisani-Ferry, J., Rosati, D., Viñals, J. and Wallace, H. 2003. *An Agenda for a Growing Europe: Making the EU Economic System Deliver: Report of an Independent High Level Study Group Established on the Initiative of the President of the European Commission.* Brussels: European Commission.

Sarno, L. and Taylor, M. 1999. 'Moral Hazard, Asset Price bubbles, Capital Flows and the East Asian Crisis: The First Tests'. *Journal of International Money and Finance*, vol. 18, pp. 637–57.

Wagner, M. and Hlouskova, J. 2002. 'The CEEC10s' Real Convergence Prospects'. CEPR Discussion Paper, No. 3318.

Williamson, J. 1994. 'Estimates of the FEERs'. In Williamson, J. (ed.), *Estimating Equilibrium Exchange Rates*. Washington DC: Institute for International Economics.

Zanghieri, P. 2004. 'Current Account Dynamics in New EU Members: Sustainability and Policy Issues'. CEPII Working Paper, No. 7.

Appendix A: Data

Variable	Source
Current Account	IFS, AMECO
Government deficit	IFS, AMECO
Money and quasi Money (M2)	IFS
Population	AMECO
Foreign direct investment	IFS, EBRD
GDP	AMECO
Investment	AMECO

AMECO: European Commission Annual Macroeconomic Database, available at http://europa.eu.int/comm/economy_finance/indicators/annual_macro_economic_database/ameco_en.htm.
EBRD: European Bank for Reconstruction and Development, Transition Report, various issues.
IFS: International Monetary Fund, International Financial Statistics, March 2004
WDI: World Bank, World Development Indicators, 2003 edition.

Appendix B: Short-and long-term determinants of the current account

The variables that according to standard economic theory are likely to affect the current account are different in terms of time and cross-country variation. For example, the old dependency ratio evolves very

Table 9.7. *Variance decomposition (in % points)*

	Between	Within
Government balance	43.59	56.41
Real per capita GDP	39.87	60.13
Financial deepening	30.86	69.14
Trade openness	44.23	55.67
Old dependency ratio	60.98	39.02
External debt	56.36	43.64

Notes: Financial deepening is the ratio between M2 and GDP; trade openness is the sum of import and export divided by GDP; old dependency ratio is the ratio between people above 65 and people aged between 15 and 65.

slowly, but in principle may be different across countries. The same applies to external debt. Net output growth, by contrast, is likely to be highly variable over time but to be less so if compared across countries, as the economies analysed are roughly in the same stage of economic development. Using slowly changing variables in panel regression along with more volatile variables might result in the former showing a low significance.

To overcome this problem, Alesina *et al.* (1999) propose a two-step estimation. In the first step, the dependent variable is regressed on more volatile regressors using standard fixed-effect methods. In the second step, the cross-section of the estimated fixed effects is regressed on less volatile variables.

In this chapter, a slightly modified approach has been adopted. First, the explanatory variables are divided into two subsets, according to whether their variance across time (within) is higher or lower than the variance across units (between). The former is more likely to affect the current account in the short-to-medium term; the latter has a long-term effect. Table 9.7 shows the variance decomposition for the explanatory variables considered.

Therefore, and in accordance with the theoretical model, the budget balance, real per capita GDP, the M2 to GDP ratio and the ratio between the sum of import and export and GDP are employed for the estimation of the short-term regression. The specification for the first step regression is a partial adjustment model:

$$CA_t = \alpha CA_{t-1} + \beta X_t' \omega_i \qquad (A1)$$

where X is the set of explanatory variables. It is well known (Nickell, 1981) that estimating a model by OLS containing lagged dependent variables and fixed effects would yield biased estimators. Moreover, given the small size of the sample, other methods such as Instrumental Variables or GMM were unfeasible.

Therefore, in order to get some idea of the long-term component of the current account which is not explained by the variables contained in X, the sample average of the residuals of equation (A1) was taken, and used as a sort of country fixed effects in the second step cross-section regression where the period averages of the old dependency ratio and of the external debt to GDP ratio were used as independent variables.

10 Challenges to banking sector stability in selected new Member States

Charles Movit

10.1 Introduction

Following their accession to the European Union (EU) in May 2004, the eight Central and Eastern European countries (CEEC) of the first wave, having been judged to have converged sufficiently with the fifteen existing members of the Union with regard to the political and economic criteria established in Copenhagen, are continuing to undergo structural and institutional change. Moreover, they are committed to entering a process leading to the adoption of the common currency, the euro. The EU has set a target date of 2007 for the accession of two additional countries in the region, Bulgaria and Romania, which are in the process of closing the final negotiations on chapters of the *acquis communautaire* that will define the path by which they too will harmonise their institutions. All of these countries have already made dramatic strides in improving the stability and efficiency of their banking sectors as well as in eliminating restrictions on capital flows. However, these processes are not complete and further progress along these lines, including such phenomena as increased competition in the banking sector and more substantial flows of short-term capital, in and of itself has the potential to increase the risks of instability in the banking sectors of the individual new Member States. Moreover, there may well be developments in macroeconomic trends, exchange rates and direction and composition of financial flows due to accession to the EU and preparation for eventual accession to the Euro area that could exacerbate these risks.

In this chapter, we attempt to examine the characteristics of the banking systems of selected Central and Eastern European countries to determine their relative ability to cope with these pressures and derive a set of priorities for further strengthening of the banking sectors in light of the upcoming challenges they will be facing in this critical period. We have chosen to focus on the banking sectors of Poland, the Czech Republic and Romania for a number of reasons. These three countries have followed rather different paths in the transition of their banking sectors from collections of state undertakings that largely served to intermediate between the government budget and budget-financed enterprises and institutions and collect household savings, to groups of predominantly privately held banks functioning in competitive markets for financial services. In each of the cases, extensive restructuring of the banks was required due to the substantial burden of non-performing loans that threatened their viability as financially independent institutions. The paths chosen in restructuring by these three countries have had considerable impact on the roles currently being played by the banking sectors in financial intermediation in the respective economies, and provide us with a spectrum of experience to consider in assessing their ability to withstand the strains that might develop subsequent to their accession to the European Union and in the course of their preparation to join the EMU thereafter.

10.2   Progress to date in restructuring the banking sectors

10.2.1   Privatisation of the banking sectors

At the outset of their transition from centrally planned to predominantly market-oriented economies, the new Member States of Central and Eastern Europe shared the problem that their banking sectors were characterised by a relatively small number of large, state-owned institutions that, due to political pressures and inappropriate incentives to management, had become burdened by large volumes of non-performing loans. These banks were therefore financially unviable as independent institutions without significant restructuring of their balance sheets. These banking institutions lacked not only the financial capital, but also the human and physical capital that would be necessary to compete in a liberalised market for financial services. In some of the countries, political leaders were unwilling, at least in the beginning, to accept a transformed banking sector that would be likely to be dominated by foreign banks. On the other hand, experience in other emerging markets strongly suggested that banking sector reform was only likely to achieve significant results with the entry of foreign banks and strategic foreign investors into domestic institutions, bringing the need to compete in offering financial services, as well as serving to transfer management expertise and technical know-how.

The Czech and Polish banking sectors, and to a somewhat lesser degree the Romanian banking sector, are now overwhelmingly in private hands. As of mid-2003, 83% of the authorised capital of the Polish banking sector was privately held, up from 51.1% at the end of 1995.

Of total bank capital at mid-2003, 61.2% was held by foreign investors. While banks with majority private capital accounted for only 13.0% of total assets held by Poland's commercial banks in 1993, by mid-2003 this share had reached 66.9%.

In the Czech Republic, the state held a mere 4.1% of equity capital in the banking sector at the end of 2002, down from 31.0% as late as the end of 1996. An initial privatisation effort in 1991–3 as part of the mass voucher privatisation programme was subsequently followed in 2001–2 by the privatisation of state-owned stakes in the largest banks with the participation of foreign strategic investors. As of end-2002, 81.9% of the equity in Czech banks was held by foreign entities. Among the four largest banks, the foreign equity share is a startling 95.5%, but even among the remaining banks (excluding nine foreign branch banks), foreign control exceeds 50%. In terms of bank assets, the share held by majority private-owned banks in the Czech Republic had risen to 95.4% at the end of 2002, up from 79.4% at the end of 1993.

Of Romania's thirty-one banks (excluding branches of foreign banks), only three remained controlled by the state in 2002. Romania's state savings bank remains fully in state hands, while the state retains majority stakes in the *Eximbank* and the largest commercial bank, *Banca Commerciala Romana*. Romania is currently in the process of selling 12.5% stakes in the latter to the EBRD and the International Finance Corporation of the World Bank Group, while the former is to be converted into a state export credit agency. The majority privately owned banks in the country held 59.6% of Romania's total banking assets at the end of 2002, including 7.4% held by branches of foreign banks. As of end-1994, Romania's majority privately owned banks had held a mere 19.6% of bank assets.

The privatisation of the banking systems in the transition economies of Central and Eastern Europe was aimed not only at attracting capital injections and increasing efficiency in the financial services sectors, but also at eliminating the inappropriate incentives to bank management that contributed to the burden of non-performing loans inherited from the socialist era. As we point out below, privatisation was a necessary, but not a sufficient condition for accomplishing these goals. State-owned commercial banks were under substantial pressure to extend further credits to financially troubled state-owned enterprises. In turn, state-owned banks were fairly confident of repeated government bailouts if needed. As a result, commercial banks slated for privatisation were badly under-capitalised and a programme of restructuring was required prior to and in conjunction with the privatisation process. The Polish strategy, characteristic of much of Poland's policy in regard to economic transition, was aimed at privatising the banking sector as quickly as practicable in an effort to minimise the fiscal cost of bank restructuring. By contrast, the Czech Republic and Romania stretched out the process by nearly a decade due to unrealistic expectations with regard to the potential selling prices of the assets as well as to the domestic political opposition to potential foreign domination of the banking sector.

By the end of 2000, the share of total Czech bank assets held by majority state-owned banks at 28.2% was actually higher than the 20.6% at the end of 1993. In Romania at the end of 2000, the share of total bank assets held by state-owned banks still remained at 50.0%, down from 75.3% at the end of 1998. As a result of the delays, inappropriate incentives to bank managers remained in place at key institutions and soft lending practices persisted, eventually boosting the fiscal cost of restructuring and impeding the efficiency of the domestic banking industry. By contrast, in Poland, the share of majority state-owned banks declined steadily to the neighbourhood of 24–26% in 1998–2002 from 86.2% in 1993.

10.2.2 Restructuring: the Czech case

In the Czech case, the partial privatisation of three large commercial banks that were partitioned from the once monolithic Czech National Bank, began early in the 1990s through the voucher privatisation programme. However, in this process, the large investment funds that ended up with the stakes in the banks were, in turn, managed by the banks. Thus, the banks essentially controlled their own shares and gained stakes in many of their most important debtor enterprises as well. Because of lax regulation of the financial sector, the result of the voucher privatisation process was detrimental to corporate governance in the banking sector. Moreover, as the state retained controlling stakes in a majority of banks, soft lending practices and inefficient bank operations were preserved. The state created the *Konsolidacny banka*, a so-called hospital bank, in 1991, and subsequently two other specialised asset management agencies, to take the non-performing loans off the balance sheets of the commercial banks, restructure them and attempt to recover the assets. However, the mandate for debt recovery frequently seemed weaker than an implied imperative to prolong the existence of important debtor enterprises and *Konsolidacny banka* itself was at times used for directed lending.

Even the sale of a fourth Czech bank, IPB Bank, to a foreign investor in 1998, which did not involve the removal of non-performing loans from the balance sheet or any state debt guarantees, did not produce the desired result in terms of the bank's operations. The bank's condition deteriorated further. The foreign investor chose not to undertake extensive debt restructuring, selling off the choicest assets and engaging in creative accounting. Inattentive auditing and delayed reaction by the Czech bank supervisory authority allowed a crisis to develop. In 2000, after panicked depositors staged a run on the bank, the Czech National Bank was forced to take over its administration. It was thereafter sold to a strategic foreign investor, this time with assumption by the state of bad debts and the extension of state guarantees. *Konsolidacny banka* ceased its other activities at that time, was transformed into the *Konsolidacny agentura*, and concentrated on asset recovery. The Czech Republic thereafter rapidly completed the privatisation of the remaining state-owned commercial banks the following year with sales to foreign strategic investors.

10.2.3   Restructuring: the Polish case

The Polish experience was vastly different. The Polish approach to the recapitalisation and restructuring of the banking sector was decentralised in character and, as a result, asset recovery was enhanced and the fiscal cost of the restructuring process was minimised. However, due to a strong political imperative to protect domestic banks from foreign competitors and to maintain restrictions on foreign participation in the Polish banking sector, the privatisation of the banking sector proceeded at a modest pace until 1999, as can be seen from Table 10.1 on the structure of the banking system. State-controlled banks still held 48.0% of banking assets in 1998. Nevertheless, the recapitalised commercial banks early on found it necessary to improve their investment strategy as it was made explicit that no further rounds of recapitalisation would be forthcoming from the state. The largest commercial banks participated in the Enterprise and Bank Restructuring Programme in the period 1993–6. Rather than transferring non-performing loans from their balance sheets to a state asset management agency, the state presented the banks with treasury bonds in return for which they were to pursue actively the work-out of non-performing loans with debtor enterprises, typically resulting in debt-equity swaps or bad debt write-offs. Smaller banks were restructured and sold or merged into stronger banks under the auspices of the National Bank of Poland. In addition, foreign banks applying for licences to operate in Poland were obliged to provide affordable credits to or acquire troubled banks in return.

While the operational characteristics of the Polish domestic banking system improved due to these initiatives, the continued strong role of the

Table 10.1. *Structure of the banking systems in the Czech Republic, Romania and Poland*

	1993	1994	1995	1996	1997	1998	1999	2000	2001	2002
Czech Republic										
Number of banks	45	55	55	53	50	45	42	40	38	37
domestic	33	43	32	32	26	20	15	14	12	11
foreign	12	12	23	23	24	25	27	26	26	26
Share of total assets in state-owned banks %	20.6	20.1	17.6	16.6	17.5	18.6	23.1	28.2	3.8	4.6
Banks per million inhabitants	4.4	5.3	5.3	5.1	4.9	4.4	4.1	3.9	3.7	3.6
Romania										
Number of banks	14	20	24	31	33	36	34	33	33	31
domestic	13	17	16	21	20	20	15	12	9	7
foreign	1	3	8	10	13	16	19	21	24	24
Share of total assets in state-owned banks %		80.4	84.3	80.9	80.0	75.3	50.3	50.0	45.4	41.2
Banks per million population	0.6	0.9	1.1	1.4	1.5	1.6	1.5	1.5	1.5	1.4
Poland										
Number of banks	87	82	81	81	83	83	77	74	64	59
domestic	77	71	63	56	54	52	38	27	18	14
foreign	10	11	18	25	29	31	39	47	46	45
Share of total assets in state-owned banks %	86.2	80.4	71.1	69.8	51.6	48.0	24.9	23.9	24.4	26.6
Banks per million inhabitants	2.3	2.1	2.1	2.1	2.1	2.1	2.0	1.9	1.7	1.5

Source: EBRD Transition Reports (1999, 2000, 2001, 2002, 2003); Annual Reports of respective central banks.

state meant that soft loans to state enterprises were still made and, for the most part, banks were content to concentrate their efforts on investing in treasury securities and to engage in only limited lending to the non-financial private sector in view of inadequate capabilities for assessing credit risk. With the lifting of restrictions on foreign participation in the Polish banking sector in 1998, foreign ownership increased dramatically. At the end of 1998, out of a total of eighty-three commercial banks, thirty-one banks with majority foreign ownership, including three foreign branch banks, accounted for 43.7% of bank equity and only around 17% of total net assets. By the end of 1999, thirty-nine foreign-controlled banks out of a total of seventy-seven commercial banks accounted for 50.2% of bank equity and a surprising 47.2% of total assets. The National Bank of Poland pointed out that in view of the diffuse shareholding structure of a number of additional banks, they were *de facto* controlled by foreign capital, bringing the market share of foreign-owned banks up to 70%. The official share of foreign-owned banks reached 76.3% of bank equity and 66.9% of assets by mid-2003. Sales of two additional major state-owned banks had originally been planned for 2003 together with an offering of a minority stake in one of these on the domestic stock market, but the transactions have been significantly delayed.

10.2.4   Restructuring: the Romanian case

Romania delayed the privatisation of its major state-owned commercial banks because their poor financial condition and the stop-and-go nature of the domestic economic recovery impinged on their likely market value. Instead, Romania engaged in repeated rounds of bank recapitalisation at substantial fiscal cost and with only a temporary impact on the balance sheets of the state-owned commercial banks. These recapitalisation efforts were defeated due to a number of factors, including a lack of co-ordination with enterprise restructuring, faulty internal controls and auditing practices, lax legal and regulatory regimes, and little attention to improving the management teams in the state-owned banking sector. Finally, in 1999, a recapitalisation programme was initiated that involved the transfer of assets to a state management company at the recommendation of the World Bank. By the end of 1999, the AVAB, the Romanian state asset management company, was managing a portfolio of US $ 2.3 billion in non-performing loans. It was estimated that this round of bank clean-up was accomplished at a cost of 4% of GDP. As indicated above, Romania is currently in the process of privatising the last of the majority state-owned banks. As of the end of 2002, the private banking sector in Romania was almost entirely controlled by foreign entities, as shown in Table 10.2. Of the 59.6% of bank assets controlled by majority privately owned banks, 56.4% was controlled by banks with a majority of foreign capital, including branches of foreign banks.

10.2.5   Easing the burden of non-performing loans

To gauge the scope of the bad loan problem in terms of its burden on the banking sectors and the improvements made to date, we turn to data on the quality of bank assets reported by the bank supervisory agencies, shown in Tables 10.3–10.5. Looking at the share of non-performing loans as a share of total loans in each of the countries as of the end of 2002, keeping in mind that the asset recovery rate has been the lowest of the three and the estimated fiscal cost of restructuring has been

Table 10.2. *Market share of banks and foreign bank branches in Romania*

	Net assets, end-period					
	2000		2001		2002	
	Billion lei	Share in per cent	Billion lei	Share in per cent	Billion lei	Share in per cent
Banks with majority domestic capital, of which	114,563.9	49.1	154,469.2	44.8	204,833.9	43.6
with majority state-owned capital	107,536.4	46.1	144,342.3	41.8	189,806.2	40.4
with majority private capital	7,027.5	3.0	10,126.9	3.0	189,806.2	3.2
Banks with majority foreign capital	100,565.9	43.1	163,413.9	47.3	230,207.0	49.0
I. Total commercial banks	215,129.8	92.2	317,883.1	92.1	435,040.9	92.6
II. Foreign bank branches	18,124.3	7.8	27,337.6	7.9	34,671.3	7.4
Banks with majority **private capital**, including foreign bank branches	125,717.7	53.9	200,878.4	58.2	279,906.0	59.6
Banks with majority **foreign capital**, including foreign bank branches	118,690.2	50.9	190,751.5	55.2	264,878.3	56.4
Total (I+II)	233,254.1	100.0	345,220.7	100.0	469,712.2	100.0

Source: National Bank of Romania.

Table 10.3. *Evolution of non-performing loans in the Czech Republic*

	1996	1997	1998	1999	2000	2001
Ratio of non-performing loans to total loans in per cent of which, categorised:	23.09	20.80	20.31	21.51	19.42	13.76
Substandard	3.19	2.74	3.36	4.26	6.20	3.34
Doubtful	3.25	3.03	3.65	4.16	3.08	3.05
Loss	16.64	15.03	13.30	13.10	10.14	7.37
Ratio of non-performing loans to GDP in per cent	13.39	12.58	11.09	10.54	8.77	6.25

Source: Czech National Bank.

Table 10.4. *Evolution of non-performing loans in Poland*

	1996	1997	1998	1999	2000	2001
Ratio of non-performing loans to total loans in per cent of which, categorised:	13.4	10.7	10.9	13.2	14.9	17.8
Substandard	3.9	3.8	3.9	5.0	4.2	4.7
Doubtful	1.6	1.2	1.9	3.3	5.0	4.7
Loss	7.9	5.8	5.1	4.9	5.6	8.3
Ratio of non-performing loans to GDP in per cent	2.6	2.3	2.6	3.5	4.2	5.0

Source: National Bank of Poland.

the highest as a share of GDP, Romania's reported figure for non-performing loans as a share of the total is the lowest of the three banking sectors we are examining, at only 2.3%. However, due to a change in Romanian banking regulations effective at the outset of 2003, financial performance of the debtor enterprise became a criterion in assessing the quality of bank assets, and the share of non-performing loans was expected to end the year at close to 5% of total loans. This was nevertheless down from a high of 71.7% at the end of 1998, just prior to the transfer of assets to the state asset management agency. Note that these figures are for the economy as a whole and include loans both on the balance sheets of banks and those transferred to the agency.

In the Czech Republic, the share of non-performing loans has also declined substantially in recent years, from 21.51% of the total at the

Table 10.5. *Evolution of non-performing loans in Romania*

	1996	1997	1998	1999	2000	2001
Ratio of non-performing loans to total in per cent, of which categorised:	61.2	65.0	71.7	52.7	6.4	3.4
Substandard	18.2	12.5	13.2	17.3	1.73	0.61
Doubtful	10.1	9.9	7.7	6.7	0.74	0.93
Loss	32.9	42.6	50.8	28.7	3.92	4.27

Source: National Bank of Romania.

Table 10.6. *Evolution of non-performing loans in Hungary*

	1996	1997	1998	1999	2000	2001
Ratio of non-performing loans to total loans in per cent, of which, categorised:	9.0	6.8	8.2	4.6	3.3	3.4
Substandard	1.8	1.8	2.3	1.3	0.9	1.4
Doubtful	2.0	2.3	3.7	1.6	1.1	0.7
Loss	5.2	2.7	2.3	1.8	1.3	1.3

Source: National Bank of Hungary.

end of 1999 to 8.1% at the end of 2002. In the first half of 2003, the Czech share fell further to 6.3% despite the fact that non-performing assets could no longer be transferred to the *Konsolidacny Agentura*.

While the Polish share of non-performing loans at its low point at the end of 1997 was 10.7% of the total, it increased substantially in 2001–2 due to the difficult macroeconomic situation and reached 21.9% at the end of 2002. In this period, the increased proportion of non-performing loans in Polish banks' portfolios reflected in particular bad loans to small- and medium-sized enterprises and sole proprietorships. In addition, a higher share of loans to construction enterprises fell into that category as the construction sector struggled with declining demand for its services over a two-year period.

Tables 10.6–10.7 provide data on non-performing loans in Hungary and Slovakia for the purposes of comparison. The European Central Bank (2003a, p. 19) reports that, on average, across the EU banking sectors, non-performing and doubtful assets amounted to 2.90% of total

284   *Movit*

Table 10.7. *Evolution of non-performing loans in Slovakia*

	1996	1997	1998	1999	2000	2001
Ratio of non-performing loans to total in per cent, of which categorised:	19.76	31.19	35.69	29.46	21.93	21.86
Substandard	1.48	2.07	3.51	3.15	1.71	1.71
Doubtful	1.83	2.56	2.65	3.29	2.24	1.26
Loss	16.45	26.56	29.52	23.02	17.98	18.89

assets in 2001 and 3.06% in 2002, adding that, even within the EU, due to differences in national definitions of non-performing and doubtful loans, these ratios are not completely comparable across countries.

10.2.6   Restructuring and concentration in the banking sectors

In addition to the processes of restructuring and privatisation that were launched by the economic transition of the 1990s, the impact of increased competition in the financial services sectors has generally been to trim the number of banks after initial periods of expansion, through mergers or withdrawal of banking licences. Smaller domestic banks were particularly vulnerable in the highly risky lending environment, lacking experience in risk assessment. This process has tended to preserve a rather highly concentrated character in the banking sectors of the region. In the Czech Republic, there were thirty-seven banks operating at the end of 2002, down from a peak of fifty-five in 1995–6. In Poland, the number of banks peaked in 1997–8 at eighty-three but fell to fifty-nine by the end of 2002. In Romania, the number of banks grew through 1998, reaching thirty-six, but was trimmed to thirty-one by the end of 2002. The market shares of the five largest banks in each of the countries in recent years testify to the high degree of concentration that has resulted. (Tables 10.8–10.10) In Poland, the five largest banks accounted for 53.6% of total assets, 60.2% of total deposits and 48.6% of outstanding loans at the end of 2002. In the Czech Republic, the respective shares reached 65.8%, 77.3% and 65.5%, while in Romania they came to 66.6%, 68.5% and 58.0% for the five largest banks. For the ten largest banks in each market, the shares in each of the countries fall into the range of 75–85%. In all three countries, the consolidation of the financial sector has resulted in a large proportion of financial assets being held by foreign investors. In light of approaching EU accession, this

Table 10.8. *Concentration indicators (2000–2) Czech Republic (share of total in %)*

Date	Banking groups[a]	Assets	Deposits	Loans
December 2000	C3	53.00	70.97	52.12
	C5	66.09	77.06	68.46
	C10	78.54	87.40	82.67
December 2001	C3	58.70	69.14	59.27
	C5	68.38	76.86	70.66
	C10	80.60	87.96	82.99
December 2002	C3	57.18	64.24	53.51
	C5	65.75	77.29	65.48
	C10	79.78	85.41	79.96

Notes: [a] C3, for example, represents the group of the three largest banks according to assets, loans to clients (net), and deposits received from clients, respectively.
Source: Czech National Bank.

Table 10.9. *Concentration indicators (2000–2) Poland (share of total in %)*

Date	Banking groups[a]	Assets	Deposits	Loans
December 2000	C5	46.5	54.7	46.1
	C10	66.7	70.3	66.7
	C15	78.8	82.6	76.8
December 2001	C5	54.7	59.8	52.1
	C10	77.6	82.1	75.7
	C15	82.4	85.4	81.3
December 2002	C5	53.6	60.2	48.6
	C10	76.8	82.2	74.0
	C15	82.7	85.6	79.9

Notes: [a] C5, for example, represents the group of the five largest banks according to assets, loans to clients (net), and deposits received from clients, respectively.
Source: National Bank of Poland.

process will continue and will help to strengthen capital positions, bring about improved governance and introduce a wider range of financial services. In comparison, the degree of concentration differs widely among the individual banking sectors of the EU countries. The share of the five largest banks in total assets in 2002 ranged from 20% in Germany and 30–31% for the United Kingdom, Luxembourg and Italy to 79% in Finland and 82–83% for Belgium and the Netherlands (European Central Bank, 2003b, p. 24).

Table 10.10. *Concentration indicators (1998–2001) Romania (share of total in %)*

Date	Banking groups[a]	Assets	Deposits	Loans
December 1999	C5	61.44	61.25	57.60
	C10	77.20	77.27	78.32
	C15	83.69	82.69	85.16
December 2000	C5	65.46	67.50	59.11
	C10	82.25	84.13	78.05
	C15	89.59	90.63	87.54
December 2001	C5	66.63	68.51	58.04
	C10	83.01	85.31	78.56
	C15	90.47	91.86	88.08

Notes: [a] C5, for example, represents the group of the five largest banks according to assets, loans to clients (net), and deposits received from clients, respectively.
Source: National Bank of Romania.

10.3   Current indicators of operational efficiency and financial stability

In this section, we undertake an examination of the relevant indicators to determine the evolution of the role of banks in financial intermediation in these economies, the impact of the macroeconomic environment and growing competition in the financial services sector on the efficiency and profitability of banks, and their likely ability to withstand shocks, both direct and indirect, due to adverse developments in the economic environment.

The role of commercial banks in financial intermediation in Poland and Romania is much weaker than is typical for developed countries, thanks largely to the relatively short period that has elapsed since the restructuring of the banking sectors. While the typical ratio of broad money (M2) to GDP in more developed countries is in the neighbourhood of 70–80%, for Romania this ratio remained in the range of 23–25% throughout the period 1997–2002, having peaked at 27.9% in 1996 (Figure 10.1). In Poland, this ratio peaked at 43.8% in 2001, up from only 36.1% in 1995, and slipped modestly to 41.6% in 2002. It is only in the Czech Republic that this indicator falls in a range typical among developed economies, remaining at 70–75% in 1995–2002. Iakova and Wagner (2002), however, suggest that, rather than reflecting a stronger role due to a healthier banking system, this indicator for the Czech Republic reflects the much lower and more predictable rates of inflation there in the past decade than in many other transition

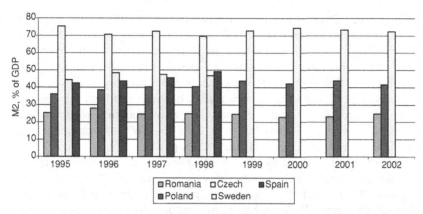

Figure 10.1. Broad money as % of GDP.

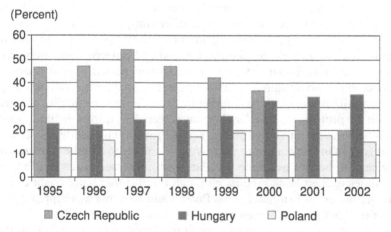

Figure 10.2. Domestic credit to private sector as % of GDP.

economies. Figures on domestic credit to the private sector as a share of GDP would seem to offer a more telling comparison (Figure 10.2). Again, the Czech Republic stands out, but far more modestly. While the international financial institutions have suggested that the volume of credit to the private sector as a share of GDP in economies at this stage of development should exceed 30%, in Romania in 2002 this ratio stood at only 8.4% (Daianu and Ionici, 2003, p. 13). For Poland, the ratio remained in the neighbourhood of 18% through 2001 before falling slightly to 15.2% in 2002, reflecting the impact of tight monetary policy. While the ratio of domestic credit to the private sector to GDP in the Czech Republic peaked at 54.3% in 1997, due partly to the recession that was setting in and an extended period required to clean up the troubled portfolios of the banking sector, it slid to only 24.3% by 2001 and further to 20.0% the following year. In sharp contrast, the comparable indicator for the aggregate of the twelve banking sectors of the EMU members rose from 103% in 1997 to 116% of aggregate GDP in 2002 (European Central Bank, 2003b, p. 25).

In difficult economic times or when concerned with meeting tighter prudential standards of bank supervisory authorities, banks in the region, which have lacked extensive experience in credit risk assessment and which might also have had reason to question the transparency of enterprise financial records, were willing to finance only the most solvent of enterprises and shifted the composition of their assets instead in favour of government securities. Lack of technical skills in assessing credit risks in a relatively unstable economic period helped to make banks reluctant to extend credit to smaller companies at such times.

An IMF working paper by Cottarelli *et al.* (2003) on the growth of bank credit to the private sector in Central and Eastern Europe concurs that 'data suggest that – in the context of increased overall financial deepening – privatisation, public sector retrenchment, and, possibly, the overall progress towards market institutions and the quality of legislation to protect creditors' rights have been key factors behind rising BCPS [bank credit to the private sector] ratios. This study also found that growth of bank credit to the private sector in most of the countries in the region did not generally correlate with increases in the net foreign liabilities of their bank sectors, although it notes that bank credit to the private sectors in Estonia, Latvia, Poland and Slovenia was supported by increased net foreign borrowing (Cottarelli *et al.*, 2003, p. 7).

While the growth of domestic credit has increased substantially in the past several years in most of the region as banks become more confident in assessing credit risks, particularly after the entry of foreign strategic investors into banking sectors bringing both capital and expertise, domestic credit growth has also reflected monetary policy swings and developments in the real economy that in some cases temporarily reversed credit growth. With improvement in both macroeconomic conditions and the health of the banking sector, credit growth *vis-à-vis* non-financial enterprises began to accelerate in Poland in 2003, offsetting a continued slowdown in lending to households and maintaining year-on-year growth in total lending at around 5%. In the Czech Republic, by contrast, retail lending, up 30% year-on-year at mid-2003, was responsible for a surge in the volume of domestic credit in 2003, with acceleration in both consumer and mortgage lending. Retail lending is attractive to Czech banks in view of the relatively low current level of indebtedness of domestic households, while corporate lending has continued to contract as banks have sought to further shore up the quality of their portfolios. The share of retail loans in total loans by Czech banks rose to 21.5% by mid-year from 19.0% at end-2002. Starting from a much lower base, domestic credit to the private sector continued to grow apace in Romania, accelerating from a year-on-year rate of 30% at end-2002. Retail lending, and mortgage lending in particular, has been growing at rates several times the growth of corporate lending, but from a much smaller base. Retail loans represented 19.7% of total loans outstanding from Romanian banks in 2002.

Developments in interest rates reflect the trends in the efficiency of the banking sectors in financial intermediation. We would expect that privatisation and increased competition in the banking sector, particularly from branches of foreign banks and banks with foreign strategic investors, as well as inflows of foreign direct investment into the corporate sector and the increased availability of credit from abroad, have compelled the banks in the new Member States to narrow the spread between their lending and deposit rates. This was hopefully made financially feasible by the increased efficiency of their operations, which we will examine in turn.

Interest rate spreads have narrowed modestly in the Czech Republic, from 5.8% on average in 1995 to 3.8% in 2000 but rising slightly to 4.0% in 2001–2, before resuming a narrowing trend in the course of 2003, as competition for the retail lending market heated up (Figure 10.3). Interest rate spreads have narrowed in Romania as well, as bank restructuring got under way in earnest. The average interest rate spread declined to 16.1% in 2002 from 20.8% in 2000. In Poland, the average spread rose abruptly in 1998 to 7.6% from only 4.5% in 1997 as a result of the take-off of consumer lending for which much higher spreads are typical in view of the perceived greater risk. Spreads exhibited declines in 1999–2000, but a widening of the average spread in 2001–2 coincided with the difficult macroeconomic situation and rising shares of nonperforming loans. The average spread between deposit and lending rates rose to 8.5% by 2002 from 7.2% in 2000. More recently, as Polish headline policy interest rates have come down in an effort to jump-start an economic growth rebound, lending rates have followed suit, although Polish banks have found it necessary to keep deposit rates from falling as quickly in order to attract household savings. As a result, the average interest spread on local currency loans and deposits dropped by 30 basis

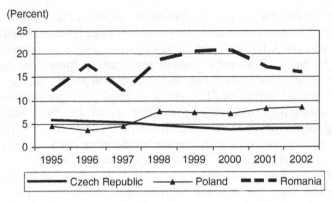

Figure 10.3. Interest rate spreads.

points in the first half of 2003. By contrast, overall for the banking sectors of the EU members, the overall interest rate spread was 3.8% by the end of 2002, but declined to 3.5% at mid-2003 (European Central Bank, 2003a, p. 20).

Despite declining interest rate spreads, higher than typical net interest margins in developed market economies suggest that competitive pressures and efficiency in the new Member States' banking sectors still compare unfavourably. Figures on net interest margins are available for Poland and the Czech Republic through 2001. The average net interest margin declined substantially in Poland in the period 1996–2001, from 5.98% to 3.38%, testifying to increasing competition in the market over that time. In the Czech Republic over this period, net interest margins remained in the range of 1.9–2.1%, with the exception of 1998–9, which was characterised by high headline policy interest rates and heightened concern over the quality of loan portfolios, when the figure pushed up to the 2.5–3.0% range. This can be compared with an average for EU banking sectors of 1.52% in 1998 (Iakova and Wagner, 2002). In addition to the influence on interest rates of increased competition in the bank sector, they will also continue to be affected by a continued reduction in rates of inflation down towards Euro-area levels and continued restructuring of the real sector which should lead to an improvement in the banks' perception of lending risks. It should be noted, however, that in most of these economies a great deal of this convergence has already taken place, and between lending rates in those countries and in the EU there is already less of an interest rate differential than existed in the late 1990s between the newer EU Member States and their predecessors in the Union.

Table 10.11. *Financial stability indicators for the Czech Republic*

	1996	1997	1998	1999	2000	2001
Net interest margin, in per cent	1.88	1.97	3.04	2.48	2.09	2.04
Ratio of non-interest income to average assets, in per cent	2.12	2.56	1.39	1.48	1.06	1.47
Ratio of operating costs to average assets, in per cent	2.21	2.24	2.24	2.24	2.07	2.13
Ratio of profit before tax to average assets (ROAA), in per cent	0.30	−0.27	−0.54	−0.29	0.69	0.45
Ratio of profit before tax to Tier 1 equity (ROE), in per cent	4.88	−4.26	−8.12	−5.12	14.99	9.99

Source: Czech National Bank.

Turning to the issue of profitability of banking activity in these economies, we have comparable data on return on assets and return on equity for the Czech Republic and Poland through 2001. For Romania, on the other hand, data are available only for 1998–2002. The data on the Czech Republic are presented in Table 10.11 for the period 1996–2001. Losses or very low rates of return in the Czech banking sector through 1999 largely reflect the results at large state-owned banks that were being restructured prior to their privatisation. In 2000–1, return on average assets for Czech banks was positive, but fell from 0.69% to 0.45%. Return on average core equity fell from 14.99% to 9.99% in 2001. Polish banks were profitable throughout the 1996–2001 period, but rates of return, presented in Table 10.12, declined monotonically thanks to increased competition in the market. The reported 3.77% return on average assets in 1996 slipped to 1.75% by 1998 and modestly further to 1.36% in 2001.

Prior to restructuring, the Romanian banking sector enjoyed rates of return above average for the region thanks to the unstable macroeconomic situation in the country that afforded the opportunity for substantial gains from foreign currency speculation and investment in government debt securities. But, as in the case of the Czech Republic, once restructuring got under way, the data also reflect losses at state-owned banks undergoing restructuring, so that rates of return were very low in 1998 and negative in 1999. Rates of return improved thereafter through 2001 following the restructuring and increased participation of foreign capital in the sector, but declined modestly in 2002 thanks to increased competition in the market. Return on average assets reached 3.1% in 2001 and slipped to 2.6% in 2002, while return on average equity hit 21.8% in

Table 10.12. *Financial stability indicators for Poland*

	1996	1997	1998	1999	2000	2001
Net interest margin, in per cent	5.98	5.23	4.58	4.01	4.26	3.38
Ratio of non-interest income to average assets, in per cent	1.81	2.04	2.01	2.48	2.73	3.05
Ratio of operating costs to average assets, in per cent	3.94	3.99	4.10	4.10	4.36	3.94
Ratio of profit before tax to average assets (ROAA), in per cent	3.77	3.00	1.75	1.60	1.51	1.36
Ratio of profit before tax to Tier 1 equity (ROE), in per cent	100.10	67.50	28.40	23.10	21.70	18.50

Source: National Bank of Poland.

Table 10.13. *Financial stability indicators for Hungary*

	1996	1997	1998	1999	2000	2001
Net interest margin, in per cent	4.9	4.5	4.5	4.1	3.9	4.1
Ratio of non-interest income to average assets, in per cent	0.1	0.7	−1.0	0.5	1.0	1.7
Ratio of operating costs to average assets, in per cent	3.7	4.0	4.0	4.0	3.7	3.7
Ratio of profit before tax to average assets (ROAA), in per cent	2.0	1.0	−2.2	0.5	1.2	1.7
Ratio of profit before tax to Tier 1 equity (ROE), in per cent	24.7	11.0	−24.7	6.3	14.4	18.3

Source: National Bank of Hungary.

2001 but declined to 18.3% in 2002. Return on average equity declined from 100.1% in 1996 to 28.4% in 1998 and then to 18.5% in 2001. Thus, in 2001, the last year in which we have data comparable across the three banking sectors, Romania actually reported the highest average rates of return. For comparative purposes, Tables 10.13 and 10.14 provide these data for two other Central European countries, Hungary and Slovakia. It should be noted that, on average, in the EU in 1998, return on average assets ran at 0.56% and return on average equity was 11.31% (Iakova and Wagner, 2002, p. 45). The European Central Bank (2003a) noted that return on average equity (in the case of the EU, after taxes and extraordinary items, unlike the Central and Eastern European data

Table 10.14. *Financial stability indicators for Slovakia*

	1996	1997	1998	1999	2000	2001
Net interest margin, in per cent	0.13	1.80	1.20	0.45	1.85	2.30
Ratio of non-interest income to average assets, in per cent	2.26	1.33	1.70	1.75	1.14	1.06
Ratio of operating costs to average assets, in per cent	2.35	2.35	2.40	2.69	2.55	2.45
Ratio of profit before tax to average assets (ROAA), in per cent	−0.43	−0.18	0.04	−3.99	0.54	1.15
Ratio of profit before tax to Tier 1 equity (ROE), in per cent	−11.92	−4.97	−0.08	−61.20	8.90	19.29

Source: National Bank of Slovakia.

that is presented before taxes) declined to 8.6% in 2002 from 10.1% in 2001 and further that these indicators varied widely among the banking sectors of the individual countries, ranging from 2% to 15%. The European Central Bank (2003a) also calculated return on equity and return on assets for an aggregation of the fifty largest banks in the EU. Return on assets for this group declined from 0.76% in 2000 to 0.39% in 2002, while return on equity fell from 14.6% in 2000 to 8.5% in 2002. Data for mid-2003 showed an improvement in both these indicators for the fifty largest banks with the return on assets rising to 0.43% and the return on equity to 11.4%.

It is interesting to note that, in the data available for Poland on operating costs as a share of total assets over this period, no significant decline was evident despite the apparent impact of competitive pressures on net interest margins. The ratio of operating costs to average assets improved modestly over this period in the Czech Republic, from 2.24% in 1997–8 to 2.13% in 2001, and not at all in Poland. This would suggest that banks in the region have so far sought to rely on improved asset management in responding to downward pressures on profitability, either neglecting or having little success in improving efficiency through lower operating costs; and, further, that reducing operating costs in the future, such as through the introduction of more modern banking information technology, might be a prime source for maintaining competitiveness in the enlarged European market post-accession. In comparison, the ratio of operating costs to assets for EU banks fell on average to 1.68% in 2002 from 1.74% a year earlier. It should be noted that, in the case of Poland, income from other activities was rising over the period as a share of total assets, which nearly compensated for the decline in net interest margin. The ratio of combined income to total assets remained in the range of 6.4–7.0% throughout 1998–2001. In the Czech case, there was no offsetting impact from sources of income other than interest, and the combined income ratio declined from 4.5% in 1997 to 3.5% in 2001. On average in the EU, the ratio of net interest income to total assets rose to 1.57% in 2002 from 1.51% a year earlier while the ratio of total income to assets fell to 2.55% in 2002 from 2.62% in 2001.

Turning to the issue of the financial stability of these banking sectors, having noted the decline in non-performing loans as a share of assets following restructuring in section 10.2 above, we now look at the issue of capital adequacy. All three of the banking sectors have consistently exceeded the minimum international standard of 8% capital adequacy in 1996–2002. However, it must be noted that the national methodologies used in calculating risk-weighted capital-asset ratios make the figures somewhat incomparable among the banking sectors in the region and with banking sectors in developed market economies. Due to lack of the necessary data, none of these three countries takes market risk into account in classifying assets, nor do they represent consolidated capital adequacy statistics. At least in the cases of Romania and Poland, we know in addition that, through 2002, no capital charges against the assets of subsidiaries or any explicit charges for foreign currency, interest rate or equity positions were considered in the calculations. These represent substantial risks for the region's banks. Furthermore, due to the relatively high rates of inflation in Romania in the post-transition period, fixed capital has been included in the calculations at inflated prices, overstating the capitalisation of the banking sector. Romania's loan classification scheme was revised in 2000 to incorporate stricter standards. Nevertheless, it is illustrative to examine the published capital adequacy figures, presented in Tables 10.15 to 10.17. In the Czech Republic, the ratio of core capital to risk-weighted assets increased from 9.3% in 1996 to 15.5% in 2001, before dipping to 14.2% in 2002. In Poland, this ratio rose modestly from 12.3% in 1996 to the neighbourhood of 13% in 1999–2000, and then improved markedly to 15.0–15.5% in 2001–2, although the data in the later years do not adequately reflect the risk associated with the growing volume of consumer credit in that period. The European Central Bank (2003a) reports that the average capital adequacy ratio (Tier 1 capital to total assets) across the EU in 2002 was 8.3%, unchanged from a year earlier, and varied only slightly among the banking sectors of the individual countries.

Table 10.15. *Capital adequacy in the Czech Republic, end-period, in %*

	1996	1997	1998	1999	2000	2001	2002
Risk-weighted capital/asset ratio	9.3	9.7	12.0	13.6	14.9	15.5	14.2

Source: Czech National Bank.

Table 10.16. *Capital adequacy in Poland, end-period, in %*

	1996	1997	1998	1999	2000	2001	2002
Risk-weighted capital/asset ratio	12.3	12.5	11.7	13.2	12.9	15.0	15.5

Source: National Bank of Poland.

Table 10.17. *Capital adequacy in Romania, end-period, in %*

	1995	1996	1997	1998	1999	2000	2001	2002
Risk-weighted capital/asset ratio	13.8	13.3	13.6	10.3	17.9	23.8	28.8	24.8

Source: National Bank of Romania.

10.4   Bank regulation and supervision

Improved bank regulation and supervision have been primary factors in shoring up the stability of the financial sectors of the economies in transition to date. Because of substantial surviving state-owned stakes in major commercial banks and politically sensitive state-owned enterprises through much of the period in a number of countries, the situation in their banking sectors was fraught with moral hazard. Poor corporate governance and expectations of repeated government bailouts did not provide bank managements with appropriate incentives. In many cases, government officials used bureaucratic power to direct lending with soft repayment terms to financially troubled state enterprises. Bankers found it necessary to rely on implicit government guarantees on credits as bankruptcy procedures seldom provided resort to collateral if necessary to recover assets. Auditing practices initially fell far short of international standards. Inadequate scrutiny in licensing new banks with insufficient capital to operate in an environment of lax supervision resulted in a rash of bank failures in some of the economies in the early post-transition.

Bank supervisory efforts suffered from lack of independence, resources and expertise. The result was the heavy burden on the banking sectors of significant shares of non-performing loans that we have described above and that served as a brake on economic recovery and growth due to inadequate financial intermediation.

In the post-transition period, the new Member States benefited from the advice of the international financial institutions in regard to improving the stability of their financial sectors. Joint working groups of the IMF and the World Bank, under the Financial Stability Assessment Program, have conducted reviews of bank supervision in individual countries, measuring conformance with the twenty-five Basel Core Principles for Effective Bank Supervision established under the auspices of the Bank for International Settlements, and have made recommendations where such conformance was incomplete. The working groups also conducted simulated stress tests for the individual banking sectors to determine if they would remain stable after suffering particular shocks. The Financial Stability Assessment Programs for Poland, the Czech Republic and Romania were completed in February 2001, June 2001 and September 2003, respectively. In each case, the working group determined that the bank regulation and supervision functions being carried out were generally compliant with the Basel Core Principles. However, further specific steps were recommended.

In the case of Poland, the assessment of bank supervision resulted in recommendations that more autonomy be granted to supervisory agencies with legal protection for supervisors, that information exchange be improved among the agencies supervising the bank and non-bank financial sectors, that frequent, consolidated reporting be required, that corporate governance principles be instilled and enforced, and that stronger powers to intervene and enforce regulations in banking institutions be granted (International Monetary Fund, 2001a). The assessment noted that these judgments were based on legislation and regulations rather than actual practice, and that, in fact, regulators had made considerable efforts to compensate for these shortcomings.

In the case of the Czech Republic, the working group recommended that supervisors make additional progress in adopting a risk-based approach, including risks other than just credit risk, apply capital charges for risk on a consolidated basis, require approval of explicit loan and investment and risk management policies at banks, strengthen regulations with respect to anti-money-laundering measures, and add human capital and technical resources to the supervisory effort for the assessment of market risk and risk management systems (International Monetary Fund, 2001b).

In the case of Romania, the working group also cited the need for greater legal protection of supervisors, to expand supervisory efforts to credit unions, to require consultation with home country supervisors before authorising foreign participation in the Romanian banking sector, and to require banks to hold capital against market risk. The working group noted that most of the issues would be addressed in upcoming amendments to the country's Bank Act and through harmonisation with EU regulations scheduled for 2004 (International Monetary Fund, 2003).

Improvements in bank supervision legislation and practice have been achieved in the process of harmonising domestic legislation with the *acquis communautaire*, as the new Member States have moved towards meeting the requirements of the eight directives that govern the financial sectors of Member States. A number of the provisions relate directly to bank regulation and supervision. The first and second directives set the rules for licensing new banks, including minimum capital requirements, and provide for cooperation between national bank supervisory authorities while retaining home country responsibility for the single licence required to operate anywhere within the EU. The Bank Account Directive establishes a common form of annual accounts for financial institutions, and the Consolidation Supervision Directive requires that supervision of banks be conducted via prudential measures compiled on a consolidated basis for all of the institutions' activities. The Own Funds Directive establishes the criteria for calculating this concept for use in prudential considerations, while the Solvency Ratio Directive sets a minimum level for the risk-adjusted capital asset ratio at 8%, the international standard. In addition, the Large Exposure Directive restricts a bank's exposure to a single client to no more than 25% of its own funds and the total of all loans amounting to 10% or more of the bank's own funds to be less than eight times the bank's own capital.

Progress in these countries on meeting these directives has been reported by the European Commission in its annual country reports on the state of preparedness for accession. It should be noted that negotiations on Chapter 1 of the *acquis* on the free provision of services, which addresses the financial services sector, were closed provisionally for Poland in November 2000 and for the Czech Republic in March 2001, and closed in December 2002 along with all negotiations on accession for the ten new Member States. The 2003 progress report from the European Commission on the preparedness of the Czech Republic notes that Czech banking sector legislation is mostly in line with the *acquis* and bank supervision is satisfactory, but that capital adequacy rules have not been implemented completely. The report notes the February 2003 agreement that is to bring about greater cooperation between the bank and financial market supervisory agencies, deemed of particular importance because of the nature of Czech banks that operate as broad-ranging financial conglomerates. In the case of Poland, the commission noted a number of the same shortcomings cited in the 2001 IMF–World Bank assessment, including the inadequate legal protection of supervisors and the incomplete calculation of capital adequacy but noted progress in conducting the consolidated supervision of financial services. Romania's negotiations on Chapter 2 were opened only in December 2002 and remain open. While the 2003 progress report notes that banking sector supervision is much closer to meeting EU standards than supervision of other segments of the financial services sector in Romania, recent progress has been slow and limited to implementing legislation. The report identifies remaining shortcomings in the areas of capital adequacy regulation, supervision of financial conglomerates and liquidation of credit institutions.

In conclusion, these detailed assessments of the banking regulation and supervision efforts in the new Member States have generally testified to significant progress made in recent years and have indicated that for the most part these activities live up to accepted international standards. The remaining shortcomings relate primarily to limited consideration of categories of risk in connection with determining capital adequacy, linked to insufficient skills and information available for the task, failure to make explicit in legislation expectations for corporate governance and investment and risk management policies of banking institutions, inadequate coordination of information and supervision across the various segments of the financial services market to assess capital adequacy on a consolidated basis, and a need to improve the independence of and legal protection for supervisors.

10.5   Challenges to the banking sectors in the run-up to accession and the euro, and policy implications

Accession to the EU is likely to present the banking systems of Central and Eastern Europe with the potential need to cope with a new set of stresses. The banking systems will face growing capital inflows together with possible changes in exchange rate regimes as well as downward adjustment of interest rates in the convergence towards Euro area rates. By the time of accession, all constraints on capital account flows (with the potential exception of temporary restrictions permitted in extraordinary situations) and barriers to foreign competition in the financial sector will have been lifted.

Substantial capital inflows, initially largely in the form of direct investment, will fuel growth in domestic investment and consumption, in turn widening current account deficits. To the extent that current account deficits would come to be financed to a significant extent with short-term debt, the potential for sudden, sharp reverse flows of capital is created if foreign investors come to change their sentiment about the country. Brouwer *et al.* (2002) note that to some extent the vulnerability of local banks to such a sudden withdrawal of short-term foreign capital is being diminished by the increasing role of foreign branch banks and subsidiaries in intermediating foreign capital inflows to the non-financial private sector. Nevertheless, to maintain stability in the financial sector it will behoove national policy-makers to manage carefully domestic demand, first of all through cautious fiscal and monetary policies, to avoid accelerated widening of payments imbalances, particularly if there is a growing tendency to finance them with debt of short maturity.

While deposits in foreign currency declined as a share of total deposits as confidence in a fairly stable exchange rate increased, in the run-up to EMU accession, euro deposits may become increasingly popular. Sensitivity to interest rate differentials among local currency and euro deposits in domestic banks and between euro deposits at home and those held abroad could generate destabilising capital flows. To the extent that banks' balance sheets are asymmetric in terms of their assets and liabilities denominated in foreign currencies, sharp movements in exchange rates can have a substantial impact on their financial situation. Additionally, sharp exchange rate movements may also have serious consequences for the financial conditions of the banks' major customers, their ability to repay loans denominated in foreign currency, and hence for the quality of the banks' assets. Tables 10.18–10.20 present the trends in the share of foreign currency denominated credits to and deposits received from the non-financial private sectors by commercial banks in each of the three countries. Note that the share of foreign currency is lower the greater the degree of macroeconomic and exchange rate stability, although it is not possible to draw a robust conclusion on the basis of such a limited sample.

Entering into the ERM-II mechanism, a requirement for the two-year period preceding the scheduled accession of the country to the EMU, is likely to make only rather modest exchange rate flexibility practicable, but the exchange rate will technically be permitted to fluctuate within 15% bands around the central rate. It will continue to be necessary for bank supervisors to monitor banks' open foreign currency positions and limit them if they threaten to create serious exchange rate risk to the balance sheets. It will also be necessary to monitor vulnerability to asset

Table 10.18. Czech Republic, currency composition of credits to and deposits from the non-financial private sector

	Units	1997	1998	1999	2000	2001	2002	2003
Koruna credits	Billion koruna	912.6	860.0	838.5	838.3	627.2	813.8	750.6
Foreign currency credits	Billion koruna	200.3	213.8	193.9	160.5	155.6	133.1	124.1
of which, in euro	Billion koruna						88.6	89.8
Total	Billion koruna	1112.9	1073.8	1032.4	998.8	782.8	946.9	874.7
Koruna credits	% share	82.0	80.1	81.2	83.9	80.1	85.9	85.8
Foreign currency credits	% share	18.0	19.9	18.8	16.1	19.9	14.1	14.2
of which, in euro	% share						9.4	10.3
Koruna deposits	Billion koruna	962.0	985.3	983.3	1027.2	1169.3	1310.2	1415.6
Foreign currency deposits	Billion koruna	138.5	142.5	147.9	157.5	176.0	166.7	166.2
of which, in euro	Billion koruna						98.0	100.8
Total	Billion koruna	1100.5	1127.8	1131.2	1184.7	1345.3	1476.9	1581.8
Koruna deposits	% share	87.4	87.4	86.9	86.7	86.9	88.7	89.5
Foreign currency deposits	% share	12.6	12.6	13.1	13.3	13.1	11.3	10.5
of which, in euro	% share						6.6	6.4

Source: Czech National Bank.

Table 10.19. *Poland, currency composition of credits to and deposits from the non-financial private sector*

	Units	1997	1998	1999	2000	2001	2002
Zloty credits	Billion zloty	80.1	94.8	122.2	139.0	142.0	137.5
Foreign currency credits	Billion zloty	16.4	28.3	33.0	41.2	50.1	55.6
Total	Billion zloty	96.4	123.1	155.2	180.2	192.1	193.1
Zloty credits	% share	83.0	77.0	78.7	77.1	73.9	71.2
Foreign currency credits	% share	17.0	23.0	21.3	22.9	26.1	28.8
Zloty deposits	Billion zloty	104.4	143.6	168.6	197.0	218.2	212.2
Foreign currency deposits	Billion zloty	32.4	34.2	41.3	43.9	52.8	48.9
Total	Billion zloty	136.8	177.7	209.9	241.0	271.0	261.2
Zloty deposits	% share	76.3	80.8	80.3	81.8	80.5	81.3
Foreign currency deposits	% share	23.7	19.2	19.7	18.2	19.5	18.7

Source: National Bank of Poland.

quality in the form of foreign currency lending to customers who might be unable to repay in case of unfavourable movements of the exchange rate.

EU membership means opening the banking and financial services market widely to foreign competitors. Local banks will see net interest margins narrow and will seek to achieve greater efficiency by reducing the ratio of operating costs to assets, perhaps by growing assets rapidly through risky lending behaviour. Under this scenario, domestic banks may more rapidly approach a threatening proportion of troubled loans in their portfolios to the extent they have engaged in insider lending or implicit government-directed lending, although, because state-owned stakes in banks in the region have dwindled, this is less likely to be a problem in the extension of new credits but relates more to possible inherited burdens of troubled loans. Thus, it will be crucial to strengthen the independence of supervisory agencies, to enforce the avoidance of the conflict of interests and to impose exposure limits, encourage the principles of good corporate governance and improve standards for auditing. It should be noted that a greater preponderance of foreign banks operating in the region widens the possibility for cross-country contagion of instability in the banking sectors, as the foreign banks tend to have operations in several of the countries of the region. If significant outflows of capital are generated by losses of confidence in one or more of the banking sectors, the impact on exchange rates could well affect the timing of euro adoption.

Table 10.20. *Romania, currency composition of credits to and deposits from the non-financial private sector*

	Units	1997	1998	1999	2000	2001	2002	2003
Leu credits	Billion lei	16232	24273	24445	30411	47533	66729	135292
Foreign currency credits	Billion lei	19668	34814	33274	44596	70721	112897	170189
Total	Billion lei	35901	59086	57720	75007	118254	179626	305482
Leu credits	% share	45.2	41.1	42.4	40.5	40.2	37.1	44.3
Foreign currency credits	% share	54.8	58.9	57.6	59.5	59.8	62.9	55.7
Leu deposits	Billion lei	5568	9252	14774	19324	26713	49702	76738
Foreign currency deposits	Billion lei	17686	30202	50482	74856	115784	146812	171169
Total	Billion lei	23253	39453.5	65256	94180	142497	196514	247907
Leu deposits	% share	23.9	23.5	22.6	20.5	18.7	25.3	31.0
Foreign currency deposits	% share	76.1	76.5	77.4	79.5	81.3	74.7	69.0

Source: National Bank of Romania.

In acceding to the EU, these countries will be instituting a more substantial financial safety net. In harmonising legislation with the EU norms, the new Member States will have instituted deposit insurance equal to the EU minimum of €20,000. This level is quite high relative to the levels of average income and average size of individual deposits. Providing insurance at this level has the potential to provide mixed incentives to bank management to act responsibly if their depositors are not expected to pay the price for risky behaviour. The other component of the safety net is the lender of last resort. This will remain strictly a central bank function. The fact that banking sectors in these countries are for the most part highly concentrated increases the likelihood that financing would be provided to a domestic bank in serious difficulty as it would represent a serious systemic threat. On the other hand, after accession, the supervision of EU-based foreign branch banks and foreign strategic bank investors will be within the purview of their home country. Thus, cooperation and harmonisation of incentives across national boundaries for bank supervisory agencies will be increasingly important.

We have seen that capital adequacy as measured by national supervisory agencies is currently well above the 8% standard in the new Member States. On the other hand, we have also catalogued the remaining inadequacies in auditing standards, the inadequacies in the assessment of a broad category of risks for the purpose of capital charges, the dearth of information-sharing on credit risk among credit institutions, the less-than-adequate corporate governance to discourage insider lending, and the problems in the judicial system that undermine the protection of creditors' rights and their resort to collateral (including real estate) in an effort to recover assets. Moreover, as noted above, the banking sectors are for the most part highly concentrated, which increases the likelihood that the national safety net (the lender of last resort) would kick in, and this represents a greater moral hazard. One suggested approach to buffering against these uncertainties in assessing the condition of banks is to increase the statutory minimum capital adequacy ratio.

More limited resources and skills are likely to characterise bank supervisory agencies in the new Member States for some time to come. This will become an even more critical limitation as the regulatory standards are harmonised with the provisions of the Basel II capital adequacy regulations that will become compulsory in 2007. The new regulatory scheme is designed to address a wider spectrum of risk assessment in weighting assets and enforcing increased transparency to bring to bear the discipline of markets to contain risk-seeking by banks. These new standards will require even more sophistication in banks' asset and risk management strategies and in information technologies that will have to be matched in the supervisory agencies as well. Within these agencies, it will be necessary to shift scarce resources to review higher risk activities and banks' policies for controlling their risk exposure. It has been suggested that in light of this necessity, banks in relatively poor financial shape should be required to pay higher premiums for deposit insurance because of their risk-seeking behaviour. Banks should also be required to provide more information about their risk-taking for the public record so that limited supervisory resources can be supplemented by scrutiny on the part of depositors concerned for the safety of their funds. Higher levels of concern by depositors would raise the cost of financing for banks. To the extent that levels of deposit insurance are high relative to the size of average individual deposits, however, the incentives for this type of scrutiny are reduced.

10.6   Conclusions

In examining the recent developments in the banking sectors of three selected Central and Eastern European countries which have acceded to or are scheduled to accede to the European Union, we have noted significant achievements in improving the efficiency and scope of their roles in financial intermediation through restructuring and privatisation, the opening of the banking sectors to foreign participation and the enhancement of bank regulation and supervision, both in principle and in practice. In these efforts, these countries have been aided by technical advice and resources from the international financial institutions and the European Union. Most usefully, the process of harmonising the national legislation and practice with the EU's banking directives has provided a critical road map for domestic policy-makers and legislators in preparing the banking sectors to cope with the stresses and opportunities of the post-transition and post-accession economic and financial environment. We have also noted areas where additional progress is required if there is to be substantial certainty that these banking sectors will continue to promote financial stability, provide an improved financial intermediation function and help to drive robust economic growth. Improved corporate governance and auditing standards will be critical not only in the banking sector but across the economy. Should banks find it preferable to boost lending to households rather than to a corporate sector that may be masking the actual risks involved, a costly misallocation of capital on a large scale could result in these economies.

Whatever the sources of potential instability in the banking sector considered here, it remains the case that the most critical element in ensuring that instability is minimised upon EU accession is bank regulation and supervision. A regular process of stability analysis and stress-testing on banking-sector data should be maintained. The supervisory agencies can be instrumental in directing banks to increase provisioning against risks, and to gain greater skill in assessing and managing credit risks and managing their assets to ensure the necessary liquidity. Legislation and regulations having been strengthened, but resources, including both professional skills and technology, and time are also necessary in the case of both the supervisory agencies and the judicial systems to get up to speed in implementing them. It should clearly be a high priority for the EU to ensure that resources, both technical and in the form of human capital, available to the supervisory agencies are supplemented.

References

Brouwer, H., de Haas, R. and Kiviet, B. 2002. *Banking Sector Development and Financial Stability in the Run-Up to EU Accession*. The Hague: Bank of the Netherlands.

Cottarelli, C., Dell'Ariccia, G. and Vladkova-Hollar, I. 2003. 'Early Birds, Late Risers, and Sleeping Beauties: Bank Credit Growth to the Private Sector in Central and Eastern Europe and the Balkans'. International Monetary Fund Working Paper, No. 03/213.

Daianu, D. and Ionici, O. 2003. *Achievements and Challenges for Banking Sector Development in EU Acceding Countries: Southeast Europe and Baltic Countries*. Bucharest: OECD Forum on Trade in Services in South Eastern Europe.

European Central Bank. 2003a. *EU Banking Sector Stability*. Frankfurt: European Central Bank.

2003b. *Structural Analysis of the EU Banking Sector*. Frankfurt: European Central Bank.

Iakova, D. and Wagner, N. 2002. 'Financial Sector Evolution: Challenges in Supporting Macroeconomic Stability and Sustainable Growth'. In Feldman, R. and Watson, M., *Into the EU: Policy Frameworks in Central Europe*. Washington DC: International Monetary Fund.

International Monetary Fund. 2001a. 'Republic of Poland: Financial System Stability Assessment'. International Monetary Fund Country Report, No. 01/67.

2001b. 'Czech Republic: Financial System Stability Assessment'. International Monetary Fund Country Report, No. 01/113.

2003. 'Romania: Financial System Stability Assessment'. International Monetary Fund Country Report, No. 03/389.

11 Infrastructure investments as a tool for regional development policy: lessons from the Spanish evidence

*Rosina Moreno, Enrique López-Bazo and Manuel Artís**

11.1 Introduction

Within the European Union interest in the effects of public capital investments on economic development has grown as a result of the increase in funds assigned to finance infrastructure projects in less developed regions in an ongoing attempt to promote the growth and, hence, the convergence and cohesion of the territories of the EU. It is well documented that, in response to the diversity of income and welfare levels prevailing in the Union following the accession of Greece, Spain and Portugal, the European institutions adopted a set of measures to ensure the integration of peripheral areas within the Community. Among these measures, basic infrastructure investments in 'Objective 1' regions accounted for 35% of the total expenditure of Structural Funds between 1989 and 1993. The further enlargement of the EU is set to exacerbate regional problems in the Union given that the mean GDP per capita of the new Member States stands at approximately 40% of the EU average. These economies are characterised by a predominance of primary and secondary activities, with industry highly concentrated in specific locations, together with an insufficient infrastructure endowment. A restructuring process is therefore required in order to guarantee suitable conditions for future growth. Those regions which fail to restructure might well pay the price of recession and thus be deprived of the potential for future growth. Only those regions that successfully restructure will have some chance of catching up with their more affluent counterparts.

The importance that the EU ascribes to infrastructure is more a matter of conviction than a policy underpinned by the results of analytical

* Authors acknowledge financial support from Ministerio de Ciencia y Tecnología, Programa Nacional de I+D+I, SEC 2002-00165.

studies; indeed, the actual effects of such investment projects have yet to be clearly identified. Most studies analysing their impact on regional growth show the relationship to be positive. However, the public capital elasticity estimated in a Cobb-Douglas function – the most common specification adopted in such studies – is often too large to be credible (Aschauer, 1989),[1] which has led to the partial discrediting of their results. For instance, Holtz-Eakin (1994) and Garcia-Milà et al. (1996) criticise initial findings that point to the positive effects of infrastructure investment projects in the case of the US on econometric grounds, and present estimates of regional production functions, using standard techniques to control for state-specific characteristics, that reveal essentially a zero role for public capital. Furthermore, Crihfield and Panggabean (1995), using a neoclassical growth model, observe that public capital has a weak effect on growth in per capita product of US metropolitan economies in terms of both indirect action (factor markets) and direct action (rates of public investment). Ciccone and Hall (1996) draw the same conclusion in accounting for differences in labour productivity across US states in a model that accounts for the effects of spatial density.

In this chapter we present new evidence regarding the effect of public capital on productivity and economic growth in the case of the Spanish regions, and discuss the implications for regional policy.

First, in order to understand the impact of public infrastructure on economic growth, we describe the capitalisation process that the Spanish regions have undergone over the last forty years and, in particular, since the country's accession to the EU in 1986, in order to analyse its relationship with the geography of economic activity. We focus our attention on the importance of the spatial dimension of the impact of infrastructure, since we believe this to be an essential factor in the study of the productivity impact of infrastructure investments. We therefore start the study of this relationship by mapping the distribution of economic activity and infrastructure endowment in the Spanish regions by means of an exhaustive exploratory spatial analysis based on several global indicators of spatial dependence. The analysis is carried out for different time periods starting from the mid-1960s and finishing at the end of the 1990s.

Secondly, it is assumed that the effects of infrastructure on productivity are dependent on the various types of public infrastructure. Different

---

[1] Papers that analyse the effect of public infrastructure by estimating a cost function include Morrison and Schwartz (1996), Morrison and Siegel (1997), Moreno et al. (2002), Boscá et al. (2002) and Moreno et al. (2003). All report a positive shadow price for public capital.

categories of basic infrastructure may not have the same kind of impact on output since they are believed to fulfil different purposes: local infrastructure enhances economic activity in the area in which it is located, whereas transport and communication infrastructure may produce benefits locally as well as having spillover effects on other regions. Such spillovers can be either positive or negative. Positive spillovers may arise from improved network connectivity whereby any single section of a network is related and subordinated to the whole, thus strengthening the interrelationship between regions. Hence, part of the benefits arising from infrastructure improvements (if they can really be said to exist) are felt beyond the limits of the region in which the infrastructure is located. Negative spillovers, by contrast, may be caused by the migration factor, in the sense that the transport infrastructure in one region might have a negative effect on the labour and mobile capital of the region's closest competitors. In this chapter, we seek to verify which of these two hypotheses regarding the spillover effect of transport infrastructure is most prevalent in the case of the Spanish regions.

In addition, we wish to analyse the extent to which the effect of public infrastructure is dependent on the level of economic development and on the existing endowment of public capital in a region. These results will provide evidence as to the effectiveness of infrastructure investment in the less developed regions compared to those made in regions with higher levels of productivity. It will also enable us to draw conclusions on the question as to whether the link between growth and public capital is dependent on the amount of existing public capital stocks. For instance, it seems sensible to think in terms of the existence of a threshold level for the provision of public capital after which returns would rapidly decrease. In other words, infrastructure may play a significant role during the takeoff of a less developed economy but the impact will decrease over time.

In this chapter, we provide evidence of the aforementioned issues for the Spanish regional economies (NUTS III level) over the last four decades. It should be borne in mind that the levels of government capital endowment and economic activity in all Spanish regions in the early 1960s were far below those of other European economies and that both these levels have undergone a significant increase during the period under consideration, especially following Spain's accession to the EU. To a certain extent, it has been argued that the new EU Member States stand, in relation to the mean figures for the EU-15, in the same position as that in which about twenty years ago Greece, Portugal and Spain stood in relation to the then older members of the EU. Boldrin (2006), deploying a number of aggregate statistics (GDP per capita, labour productivity, share of employment in agriculture and openness of the economy) demonstrates that the macroeconomic conditions of the new Member States are similar to those of previous entrants and that the gains to be enjoyed from joining the EU will probably be comparable to those experienced by the previous three newcomers. Indeed, these new Member States present a number of cultural and historical features that very much resemble those of Spain at the time of accession to the EU: about a decade has elapsed since previous regimes collapsed and a number of reforms have already been implemented. However, the present environment within the EU is marked by much higher levels of economic integration than in the 1980s, while the new Member States will be entering a larger and richer market (Boldrin and Canova, 2003). Such conditions should benefit these states and ease their integration. A further potential difference is the fact that the level of infrastructure stock in the new Member States may differ from the level of public capital in Spain at the time of accession, but, because of the paucity of monetary data on infrastructure stocks in the accession countries, we cannot conclude whether this is a real difference or not. What we do know is that the level of infrastructure endowment in Spain at the time of accession had increased considerably if compared with levels recorded during the 1970s and early 1980s. This means that the benefits accrued from investing in infrastructure in this country were not only attributable to entrance into the EU. Therefore, Spain's experience should, to a certain extent, provide some general pointers as to what may happen to the new entrants when they obtain new investments in public capital. The empirical results in this chapter can be understood, therefore, as demonstrating the effects of infrastructure on the takeoff of less developed economies that are just beginning to open up and modernise their productive structures.

This chapter is organised as follows. Section 11.2 presents the model specification based on the assumption that competition between regions is made manifest when the endowment of public infrastructure is increased. Section 11.3 describes the database and its main spatial features. The empirical results for the industrial sector in the Spanish regions are presented and discussed in section 11.4. Finally, some concluding remarks and suggestions for policy-makers are given in section 11.5.

11.2   Model specification

This section presents an outline of a classical production model, in which public capital stock is a quasi-fixed input for regional production.

Furthermore, the output in each region (Y) is produced according to a classical production model that relates output with the amounts of labour (L), private capital (K) and public capital (G):[2]

$$Y = f(L, K)g(G) \qquad (1)$$

and in which the factors of production meet the following conditions:

$$
\begin{aligned}
& g'(G) > 0 \\
& f_K > 0; \ f_{KK} < 0 \\
& f_L > 0; \ f_{LL} < 0
\end{aligned}
\qquad (2)
$$

The model assumes that public infrastructure is complementary to labour and capital. If the markets are competitive and the factors of production are mobile, each factor will be paid its marginal revenue product, given a certain amount of public capital, the choice over which is considered to be external to the firms of the regions:

$$
\begin{aligned}
\frac{\partial Y}{\partial L} &= f_L(L, K)g(G) \\
\frac{\partial Y}{\partial K} &= f_K(L, K)g(G)
\end{aligned}
\qquad (3)
$$

Once the supply and demand for each input are balanced, the factor prices will be equal to their respective marginal revenue, so that:

$$
\begin{aligned}
p_L &= p_Y f_L(L, K)g(G) \\
p_K &= p_Y f_K(L, K)g(G)
\end{aligned}
\qquad (4)
$$

where p_Y, p_L and p_K are the prices of output, labour and capital, respectively.

In line with Boarnet (1998) and focusing our attention on the effect of an increase in public capital, let us suppose that a region i increases its public capital endowment. Following the above reasoning, the price of labour and capital in region i will increase accordingly, so that, if these factors were perfectly mobile, the factor–price differential would induce labour and capital migration from other regions to region i. This migration would imply a new output level in region i:

$$Y_i = f(L_i + \Delta L, K_i + \Delta K)g(G_i + \Delta G) \qquad (5)$$

---

[2] As is standard in the literature, we assume that firms do not pay for the services provided by public capital. However, while firms do not have to face the direct costs of accumulating this input, they do pay for infrastructure in terms of taxes, so a social cost is incurred in obtaining adequate public capital endowment.

along with a lower output level in those regions that have lost production factors. In other words, an increase in public capital leads to a rise in output in region i and a reduction in output in the other regions, with some labour and capital migrating from these regions to region i. Therefore, the migration of inputs leads to output increases in regions with good public capital endowments and reduced output in the others.[3]

The above model would, therefore, seem to point to the existence of negative output spillovers associated with public infrastructure, since mobile factors tend to move to the region with good infrastructure endowments. In this way, the total output in a region would depend positively on its stock of infrastructure and negatively on the stock of infrastructure in other regions.

Yet, there are reasons to believe that public infrastructure, in particular that associated with transportation, may have a positive impact not only in the region in which it is located but also in adjacent regions. This is due, as mentioned earlier, to improved network connectivity whereby any single section of a network is related and subordinated to the whole, thus strengthening the interrelationship between regions. The importance of this spatial dimension in infrastructure studies was first considered after noting the reduction in the effects of public capital at the territorial level (Duffy-Deno and Eberts, 1991; Eberts, 1990; Munnell, 1990; Garcia-Milà and McGuire, 1992). Economists began to suspect the existence of spillover effects that spread the impact of public capital among neighbouring regions. These effects are due either to the network characteristics of the infrastructure, or to the fact that regions are administrative areas whose boundaries tend to break forward and backward linkages, thereby attributing regions with an inadequate infrastructural effect. Thus, a number of studies of the Spanish regions (e.g. Mas *et al.*, 1996) have demonstrated that productivity depends not only on infrastructure but on the overall provision throughout the country, especially in bordering regions. However, Holtz-Eakin and Schwartz (1995) report no evidence in favour of the idea that the US highway stock has significant effects on productivity across states, and Kelejian and Robinson (1997) report a negative spillover effect of infrastructure, which is more in line with the migration effects outlined in the above model. In short, the fact is that there is no empirical consensus on the existence of spillovers or on their effects, positive or otherwise.

---

[3] Some extensions to the case where factors of production are imperfectly mobile are given in detail in Boarnet (1998).

In order to test the effects of the spillover of public infrastructure, the production function for a region i after including the spatial spillover can be written as:

$$Y = f(L, K)g(G, G_\rho) \qquad (6)$$

where G_ρ is the public capital infrastructure in the other regions, which should reflect the spillover impact of infrastructure. Were a positive spillover to exist, then it might be assumed that the closer the two regions were to each other, the stronger the interaction would be. By contrast, in the case of the prevalence of negative spillover, it seems logical to assume thats the spillover would be stronger between regions that are close substitutes as locations for production.

Independently of the reasoning underlying the similarity or proximity between regions, the empirical model we estimate here is based on the log-linear Cobb-Douglas production function in which public capital is disaggregated into two main components, local (*G_local*) and transportation (*G_trans*):

$$log(Y_{it}) = \beta_0 + \beta_1 log(L_{it}) + \beta_2 log(K_{it}) + \beta_3 log(G\_local_{it})$$
$$+ \beta_4 log(G\_trans_{it}) + \varepsilon_{it} \qquad (7)$$

where log denotes logarithm and ε_{it} is a well-behaved error term, and where i denotes regions and t time periods. This expression allows us to isolate the effect of the two types of infrastructure.

In a subsequent step, we can add a spillover variable for transportation public infrastructure (*G_trans$_\rho$*) to expression (7):

$$log(Y_{it}) = \beta_0 + \beta_1 log(L_{it}) + \beta_2 log(K_{it}) + \beta_3 log(G\_local_{it})$$
$$+ \beta_4 log(G\_trans_{it}) + \beta_5 log(G\_trans_{\rho_{it}}) + \varepsilon_{it} \qquad (8)$$

In the estimation of the above equation, the calculation of the spillover variable is computed using a spatial lag provided by Spatial Econometrics (Anselin, 1988): $G_{\rho t} = W \cdot G_t$. Different definitions for proximity and/or similarity are used in constructing the weighting matrix W that will reflect the infrastructure spillover and enable us to test its sign and magnitude.

The first three definitions of the W matrix consider geographical proximity as an important factor in the interaction between regions. The first (W_{bin}) is a physical contiguity matrix that gives rise to a symmetrical binary matrix in which its elements are 1 when two regions are bordering and 0 when otherwise. The second matrix represents the inverse of the distance (W_{dist}), while the third represents the inverse of the square of the distance (W_{dist2}).

The definition based on physical proximity presents certain problems. First, the symmetrical nature of the contiguous matrix is debatable, because it supposes that the influence that region j receives from region i is the same as that received by i from j, whereas the influence between two regions is not always reciprocal in its intensity. Secondly, interrelationships are due not only to geographical proximity. For these reasons, even though the contiguity matrix seems to be the one best suited to the study of the effects of infrastructure, other criteria need to be taken into consideration. We, therefore, constructed a fourth matrix on the basis that the more similar the economies of two regions are, the higher the values in the weight matrix should be. For our purposes here, agglomeration economies are taken into account by considering the density of population (inhabitants per square kilometre for 1981). In order to exhibit a similarity in population density, the weights in the W matrix were constructed as follows:

$$w_{ij} = \frac{1}{|Density_i - Density_j|} \qquad (9)$$

In this way, the matrix (W_{dens}) reflects the similarity in the population density of two regions, irrespective of their geographical proximity.

Finally, we need to construct a matrix based on the fact that economically powerful regions will have a greater impact on other regions than their economically weaker counterparts, while weighting this impact according to the distance between regions. Thus, the matrix will display higher weights in the case of a high value added in region j and physical proximity to region i (W_{va_d}, W_{va_d2}):

$$w_{ij} = \frac{VA_j}{d_{ij}} \text{ or } w_{ij} = \frac{VA_j}{d_{ij}^2} \qquad (10)$$

11.3 Data and spatial exploratory analysis

Our data refer to the fifty regions of Spain (NUTS III level, known as provinces) for the period 1965–97: value added at factor cost and labour (total number of employees) figures are obtained from the 'Renta Nacional de España y su Distribución Provincial',[4] which is published every two years; while the series of private and public capital stocks are taken from 'El Stock de Capital en la Economía Española'.[5,6]

---

[4] National Wealth of Spain and Its Distribution by Provinces, BBVA.
[5] Capital Stock in the Spanish Economy.
[6] These stocks are calculated using the Perpetual Inventory Method (see Mas et al., 1995). Thus, we use data for public capital stocks (not investments) in monetary terms.

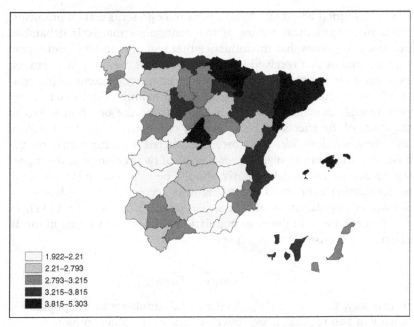

Figure 11.1. Value added per capita 1965–73: annual average.

As local public capital, we considered water and sewage facilities and urban structures. For the transportation component, we considered the stock of roads and highways, railways, harbours and maritime signalling and airports. All variables are expressed at constant prices for 1986, with seventeen temporal biennial observations and fifty cross-section observations.

This section sets out to describe the capitalisation process that the Spanish regions have undergone during the period under analysis in order to examine the extent to which it corresponds to the geography of economic activity. The geographical distribution of production and public capital (both its local and transportation components) across Spain can be analysed by comparing their respective mappings. The first two distributions (Figures 11.1 to 11.3 for value added per capita and Figures 11.4 to 11.6 for transportation infrastructure) present a number of common features, with a similar contrast between the North-East and South, although certain specific differences are worth mentioning. Most of the rich regions lie in the north-east quadrant (the provinces of Catalonia, the Basque Country, Navarre and the Balearic Islands plus the capital region in the centre, Madrid), in which a large part of the

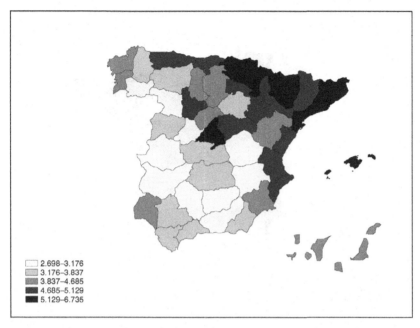

Figure 11.2. Value added per capita 1975–83: annual average.

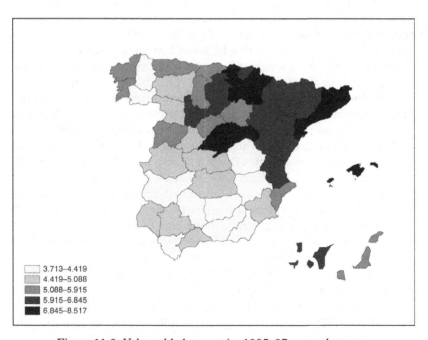

Figure 11.3. Value added per capita 1985–97: annual average.

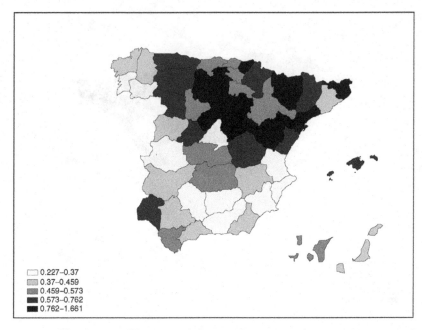

Figure 11.4. Transport infrastructure per capita: 1965–73: annual average.

transportation infrastructure endowment is also concentrated. However, some of the other regions with a high stock of public capital are among the poorest regions, though still, it must be said, concentrated in the northern half of the Spanish peninsula. The south of Spain comprises the provinces with the lowest value added, together with the poorest endowment of transport infrastructure. However, such poor endowment of transportation public capital per capita is also true for regions such as Madrid and Barcelona, which, according to their level of economic activity, present a low stock of public transportation infrastructure. It is also interesting to highlight that, whereas the pattern of economic activity does not vary greatly over time, the distribution of transportation public capital has undergone a marked process of centralisation in the north-east quadrant. By contrast, in the case of local public infrastructure (Figures 11.7 to 11.9), it can be seen that its distribution has little to do with that of economic development.

    The picture obtained from these maps can be summarised using a number of measures of spatial association of the regional distribution of economic activity and public capital. One of the most frequently used spatial dependence statistics is Moran's I statistic. Specifically,

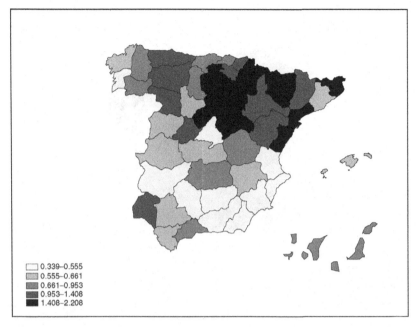

Figure 11.5. Transport infrastructure per capita: 1975–83: annual average.

the presence of spatial dependence implies that the value of a variable at a given geographical point is functionally related to the value of the same variable in other locations, $Y_i = f(Y_1, Y_2, \ldots, Y_N)$. In the case of positive spatial autocorrelation, similar characteristics are spatially concentrated; in the case of negative spatial autocorrelation, the phenomenon is disseminated throughout the space. In order to test the presence of global spatial dependence among the variables used here, Moran's standardised I statistic (Moran, 1948) was used. This can be defined as:

$$I = \frac{N}{S_0} \frac{\displaystyle\sum_i^N \sum_j^N w_{ij}(x_i - \bar{x})(x_j - \bar{x})}{\displaystyle\sum_{i=1}^N (x_i - \bar{x})^2} \qquad (11)$$

where x_i and x_j are the observations for region i and j of the variable under analysis; $\bar{x}$ is the average value of the variable in the sample of regions; and w_{ij} is the i-j-th element of the row-standardised W matrix of weights. $S_0 = \sum_i \sum_j w_{ij}$ is a standardisation factor that corresponds to

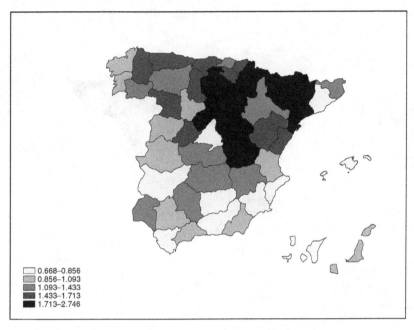

0.668–0.856
0.856–1.093
1.093–1.433
1.433–1.713
1.713–2.746

Figure 11.6. Transport infrastructure per capita: 1985–97: annual average.

the sum of the weights. As it equals the number of observations, N, in case of a row-standardised W matrix, N/S_0 is equal to 1 in our analysis. In Moran's test, the null hypothesis is spatial independence and the weight matrix representing the interaction between regions was chosen on the basis of geographical contiguity.

The use of Moran's index (see Table 11.1) shows a clear rejection of the null hypothesis of the absence of spatial autocorrelation with a positive value of the statistic for all the variables under consideration except for local infrastructure. Production activity measured as value added per capita appears to be strongly and positively correlated in space, confirming the picture of spatial clustering given by the map. Moreover, it seems that the value of Moran's index increases over time, indicating a possible increase in the level of spatial dependence in all the variables under consideration. The same conclusions are obtained for both private and transportation capital per capita. By contrast, local infrastructure presents a non-significant value of Moran's I test, pointing to a random distribution of this variable in space.

The degree of regional dispersion of value added and the two types of infrastructure in per capita terms, measured by the coefficient of

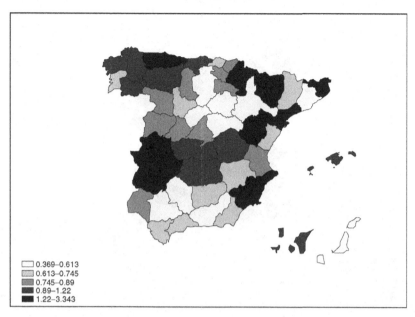

Figure 11.7. Local infrastructure per capita: 1965–73: annual average.

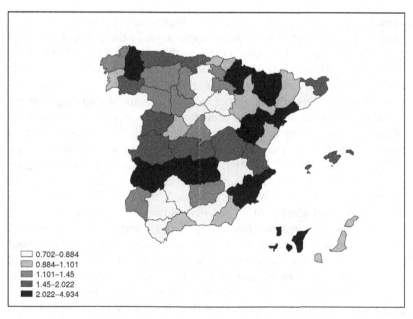

Figure 11.8. Local infrastructure per capita: 1975–83: annual average.

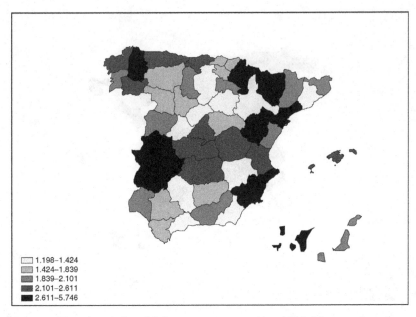

Figure 11.9. Local infrastructure per capita: 1985–97: annual average.

variation, is shown in Table 11.2. The dispersion of economic activity is markedly lower than that of public capital, while the convergence process (the coefficient of variation having fallen from 0.34 in 1965 to 0.21 in 1997) has taken place almost uninterruptedly throughout the whole period. As for public capital, the dispersion of transportation infrastructure is markedly lower than that of local public capital. Although a significant convergence process has occurred in both magnitudes, a number of differences in their dynamics should be highlighted. Transportation public infrastructure presents several major changes over time so that, while the coefficient of variation fell slightly in the late 1960s, it grew considerably during the 1970s, with the 1980s experiencing significant structural changes in this respect. Indeed, the coefficient of variation fell from 0.48 in 1965 to 0.36 in 1997. However, the highest degree of dispersion is observed for local public capital, with a slight increase in the late 1960s but with a permanent and major decrease throughout the rest of the period under consideration (from 1.06 to 0.51 at the end of the period). It can be argued that this convergence process in the distribution of public infrastructure within Spain is the result of the policy of cohesion and restructuring that the Spanish economy adopted over the last few decades, especially following the accession to the EU,

Table 11.1. *Moran's I test for spatial autocorrelation*

Variable	W	1965–1973		1975–1983		1985–1997	
		Z-value	Prob	Z-value	Prob	Z-value	Prob
VA pc	1st order contiguity	6.255	0.000	6.838	0.000	7.509	0.000
K pc	1st order contiguity	6.409	0.000	7.237	0.000	6.829	0.000
G_trans pc	1st order contiguity	4.144	0.000	5.889	0.000	5.026	0.000
G_local pc	1st order contiguity	−0.049	0.960	0.125	0.900	0.651	0.515

Table 11.2. *Coefficient of variation, regional averages*

	VA pc	G_trans pc	G_local pc
1965	0.34	0.478	1.005
1967	0.32	0.459	1.044
1969	0.301	0.444	1.066
1971	0.281	0.472	1.033
1973	0.265	0.535	0.976
1975	0.273	0.54	0.946
1977	0.249	0.54	0.894
1979	0.239	0.574	0.896
1981	0.243	0.557	0.879
1983	0.241	0.525	0.825
1985	0.238	0.503	0.797
1987	0.237	0.479	0.743
1989	0.231	0.444	0.668
1991	0.222	0.403	0.62
1993	0.213	0.38	0.572
1995	0.224	0.363	0.534
1997	0.211	0.358	0.506

a period in which the less developed regions enjoyed high funding levels for public infrastructure.

11.4 Empirical analysis

Access to data for several regions at different points in time permits estimation by panel data techniques. These techniques have the advantage of including within the specification of the error term a specific regional component, which controls the unobservable characteristics of each region in such a way that each is included within the function in accordance with its own peculiarities (resource endowment, industrial mix, etc.), as well as a time-specific component, which accounts for changes in the overall economy in each period, thereby reflecting cyclical effects and changes in technology.[7] In order to select the most accurate estimation method from the various possibilities, a Hausman test is considered together with an F-statistic to verify the need to introduce regional and temporal effects. The use of either the fixed or the random effect models may provide better estimates than the OLS method, since they take into account the characteristics of each region likely to be present in any regional study. In fact, Holtz-Eakin (1994) and Garcia-Milà *et al.* (1996) argue that early studies of the impact of public capital failed to control for regional effects and obtained a large, positive and significant coefficient for public capital because they used the wrong estimation method. Therefore, the positive relationship between regional growth and infrastructure reported in some studies could be the result of a spurious correlation, given that these controls were not taken into consideration. Thus, we adopt here the method of estimation that best suits our data according to the tests described above. The different models outlined in section 11.2 were estimated for the case of Spanish manufactures, and in all cases the fixed effect model was chosen for the individual and time effects.

The results of the estimation of the different models outlined in section 11.2 are shown in Table 11.3. In each it can be concluded that private capital and labour elasticities are approximately 0.24 and 0.78, which is similar to the share of these two inputs in aggregate output. Constant returns to scale were not rejected for private inputs when applying an F-test (with a value of 0.551, p = 0.458), while slightly increasing returns were obtained for all productive inputs (rejection of the F-test for constant returns to scale for all productive inputs, presenting a value of 8.680, p = 0.003), concluding that both public capital components (local and transportation) are important for regional productivity since the external economies that they generate mean that slight increases can be achieved in returns. For the specification in (7) that does not include spillover effects (results in the first column of Table 11.3), the estimate of the elasticity of the local public capital is almost 6%, so that an increase of 1% in the stock of local public capital would increase value added by 0.06%, an elasticity that is quite different from

---

[7] Including a linear trend as an approximation to the level of technology was initially considered here. However, this was rejected and the use of time effects preferred, since time dummies reflect technological change as well as other possible effects common to all regions in each year.

Table 11.3. Estimates of the effects of public capital [a,b]

	No spillover	W_{bin}	W_{dist}	W_{dist2}	W_{va_d}	W_{va_d2}	W_{dens}
L	0.779[c]	0.786	0.782	0.784	0.782	0.784	0.784
	(0.046)**	(0.046)**	(0.046)**	(0.04)**	(0.046)**	(0.046)**	(0.046)**
K	0.248	0.242	0.245	0.244	0.245	0.244	0.239
	(0.026)**	(0.026)**	(0.026)**	(0.026)**	(0.026)**	(0.026)**	(0.026)**
G_local	0.058	0.062	0.058	0.058	0.058	0.059	0.065
	(0.012)**	(0.012)**	(0.012)**	(0.012)**	(0.012)**	(0.012)**	(0.012)**
G_trans	0.029	0.049	0.038	0.041	0.037	0.042	0.037
	(0.017)*	(0.018)**	(0.018)**	(0.018)**	(0.018)**	(0.018)**	(0.017)**
W*G_trans	—	-0.104	-0.189	-0.105	-0.189	-0.105	-0.101
		(0.033)**	(0.107)*	(0.050)**	(0.107)	(0.050)	(0.042)**
R^2	0.99	0.99	0.99	0.99	0.99	0.99	0.99

Notes: [a] Dependent variable is the log of output.
[b] All the specifications include province and time dummies.
[c] * and ** denote significant at 10% and 5%, respectively.

that reported in earlier studies of the impact of public capital, albeit still a significant value. The estimate for the parameter of transportation infrastructure is also significant, although of a somewhat lower value than the local one (elasticity of 3%). In conclusion, although public capital seems to have had a positive impact on the growth in Spanish productivity, this impact is lower than that reported in earlier public capital studies. This finding is more closely in line with recent studies which conclude that the role of infrastructure is in fact a more subtle one. Furthermore, in contrast to the US economy (Holtz-Eakin, 1994; Garcia-Milà *et al.*, 1996) where controlling for state effects reduces or invalidates public capital impact, in the case of Spain the use of panel data techniques presents credible values, not only for public capital elasticities, but also for labour and private capital shares. It is our belief that this could be due to the fact that at the beginning of the period under consideration Spain's regions were lacking in infrastructure; however, as this increased, a positive influence was recorded on productivity growth. Conversely, with large initial infrastructure endowment, the US states may have reached a saturation point.[8]

To examine the sign and importance of the externality of infrastructure, we estimated equation (8), which includes the spatial lag of transport infrastructure endowment as an additional explanatory variable, and analysed the sign and magnitude of the estimate of its associated parameter, β_5. Our results are summarised in columns 2 to 7 of Table 11.3, according to the weighting matrix used to compute the spillover variable. The public infrastructure of the geographical neighbour presents a significantly negative value regardless of the weight matrix considered. The coefficient ranges from between -0.10 in the case of the physical contiguity matrix to -0.19 in the case of the inverse of distance. Thus, not only does the proximity concept seem to support the negative spillover hypothesis, but when considering the other three weight matrices, based on similarities across regions, the spillover effect is also significantly negative with a magnitude similar to that specified earlier. In sum, the negative spillover arising from factor migration from regions with a poor endowment of transport infrastructure to regions with good endowments seems to override the positive spillover caused by the

---

[8] It could be argued that simultaneity or reversed causality might cause an upward bias in the estimate of public capital coefficients. However, studies that have corrected for such a bias have only obtained a minor change in the estimated rates of returns on public infrastructure. Additionally, it has been reasoned that individual industry productivity would not simultaneously determine the overall stock of public capital. Thus, a large bias is unlikely in our estimates. Further discussion can be found in Gramlich (1994).

connectivity characteristic of most transport public capital. This result is in line with those obtained in the US by Holtz-Eakin and Schwartz (1995), Kelejian and Robinson (1997) and Boarnet (1998) for the case of state roads and highways. Additionally, it should be noted that the estimate of private input elasticities and the estimate of the effect of local public capital are quite robust to the inclusion of the spillover in transport infrastructures. The only significant change is the increase in the magnitude of the elasticity to that of transport infrastructure endowment, which suggests that the omission of its spillover effect leads to its magnitude being underestimated.

Due to the presence of global spatial association in the variables considered in our regressions, some kind of spatial dependence may appear in them. For this reason, and due to the problems to which this can give rise, such as the invalidation of standard econometric techniques (Anselin, 1988), we tested for the presence of a remaining problem of spatial dependence in the model. Moran's I test for the estimated errors was obtained to test the null hypothesis of the lack of spatial residual correlation. In all cases, the assumption of spatial independence was not rejected, indicating that our results would be unaffected by a remaining problem of spatial dependence in the error term.

To what extent the output effect of an increase in the stock of public infrastructure is the same for both transport and local public capital, and whether they depend on the existing stock of infrastructure and the level of development of the region, is discussed below. These issues can be analysed by estimating the marginal effect of output to public capital ($\partial Y/\partial G$), given that the general pattern described above may present some interesting regional differences. Thus, a return for each region in each time period is obtained, and this is compared with the existing stock and with the level of productivity.[9] Figure 11.10 shows the returns for an average province both for transport and local public capital in the period analysed, using the elasticities reported in the second column of Table 11.3. The first result of interest is concerned with the different magnitude of returns on both types of public capital. Returns on regional investments in local infrastructure are more than twice as great as those obtained from investments in transport public capital. The average for the whole period in a representative province is 19% in the case of the former while it is just 7% for the latter. The significance of this result is

---

[9] These marginal effects are computed from the results obtained from the estimation of equation (8) and the use of W_{bin} for the spillover effect.

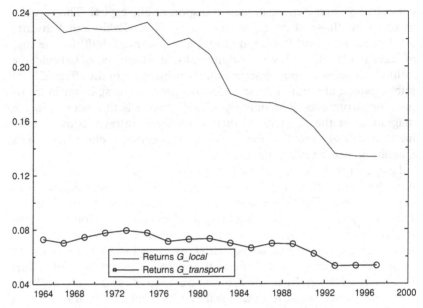

Figure 11.10. Returns to transport and local public capital: regional average.

worth stressing as most of the existing literature places an emphasis on the role of transportation infrastructure (Blum, 1982; Vickerman 2000; Henderson, 2000; OECD, 2002), and policies aiming at promoting growth in the less developed regions have mainly focused on financing this type of capital (European Commission, 2001). By contrast, our results suggest that investments in local public capital may be more effective in increasing productivity, and thus in promoting economic growth.

A second finding (see Figure 11.10) is the sharp decrease over time in the returns on both types of capital. This decrease is higher in the case of local infrastructure, where the return has fallen in a constant pattern from 24% to 13% (a 45% decrease). In the case of transportation capital, the decrease represents a 27% drop, from 7.3% to 5.3%, and with the sharpest fall being recorded following Spain's accession to the EU in 1986 – the beginning of a period in which the Spanish provinces benefited from large investments in transport infrastructures financed by EU regional policies. Hence, it could be said that, although infrastructure in Spain has played a significant role during the period analysed, its importance has declined over time, and is unlikely to have the same impact in the future. In fact, the pattern recorded suggests that large decreasing returns on infrastructure investments are at work, in agreement with the idea that the output effect of an increase in the public capital stock depends on the size of the existing endowment. This can be verified by comparing the estimated return with the ratio of the existing stock of public capital to the endowment of private capital in the average Spanish regions at different points in time. While the return on local infrastructure was as high as 21.9% in 1965 with a ratio of 0.20, this had fallen to 15.9% in 1985 and to 12.2% in 1997 in accordance with continuous improvements in the ratio (0.32 and 0.36, respectively). A similar behaviour is observed for transport infrastructure: returns of 7.2%, 6.6% and 5.3% in 1965, 1985 and 1997, with ratios of 0.38, 0.60 and 0.75, respectively.

However, the issue of differences in the impact of public capital investments depending on the level of development of the recipient region is a controversial one. It can be argued that adding capacity to an uncongested endowment due to the fact that the private economy is not highly developed would not affect private productivity, while the benefits from an increase in the amount of public capital would be large when congestion is high, which is more common in highly developed areas. However, those supporting investments in infrastructures in less developed regions stress that public capital is a necessary condition for regional economic development. In their absence it would be almost impossible for a poor region to take off. Here we relate the estimate of the return on public capital in each Spanish region to the level of value added per capita to shed some light on the debate and to draw some conclusions on the effectiveness of infrastructure investments as a regional development policy. The time average of value added per capita for each province is represented along the x-axis while the corresponding average return on local (Figure 11.11) and transport (Figure 11.12) infrastructure is shown on the y-axis. A positive relationship between returns and level of economic development was obtained – this being most clearly shown in the case of local infrastructure. Regions for which production per capita was well below the average presented rather small returns on both local and transport public capital, while regions with high levels of production presented large returns for local infrastructure, though this was not so clear in the case of transport infrastructure.

11.5   Conclusions

The results in this chapter confirm that improvements in public infrastructure endowment in recent decades have played a major role in the

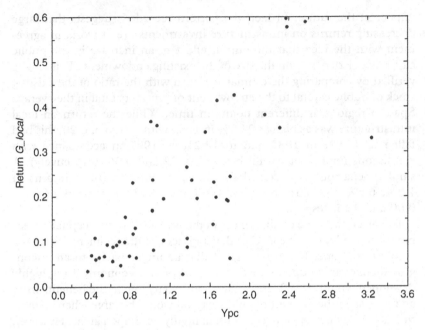

Figure 11.11. Returns to local infrastructure and economic development in the Spanish regions.

development of the Spanish regional economies. In fact, given the evidence for the existence of a positive impact of public infrastructure on industrial output, we can conclude that EU policies aimed at reducing regional disparities should renew their interest in ensuring that infrastructure policy, at the very least, does not hinder economic development. This could be of particular relevance to the new Member States which are, in general, less developed than existing members and have poorer endowments of public capital. Given the similarities observed between Spain at the time of its accession and the new Member States today, there still seems to be potential for industry in these countries to obtain output benefits from public capital, from both local and transport infrastructure, albeit that these benefits tend to fall with increases in the stock of public capital.

However, evidence from Spain reveals that local infrastructure gives larger returns than those obtained from public capital investments in transport. It is our belief that this is a significant finding given that policies aimed at promoting growth in the less developed regions have tended to focus on the latter type of investment, because, it would seem,

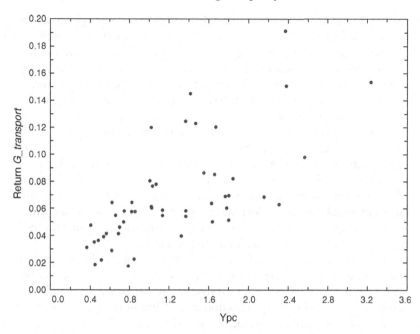

Figure 11.12. Returns to transport infrastructure and economic development in the Spanish regions.

of the emphasis attached to the role of transport infrastructure in the existing literature. By contrast, our results suggest that investments in local public capital may be more effective in increasing productivity, and thus in promoting economic growth in the less developed regions. Indeed, our findings support the prediction of the theoretical model developed by Martin and Rogers (1995) which shows that a regional aid programme aimed at improving domestic infrastructure will encourage industry to relocate to this region. However, a regional policy that improves international infrastructure in poor regions (i.e. infrastructure connecting regions with each other) exacerbates agglomeration economies in the advanced areas, and may therefore contribute to regional divergence. Undoubtedly, the significance of this result from a policy point of view requires that further evidence is provided from other sets of regional economies.

A further finding of interest is related to regional differences in the impact of infrastructure investments. The estimated return on local and transport public capital was found to be larger in those Spanish regions with higher levels of development. This contrasts with a regional assignment of infrastructure investments based on a policy of favouring the less developed areas. Returns were higher when investments were made in public capital in the more advanced Spanish regions than when made in the less developed provinces. Therefore, if the objective is to promote growth in the new Member States, investments should be directed to those areas with the potential to obtain a higher return, in other words, in those with better endogenous conditions and higher agglomeration economies. Undoubtedly, this will be at the cost of larger internal regional disparities within each of the new Member States, which could be exacerbated in the case of transport infrastructure by the existence of negative spillovers. In this case, improvements in the infrastructure endowment of the most fortunate regions of those countries might, at least temporarily, cause firms and labour to migrate from the poor regions, and thus increase regional disparities.

The negative output spillover from public capital investments in transport detected for the Spanish regions may be due to the fact that when input factors are mobile, transport infrastructure in one region is able to draw industrial production away from other regions. In other words, regions with similar infrastructure compete for mobile factors of production. Therefore, in the initial stages, the use of public investment to strengthen integration may increase disparities, as regions that cannot compete so strongly may be adversely affected. Politically, the presence of negative spillovers means that regions might use infrastructure as a competitive tool for attracting factors of production and thus increase their own industrial output at the expense of that of other regions.

References

Anselin, L. 1988. *Spatial Econometrics: Methods and Models.* Dordrecht: Kluwer Academic Publishers.

Aschauer, D. 1989. 'Is Public Expenditure Productive?'. *Journal of Monetary Economics*, vol. 23, pp. 177–200.

Blum, U. 1982. 'Effects of Transportation Investments on Regional Growth: A Theoretical and Empirical Investigation'. *Papers and Proceedings of the Regional Science Association*, vol. 49, pp. 169–84.

Boarnet, M. 1998. 'Spillovers and the Locational Effects of Public Infrastructure'. *Journal of Regional Science*, vol. 383, pp. 381–400.

Boldrin, M. 2006. 'Regional Policies After the EU Enlargement', chapter 13, this volume.

Boldrin, M. and Canova, F. 2003. 'Regional Policies and EU Enlargement'. CEPR Discussion Paper, No. 3744.

Boscá, J., Escribá, F. and Murgui, M. 2002. 'The Effect of Public Infrastructure on the Private Productive Sector of Spanish Regions'. *Journal of Regional Science*, vol. 42, pp. 301–26.

Ciccone, A. and Hall, R. 1996. 'Productivity and the Density of Economic Activity'. *American Economic Review*, vol. 86, pp. 54–70.

Crihfield, J. and Panggabean, M. 1995. 'Is Public Infrastructure Productive? A Metropolitan Perspective Using New Capital Stock Estimates'. *Regional Science and Urban Economics*, vol. 25, pp. 607–30.

Duffy-Deno, K. and Eberts, R. 1991. 'Public Infrastructure and Regional Economic Development: A Simultaneous Equations Approach'. *Journal of Urban Economics*, vol. 30, pp. 329–43.

Eberts, R. 1990. 'Cross-Sectional Analysis of Public Infrastructure and Regional Productivity Growth'. Federal Reserve Bank of Cleveland Working Paper, No. 4.

European Commission. 2001. *Unity, Solidarity, Diversity for Europe, Its People and Its Territory: Second Report on Economic and Social Cohesion.* Luxembourg: Office for Official Publications of the European Commission.

García-Milà, T. and McGuire, T. 1992. 'The Contribution of Publicly Provided Inputs to States' Economies'. *Regional Science and Urban Economics*, vol. 22, pp. 229–41.

García-Milà, T., McGuire, T. and Porter, R. 1996. 'The Effect of Public Capital in State-Level Production Functions Reconsidered'. *Review of Economic and Statistics*, vol. 78, pp. 177–80.

Gramlich, E. 1994. 'Infrastructure investment: A Review Essay'. *Journal of Economic Literature*, vol. 32, pp. 1176–96.

Henderson, V. 2000. 'The Effects of Urban Concentration on Economic Growth'. NBER Working Paper, No. 7503.

Holtz-Eakin, D. 1994. 'Public-Sector Capital and the Productivity Puzzle'. *Review of Economics and Statistics*, vol. 76, pp. 12–21.

Holtz-Eakin, D. and Schwartz, A. 1995. 'Infrastructure in a Structural Model of Economic Growth'. *Regional Science and Urban Economics*, vol. 25, pp. 131–51.

Kelejian, H. and Robinson, D. 1997. 'Infrastructure Productivity Estimation and Its Underlying Econometric Specifications: A Sensitivity Analysis'. *Papers in Regional Science*, vol. 76, pp. 115–31.

Martin, P. and Rogers, C. 1995. 'Industrial Location and Public Infrastructure'. *Journal of International Economics*, vol. 39, pp. 335–51.

Mas, M., Pérez, F. and Uriel, E. 1995. *El stock de capital en la economía española.* Bilboa: Fundación BBVA.

Mas, M., Maudos, J., Pérez, F. and Uriel, E. 1996. 'Infrastructures and Productivity in the Spanish Regions'. *Regional Studies*, vol. 30, pp. 641–9.

Moran, P. 1948. 'The Interpretation of Statistical Maps'. *Journal of the Royal Statistical Society*, vol. 10, pp. 243–51.

Moreno, R., Artís, M., López-Bazo, E. and Suriñach, J. 1997. 'Evidence on the Complex Link Between Infrastructure and Regional Growth'. *International Journal of Development Planning Literature*, vol. 12, pp. 81–108.

Moreno, R., López-Bazo, E. and Artís, M. 2002. 'Public Infrastructure and the Performance of Manufactures: Short and Long Run Effects'. *Regional Science and Urban Economics*, vol. 32, pp. 97–121.

2003. 'On the Effectiveness of Private and Public Capital'. *Applied Economics*, vol. 35, pp. 727–40.

Morrison, C. and Schwartz, A. 1996. 'State Infrastructure and Productive Performance'. *American Economic Review*, vol. 86, pp. 1095–111.

Morrison, C. and Siegel, D. 1997. 'External Capital Factors and Increasing Returns in US Manufacturing'. *Review of Economics and Statistics*, vol. 79, pp. 647–54.

Munnell, A. 1990. 'How Does Public Infrastructure Affect Regional Economic Performance?'. *New England Economic Review*, September/October, pp. 11–32.

OECD. 2002. *Impact of Transport Infrastructure Investment on Regional Development*. Paris: OECD.

Vickerman, R. 2000. 'Economic Growth Effects of Transport Infrastructure'. *Jahrbuch für Regionalwissenschaft*, vol. 20, pp. 99–115.

12 TFP, costs and public infrastructure: an equivocal relationship

*Eliana La Ferrara and Massimiliano Marcellino**

12.1 Introduction

The role of public infrastructure in stimulating productivity growth and reducing production costs has received increasing attention from both policy-makers and researchers. The former have generally maintained that public capital enhances economic performance, and have been mainly concerned with where to invest, in what, and how much. The latter, on the other hand, have recently taken a step back and investigated whether a positive effect of public capital can indeed be taken for granted. Findings on this point have been mixed, depending on the theoretical models, econometric techniques and datasets used. The ambivalence of the results challenges the rationale for public infrastructure provision as an input in the growth process, a serious issue for policy-makers. This chapter attempts to shed light on the relationships between public infrastructure, total factor productivity and production costs, both in theory and in practice. From a methodological point of view, our contribution is a critical comparison of the main competing approaches to evaluating the returns to public investment, highlighting the conditions under which they should yield the same results. On the empirical side, we implement the different methodologies using the same dataset, a task that, to the best of our knowledge, has not yet been undertaken.

The setting in which our empirical analysis is carried out is the Italian regions in the period 1970–94. This setting is particularly interesting in view of the growing efforts on behalf of European institutions to integrate the economies of the new Member States, and promote growth in

* We are grateful to Tito Boeri, Francesco Daveri, Riccardo Faini, Francesco Giavazzi, Vittorio Grilli, Lucio Picci, Guido Tabellini and participants of an IGIER–Ministero del Tesoro Conference and of a seminar at Harvard University for useful comments on an earlier version. We also thank Federico Bonaglia for outstanding research assistance, and Luca Opromolla and Andrea Ghiringhelli for editorial assistance. Financial support by Bocconi University is gratefully acknowledged.

relatively backward areas. In fact, Italy reproduces within itself many of the contrasts and differences that exist among European countries: the productive structure and the level of development of Italian regions varies widely, ranging from the rich and industrialised regions of the North to the relatively poor regions of the South. Understanding the differential impact of infrastructure investment in these areas can therefore shed some light on the role that public investment at the European level can play in promoting economic growth in relatively backward regions. In this sense, our analysis shares the motivation of the work by de la Fuente and Vives (1995) and Moreno *et al.* (2005), who have studied the role of public investment in education and infrastructure in reducing regional disparities in Spain.

Broadly speaking, the existing empirical literature can be grouped into three methodological strands. First, there have been studies relating public capital accumulation to the growth rate of total factor productivity (TFP), computed as a residual from growth accounting (Hulten and Schwab, 1984, 1991). Secondly, public capital has been included as an input in the production function, and its marginal returns have been estimated (e.g. Aschauer (1989a, 1989b), Munnell (1990a, 1990b), Holtz-Eakin (1994), Evans and Karras (1994) and Bradley *et al.* (2003)). Thirdly, the contribution of infrastructure investment to reducing production costs has been assessed (e.g. Morrison and Schwartz (1994, 1996), Seitz and Licht (1995)). The empirical results differ not only across methodologies, but also within the same approach. Hulten and Schwab (1991) find a weak relationship between the growth rates of TFP and of public capital. Aschauer (1989a), on the contrary, reports evidence in favour of a high and significant elasticity of production to public capital, i.e. approximately 0.35. Munnell (1990a) also finds a similar estimate for this elasticity when using data for the US as a whole, but a lower value (around 0.15) when using state level data. Within the same production function framework, Holtz-Eakin (1994) and Evans and Karras (1994) show that, when controlling for state-specific effects, public capital does not seem to play a significant role. Finally, Morrison and Schwartz (1994, 1996) report a positive but quantitatively limited impact of public infrastructure on cost reduction but find that, when they take into account the efficiency loss due to financing public investment through taxation, the net effect is close to zero.[1]

---

[1] For a model in which the costs and benefits of public capital are embodied in an endogenous growth framework, see Barro (1990).

While the above studies use data from the United States, recently there have been studies on Italy (e.g. Picci (1995a), Rossi and Toniolo (1993), Bonaglia, La Ferrara and Marcellino (2000)). Within the production function approach, Picci (1995a) uses regional data for Italy and reports an elasticity of production to public capital of 0.43 and 0.35 with fixed and random effects, respectively. When performing robustness checks, however, he finds that this result is weakened. Rossi and Toniolo (1993), following a cost function methodology with a century-long dataset (1880–1980), focus more on the relationships among production inputs, and find that public and private capital are substitutes in the short run but become complements in the long run for most of the sample period. Finally, Bonaglia *et al.* (2000) estimate the impact of different categories of public capital (e.g. transportation, sanitation and education) on economic performance, and find different results depending on the methodology used.

It is difficult to assess whether the discrepancy in the above results, both for Italy and for the US, is due to the different methodologies used by the various studies, to different data sets, or to some other factor. A first goal of the present study is to apply all the existing approaches consistently to the same data set (Italian regional data for the period 1970–94), in order to isolate potential sources of ambiguity in the results. Furthermore, we specify the conditions under which, from a theoretical point of view, we can expect to find a correspondence among the quantitative values of the parameters estimated with the various approaches, and we test these correspondences in our data. Finally, we attempt to analyse the impact of infrastructure at a more detailed level than the simple national level, by disaggregating our data in two ways. First, we run our regressions separately over various sub-periods, to allow for structural changes in the parameters over time. Secondly, we consider four Italian 'macro-regions' separately, to account for the different economic and production structures that may prevail in those areas. In all cases, we control for potential endogeneity problems of the public capital variable by applying two stage least squares, and we check the robustness of our results.

Our findings show first of all marked differences in the sources of growth in different geographic areas. Overall, the relatively high growth rates of the north-east and the centre are mostly attributable to higher than average total factor productivity growth. Both labour and private capital in fact grew very little in those regions in the sample period. The south, on the contrary, had extremely low TFP growth rates and managed to achieve an average growth rate of real value added between 2% and 3% per year only thanks to significant private capital accumulation.

Starting from these facts, we can expect to find interesting differences in the impact of public infrastructure on productivity in northern, central and southern regions.

On the pooled sample (regional time series data for the whole of Italy) the three methodological approaches yield different results. Overall, public investment in infrastructure seems to have contributed positively to TFP growth (the share of TFP growth that can be attributed to public capital accumulation is estimated to be 0.45), while we fail to find a positive role for public capital as an input in the production function and in reducing costs. The estimated elasticity of costs to public capital for Italy as a whole is in fact −0.02.

When we turn to disaggregated analysis, the results are more coherent across methodologies. Both the growth accounting and the production function approach suggest that public capital was least effective in the 1970s, and that its effectiveness has been improving over time. In terms of regional disaggregation, all three approaches indicate the centre and the south as the areas where infrastructure investment yields the highest benefits. This is particularly relevant in that those areas (especially the south) are less economically advanced compared to the north of Italy, so our analysis seems to support the scope for public investment in fuelling the economic development of relatively backward areas.

The remainder of this chapter is organised as follows. In section 12.2, we present a theoretical framework for the analysis of the effects of public infrastructure. In section 12.3, we briefly comment on the Italian regional data set that we use (more details can be found in Appendix A to this chapter) and present descriptive statistics on the main variables of interest. In section 12.4, we develop the empirical analysis and discuss the results, addressing issues of the endogeneity and robustness of our estimates. Finally, in section 12.5, we summarise the main conclusions of this study and highlight its limitations and scope for future research.

12.2   The theoretical framework

In this section, we briefly review the economic theory underlying the growth accounting, the production function and the cost function approaches to infrastructure investment evaluation, both to provide a background for the interpretation of the results of the ensuing empirical analysis, and to highlight relationships, pitfalls and opportunities of the alternative methods.

12.2.1 The Total Factor Productivity approach

In the growth accounting literature (e.g. Hulten and Schwab (1984, 1991), the starting point is a production function that links real inputs to real output, under the assumption that factor remuneration equals its marginal product. With these hypotheses it is relatively straightforward to derive total factor productivity, and the question of interest is whether TFP can be explained at least in part by changes in the pattern of infrastructure investment.

Let us define the factor inputs labour, private capital (capital henceforth), and public capital by L, K and KG, while Q denotes gross output. Inputs are transformed into output according to the production function $Q = AF(L, K)$, where A indicates Hicks neutral technological progress.[2] Under the hypothesis of profit-maximising behaviour and competitive markets, the growth rate of A is

$$\dot{A} = \dot{Q} - S^L \dot{L} - S^K \dot{K} \tag{1}$$

with S^L and S^K being the output shares of labour and capital. With constant returns to scale, the sum of S^L and S^K is 1. All the terms in the right-hand side of equation (1) are known, and can be used to measure the growth in the index of technological progress, $\dot{A}$, usually referred to as TFP growth.

So far, we have not considered the role of public capital, KG, which can affect both A, i.e. increase the productivity of the other factors as an externality, and it can be a direct (unpaid) input in the production function F, e.g. $Q = \tilde{A}(KG) \, F \, (L, K, KG)$, with $\tilde{A}(KG) = \tilde{A} KG^\eta$. In this case, the growth rate of TFP is:

$$\dot{A} = \dot{Q} - e^L - e^K \dot{K} - (\eta + e^{KG}) \dot{K}G \tag{2}$$

where η is the elasticity of A with respect to KG, e^x is the elasticity of output to input x ($x = L, K, KG$), and $\tilde{A}$ is 'true' technological progress. Combining (1) and (2), we get:

$$\dot{A} = (e^K - S^K) \dot{K} + (e^L - S^L) \dot{L} + (\eta + e) \dot{K}G + \dot{\tilde{A}} \tag{3}$$

Equation (3) is more general than standard specifications in the growth accounting literature. For example, according to Hulten and

---

[2] Energy and intermediate inputs should also appear as arguments of F (e.g. Berndt and Wood (1975)). Since data on these variables are not available on a regional basis for Italy, we make the usual assumption of separability (e.g. Chambers, 1988), and use data on value added instead of gross output in the empirical implementation.

Schwab (1991), it is:

$$\dot{A} = (\eta + e^{KG})\dot{K}G + (e^L + e^K - 1)\dot{K} + \dot{A}^* \tag{4}$$

This simplification is valid when $e^L = S^L$ and $S^K = 1 - S^L$. Otherwise, biased estimators for the coefficients are obtained, and the direction and magnitude of the biases depend on the correlations among $\dot{L}$, $\dot{K}$ and $\dot{K}G$, and on the difference $e^L - S^L$.

Given the above arguments, the role of public infrastructure can be evaluated on the basis of the sign and significance of the coefficient of $\dot{K}G$ in a regression of $\dot{A}$ on $\dot{K}G$, $\dot{K}$ and $\dot{L}$, where $\dot{A}$ is computed from equation (1). From now on, we will refer to this approach as growth accounting.

12.2.2 The production function approach

A second way to evaluate the role of public capital is through what we may term a 'production function approach'. In agreement with the production function literature (e.g. Aschauer (1989a, 1989b) and Holtz-Eakin (1994)), a Cobb-Douglas specification is adopted. Services from public capital are considered as a direct factor input, usually proxied by the stock of available infrastructure, and the main question is whether the elasticity of output to this input is positive and significant.

Assuming that KG is a direct input, and under the hypothesis on technological progress we made in the growth accounting framework $A(KG)) = A^*KG^\eta$, we have:

$$q = a^* + (\eta + e^{KG})kg + e^K k + e^L l \tag{5}$$

where lower case letters denote logarithms. The question of interest is whether the overall elasticity of production to public capital, $\eta + e^{KG}$, is positive and significant.

Introducing hypotheses on the returns to scale, different specifications are obtained. With constant returns to private inputs only, it is:

$$q - l = a^* + e^K(k - l) + (\eta + e^{KG})kg \tag{6}$$

When there are constant returns to all inputs, we get the specification in Aschauer (1989b):

$$q - l = a^* + e^K(k - l) + (\eta + e^{KG})(kg - l) \tag{7}$$

In the case of overall decreasing returns to scale,

$$q - l = a^* + e^K(k - l) + (\eta + e^{KG})(kg - l) - \lambda l \qquad (8)$$

where $\lambda = 1 - e^K - e^{KG} - e^L - \eta > 0$. For increasing returns, it is $\lambda < 0$. In all cases, the coefficient of kg (or of $kg - l$, depending on the specification) is equal to that of $\dot{KG}$ in the growth accounting framework, equation (4). Yet, if invalid hypotheses on the returns to scale are made, the estimator of the coefficient of kg can be biased, as stressed by Holtz-Eakin (1994). Hence, if the hypothesis of a Cobb-Douglas specification is correct and no invalid assumptions on the return to scale are made, the growth accounting and the production function approaches should lead to the same conclusions about the effects of public capital on TFP and output growth.

12.2.3 The cost function approach

The dual problem, i.e whether there are substantial cost savings in the presence of public infrastructure, has also received attention (e.g. Morrison and Schwartz (1994, 1996), Seitz and Licht (1995)). The starting point is the specification of a cost function:

$$c = G(K, KG, w, t, Q) + cK \qquad (9)$$

where G is a variable cost function. Private capital, infrastructure and output are included among its arguments to take into account fixity, availability of (free) public capital, and scale economies. Other arguments are the price of labour, w, and a linear trend, t, that proxies for technology improvements.[3]

The counterpart of marginal product in the cost function framework is the shadow value, i.e the change in variable costs due to a marginal variation in an input. We label the shadow values of private and public capital as z_K and z_{KG}, respectively, and define them as:

$$z_K = -\frac{\partial G}{\partial K}, z_{KG} = -\frac{\partial G}{\partial KG} \qquad (10)$$

---

[3] Notice that we are assuming that KG_t has a price of zero, so that it does not appear as a paid input in the total cost function C. Notice also that, while in the estimation of the production function output is endogenous and input quantity is exogenous, estimating a cost function implies the more realistic assumption that input quantities are endogenously determined, taking as given input prices (Berndt, 1991).

The corresponding elasticities are:

$$\varphi^K = -\frac{\partial \log C}{\partial \log K}, \quad \varphi^{KG} = -\frac{\partial \log C}{\partial \log KG} \tag{11}$$

Because KG only affects variable costs, it is $\varphi^{KG} = z_{KG}\, KG/C$, that can be interpreted as the shadow share of public capital.

The first order conditions for cost minimisation imply that the optimal level of K satisfies $z_K = c$, where c is the user cost of private capital. Unfortunately, a similar condition cannot be directly employed for the determination of public capital, first because the level of KG cannot be decided by the firm, and, secondly, because its price for the firm itself is zero, assuming no direct links between the tax bill and infrastructure usage. Nonetheless, it makes sense to compare the shadow value of KG with a measure of its opportunity cost, say c_{KG}, in order to determine the optimal level of KG. A positive shadow value indicates that public capital reduces costs, but z_{KG} should be at least as big as the social user cost, c_{KG}, for the investment to be convenient. Synthetic indexes to evaluate investment are:

$$E^K = (c - z_K)K/C \qquad E^{KG} = (c_{KG} - z_{KG})KG/C \tag{12}$$

A positive value of E signals over-investment, and a negative value under-investment.

To obtain an estimate of each of the quantities in (10), (11) and (12), we adopt first a Cobb-Douglas cost function, in order to obtain results that are qualitatively comparable to those from the production function (see Appendix B to this chapter for more details). Then we follow Morrison and Schwartz (1994, 1996) and assume a more flexible functional form, namely a generalised Leontief cost function (see Appendix C to this chapter for details).

12.3   The data

In this section, we briefly describe the data we use in our empirical analysis and then present some descriptive statistics and simple correlations to get a sense of the main patterns. For a full definition of the variables and sources, the reader is referred to Appendix A to this chapter.

12.3.1 Data sources and definitions

Throughout the analysis, we use yearly data at the regional level, currently the smallest disaggregation level available in Italy for which there is sufficient time series data for all the variables. The sample period is 1970–94.[4] We concentrate on the regional industrial sector, which includes Industry in the strictest sense, Energy, and Constructions. Our output measure is regional value added at constant 1990 prices. The series is built merging the ISTAT (1997a, 1997b) data for 1980–95 with data from Fondazione Eni-Enrico Mattei. Labour input is measured as total labour units, i.e. dependent and autonomous workers, in the industrial sector. Wages are taken to be equal to those of dependent workers, due to the absence of data on incomes of autonomous workers disaggregated by sector and region.

The stock of private capital is constructed using the perpetual inventory method. First, a benchmark stock of capital is constructed by summing investment flows over a number of years equal to the average economic life of the investment goods under consideration (e.g. fifteen years for equipment and machinery, ten years for transportation, fifty years for constructions).[5] Starting from this initial value, the capital stock for every year is obtained by adding investment in that year, and subtracting the value of capital goods that become obsolete in that year.

The stock of public capital disaggregated by region and category is taken from Bonaglia and Picci (1999). They apply the perpetual inventory method to regional time series for executed public investment (published in ISTAT (1954–92)) to apportion the aggregate capital stock estimated by Rossi et al. (1993). The categories of public capital included are the following: Land (e.g. land reclamation and irrigation); Communications; Education (e.g. buildings for educational and social activities); Water (e.g. river planning); Sanitation (e.g. sewers, water filtering, hospitals); Roads; Railways (e.g. railways and subways); Marine (e.g. ports, lake and river navigation); and Other (e.g. gas pipelines, infrastructures for tourism). As for the source of financing, the data include public works financed by the state (Ministries and Cassa per il Mezzogiorno); Public Administration (Regional, Provincial and Municipal governments; INPS, INAIL); Public Companies and other public organisations.

A drawback of using the permanent inventory method to measure public capital is that the resulting stock is systematically overestimated

---

[4] Of course, to build capital stocks we use data going back to before 1970, so 1970–94 must be intended as the period covered by our regressions. Unfortunately, data availability on public capital constrains our period to end in 1994.

[5] For a review of the average lives of different categories of investment goods in various countries, the reader is referred to Rosa and Siesto (1985). Another useful reference on the perpetual inventory method is ISTAT (1995).

for those regions that are least efficient in the use of public funds. Ideally, one would want a physical index of public capital stock for each region and each year. Unfortunately, such data do not exist for Italy: the only physical indexes we are aware of are those by Bracalente and Di Palma (1982) for the year 1977, and by Biehl *et al.* (1990) for 1970 and 1987. Preliminary evidence by Picci (1995b) shows that southern regions are ranked systematically higher with the permanent inventory method than with a physical index. Despite these discrepancies, we are forced to use the investment-based measure due to lack of data. Notice that, as a consequence of the possible over-estimation of *KG* for southern regions, one could find downward biased regression coefficients.

Next, following Hall and Jorgenson (1967) and King (1972), we define the user cost of private capital as:

$$c = p_K^E(r + \delta) \tag{13}$$

where p_K^E is the 'effective price' of private capital, i.e. the investment deflator adjusted for taxation and subsidies (see Appendix A to this chapter for a precise definition); r and δ are, respectively, the rate of return and the depreciation rate. The construction of a 'social user cost' of public capital, c_{KG}, is a controversial issue (see e.g. Harper *et al.* (1989) and Ballard and Fullerton (1992)). We choose to compute c_{KG} with a similar formula to (13), except that in place of p_K^E we use the public investment deflator; r and δ, instead, are assumed to be the same as for c.[6]

Finally, TFP growth is calculated as in equation (1), where S^L is the share of total labour compensation in value added, and $S^K = 1 - S^L$. Notice that S^L includes compensation for both employees and self-employed, where average earnings for self-employed are assumed to be the same as for employees. We cannot adjust for factor utilisation, due to the lack of data. In fact, the two most commonly used corrections for factor utilisation, namely hours worked for labour and electricity consumption for capital, are not available at the regional level for the whole sample, to the best of our knowledge. Yet, inclusion of time dummies in the regressions may capture cyclicality and attenuate the problem.

---

[6] Morrison and Schwartz (1996a, 1996b) compute the user cost of public capital in a similar way, but they adjust it for the marginal efficiency cost of financing public investment through taxation. We do not know of any reliable estimate of the latter for Italy, hence we omit this adjustment in our calculation.

12.3.2 Output, private inputs and TFP

In Table 12.1, we present descriptive statistics on the growth rate of real value added, and on its decomposition into the share attributable to private capital, labour and TFP. These values correspond, respectively, to $\dot{Q}$, $S^K\dot{K}$, $S^L\dot{L}$ and $\dot{A}$ in expression (1). We also report the growth rate of public capital. The figures are disaggregated by period, and by macro-region, i.e. North-West, North-East, Centre and South. Details on the composition of the macro-regions can be found in Appendix A to this chapter.

Over the whole period 1970–94, the annual growth rate of real value added was on average 2%. The worst performance was in the North-West (0.9%), the best one in the North-East (2.9%) and the Centre (2.5%), while the South grew at 1.9%. These figures, however, hide substantial differences over sub-periods: between 1970 and 1979; in fact, Italian regions grew on average at a fast 3.1%, while growth slowed down in 1980–89 to about 1.7%, and nearly stopped in 1990–94, when on average it was only 0.7% per year.

Turning to capital and labour, over the whole period the contribution of private capital to growth was one percentage point, while that of labour was −0.3 percentage points. The South is the area where the contribution of capital and labour was highest, respectively, 1.3 and −0.1 percentage points, while the North-West suffered most from the decrease in occupation in the industrial sector. The outstanding growth performance of the North-East in general cannot be attributed only to higher investment, since average private capital accumulation accounted for only 0.9 percentage points of growth. Over time, there is a clearly decreasing trend in the contribution of both capital and labour to growth.

Average TFP growth is rather low (1.3%), and constant across sub-periods for the whole of Italy. Yet, it is higher in the North-East, where it reaches 2.2%, and it is close to zero in the South (0.6%). The Centre has similar average TFP growth rates to the North-West, though the temporal pattern is rather different, with higher growth in the Centre in the 1970s, and vice versa in the 1980s. The relative advantage of the North-East – and disadvantage of the South – holds across all sub-periods.

Overall, the good relative performance of north-eastern and central regions seems to be mostly attributable to higher than average TFP growth. The North-West had a respectable TFP growth rate, but did markedly worse in terms of labour (and partly capital) accumulation. But the most striking fact is that overall the South had higher labour and capital growth rates than the North-East (4.4% and −0.2% for the South

344   *La Ferrara and Marcellino*

Table 12.1. *Summary statistics*

Average annual growth rate of:	Italy	North-West	North-East	Centre	South
Full sample[b]					
Real value-added	.020	.009	.029	.025	.019
	(.057)	(.059)	(.053)	(.047)	(.062)
Private capital[a]	.010	.006	.009	.009	.013
	(.012)	(.007)	(.005)	(.007)	(.017)
Labour[a]	−.003	−.012	−.002	−.001	−.001
	(.025)	(.023)	(.022)	(.024)	(.027)
Total factor productivity	.013	.015	.022	.017	.006
	(.050)	(.056)	(.044)	(.036)	(.056)
Public capital	.027	.030	.031	.023	.025
	(.014)	(.015)	(.013)	(.012)	(.014)
1970–1979					
Real value-added	.031	.007	.046	.041	.030
	(.070)	(.083)	(.066)	(.059)	(.068)
Private capital[a]	.014	.007	.010	.010	.022
	(.013)	(.005)	(.005)	(.005)	(.017)
Labour[a]	.004	−.008	.006	.009	.006
	(.022)	(.016)	(.015)	(.027)	(.022)
Total factor productivity	.013	.007	.030	.022	.002
	(.062)	(.076)	(.059)	(.047)	(.060)
Public capital	0.32	.027	.030	.029	.037
	(.014)	(.008)	(.013)	(.015)	(.015)
1980–1989					
Real value-added	.017	.017	.020	.018	.015
	(.048)	(.040)	(.043)	(.037)	(.059)
Private capital[a]	.009	.007	.009	.011	.008
	(.012)	(.008)	(.004)	(.009)	(.017)
Labour[a]	−.006	−.013	−.003	−.008	−.003
	(.025)	(.026)	(.023)	(.022)	(.027)
Total factor productivity	.014	.023	.014	.015	.010
	(.046)	(.041)	(.034)	(.029)	(.059)
Public capital	.025	.033	.033	.020	.020
	(.014)	(.020)	(.013)	(.007)	(.007)
1990–1994					
Real value-added	.007	−.003	.015	.012	.006
	(.042)	(.040)	(.031)	(.032)	(.052)
Private capital[a]	.005	.001	.005	.004	.007
	(.008)	(.006)	(.006)	(.005)	(.009)
Labour[a]	−.011	−.018	−.014	−.006	−.007
	(.027)	(.025)	(.026)	(.018)	(.032)
Total factor productivity	.013	.014	.024	.014	.006
	(.034)	(.040)	(.025)	(.027)	(.038)
Public capital	.021	.030	.028	.017	.014
	(.012)	(.014)	(.010)	(.008)	(.006)

Notes: [a] private capital is $S^K K$; Labour is $S^L L$.
[b] standard deviations are in parentheses.

versus 3.4% and −0.3% for the North-East), yet grew almost one percentage point less per year. A possible explanation for this pattern is the policy of incentives to private investment and hiring in the South. Some authors (e.g. Prosperetti and Varetto (1991)) argue that this policy has led to 'overcapitalisation' and, in general, to a relative inefficiency of southern firms compared to northern ones. Others (e.g. del Monte and Giannola (1997)) view the relatively high capital labour ratio in the South as a rational response by firms to the presence of higher costs of intermediate goods.[7]

The single most important factor responsible for the regional growth differentials appears to be TFP growth. It has been widely recognised in the literature that public investment in infrastructure is one of the main potential determinants of TFP. As we can see from Table 12.1, the average annual growth rate of public capital in Italy was 2.7% over the period 1970–94, more than 1.5 percentage points higher than that of private capital. It is also worth pointing out that, in all sub-periods, public capital growth was higher in the northern regions (about 3%) than in the Centre and in the South (2.3% and 2.5%, respectively). The widely held notion that the South receives a disproportionate share of public spending compared to the Centre and especially the North must be understood as related to transfer payments as opposed to public investment in capital goods.

The pattern of growth of public capital over time is decreasing, with values of 3.2% in the 1970s, 2.5% in the 1980s and 2.1% in the early 1990s. Though such a pattern could be correlated with the decrease in output growth, the decline is also present in the growth rates of private inputs. Hence, before drawing any conclusions on the role of public capital in enhancing growth, we need to take into account the interaction among all productive inputs, and turn to multivariate analysis.

12.4   The role of public capital

12.4.1   Results from growth accounting

In Table 12.2, we report estimates of equation (4), namely, we regress TFP growth on the growth rate of public capital ($\dot{G}$) and of private capital ($\dot{K}$), with fixed effects included in the regressions.[8]

---

[7] In del Monte and Giannola's (1997) view, the relative 'inefficiency' of southern firms is due to the fact that the latter are forced to integrate vertically, due to the higher costs of intermediate inputs, and hence cannot take full advantage of specialisation.
[8] We started with the more general equation (3), but L_t was never significant (results are available). There also appears to be no need for random effects (the Breusch Pagan test

Table 12.2. Growth accounting[a]

	Italy	Italy 1970–9	Italy 1980–9	Italy 1990–4	North-West	North-East	Centre	South
KG	.471**[b]	.240	.820**	.535	.449	-.144	.398	.616**
	(.188)[c]	(.437)	(.381)	(.639)	(.448)	(.463)	(.338)	(.313)
K	-.138**	.023	-.44**	.035	-.317	.276	-.022	-.178**
	(.061)	(.121)	(.145)	(.219)	(.262)	(.227)	(.141)	(.08)
Const	.006	.004	.005	.001	.009	.017	.009	-.001
	(.006)	(.017)	(.011)	(.013)	(.017)	(.016)	(.009)	(.008)
R^2	.02	.01	.07	.01	.02	.01	.01	.04
Observations	480	180	200	100	96	96	96	192

Notes: [a] dependent variable is TFP growth.
[b] * and ** indicate significance at the 10% and 5% level, respectively.
[c] standard errors are in parentheses.

As already mentioned in section 12.2, the coefficient on KG measures the overall elasticity of output with respect to public capital, $\eta + e^{KG}$. It is clear from the first column of Table 12.2 that the elasticity is positive, rather high, 0.47, and significant at 5%. This means that, *ceteris paribus*, the effect of an increase of one percentage point in $\dot{K}G$ (e.g. from 2% to 3%) on TFP growth – and therefore on output growth – is about 0.47 percentage points. The coefficient on $\dot{K}$ is negative, suggesting that the returns to private capital may be decreasing.

We then estimate the regression separately for the periods 1970–79, 1980–9 and 1990–4; the results are reported, respectively, in columns 2, 3 and 4 of Table 12.2 The maximum impact obtains in the 1980s, with an elasticity of TFP to KG of 0.82; the lowest one is the 1970s, with an elasticity of 0.24, while the estimated value for the first half of the 1990s is 0.53. In the light of this pattern, we can think that most of the scepticism regarding the productivity-enhancing role of public capital comes from the experience of the 1970s, rather than from more recent years. As we will see, the temporal pattern of increasing effectiveness of public capital in recent years will also emerge from the production function approach. Among the potential explanations for such a pattern, improved administrative efficiency is likely to have played a non-negligible role.

In the last four columns of Table 12.2, we pool the years again and disaggregate over macro-regions. The coefficient on $\dot{K}G$ is positive (but not significant at conventional levels) for the North-West and the Centre, positive and significant for the South, and negative and insignificant for the North-East. The estimated elasticity is particularly high for the South, 0.62. On the other hand, the impact of $\dot{K}$ is generally negative (positive for the North-East), though again not significant, except for the South. The fact that we find statistically significant values for Italy and for the South, but not for the other macro-regions, is likely to be due to the different sample sizes.

12.4.2 Results from the production function approach

We now illustrate the empirical results that arise from the production function approach. Table 12.3 reports the estimated coefficients for a

yields a p-value of 0.53). The low values of R^2 obtained in our regressions are common to the literature (e.g. Hulten and Schwab, 1991), and likely depend on the fact that the dependent variable is a residual. The empirical results for the growth accounting and the production function approaches are obtained with Stata 5.0. For the cost function estimation, we used TSP 4.1. The programmes and detailed results are available upon request.

Cobb-Douglas specification as in equation (5), using fixed effects and time dummies.[9] From the first column of Table 12.3, the elasticity of output to public capital, e^{KG}, for Italy is negative, while that to private capital is positive and significant, 0.14. Repeating the analysis over different sub-periods, however, we can see that the negative impact of public capital on output only holds for the 1970s, while in the 1980s and 1990s such impact is significantly positive and increasing (the estimated coefficient on the log of KG for these periods is, respectively, 0.17 and 0.56). The temporal pattern of the effect of public capital is broadly similar to that of the growth accounting approach.

Further useful information can be gained from regional disaggregation. Columns 5–8 of Table 12.3 report results for the four macro-regions, using regional and time dummies. It turns out that public capital is mostly productive in the South, followed by the Centre, and not productive in the North-East and North-West.

The last row of Table 12.3 reports the p-value for the test of constant returns to all inputs. The null of constant returns is accepted at the 5% level for the 1970s and the 1990s, and rejected for the 1980s. In terms of geographical areas, the hypothesis is accepted for the Centre and the South, but rejected for northern regions.

A potential objection to our interpretation of the above results is that the positive correlation between public capital and production may work through demand as opposed to supply. To discriminate among the two channels, one may want to exploit the fact that demand effects are likely to take place at the time the investment is undertaken, while the impact on supply can be expected to last longer. To perform a test along these lines, one would need either project level data or a sufficiently long time series to allow for estimation of dynamic models with a number of lags. Unfortunately, neither is currently available. However, we believe that the supply side interpretation can be maintained for two main reasons. First, to the extent that the expansionary effects of public investment translate into increased labour demand and private investment, they

---

[9] The hypothesis of fixed versus random effects is often rejected, yet the regressors appear to be correlated with the random regional errors. Hence, we prefer to focus on the fixed-effects model, that yields consistent, even though not efficient, estimators. Cyclical fluctuations also need to be accounted for, in order to avoid spurious correlations. To evaluate whether there is any cyclicality left after inclusion of the time dummies (which also allow us to account for exogenous changes in the rate of growth of technological progress), we have tried including inventories as an explicit cyclical variable. However, inventories do not improve our explanatory power in any way, hence we do not keep them in the final specification. Notice that the reported high values of R^2 in Table 12.3 are due to the time dummies.

Table 12.3. *Production function*[a]

	Italy	Italy 1970–9	Italy 1980–9	Italy 1990–4	North-West	North-East	Centre	South
KG	-.148**[b]	-.085	.176*	.559**	-.139	-.141*	.147	.367**
	(.048)[c]	(.132)	(.094)	(.194)	(.113)	(.072)	(.206)	(.151)
K	.144**	.082**	.022	.418**	-.349**	-.325**	.370**	.216**
	(.020)	(.037)	(.053)	(.126)	(.143)	(.087)	(.043)	(.025)
L	.748**	1.189**	.465**	.490**	.907**	.938**	.454**	.289**
	(.043)	(.101)	(.076)	(.081)	(.202)	(.083)	(.082)	(.087)
Const	2.657**	1.349	3.758**	-3.256	6.701**	9.593**	1.860	1.516
	(.536)	(1.225)	(1.113)	(2.690)	(1.574)	(.808)	(1.865)	(1.507)
R^2	.98	.98	.94	.94	.91	.93	.99	.96
Observations	500	200	200	100	100	100	125	200
CRS (p-value)[d]	.00	.16	.01	.07	.01	.00	.87	.33

Notes: [a] dependent variable is (log of) value added; KG, K and L are in logarithms.
[b] * and ** indicate significance at the 10% and 5% level, respectively.
[c] standard errors are in parentheses.
[d] the null hypothesis is constant returns to scale to KG, K and L.

should already be taken into account by the fact that we include L and K as inputs in the production function (and explanatory variables in the regressions). Secondly, our empirical results on the time pattern of public capital effectiveness go in the opposite direction to what a demand side interpretation would suggest. In fact, public investment was higher in the 1970s than in the 1980s, which should have led to a bigger impact on demand, while both the production function and the growth accounting approaches yield higher coefficients on public capital for the 1980s as compared to the 1970s.

12.4.3 Results from the cost function approach

Having considered the effects of public capital on output growth, we now evaluate its role in cost reduction. This requires estimating the system of equations reported in Appendix B to this chapter. The resulting parameter estimates are not of direct interest (they are available upon request), but they are useful to calculate the shadow values of the capital inputs (z_{KGt}, z_{KMt}, z_{KBt} in (10), where KM and KB are private capital in equipment/machinery and buildings, respectively), and the cost elasticities, φ^{KG} in particular (equation (11)). A comparison of the shadow values with the user costs of private and public capital then provides information on whether under-investment ($E < 0$ in (12)) or over-investment occurred ($E > 0$). These quantities are calculated for each year, but, due to the space constraint, we only report the average values over the sample under analysis.

The first column of Table 12.4 presents results from panel fixed effects estimation, for the whole period 1970–94.

The variable φ_{KG}, which is the cost elasticity to public capital taken with the opposite sign, should be positive for KG to be cost reducing.

Table 12.4. *Cost function (Cobb-Douglas)*

	Italy	Italy 1970–9	Italy 1980–9	Italy 1990–4	North-West	North-East	Centre	South
φ_{KG}	−.029	.049	−.085	−.029	−.171	−.086	.202	.016
E_{KG}	.275	.181	.338	.298	.491	.300	.092	.371
E_{KM}	−.022	.051	−.057	.179	−.090	.177	.041	.088
E_{KB}	.198	.029	.395	−.115	.223	−.027	.128	.149
Observations	500	200	200	100	100	100	100	200

Notes: φ_{KG} is the shadow share of input x; E_X is $(U_X - Z_X)x/C$, where U_X is the user cost of x, and C represents total costs.

Instead, the estimated value for Italy is negative, though very close to zero. As a result, E^{KG} is positive, 0.27, suggesting over-investment in KG at the national level. E^{KB} is also positive, while $E^{KM} = -0.02$, suggesting under-investment in machinery.

Repeating the analysis over sub-periods, φ_{KG} is positive only in the 1970s, and negative in later periods. Even for the first period, however, the cost reducing effect of public capital is not sufficient to cover its social user cost: in fact, E^{KG} remains positive. On the other hand, E^{KM} and E^{KB} are only negative, respectively, in the 1980s and in the early 1990s.

Noticeable differences across macro-regions also emerge. From Table 12.4, columns 5–8, the best performance is in the Centre, followed by the South, while the estimated values of φ_{KG} are negative for the North-East and, in particular, for the North-West. Again, when we take into account the opportunity cost of infrastructure investment, E^{KG} is positive even for the Centre. The latter results could be due to overestimation of the user cost of public capital, c_{KGt}, that is substantially higher than its private capital counterpart, c. As far as private capital is concerned, there appears to be under-investment in machinery in the North-West and in buildings in the North-East.

12.4.4 Comparing the results

We should now pause to compare the estimates obtained under the three approaches. Comparing the TFP and the production function methods (Tables 12.2 and 12.3, respectively), it is apparent that the latter gives estimates on the coefficient of KG that are systematically lower than the former. Vice versa, the estimated coefficient on private capital in the production function approach is generally higher than in the growth accounting (notable exceptions are the North-West and North-East).

This second result is not surprising. In fact, we can see from equation (5) that the coefficient on k in the production function approach is the elasticity e^K, while that on K is $(e^K - S^K)$ or $(e^L + e^K - 1)$, depending on whether (3) or (4) is estimated. Therefore, we should always be getting a lower coefficient on private capital from the growth accounting approach, possibly negative when there are decreasing returns to K and L (and in fact we can see from the last row of Table 12.3 that a negative coefficient on K occurs whenever the hypothesis of constant returns to scale is rejected and there appear to be decreasing returns to K and L).

The different coefficients on public capital, on the other hand, are much harder to explain. In fact, as we showed in section 12.2, both approaches should yield the same estimates, equal to $(\eta + e^{KG})$. The only cases in which we obtain virtually identical estimates are the period 1990–4 for Italy, and the North-East. In all other cases, the growth accounting method yields higher coefficients than the production function one. A possible reason is that in the production function specification we include a set of time dummies that may attenuate the explanatory power of *KG* (in fact, when we leave the time dummies out, the coefficient on public capital increases substantially). Other reasons may have to do with influential observations or endogeneity, and we will address these points in the next section.

Overall, we can see that, despite the discrepancy in the quantitative impact of public capital which we observe in some cases, the qualitative pattern that emerges from the two approaches is very similar. The effectiveness of public investment has increased over time (in particular, compared to the 1970s), and the macro-regions where such effectiveness is highest are, in order, the South and the Centre.

Turning to the cost function methodology, we cannot directly compare the estimates in quantitative terms, but again some qualitative features remain the same as in the other approaches. In particular, the South and the Centre are still the areas where public capital is most effective (though the ranking among the two is now reversed). The time pattern is now markedly different, suggesting a *decrease* in the cost saving role of public capital from the 1970s to the 1980s, and a slight improvement from the 1980s to the 1990s (though still lower effectiveness than in the 1970s). This difference may be due to differences in the specification of the model,[10] and also to the few degrees of freedom that remain when we estimate the cost system on subsets of the sample. In the next section, we experiment with a more flexible functional form for the cost function, and we find that the temporal pattern found for the other approaches is reinstated.

12.4.5 Causality and sensitivity analysis

In this section, we explore the robustness of our estimates to the presence of outliers, we deal with potential endogeneity problems and/or measurement error, and we address the issue of the functional form for the cost function approach.

In order to control for influential observations whose presence can clearly bias the estimators, we follow the procedure in Belsley *et al.*

---

[10] In order to separate between variable and fixed costs, the Cobb-Douglas in this approach includes private capital only in transportation, and not the total stock of private capital.

(1980, p. 28) and drop the observations that lead to major changes in the parameters when included in the sample. Table 12.5 reports our estimates of the production function for the sample purged of influential observations.[11]

Comparing these results with those obtained from the full sample (Table 12.3), we find that the estimated coefficient on KG is very similar for Italy as a whole, and fairly similar for the South (0.28, as compared to 0.37, both significant at the 5% level). The coefficient for the Centre is also positive, though not statistically significant, and that for the North is virtually zero. The most important difference emerges with respect to north-eastern regions. While in the full sample we found a coefficient of −0.14 on KG, when we drop influential observations the same coefficient is estimated to be 0.16 (significant at the 10% level). Nonetheless, the qualitative pattern of highest effectiveness of public capital in the Centre and South as opposed to the North remains unchanged.

We next turn to the issue of potential endogeneity of public capital. We can think of two reasons why the link between output and public capital may go in the opposite direction to that hypothesised here. First, regions with higher output may be regions where KG is systematically higher, for example because those are fast growing regions and public investment is more productive in an environment where technology grows faster. Secondly, public intervention may be targeted towards relatively poorer areas with the aim of improving incentives for private investment. In the former case, we can expect the OLS coefficient on KG to be upward biased, in the latter to be downward biased. Another source of bias in the OLS coefficient for KG would be measurement error. To cope with these problems, in Table 12.6 we present two stage least squares of the role of public capital in production.

We use two instruments for KG: (i) a one-year lag of the stock of public capital for a given region (in logs), which we call $KGlag$; and (ii) the average contemporaneous stock of public capital in neighbouring regions (still in logs), which we denote $KGnb$. Notice that with the latter instrument we lose two regions which are islands (Sicily and Sardinia). From the first column of Table 12.6, the coefficient on public capital for Italy is virtually identical to that found without instrumenting (first column of Table 12.3). When we disaggregate the sample over

---

[11] In this section, for expositional purposes we concentrate on the production function approach and perform the various possible tests. We have also repeated similar tests for the other approaches, and no significant differences emerged. The disaggregation into sub-periods is not reported because, once we drop the influential observations, we are left with too few observations for 1990–4.

Table 12.5. *Production function, no influential observations[a]*

	Italy	North-West	North-East	Centre	South
KG	-.182**[b]	.021	.164*	.348	.283**
	(.048)[c]	(.172)	(.086)	(.231)	(.143)
K	.166**	-.379**	-.478**	.297**	.195**
	(.018)	(.172)	(.100)	(.041)	(.025)
L	.683**	1.055**	.872**	.611**	.265**
	(.042)	(.207)	(.084)	(.077)	(.082)
R^2	.97	.98	.81	.99	.94
Observations[d]	471	90	88	115	190
CRS (p-value) [e]	.00	.21	.00	.19	.04

Notes: [a] dependent variable is (log of) value added; KG, K and L are in logarithms.
[b] * and ** indicate significance at the 10% and 5% level, respectively.
[c] standard errors are in parentheses.
[d] outlying observations are discarded using the method in Belsley et al., (1980, p. 28).
[e] the null hypothesis is constant returns to scale to KG, K and L.

macro-regions, we find again a positive (though not statistically significant) coefficient on public capital for central and southern Italian regions, and negative coefficients for the North-West and North-East (the latter two being very similar in magnitude to those obtained without instrumentation). We therefore conclude that our results hold when controlling for the potential endogeneity and measurement error in public capital, which is nonetheless important according to the outcomes of the Hausman test, reported in the last row of Table 12.6. Two stage least squares on the sample purged of influential observations are reported in Table 12.10 of Appendix C to this chapter. In that table, no significant difference emerges.

Finally, in Table 12.7 we explore the robustness of our results to the specification of a different functional form in the cost function approach. Following Morrison (1988) and Morrison and Schwartz (1994, 1996b), we assume that the variable cost function is a Generalised Leontief (analytical details are provided in Appendix C to this chapter).

Compared to the results in Table 12.4, where a Cobb-Douglas specification was adopted, two main differences emerge. First, the temporal pattern is now in line with that suggested by the growth accounting and the production function approach: the effectiveness of public capital is now generally increasing over time, leading to the highest cost savings in the 1990s. Secondly, the pattern across macro-regions is now different: the North-East is now the area where public investment has the largest

Table 12.6. *Production function, two stage least squares*[a]

	Italy	North-West	North-East	Centre	South
KG	−.161**[b]	−.159	−.134*	.221	.184
	(.048)[c]	(.108)	(.075)	(.224)	(.174)
K	.173**	−.331**	−.342**	.382**	.242**
	(.022)	(.145)	(.091)	(.044)	(.028)
L	.702**	.850**	.927**	.482**	.314**
	.045	(.196)	(.083)	(.074)	(.096)
Const	1.229**	1.366**	−1.972**	−1.487**	1.064**
	(.022)	(.067)	(.035)	(.049)	(.057)
R^2 adj	.99	.99	.99	.99	.99
Observations[d]	432	96	96	96	144
Hausman (p-value)[e]	.01	.43	.09	.05	.00

Notes: [a] dependent variable is (log of) value added; KG, K and L are in logarithms, instruments are KGlag and KGnb.
[b] * and ** indicate significance at the 10% and 5% level, respectively.
[c] standard errors are in parentheses.
[d] outlying observations are discarded using the method in Belsley *et al.*, (1980, p. 28).
[e] the null hypothesis is constant returns to scale to KG, K and L.

Table 12.7. *Cost function (Generalised Leontief)*

	Italy	Italy 1970–9	Italy 1980–9	Italy 1990–4	North-West	North-East	Centre	South
φ_{KG}	−.139	−.155	−.223	.139	−.252	.190	−.003	−.259
E_{KG}	.385	.374	.500	.137	.395	.021	.294	.660
E_{KM}	.035	.076	.208	.199	.093	.472	.195	.265
E_{KB}	.190	.239	−.004	.385	−.171	.125	.234	178
Observations	500	200	200	100	100	100	100	200

Notes: φ_X is the shadow share of input x; E_X is $(U_X - Z_X)/C$, where U_X is the user cost of x, and C represents total costs.

impact, while such impact is basically zero (or even negative) for the Center and the South.

12.5 Conclusions

The potential for a productivity-enhancing role of public infrastructure has been greatly emphasised in recent years, and is a key policy issue for the new members of the European Union. Yet, empirical evidence has been mixed at best. This chapter attempts to conduct a systematic analysis of the impact of public capital on TFP, production, and costs by comparing the three main existing theoretical approaches, and implementing them with regional data for Italy. The empirical results for Italy can be of more general interest, since many of the contrasts and differences that exist among European countries are reproduced within Italy. In particular, the productive structure and the level of development of Italian regions varies substantially, going from the rich and industrialised regions of the North to the relatively poor regions of the South.

At the national level, the total factor productivity approach indicates a strong positive effect of public capital accumulation; the production function approach yields a (small) negative elasticity of production to public capital; and the cost function approach indicates virtually no effect of public capital on variable costs. The results are more coherent across methodologies when we disaggregate the sample by time periods and by geographical areas. According to all three methodologies, the effectiveness of public infrastructure has increased over the years, especially in the 1980s compared to the 1970s. Also, all three methods indicate central and southern Italian regions as the areas where public capital is most productive.

An important caveat is in order. Our analysis is confined to the *manufacturing* sector, in the sense that the output measures or the costs which we use as dependent variables refer to that sector only. We cannot infer that our results would remained valid if a broader measure of output were used. Indeed, certain types of public investment (e.g. irrigation, land reclaimation, etc.) are more likely to have an impact on agricultural production than on the output of the manufacturing sector. Also, there are a large amount of additional factors at play which are difficult to capture by the methods described in this chapter. These other factors play a key role in determining for example the efficiency with which the infrastructure funds are spent. A study by Ederveen *et al.* (2002) on the effectiveness of the EU cohesion policy stressed that the impact of structural fund spending in terms of the overall growth performance of countries is significantly dictated by the quality of the institutional set-up in the country in question. There are a range of variables, such as the openness of the economy and an absence of corruption, which are vital in extracting positive benefits from infrastructure investments. In fact, the 'right' institutions are, according to the authors, more important than the infrastructure spending itself in determining the overall productivity effects of such investments. These considerations need to be borne in mind in drawing implications from the present chapter for cohesion policy for the new Member States.

Scope remains for further work in several directions. First, it would be important to compare the benefits with an appropriate measure of the costs of public capital, taking into account for example the distortionary effects of financing public investment through taxation. Secondly, the criteria and procedures for financing public investment are likely to play a role in the efficiency of its allocation, and it could be interesting to explore these links. Thirdly, analogous procedures to those we use could be employed to assess the impact of other types of public expenditures which in theory should be productivity enhancing, e.g. in law and order or higher education. Finally, a wider and more detailed set of data (e.g. at the provincial level) would be helpful in enabling us to draw more accurate conclusions.

References

Aschauer, D. 1989a. 'Is Public Expenditure Productive?'. *Journal of Monetary Economics*, vol. 23, pp. 177–200.

1989b. 'Does Public Capital Crowd Out Private Capital?'. *Journal of Monetary Economics*, vol. 24, pp. 171–88.

Ballard, C. L. and Fullerton, D. 1992. 'Distortionary Taxes and the Provision of Public Goods'. *Journal of Economic Perspectives*, vol. 6, pp. 117–31.

Barro, R. 1990. 'Government Spending in a Simple Model of Endogenous Growth'. *Journal of Political Economy*, vol. 98, pp. 103–25.

Belsley, D., Kuh, E. and Welsch, R. 1980. *Regression Diagnostics*. New York: John Wiley and Sons.

Berndt, E. 1991. *The Practice of Econometrics*. Reading, MA Addison-Wesley.

Berndt, E. and Wood, D. 1975. 'Technology, Prices and the Derived Demand for Energy'. *Review of Economics and Statistics*, vol. 57, pp. 259–68.

Biehl, D., Bracalente, B., Di Palma, M. and Mazziotta, C. 1990. 'La Diffusione Territoriale delle Infrastrutture: un'analisi per l'Europa e per l'Italia'. In Di Palma, M. (ed.), *Le Infrastrutture a Rete: Dotazioni e Linee di Sviluppo*. Rome: Centro Studi Confindustria.

Bonaglia, F. and Picci, L. 1999. 'Lo stock di capitale nelle regioni italiane'. *Mimeo*.

Bonaglia, F., La Ferrara, E. and Marcellino, M. 2000. 'Public Capital and Economic Performance: Evidence from Italy'. *Giornale degli Economisti*, vol. 60, pp. 221–44.

Bracalente, B. and Di Palma, M. 1982. 'Infrastrutture e Sviluppo Regionale in Italia: un'Analisi Multidimensionale'. *Note Economiche*, pp. 13–42.

Bradley, J., Morgenroth, E. and Untiedt, G. 2003. 'Macro-Regional Evaluation of the Structural Funds Using the Hermin Modelling Framework'. Mimeo, paper presented at the 43rd Congress of the European Regional Science Association.

Chambers, R. 1988. *Applied Production Analysis*. New York: Cambridge University Press.

358   *La Ferrara and Marcellino*

De la Fuente, A. and Vives, X. 1995. 'Infrastructure and Education as Instruments of Regional Policy: Evidence from Spain'. *Economic Policy*, vol. 20, pp. 13–51.

Del Monte, A. and Giannola, A. 1997. *Istituzioni economiche e Mezzogiorno: analisi delle politiche di sviluppo.* Rome: La Nuova Italia Scientifica.

Ederveen, S., de Groot, H. and Nahuis, R. 2002. 'Fertile Soil for Structural Funds? A Panel Data Analysis of the Conditional Effectiveness of European Cohesion Policy'. Central Planning Bureau Discussion Paper No. 10.

Evans, P. and Karras, G. 1994. 'Are Government Activities Productive? Evidence from a Panel of US States'. *Review of Economics and Statistics*, vol. 76, pp. 1–11.

Greene, W. 1997. *Econometric Analysis* Upper Saddle River, NJ: Prentice-Hall.

Hall, R. and Jorgenson, D. 1967. 'Tax Policy and Investment Behaviour'. *American Economic Review*, vol. 57, pp. 391–414.

Harper, M., Berndt, E. and Wood, D. 1989. 'Rates of Return and Capital Aggregation Using Alternative Rental Prices'. In Jorgenson, D. and Landau, R. (eds.), *Technology and Capital Formation.* Cambridge, MA: MIT Press, pp. 331–72.

Holtz-Eakin, D. 1994. 'Public-Sector Capital and the Productivity Puzzle'. *Review of Economics and Statistics*, vol. 76, pp. 12–21.

Hulten, C. and Schwab, R. 1984. 'Regional Productivity Growth in US Manufacturing: 1951–78'. *American Economic Review*, vol. 74, pp. 152–62.

1991. 'Public Capital Formation and the Growth of Regional Manufacturing Industries'. *National Tax Journal*, vol. 44, pp. 121–34.

ISTAT. 1995. 'Investimenti, stock di capitale e produttività dei fattori. Anni 1980–1994', Note e relazioni, No. 2.

1997a. *Contabilità Nazionale*, Tomo 1, *Conti Economici Nazionali Anni 1970–95.*

1997b. *Contabilità nazionale*, Tomo 3, *Conti economici regionali.*

Annuario Statistico Italiano, various years.

King, M. 1972. 'Corporate Taxation and Dividend Behaviour: A Further Comment'. *Review of Economic Studies*, vol. 39, pp. 231–4.

Moreno, R., López-Bazo, L. and Artís, M. 2005. 'Infrastructure Investments as a Tool for Regional Development Policy: Lessons from the Spanish Evidence'. Chapter 11, this volume.

Morrison, C. 1988. 'Quasi-Fixed Inputs in US and Japanese Manufacturing: A Generalized Leontief Restricted Cost Function Approach'. *Review of Economics and Statistics*, vol. 70, pp. 275–87.

Morrison, C. and Schwartz, A. 1994. 'Distinguishing External from Internal Scale Effects: The Case of Public Infrastructure'. *Journal of Productivity Analysis*, vol. 5, pp. 249–70.

1996a. 'Public Infrastructure, Private Input Demand, and Economic Performance in New England Manufacturing'. *Journal of Business and Economic Statistics*, vol. 14, pp. 91–101.

1996b. 'State Infrastructure and Productive Performance'. *American Economic Review*, vol. 86, pp. 1095–112.

Munnell, A. 1990a. 'Why Has Productivity Growth Declined? Productivity and Public Investment'. *New England Economic Review*, January/February 1990, pp. 3–22.

1990b. 'How Does Public Infrastructure Affect Regional Economic Performance?'. In Munnell, A. (ed.), *Is There a Shortfall in Public Capital Investment?*. Boston: Federal Reserve Bank of Boston.

Picci, L. 1995a. 'Productivity and Infrastructure in the Italian Regions'. Dipartimento di Scienze Economiche, Università di Bologna, working paper.

1995b. 'Il "capitale mancante" nel Mezzogiorno italiano'. Dipartimento di Scienze Economiche, Università di Bologna, working paper.

Prosperetti, L. and Varetto, F. 1991. *I differenziali di produttività Nord-Sud nel settore manifatturiero*. Bologna: Il Mulino.

Rosa, G. 1979. *Lo stock di capitale nell'industria italiana: Nuove stime settoriali e territoriali*. Rome: SIPI.

Rosa, G. and Siesto, V. 1985. *Il capitale fisso industriale: Stime settoriali e verifiche dirette*. Bologna: Il Mulino.

Rossi, N. and Toniolo, G. 1993. 'Un secolo di sviluppo economico'. *Rivista di Storia Economica*, vol. 10, pp. 145-75.

1993. 'I conti economici italiani: una ricostruzione statistica'. *Rivista di Storia Economica*, vol. 10, pp. 1–47.

Seitz, H. and Licht, G. 1995. 'The Impact of Public Infrastructure Capital on Regional Manufacturing Production Costs'. *Regional Studies*, vol. 29, pp. 231–40.

SVIMEZ. 1993. *I conti economici del Centro-Nord e del Mezzogiorno nel ventennio 1970–1989*. Bologna: Il Mulino.

Appendix A: The data

Output: regional series for manufacturing value-added in current and constant 1990 prices are obtained from ISTAT (1997b) for the period 1980–94 and from Fondazione Eni-Enrico Mattei, for previous years. Time series data on expenditures on energy and intermediate inputs for the manufacturing sector are not available on a regional basis. The price of output is measured as the implicit price deflator computed for each region as the ratio of current and constant liras value added.

Labour: number of workers employed in the manufacturing sector is obtained by combining data from *Annuario Statistico Italiano* (ISTAT, various years) and SVIMEZ (1993). The nominal value of wages for production and non-production workers is taken to be the same, since no data are available for the latter. Regional consumer price indexes (ISTAT, 1997a) are used to obtain real wages.

Private capital: the quantity of private capital, K, is measured as the private capital in the manufacturing sector in 1990 liras. We have estimated regional stocks of capital for each category of capital good (buildings, plant, equipment and machinery, transportation) applying the perpetual inventory method (assuming constant depreciation within each group). ISTAT (1997b) provides regional investment data on nominal and constant investment over the period 1980–97. Different

360   *La Ferrara and Marcellino*

Table 12.8. *Data set*

Variable name	ISTAT category	Description
Roads	1. Roads	Highways and all kinds of roads
	2. Airports	Landing strips, buildings
Rail	3. Railways	Railways, subways, cable-railway
Mar	4. Marine	Ports, lake and river navigation
Water	5. Water	River planning
	6. Energy	Electric grid, power plants
Com	7. Communications	Telecommunications plants
Educ	8. Schools and social facilities	Schools, universities
	9. Public buildings	Monuments, penitentiaries
	10. Residential buildings	Subsidised buildings, reconstruction after calamity
San	11. Sanitation	Hospitals, water-filtering, water cisterns, sewers
Land	12. Land reclaimation	Land reclamation and irrigation
	13. Land transformation	Land improvement
Other	14. Other	Gas pipelines, infrastructures for tourism

sources have been used to build regional series covering the whole period needed in order to apply the perpetual inventory method. Regional investments on the three categories are obtained by applying to these series the same weights observed at the national level over the same period. The usual hypotheses on depreciation are made. The benchmark for the capital stock in buildings is taken from ISTAT (1995).

Factor prices for capital inputs: we use the concept of user cost of private capital. The effective rental price of capital, p_K^E, is obtained by adjusting the implicit price deflator for taxation and subsidies:

$$p_K^E = p_K[1 - us]$$

with *us* standing for savings per unit, i.e.,

$$us = \frac{1}{1 + \rho(1 - \tau)} \left[\frac{CC}{I} + \sum_{i=1}^{n} \frac{a_i + b_i}{(1 + \rho)^i} \right]$$

where ρ is the discount rate (which we assume is equal to the interest rate charged by special investment banks called Istituti di Credito Speciale), τ is the tax rate on profits, CC are government contributions to buy industrial capital given through Cassa del Mezzogiorno,[12] I are

[12] We use commitments rather than disbursements because the former are more relevant for investment decisions by firms.

Table 12.9. *Macro-regions*

Macro-region	Regions included
North-West	Piemonte, Val d'Aosta, Lombardia, Liguria
North-East	Trentino Alto Adige, Veneto, Friuli Venezia Giulia, Emilia Romagna
Centre	Toscana, Umbria, Marche, Lazio
South	Abruzzo, Molise, Campania, Puglia, Basilicata, Calabria, Sicilia, Sardegna

Table 12.10. *Production function, 2SLS without influential observations*[a]

	Italy	North-West	North-East	Centre	South
KG	−.219**[b]	−.062	−.190**	.144	.089
	(.048)[c]	(.160)	(.090)	(.257)	(.164)
K	.183**	−.296*	−.428*	.356**	.188**
	(.019)	(.171)	(.101)	(.043)	(.029)
L	.670**	.946**	.855**	.647**	.380**
	(.043)	(.194)	(.087)	(.076)	(.089)
Const	−1.692**	1.354**	1.440**	1.025**	−1.338**
	(.022)	(.064)	(.030)	(.049)	(.054)
R^2 adj	.99	.99	.99	.99	.99
Observations[d]	406	86	86	86	137
Hausman (p-value)	.00	.32	.05	.01	.00

Notes: [a] dependent variable is (log of) value added; *KG*, *K* and *L* are in logarithms, instruments are *KGlag* and *KGnb*.
[b] * and ** indicate significance at the 10% and 5% level, respectively.
[c] standard errors are in parentheses.
[d] outlying observations are discarded using the Dfbeta method.

investments in the industrial sector, *a* and *b* are normal and ahead depreciation coefficients.

Public capital: the stock of public capital is measured as end-of-year public-capital stock of Communications, Public Buildings, Water, Sanitation, Roads, Railways, Marine, and Other (e.g. gas pipelines, infrastructures for tourism). These data are computed by Bonaglia and Picci (1999) applying the perpetual inventory method to the series of public spending in infrastructure ("lavori eseguiti", ISTAT, *Opere Pubbliche*).

Appendix B: Cobb-Douglas cost function

In our analysis, we distinguish between variable inputs (labour, *L*, and private capital in transportation, *KT*), and quasi-fixed inputs (public capital, KG, and private capital in buildings and machinery, KB and KM respectively, with $KB + KM + KT = K$). Variable costs, G, depend on the price of the variable factors, on the level of output, on the state of technology, and on the level of the quasi-fixed inputs:

$$G = G(p_L, p_{KT}, Q, A, KM, KB, KG) \tag{14}$$

Total costs are given by:

$$C = G + p_{KM}KM + p_{KB}KB \tag{15}$$

where we are assuming that KG has a price of zero for the firm.

For a Cobb-Douglas technology, $Q = AKT^a L^b KG^g KM^m KB^d$, conditional factor demands for variable inputs are given by:

$$X_L^* = A^{-\frac{1}{a+b}} \left[\frac{a}{b} \frac{p_L}{p_{KT}} \right]^{-\frac{a}{a+b}} Q^{\frac{1}{a+b}} KG^{-\frac{g}{a+b}} KM^{-\frac{m}{a+b}} KB^{-\frac{d}{a+b}} \tag{16}$$

$$X_{KT}^* = A^{-\frac{1}{a+b}} \left[\frac{a}{b} \frac{p_L}{p_{KT}} \right]^{\frac{b}{a+b}} Q^{\frac{1}{a+b}} KG^{-\frac{g}{a+b}} KM^{-\frac{m}{a+b}} KB^{-\frac{d}{a+b}} \tag{17}$$

and

$$G(p_L, p_{KT}, Q, A, KG, KM) = p_L X_L^* + p_{KT} X_{KT}^* \tag{18}$$

Assuming constant returns to variable inputs, $a + b = 1$, and taking logs, yields:

$$\log G/Q = -A - g\log KG - m\log KM - d\log KB + \log \Psi + b\log p_L + a\log p_{KT} \tag{19}$$

where $\Psi \equiv (a^a b^b)^{-\frac{1}{v}}$. Then, by Shepard's Lemma:

$$\beta_j = \frac{\partial \log G}{\partial \log p_j} = \frac{\partial G}{\partial p_j} \frac{p_j}{G} = \frac{p_j X_j}{G} = S_j, \ j = 1, 2 \tag{20}$$

where $X_1 = L$, $X_2 = KT$, $p_1 = p_L$ and $p_2 = p_{KT}$.

We estimate the system of equations formed by the log cost function (19), a factor share equation (20) and the optimality condition (the price of output equals the marginal cost).[13]

We add fixed effects, a time trend to proxy for technological improvements, and estimate the resulting three equation system by (iterative)

[13] Notice that, by construction, the two share equations in (20) have the property that, in each time period, the sum of the dependent variables equals one. Hence, we can drop one share equation.

SUR (see e.g. Greene (1997), pp. 689–98, or Berndt (1991) for details). Using the estimated parameters, we can calculate the quantities in (10), (11) and (12).

Appendix C: Generalised Leontief cost function

Following Morrison (1988) and Morrison and Schwartz (1994, 1996a, 1996b), a Generalised Leontief specification for the variable cost function G in (9) is:

$$
\begin{aligned}
G(x, p, t, Q) = Q\bigg(\sum_i \sum_j \alpha_{ij} p_i^{0.5} p_j^{0.5} + \sum_i \sum_m \delta_{im} p_i s_m^{0.5} \\
+ \sum_i p_i \sum_m \sum_n \gamma_{mn} s_m^{0.5} s_n^{0.5}\bigg) + Q^{-0.5}\bigg(\sum_i \sum_k \delta_{ik} p_i x_k^{0.5} \quad (21) \\
+ \sum_i p_i \sum_m \sum_k \gamma_{mk} s_m^{0.5} s_k^{0.5}\bigg) + \sum_i p_i \sum_k \sum_h \gamma_{hk} x_k^{0.5} x_h^{0.5}
\end{aligned}
$$

with symmetry in the parameters imposed, e.g. $\alpha_{ij} = \alpha_{ji}$. In (21), x indicates quasi-fixed inputs subject to homogeneity conditions: KG, KB and KM; p are the prices of variable inputs (L and KT); s denotes the remaining arguments: a time trend (t), that proxies technological progress, and output (Q).[14]

To estimate all the parameters of (21), we construct a system that includes the two variable input demand equations, the profit maximisation condition, and (21) itself. The variable input demand equations are the derivatives of G with respect to p (by Shepard's lemma):

$$
\begin{aligned}
\frac{V_j}{Q} = \frac{\partial G}{\partial p_j}\frac{1}{Q} = \sum_i \alpha_{ji}\frac{p_i^{0.5}}{p_j^{0.5}} + \sum_m \delta_{jm} s_m^{0.5} + \sum_m \sum_n \gamma_{mn} s_m^{0.5} s_n^{0.5} \\
+ Q^{-0.5}\bigg(\sum_k \delta_{jk} x_k^{0.5} + \sum_m \sum_k \gamma_{mk} s_m^{0.5} x_k^{0.5}\bigg) \quad (22) \\
+ Q^{-1}\sum_k \sum_h \gamma_{hk} x_k^{0.5} x_h^{0.5}
\end{aligned}
$$

for $j = 1, 2$

[14] Notice that this specification for the cost function only ensures linear homogeneity in prices. Convexity in the quasi-fixed inputs and concavity in prices are not guaranteed. It can be either imposed *a priori* by imposing sign constraints on certain parameters, or checked *ex post*; see Morrison (1988) for details.

where $V_1 = L$, $V_2 = KT$, and we standardise by Q to reduce problems of heteroskedasticity.

Next, profit maximisation requires equality of output price and marginal cost, so that:

$$p_Q = \frac{\partial G}{\partial Q} = \sum_i \sum_j \alpha_{ij} p_i^{0.5} p_j^{0.5} + \sum_i \sum_m \delta_{im} p_i s_m^{0.5} + \sum_i p_i \sum_m \sum_n \gamma_{mn} s_m^{0.5} s_n^{0.5}$$

$$+ 0.5 Q^{-0.5} \left(\sum_i \sum_k \delta_{ik} p_i x_k^{0.5} + \sum_i p_i \sum_m \sum_k \gamma_{mk} s_m^{0.5} x_k^{0.5} \right)$$

$$+ 0.5 Q^{0.5} \left(\sum_i \delta_{iQ} p_i + \sum_i p_i \sum_m \gamma_{mQ} s_m^{0.5} \right) + 0.5 \sum_i p_i \sum_k \gamma_{Qk} x_k$$

$$(23)$$

To conclude, notice that the four equation system made up of (21), (22) and (23) has a rather complex structure, but it is linear in the parameters. Hence, we can estimate it by (iterative) SUR, after adding fixed effects to account for regional disparities. Using the estimated parameters, we calculate the quantities in (10), (11) and (12).

13   Regional policies after the EU enlargement

*Michele Boldrin**

13.1   Introduction

In this chapter, I try to address the following question: which, among the structural policies currently in place should the EU maintain, which should it reform and which should it altogether abandon in order to fuel real convergence at the national and regional level?

My focus will be on economic convergence, but, in the EU, convergence is seldom addressed at the national level. For the EU, and the European Commission in particular, economic convergence is a regional issue and must be addressed at that level. The word 'regional', here, refers to NUTS-2 territorial units or lower, as this is the level at which EU structural policies are designed and evaluated. I have argued elsewhere (see e.g. Boldrin and Canova (2001)) against the choice of such policy objective, as NUTS-2 units are too small and too varied in size for convergence to make any sense. Taking this policy objective at face value, I ask how Structural and Cohesion Funds and their allocation should be modified to reach it, and what kind of policies may create the environment most conducive to economic growth at the NUTS-2 territorial level. My attention concentrates on the twin issues of economic growth and convergence, for the new Member States after joining the EU.

I proceed through the following steps. In section 13.2, I show that new Member States stand, relative to the EU-15 average member, roughly in the same position in which, about twenty or so years ago, Greece, Ireland, Portugal and Spain stood in relation to the then older members of the EEC. This explains our simulations, the sombre results of which are summarised at the end of section 13.2. The mole of previous studies on regional convergence is briefly summarised in

* This material is based upon work supported by the National Science Foundation under Grant SES-0114147.

section 13.3, which also argues that the economic logic supporting the three-decade-long EU approach to the problem is seriously at odds with the facts. In section 13.4, I conclude with a number of policy recommendations.

13.2   Initial conditions and simulations of the future

Unless otherwise noted, data for the year 2000 are used to provide a snapshot characterisation of initial conditions, while the evolution over the decade 1990–2000 is used to gauge the underlying tendencies. Where relevant, I report the most recent (i.e. 2002 or 2003) values. Due to both lack of data and their economically negligible size, I leave Cyprus and Malta out of the picture, while Romania and Bulgaria, which should join the EU only in 2007, are often mentioned.

13.2.1   Per capita income and labour productivity

New Member States are poor according to GDP per capita, measured in Purchasing Power Standards (PPS). In 2001, and relative to the EU-15 average, their GDP per capita goes from 36% (Latvia) and 39% (Lithuania) to 75% (Slovenia) and 86% (Cyprus). As a group, the average is substantially below 50%. Labour productivity measures paint the very same scenario. For the 1990s as a whole, average growth rates in the EU-15 and the new Member States have been close, so that relative distances have not changed much; still, this similarity is misleading, and it is not obvious at all whether it should be projected into the near future. New Member States grew little or contracted in the early 1990s, as their economic and political systems underwent the transition shock. Since the middle 1990s, and particularly after 1999/2000, they have persistently outpaced the growth rate of the EU-15. So, for example, during 2002–4, the EU-15 has grown at 1.3% a year on average, while the slowest among the newcomers (the Czech Republic) has grown at 2.6% and the fastest (Lithuania) at 6.5%. A sizeable degree of catching up is therefore apparent, and, while this is far from being an established and uniform trend, it cannot be underestimated. I predict it will continue.

13.2.2   Saving and investment

The empirical literature on economic growth has consistently reported strong correlations between the rate of investment, the growth rates of labour and total factor productivity, and subsequent growth in per capita income (Miles and Scott (2002) is a recent reference). While the theoretical reasons for this correlation are far from obvious, and abundant evidence shows that capital accumulation per se is not to be looked upon as the main cause of high labour productivity, it is important to recognise that a high investment rate provides a reliable signal of both short- and long-term potentials for growth. All the evidence, and an abundant amount of theory, suggests that the often invoked distinction between a growth model that is 'investment intensive' and one that is 'TFP intensive' is misplaced and misleading. TFP growth is the result of a process of dismissal of old methods of production and adoption of different and more productive ones, and the latter can only take place through a massive flow of investments. Disembodied TFP is mostly a myth, which evaporates quickly in the heat of macro and micro data; TFP is mostly embodied in capital, and the latter comes around only through the investment process.

Capital comes in two forms, human and physical. When one looks at the average years of school attendance, the new Member States, with 9.8 years of schooling on average, are ahead of the EU-15, which had only 9.5 years in 1999. After controlling for content and for quality of schooling, the average new Member State may be somewhat below the EU-15 average, but this residual difference is unlikely to be close to 60%. Currently, hourly labour costs in the new Member States are roughly 60% lower than in the EU-15. This is important; the quality of the labour force of the new Member States is comparable to that of the EU countries, and it costs a lot less.

The picture is less rosy when one looks at machines, equipment, plants, infrastructures and so forth. There are two problems in this respect: bad initial conditions (obsolete factories and infrastructure) and relatively low investment rates since the transition started. In the EU, the investment rate has been 17.6% on average over the last ten years, with little variations around that level. The four Cohesion countries all had investment rates in excess of 20% during the 1990s. A similar calculation can be performed for the new Member States. For the latter, the average rate of gross capital formation was 24.5% in 2000, and above 20% for most of the last decade, but there are remarkable differences across countries and time. For example, the Czech Republic and Slovakia have investment rates in excess of 30% on average, while Latvia, Romania and Bulgaria average only 14%. High investment rates can be financed either by local or by foreign savings. The openness of capital markets and the security of the legal system play an important role in determining the extent to which investment is financed by foreign savings. In all countries, domestic savings are the major source of funds for investment and only in the Czech Republic a sustained flow of foreign saving allows investment rates to exceed domestic savings by about 3–4% in every year of the sample. In fact, direct portfolio investments have been relatively small in the area, and their magnitude is completely dwarfed by the magnitude of FDI (Eurostat, 2002c).

The proportion of FDI in total investment of new Member States displays an increasing trend, in particular after 1995–6. The ratio of FDI to GDP is, on average, more than twice as large as the corresponding number for the EU (5% as compared to 2%). For some countries, the net FDI inflow as a percentage of GDP has reached fairly high levels (11% in Slovakia, 8% in the Czech Republic and 8% in Estonia). For others, it is still around 2–3% of GDP. A 5% average, however, is substantially better than that recorded in, for example, Russia, where in the 1990s the FDI rate was smaller than 1%. It is also about ten times better than the rate recorded by Greece, Portugal and Spain in the early 1980s, that is at the time or just before they entered the EU. Over two-thirds of FDI in the new Member States comes from the EU; Germany, the Netherlands and Austria are providing the largest amounts, while Poland, the Czech Republic and Hungary are the largest recipients, taking about 70% of total FDI flow to the region (see Eurostat, 2000a, 2000b).

13.2.3 Labour market

Even if now equal to those in the EU-15, employment and participation rates have declined substantially over the decade, and are currently about 5% lower than in 1991 in the new Member States. In general, the declining participation rates are the product of two phenomena. The first, common to the EU-15, is the aging of the population accompanied by a tendency to early retirement for old workers displaced by industrial restructuring. A second factor, also present in some EU countries, but exacerbated in the CEEC-10 by the transition process, is the exit of many workers from the legal labour markets and towards underground activities. Overall, the dynamics of labour market indicators in the new Member States and the EU-15 are remarkably similar.

Although along this dimension the new Member States are not so different from their EU-15 counterparts, one may wonder as to why, also in countries that are relatively much poorer than the EU-15, wage growth has exceeded labour productivity growth so much in the presence of high and rising unemployment rates. In general, I share the view of the specialised literature, according to which, while some non-competitive aspects still remain in the labour markets of new Member States, high unemployment compensations and the high level of labour income (or payroll) taxation are the main culprits for the current situation, making the switch from unemployment to employment un-attractive for certain types of workers (see, for example, World Bank, 2001a, 2001b). The level and duration of unemployment compensations in transition countries with high unemployment rates clearly reflects political and social pressures, and does not require further discussion here. Detailed examinations of these issues appear in the above publications, and in Vaitilingam (2001).

13.2.4 Growth accounting

A growth accounting exercise requires several assumptions, most of which are somewhat heroic when applied to new Member States. I make the following set of assumptions:

- The share of labour in national income is 70%. This roughly corres-ponds to the estimate obtained using data for the Czech Republic, Hungary and Poland.
- Capital stock increments are computed summing up investment over the period and subtracting yearly depreciation. Data for depreciation is available only for the three Baltic States, in which the depreciation rate is estimated to be 40%, 47% and 52% of the gross investment rate, respectively. These estimates seem to be on the high end of the distribution, hence we use a value of 45% for the remaining countries.
- Since no information about part-time versus full-time labour is avail-able, the increments of the labour input are computed using bodies. Data for Hungary indicate that the accounting discrepancy between using bodies and hours is small. We expect the same to hold for the remaining nine countries.
- The increment in the domestic stock of capital is calculated as a residual, subtracting FDI increments from total increments. The same depreciation rate is applied to domestic capital and FDI. Since the technological content of FDI is higher and its depreciation is probably lower, this procedure biases FDI's contribution downward.

Table 13.1 reports the results. Since the first (and, at times, the last) year of the sample period differs across countries, the first column reports the range of years for each country. Average growth rates of GDP vary substantially, from a value of −4.0% per year in Bulgaria to a 7.7% per year in Latvia. Apart from Latvia, success stories appear to be Slovenia, with an average growth rate of 5.0%, and Lithuania with 4.9%. After Bulgaria, the worst performers are Romania (−0.4%) Estonia (2.0%) and the Czech Republic (2.0%). In recent years, Estonia and Slovakia have also had growth rates above 4.0% per year.

Table 13.1. *Growth accounting*

	Time period	Δy/y	Δk/k	Δn/n	Δtfp	ΔFDI/FDI	AGR Δn/n[a]
Bulgaria	1991–2001	−0.040	0.006	−0.04	−0.006	0.001	−0.0008
Czech Republic	1993–2000	0.020	0.020	−0.002	0.002	0.003	−0.0006
Estonia	1992–2001	0.020	0.015	−0.015	0.020	0.004	−0.0055
Hungary	1992–2001	0.023	0.014	−0.004	0.013	0.003	−0.0008
Latvia	1991–2000	0.077	0.008	−0.013	0.082	0.002	−0.0027
Lithuania	1991–2000	0.049	0.018	−0.014	0.044	0.002	−0.0026
Poland	1991–2001	0.032	0.012	−0.006	0.040	0.001	0.0002
Romania	1991–2001	−0.004	0.010	0.000	−0.015	0.001	0.0000
Slovakia	1993–2000	0.030	0.022	−0.010	0.017	0.003	−0.0017
Slovenia	1992–2000	0.050	0.017	−0.010	0.042	0.001	−0.0016
CEEC average		0.025	0.014	−0.011	0.022	0.002	−0.0016

Notes: [a] Δn/n stands for the contribution of agricultural employment. The increments in capital stock are computed summing up investment over the period and subtracting yearly depreciation. Data for depreciation is available only for the three Baltic States: the depreciation rate is estimated to be around 40–50% of the investment rate. We apply a value of 45% to the other seven countries. The increments on the labour input are computed using bodies and not hours which are not available in many countries. Data for Hungary indicate that the difference is small. The domestic increment in the capital stock is calculated as residual. The same depreciation rate is applied to domestic capital and FDI, therefore biasing downward the contribution of FDI to growth. The contribution of agriculture to growth is calculated multiplying Δn/n by the decrement in the population employed in agriculture.

The relative contributions of labour and capital follow analogous patterns across countries: the capital stock has a small influence, while the contribution of labour to growth is negative. To be precise, the contribution of capital to aggregate growth is fairly constant and centered at around 1.4% on average. Exceptions are Bulgaria (0.6%) and Latvia (0.8%) on the negative side, and Slovakia (2.2%) and the Czech Republic (2.0%) on the positive side. In the latter two countries, growth in capital accounts almost entirely for the growth in aggregate output, with variations in labour inputs or TFP playing a secondary role. As already mentioned, labour dismissals were intense during the 1990s. This is reflected in the uniformly negative contribution of labour input, which averages about −1.1%.

Qualitatively speaking, these patterns are not dissimilar from those observed in Spain and Portugal post-1975. Quantitatively, the difference is one of speed and magnitude, both of which appear to be higher in the new Member States, making their transition process even more remarkable. On average, the seriously downward phase of the transition process lasted about seven years in the CEECs: this is about half the time it took to either Spain or Portugal to start growing faster than the EU average after their transition began. The relative size of the sectors affected by the transition is also much larger in the new Member States. The Spanish and Portuguese economies were heavily protected from foreign competition, had a strong presence of the state in all sectors, but, nevertheless, they were market economies to a substantial extent. State-controlled firms never accounted for more than 20–25% of gross value added in the tradable sector. On the contrary, and excluding perhaps Hungary, private enterprises never came to control more than 20% of tradable economic activity in the CEECs before the socialist system collapsed.

An alternative measure of the relative size of the two transitions can be gathered by looking at the drop in total employment during the first decade. From 1975 to 1985, Spain, which suffered more than Portugal, lost 2 million workers out of an initial labour force of 12 million, that is, about 16%. Among the CEECs, the one with the smallest percentage drop in employment, during the decade of 1990–2000, is Poland (−11%) followed by Latvia (−14.5%), the Czech Republic (−15%) and Slovakia (−16%). All the others have larger percentage drops, with Bulgaria the worst affected (a 33% loss in total employment).

We move next to the contribution of Total Factor Productivity (TFP). Averaging over the whole CEEC-10, TFP changes have contributed to growth for about 2.2% per year out of a total of 2.5% per year (roughly 88%). This result is not unusual. With few exceptions, TFP invariably accounts for most of the growth in per capita output when one cannot control for the micro details of labour and capital improvements. However, this average masks substantial cross-country differences. For example, in Lithuania, Latvia, Slovenia and Poland, TFP growth would have implied GDP growth in excess of 4.0%, had the two production inputs remained constant, while in Bulgaria, Romania and the Czech Republic the contribution of TFP changes to growth has been either negative or negligible. But this kind of counter-factual should not be pushed too far: micro-evidence, and economic theory, suggest that Slovenia and Poland performed so well on the TFP growth side precisely because they performed badly on the capital and labour side: TFP grew because inefficient firms and plants were shut down. Symmetrically, the Czech Republic did poorly on the TFP side and very well on the capital and labour side because very few inefficient plants were dismissed. For Hungary and Poland, two of the largest recipients of FDI in the group, the TFP contribution is positive but not large.

Table 13.2. *Institutional indices*

	Capital flows rest[a]	Structural reforms[b]	Legal proxies[c]
Bulgaria	1.01	0.79	NA
Czech Republic	0.05	0.90	3.40
Estonia	0.00	0.93	3.33
Hungary	0.62	0.93	3.30
Latvia	0.50	0.86	3.77
Lithuania	1.40	0.82	3.76
Poland	1.03	0.86	3.66
Romania	1.90	0.82	NA
Slovakia	0.75	0.90	3.78
Slovenia	1.35	NA	NA
CEEC average	NA	NA	3.66
EU		1	

Notes: [a] The capital flow index varies from −0.2 to 6, 6 is most restrictive (source Garibaldi *et al.* (2001)).
[b] The reform index weights price liberalisation and competition policies (0.3), trade and exchange rate liberalisation (0.3) and privatisation and banking reform (0.4). A value of 1 is a market economy.
[c] The index of legal proxies weighs predictability of law and policies, political stability and security of properties, government/business interface, red tape and efficiency of government infrastructure. The scale goes from 0 to 6 with 6 being the worst performer (from Aslund *et al.* (2001) and Garibaldi *et al.* (2001)).

In an attempt to find some evidence on the sources of cross-country variability in TFP changes, we look at where the CEEC-10 stand as far as trade liberalisation, capital flows, privatisation of firms, banking and legal systems reforms in relation to the EU. Table 13.2 summarises the relevant information. We report three indices: a capital flow restriction index, an index of institutional reforms and an index of legal proxies. The capital flow index refers to data for 1997 and ranges from −0.2 to 6, with 6 indicating the most restrictive institutions and negative numbers indicating the presence of positive incentives to capital (in)flows. The reform index refers to 1999 and weighs price liberalisation and competition policies (0.3), trade and exchange rate liberalisation (0.3) and privatisation and banking reform (0.4). A value of 1 corresponds to a market economy. The index of legal proxies refers to the conditions present in 1997 and equally weighs the predictability of law and policies, the political stability and the security of properties, government/business interface, red tape and the efficiencies of government infrastructures. The index ranges from 0 to 6, with 6 being the worst performer.

In general, there appear to be limited differences along institutional lines. For example, the legal proxies index varies from 3.30 (Hungary) to 3.78 (Slovakia) while the average is at 3.66. By comparison, Russia and the other CIS countries are at about the 4.0 level. The index of structural reforms also indicates that all ten countries are close to the EU, except Bulgaria (0.79), Romania (0.82) and Lithuania (0.82). Top performers in this category are Estonia and Hungary (both 0.93). Capital flow restrictions are now relatively low in all countries: the least restrictive is Estonia – which actually provides incentives to FDI – with the Czech Republic a close second (0.05). Worst performers are Romania (1.90), Lithuania (1.40) and Slovenia (1.35). Once again, by way of comparison, Russia scored 1.81 on this scale and the other CIS countries 1.33.

In sum, the examination of liberalisation indices indicates that the majority of the new Member States are already similar to current EU members. Since the data are slightly outdated, we expect the divergences to have been further reduced in the last few years. Although institutional reforms may still be sought in the future, they do not appear to constitute a fundamental stumbling block in harmonising the economies of the new Member States within that of the EU.

13.2.5 Regional inequalities in the new Member States

Regional inequalities are not very large in the group of new Member states, and, to some extent, they are smaller or at most comparable to those already present in the EU-15. There are two reasons for this: first, most new countries are small, in size and in population, and this fact limits heterogeneity among reasonably sized internal territorial units; secondly, the high level of inequality among countries (almost one to three in per capita GDP) dwarfs the within country differences. This is a crucial fact to be kept in mind when thinking about economic growth and convergence in new Member States: regional and national economic convergence are, to a first approximation, the same problem.

The basis for our statement is simple: eight of them can be treated in the same way as moderately large NUTS-2 units of the EU. Obviously, one can try to find large differences within countries by looking at smaller territorial units. Nevertheless, one needs to try hard to find differences larger than those characterising Italian and Spanish provinces, for which both unemployment and per capita GDP ratios between highest and lowest reach levels equal to 6. In Hungary and the Czech Republic, for example, the ratio between the maximum and minimum unemployment rate at the regional level is about 4. Notice also that there are seven such regions in Hungary and nine in the Czech Republic, both countries with populations of about ten million people. Slovenia is divided into three areas, the ratio in per capita income between the first and the second is 1.38, while that between the second and the third is 1.10. Poland is fairly large, with a population of 39.0 million people in a country which is approximately the size of Italy. Nevertheless, while Polish regional disparities exist, they are also small relative to those present in several of the EU countries. For example, the unemployment rates in the *voivodship* of Poland average 16% (using 2001 data), ranging from a maximum of 25% in Warminsko-Mazurskie to a minimum of 12% in the metropolitan Warsaw area of Mazowieckie. This range is smaller than those we encounter among the Spanish *autonomias* or the Italian *regioni*. In summary, the extent to which regional disparities are a problem for the new Member States is smaller than that for some of the current EU-15 members.

13.2.6 A simulation exercise

The EU has experienced several enlargements since its creation. During the period 1981–6, three countries, all poorer than the EU average, were admitted: Greece in 1981, and Portugal and Spain in 1986. We use this experience to learn about two issues: (i) how the new Member States compare, in relation to EU averages, to the three earlier entrants; (ii) if the experience of Greece, Portugal and Spain can teach us something about the future of the new EU members. The punch line is: although the historical circumstances were different, macroeconomic conditions in the CEECs resemble very much those of Greece, Portugal and Spain at the time of accession. On the ground of similar initial conditions, accession to the same free trade area, and under the assumption of similar national and supranational policies, we find that the differential effect of joining the EU will be small (both in terms of levels and growth rates) so that current inequalities are likely to be reduced, but not miraculously fast. My claim is that the economic systems of the new Member States are comparable to those of Greece, Portugal and Spain at the time of their accession to the EU.

I concentrate upon a restricted number of aggregate statistics, which can provide a parsimonious measure of the 'distance' between the CEECs and Greece, Portugal and Spain at the time of accession (see Table 13.3). The factors used to measure similarities and differences are GDP per capita relative to the EU average, labour productivity relative to the EU average, share of employment in agriculture and openness of the economy, the last measured by exports plus imports over GDP.

Table 13.3. *Indices of similarity*

	Openness	Employment in agriculture	GDP per capita	Labour productivity
Spain (1985–6)	0.29	0.15	0.62	0.95
Portugal (1985–6)	0.56	0.22	0.49	0.44
Greece (1980–1)	0.42	NA	0.55	0.52
Bulgaria	1.28	0.27	0.25	0.28
Czech Republic	1.44	0.05	0.59	0.47
Estonia	0.87	0.07	0.41	0.34
Hungary	1.23	0.07	0.53	0.47
Latvia	1.02	0.14	0.30	0.30
Lithuania	1.06	0.19	0.30	0.26
Poland	0.63	0.25	0.41	0.34
Romania	0.75	0.41	0.27	0.15
Slovakia	1.60	0.08	0.49	0.47
Slovenia	1.20	0.10	0.73	0.50

Notes: Openness is measured by export plus import over GDP. For Spain, Portugal and Greece, we average over the two years. For the CEECs, the values refer to 2000. The employment share and labour productivity for Spain, Portugal and Greece are computed using the OECD's Structural Statistics for Industry and Services database and the OECD's STAN database for industrial analysis. Values for the CEECs come from previous tables. GDP per capita is computed using the Eurostat Regio data set.

Since initial conditions in the new Member States are approximately the same as those of the old newcomers, and since, with current policies, we find it likely that joining the EU will have on these countries the same effect as it had on Spain, Portugal and Greece, we can hypothetically estimate where new Member States will be in their post-accession steady state relative to the EU average. As with all reduced form econometric exercises, this one also suffers from obvious limitations. First and foremost is the assumption of policy and behavioural invariance post-admission. What this means is that we assume that none among the new Member States will have the ability to replicate, for example, the policies that Ireland has adopted since 1986 and which led it to move, in less than twenty years, from the last to the first position in terms of per capita GDP within the EU. Rather, we assume that new Member States will behave, more or less, like Greece, Portugal and Spain, that the EU structural policies towards poorer regions will remain more or less unaltered, and that the overall degree of trade liberalisation within the EU and between the EU and the rest of the world will not change. Dull as this may sound, it should not be taken as granted: Spain and Portugal have progressively modernised and liberalised their own internal product and labour markets, slightly reduced labour taxation, improved capital mobility and implemented a fairly large, albeit not overwhelming, privatisation process.

We construct three scenarios. The first, the 'no-change scenario', assumes that the current historical conditions will endure indefinitely into the future. For this scenario, we estimate a simple AR(1) model for relative (to EU average) income per capita/labour productivity for each country and, given parameter estimates, we project past behaviour far into the future. Since the data set is short, estimates of the steady states are biased. What we call the 'steady state' is, in reality, a growth path. It can be treated as a steady state, i.e. as a fixed point of a stationary dynamic system, because we are normalising everything by the (unknown) average long-run growth rate of the EU. It is relative to this unknown growth rate, whatever it may turn out to be, that the position we compute is a steady state.

In the second, 'level-effect scenario', we assume that, after joining the EU, new Member States will settle in a steady state position which is similar (in terms of the parameters regulating the asymptotic distribution of relative growth rates) to that of Spain, Portugal and Greece since they entered the EU. Theoretically, one can justify this scenario by using either endogenous or exogenous growth models in which countries that are similar in terms of economic fundamentals face the same distribution of long-run growth rates. Notice that, because of the normalisation by the unknown EU growth rate, this reduced form statistical model makes absolutely no assumption as to what the source of growth is.

In the third, 'growth-effect scenario', we assume that joining the EU will proportionately boost the growth rate of new Member States by the same factor it boosted the growth rates of Spain, Portugal and Greece after their accession. This scenario assumes a linear production function in which the asymptotic growth rate is country-specific. The scenario assumes that, when two countries are exposed to the same change in their fundamentals, a common proportionality factor affects country-specific growth rates. To implement the idea behind this scenario, we estimate the average and dispersion of growth rates using regional data for Spain, Portugal and Greece before and after accession. We use these two distributions to estimate the common proportionality factors for the mean and for the standard deviation. As before, we use this information as a prior for the AR model we estimate using CEEC-10 data. Since we have very few data points before accession, estimates of the jump are very imprecise. The mean effect is, however, very small (1.01), probably because most growth gains in Greece, Portugal and Spain predated EU

Table 13.4. *Estimated steady states*

	No-change scenario		EU level effect		EU growth effect	
	GDP	LP	GDP	LP	GDP	LP
Bulgaria	0.23	0.26	0.34	0.35	0.37	0.37
Czech Republic	0.61	0.5	0.5	0.56	0.51	0.53
Estonia	0.33	0.33	0.39	0.38	0.4	0.39
Hungary	0.48	0.46	0.45	0.49	0.45	0.45
Latvia	0.26	0.25	0.35	0.36	0.37	0.36
Lithuania	0.28	0.26	0.37	0.35	0.36	0.37
Poland	0.48	0.34	0.46	0.39	0.47	0.37
Romania	0.27	0.23	0.42	0.31	0.38	0.33
Slovakia	0.49	0.48	0.45	0.49	0.46	0.48
Slovenia	0.8	0.61	0.76	0.68	0.74	0.6
CEEC average	0.38	0.38	0.41	0.45	0.42	0.41

Notes: Estimates obtained in the columns 'EU level effect' and 'EU growth effect' are computed using a Bayesian procedure that weighs information contained in domestic data and information in the time series of poor EU regions after they joined the EU. In the first case, it is assumed that the distribution of steady states to which the CEECs will belong is the same as that of poor EU units. In the second, it is assumed that joining the EU has a level effect on the growth pattern which is the same for the CEECs.

accession. We take into account the uncertainty present in the data by letting the dispersion of the potential jump to be relatively large (maximum range we allow is [1.00, 1.03]).

Table 13.4 provides a summary of the results. For each scenario, the first column refers to relative GDP per capita and the second to relative labour productivity. There are two results we would like to emphasise. First, in the absence of any structural change ('no-change scenario'), we should not observe significant variations either in the ranking or in the level of GDP per capita of the new Member States relative to that observed in 2000. In other words, the new members are already close to their steady state, relative to the EU-15. The only two countries which, at the steady state, seem able to reduce significantly their distance from the EU are Poland (currently at 41%) and Slovenia (currently at 73%).

Secondly, adding the information contained in the behaviour of the poor EU regions after accession does not radically alter the estimates of the relative steady states. The distribution of relative steady states in either the level or in the growth-effect scenarios is only marginally different from that estimated for the case of no change. This follows from the fact that the growth patterns experienced by the new Member States during the 1990s was not so different from the growth patterns experienced by Mediterranean regions after they joined the EU. The reason behind this finding should be kept in mind when discussing policy implications. Greece, Portugal and Spain have performed well but far from spectacularly after accession and only marginally better than they had done in earlier decades. The best among the new Members have done well in the decade since the middle 1990s, in fact they have done better than the earlier entrants did, on average, after accession. The opposite is true for the weakest five among them. Hence, applying to the new Member States the distribution of growth rates experienced by Greece, Portugal and Spain induces a 'reversion to the mean' effect in which the currently fast growers grow more slowly and the laggards accelerate. Similar steady state growth implies constant ranking in the distribution of GDP per capita and persistence of current inequalities. Integration and extension of the current EU regional policies to the CEEC countries will not sweep away income inequalities. National policies, if anything, must do the job.

13.3   Principles, instruments and jurisdiction

13.3.1   *Which economic principles?*

Probably the most important lesson that previous studies of economic growth in trade-integrated areas have taught us is that the predictions of 'new growth' or 'new trade' theory models are comfortably rejected by the data. These kinds of models almost unanimously predict that trade openness combined with increasing returns and a variety of external effects will produce agglomeration phenomena, poverty traps, economic divergence and increased inequality. Hence, when differently endowed countries start trading with each other, the richer or more advanced ones 'win' while the other 'lose'. Victory takes the form either of a higher growth rate of income (because of faster capital accumulation or a faster rate of innovation) or of a concentration of productive factors in the rich country, or both. Agglomeration theories, particularly popular among policy-makers and technocrats involved with regional and structural policies, predict that capital and labour move towards where their complementary factor of production is more abundant, thereby leading to a concentration of economic activity in a few privileged areas and leaving the rest far behind. Hence the need for active public intervention to prevent factors (especially labour) from moving around too much and for subsidising economic activity in poorer areas where it would not, otherwise, take place. These are, in a nutshell, the economic principles upon which current and, as far as I can tell, future EU regional policies are founded. I claim these principles are incorrect and they lead to badly designed and probably counter-productive policies.

I am not aware of any historical experience of trade integration showing support for this kind of prediction. In fact, all recorded episodes of increased trade openness, at the national or international level, have generated the opposite outcome: poorer areas have either strictly gained (in both absolute and relative terms) on the leader or have kept distances roughly constant. Falling behind, after trade opens up and factor mobility is allowed, has never been experienced by any country in the advanced world, absent wars or major political disasters. What I have in mind here are the increasing trade and factor mobility among the fifty states of the United States since the end of the Civil War, the increasing trade and economic integration among the initial six members of the EEC since the 1950s and then, since the end of the 1980s, among the current fifteen; the recent successful integration of Canada, the USA and Mexico in the NAFTA; and the almost fifty years of progressive and still increasing trade integration of Japan and South East Asian countries among themselves and with Europe and the USA. One is hard-pressed to find a single 'loser' in any of these episodes. It is quite important to stress that, in all but one case (the post-1980s EU), trade integration and increased factor mobility took place without any kind of regional, structural or transfer policy meant to compensate the poor countries or areas from the losses that trade integration with the richer ones is supposed to bring about according to the 'new' theories of growth and trade. While the extent to which trade openness and integration have generated convergence varies greatly from one situation to the other, divergence has never been observed at any reasonable level of spatial disaggregation. The latter is not a minor point. The EC integrated trade first among six and then among a higher number of countries for about thirty years, practising very few 'compensatory' or 'structural' policies (aside from the infamous Common Agricultural Policy, the consequences of which are well known) and income differences sharply decreased both across and within the EC countries. During the last twenty years, the EU has increased dramatically the amount of funds invested in structural and regional policies, without any visible impact on the rate of economic convergence within countries. Empirical estimates suggest in fact that regional convergence has come close to a halt just at the time structural and cohesion policies have been introduced (Boldrin and Canova, 2001). East Asian countries have practised zero compensation or structural policies. Still, their convergence to the average income of their trading partners (i.e. Europe, the USA, Canada and Japan) seems out of the question.

13.3.2   *Which policy instruments?*

One may legitimately wonder whether structural and regional policies are behind miracles or, at least, the growth convergence we observed. We doubt that this is the case for several reasons. First, as mentioned above, no regional policies were ever implemented for example among South East Asian countries and divergence was not observed. Secondly, one may think of the Marshall Plan – the historical event analogous to the current European transfer policies – as key to the European convergence to the USA. However, both the financial size and the time frame of the Marshall Plan are orders of magnitude smaller than those of the European structural policies or, at the national level, of the German transfers to the Eastern *Länder* and the Italian transfers to the southern regions. If what it takes for convergence is a Marshall Plan, then Sicily and Calabria have received approximately twenty of them since the 1950s. Furthermore, in Boldrin and Canova (2001), we have shown econometrically that, at least in the EU-15, the conjecture that regional transfer policies are behind the partial convergence episodes, is not supported by the data.

Arevalo (2003) has carried out a meticulous investigation of Spanish regional development since the late 1950s, using a high-quality data set of both provincial and regional human, public and private capital stocks, and sectorial value added. He shows that TFP growth accounts for the lion's share of economic growth and convergence across Spanish regions, with little left for public and private capital and a somewhat larger share for human capital. More importantly, he shows once again that, even at this very detailed and disaggregated level, one cannot find any sign of a positive impact of Structural Funds on provincial and regional TFP growth rates. A recent paper by Ederveen *et al.* (2002) also supports this view. They use a statistical methodology which is quite different from Boldrin and Canova (2001), but reach the same conclusions: Structural Funds by themselves are ineffective. To be precise: their estimates show a statistically significant negative effect of Structural Funds on regional growth rates and convergence.

13.3.3   Which policies?

Sometimes poorer countries grow faster than richer ones. During the 1960s and until 1974, Spain unilaterally liberalised trade and adopted internal policies that, relative to the previous situation, were market-oriented. By 1974, Spanish income per capita stood at almost 80% of the EU-15 average, which is were it still stood in 2000, after twenty-five years of oscillations, in both growth rates and internal policies. Irish relative per capita income stagnated for more than twenty years, without any apparent effect coming either from the 1973 EU accession or from having become an early beneficiary of EU Structural Funds: by the mid-1980s, Irish income per capita was around 65% of the EU average. Since then, Irish governments have fully embraced free trade, low taxes, low public spending and a set of well-known competition-oriented policies. Its income per capita now exceeds 120 per cent of the EU-15 average: in Europe only Luxembourg has a higher per capita income than Ireland.

Look next at Greece, Portugal and the Mezzogiorno. The first one now stands at about 65% of the EU average. This is exactly where it was twenty-four years ago, when it first joined the EU and began receiving transfers: all the catch-up that Greece managed to do since 1960 took place before it started to receive Structural Funds. It is also a fact that, since accession, Greece has also been the one country in Europe that has least indulged in market-friendly internal policies. Portugal seems to have done almost the opposite: it followed its neighbour Spain in unilaterally liberalising trade in 1960, shifted to a regime of high public spending and taxation coupled with heavy state intervention in labour and product markets right after the 1974 revolution and resumed liberalisation, privatisation and labour market reform in the late 1980s. Its per capita GDP, relative to the EU-15, followed a similar sequence: from 45% to 60% between 1960 and 1974, unchanged between 1974 and 1988, and from 60% to 78% between 1988 and 2000. The Mezzogiorno's itinerary is slightly more complex, as it has been the object of Italian and EU transfers at the same time. In any case, during the 1960s, the flow of external funds to the Mezzogiorno was relatively low: this and the earlier one were the decades of the labour migration to northern Italy and northern Europe. By the time of the oil crisis, 1974, the Mezzogiorno's per capita GDP was about 63% of the EU average. Since then, the Mezzogiorno has become one of the privileged targets of EU Structural Funds and the Italian government has stepped up its subsidy and transfer policies. Migration flows came to an end and official unemployment started rising. By 2000, the Mezzogiorno's per capita income is around 68% of the EU average.

The recent East German experience seems to lend further support to this claim: badly conceived, very generous and sustained transfer policies do not spur economic growth and convergence; they often retard it.

13.3.4   Which jurisdiction?

These tales of miracles, disasters and average achievements should also teach us something about who, that is: which jurisdiction, should call the shots. Both in the case of Ireland and in that of the Italian Mezzogiorno, national policies have counted for substantially more than the EU ones. The EU has, at most, made some additional funds available, conditional on certain transparency criteria and for certain kinds of investments. In environments where public administration, both local and national, is highly inefficient and corrupted (as is the case in the Mezzogiorno), imposing some degree of accountability and transparency may have a positive social value. This much should certainly be granted to the EU intervention. But the positive effects probably begin and end there. Funds are fungible, hence most countries have simply shifted their own expenditure away from those sectors and kinds of intervention where the EU Structural Funds were likely to flow, and towards other items in the public budget. When one looks at things this way, one realises that the EU Structural Funds are nothing but a generic transfer to the governments of the recipient countries. Only if one is willing to assume that, absent the structural policies, countries such as Italy, Spain, Portugal, Greece and Ireland would not have invested any funds in public transportation, water sanitation, industrial parks etc., can one conclude that it makes sense to attribute to the EU and to the European Commission the management of such funds as a way of guaranteeing that specific targets are achieved. This is a most unrealistic assumption: in practice, such investments would have taken places in any case, possibly at a slightly lower level. Once transferred from Brussels to the regional and national entities that actually spend them, the Structural Funds have, quite likely, simply been 'spread over' the overall range of public expenditure items and, ultimately, increased expenditure most uniformly in the targeted areas and in every other area.

This is an obvious consequence of the fact that the current design of the EU structural policy does not satisfy the minimal requirements for subsidiarity: there is no compelling reason, even assuming that the incorrect economic principles upon which it is founded made any sense, that regional policies should be coordinated and managed from Brussels.

They can be easily coordinated at the national level. Not doing so, i.e. pretending that growth and convergence at the regional level has little to do with national fiscal and industrial policies, obscures the political process and allows politicians to pursue damaging policies without receiving the blame for their consequences. If, and it is a big if, there is a political need for 'compensating transfers' to flow from richer to poorer EU countries, this can be easily achieved by a simple transfer mechanism among countries. At most, all that the Commission needs to do is to act as a clearing house for the fat cheques crossing over Europe from one national government to another. When it comes to defining, designing and implementing regional policies the basic subsidiarity principles recommend leaving it to national governments – barring, obviously, the claim that national governments are too corrupt to do this and that the Commission is, like the wife of Caesar, above any suspicion of corruption.

13.4   Conclusions

Although theoretically possible in special circumstances, there is no reason to expect that trade integration, per se, would lead economies to diverge. All past experiences of trade integration, especially in Europe, have led to sizeable improvements in the factor endowments of the poorest partner and in the efficiency with which such factors were allocated in production. In principle, further trade integration should therefore be pursued among European countries.

Pure trade integration generates a level – more than a growth – effect on participating countries. In particular, there is no hard evidence supporting the idea that trade integration alone may increase the long-run growth rates of participating countries in a stable form. When absolute convergence is the objective, other national policies besides liberalisation of international trade play an important role. Experience shows that reductions in fiscal pressure, accompanied by parallel reductions in public spending are among such policies. Capital and labour mobility, together with a competitive level of labour income taxation also play a role in fostering real convergence.

Both evidence and economic theory suggest that, given a stable macroeconomic environment, the presence or lack of supply-side incentives play a crucial role in determining long-run regional performances. The half-century of experience with southern Italy and more than two decades of experience with southern Spain show that the availability of large and permanent income support transfer programmes has a negative impact on economic efficiency and long-run growth. The relatively more recent experience of the East German *Länder* leads to the same conclusion: public programmes for long-term income support, corporate subsidies and other forms of income transfer have negative effects on economic growth: they hamper instead of foster economic convergence.

The experiences of Ireland, Portugal and the Italian North-East in the EU-15, and of various new members, show that sustained above average economic growth is the consequence of an attractive environment for FDI and new small firm creation, risk-taking entrepreneurial behaviour, and the exploitation of local comparative advantages via enhanced labour and capital mobility. Low marginal taxes, efficient transportation and communication infrastructures, good financial facilities, a relatively flexible supply of high-level human capital appear as the key ingredients for the establishment of a growth-friendly environment.

Labour and capital mobility are good for growth and economic convergence. Free capital movements across national borders seem now to have become an obvious and accepted policy stance in the EU. Things are different with respect to labour movements. In particular, a number of researchers are recommending the adoption or continuation of various transfer and/or regulation policies aimed at reducing or even altogether eliminating labour migration from poorer to richer European regions. We consider this policy prescription wrong and damaging. While the social and political costs of mass migration are certainly large and cannot be underestimated, one must also clearly say that a certain amount of free labour migration is necessary to a well-functioning labour market. Further, labour migration from one EU country or region to another has often been temporary and has been associated with episodes of rapid economic growth and convergence. Finally, a variety of arguments and considerations suggest that the size of the post-admission migration flows from the new Member States will be much smaller than envisaged, and will have very little impact on the labour markets of the old members of the EU-15.

Experience from earlier EU enlargements and current economic conditions within the new Member States suggest that placing too high expectations on the economic consequences of the enlargement would be misplaced. Hopes that EU regional and structural policies will be the key to fostering rapid economic growth and convergence are likely to be disappointing. Regional transfers taking place under the structural and cohesion policies are just that – transfers. To achieve long-run growth at rates higher than average, an appropriate mix of the policies just described seems to be needed.

In light of their very secondary effect on long-run growth, and of the particularly acute political tensions their availability and allocation creates among Member States, one should reconsider the very same existence of regional structural funds within the enlarged EU. This applies, with stronger force, to the funding of the Common Agricultural Policy. Theory and evidence show that Structural Funds are pure income transfers with little long-term effects. The availability of such transfers generates two very negative effects. First, it leads to rent-seeking behaviour on the part of poorer regions seeking such funds. It also creates rent-seeking coalitions of the 'half poor' against the 'even poorer' or the 'very rich', giving rise to spurious coalitions whose only objective is to increase the amount of transfers accruing to one particular region or country. Both activities cloud the political discourse. Secondly, it determines inefficient allocation of resources within those regions that are the beneficiaries of such transfers. This leads to a sub-optimal allocation of regional labour, capital and entrepreneurial resources and to a self-perpetuating system of expectations in which below average income levels are almost 'sought' by the regional administrations as a conduit for additional structural funding. In the long run, both of these effects lead to the misallocation of resources, corruption, underground activities and a lack of sustained growth that characterise and distinguish, for example, the Mezzogiorno of Italy. Structural Funds should be phased out over the next EU budget cycle (2006–12). The Cohesion Funds, whose objective has been achieved with the successful establishment of the euro, should be terminated with the end of the current spending cycle (2006).

References

Arevalo, P. 2003. 'Crecimiento y Convergencia en España y sus Regiones: 1960–2000'. Doctoral Dissertation, Universidad Carlos III de Madrid, Madrid, Spain.

Aslund, A., Boone, P. and Johnson, S. 2001. 'Escaping the Under-Reform Trap'. *IMF Staff Papers*, vol. 48, pp. 88–108.

Boldrin, M. and Canova, F. 2001. 'Inequality and Convergence in European Regions: Reconsidering European Regional Policies'. *Economic Policy*, vol. 16, pp. 207–53.

Ederveen, S., de Groot, H. and Nahuis, R. 2002. 'Fertile Soil for Structural Funds? A Panel Data Analysis of the Conditional Effectiveness of European Cohesion Policy'. Tinbergen Institute, Discussion Paper, No. 96/3.

Eurostat. 2000a. *Statistics in Focus, Economic and Finance, Theme 2, European Union FDI with Candidate Countries: An Overview*, 26/2000.
 2000b. *Statistics in Focus, General Statistics, Theme 1, Regional GDP in Candidate Countries*, vol. 2.

2001a. *Statistics in Focus, Economic and Finance, Theme 2, Value Added, Employment, Remuneration and Labor Productivity in the Candidate Countries*, vol. 13.

2001b. *Statistics in Focus, General Statistics, Theme 1, Regional GDP in Candidate Countries*, vol. 4.

2002a. *Statistics in Focus, Economic and Finance, Theme 2, Candidate Countries' National Accounts by Industry*, vol. 17.

2002b. *Statistics in Focus, General Statistics, Theme 1, Regional GDP in Candidate Countries*, vol. 2.

2002c. *Statistics in Focus, Economic and Finance, Theme 2, the Evolution of FDI in Candidate Countries: Data 1995–2000*, vol. 3.

2002d. *Free Data, General Statistics, Theme 1, Employment Rate-Total*, 12 July 2002.

2002e. *Free Data, General Statistics, Theme 1, Unemployment Rate-Total*, 12 July 2002.

Garibaldi, P., Mora, N., Sahay, R. and Zettelmeyer, J. 2001. 'What Moves Capital in Transition Economies'. *IMF Staff Papers*, vol. 48, pp. 109–45.

Miles, D. and Scott, A. 2001. *Macroeconomics: Understanding the Wealth of Nations*. London: John Wiley and Sons.

Vaitilingam, R. 2002. 'Who's Afraid of the Big Enlargement?'. CEPR Policy Paper 7. London: CEPR.

World Bank 2001a. *Poland's Labor Market*. Washington DC: World Bank.

2001b. *Employment and Labor Market in the Czech Republic*. Washington DC: World Bank.

Index